4
QUEEN SQ.
British Museum
BLOOMS-BURY SQUARE
GT. RUSSELL ST
(Lord Mansfield's)
(Bosville's)
RED LION SQUARE
Gray's Inn
HATTON GARDEN
HIGH HOLBORN
HOLBORN
HOLBORN HILL
CHANCERY LANE
LINCOLN'S INN FIELDS
Lincoln's Inn
St. Andrew's Church
FETTER LANE
GOUGH SQ.
Rolls
St. Dunstan's Church
BOLT CT.
FLEET STREET
DRURY LANE
GT. QUEEN ST.
LONGACRE
Covent Garden Theatre
Piazza Coffee-house
Shakespeare Tavern
BOW ST.
RUSSELL ST.
Drury Lane Theatre
Rose Tavern
Davies' Shop
COVENT GARDEN MARKET
HENRIETTA ST.
SOUTHAMPTON ST.
St. Anne's Church
LEICESTER ST.
LEICESTER SQUARE
(Reynolds's)
ST. MARTIN'S LA.
Clifton's Chop-house
Temple Bar
St. Clement's Church
Mitre Tavern
Temple Ch.
St. Bride's Church
WATER LA.
INNER TEMPLE LA.
Crown & Anchor
New Church
The Temple
Somerset Coffee-house
THE STRAND
Somerset House
Savoy
Temple Stairs
Whitefriars Stairs
Savoy Stairs
Somerset Water Gate
(Foote's)
(Crosbie's)
St. Martin's in-the-Fields
SUFFOLK ST.
The Adelphi, (Garrick's)
CHARING CROSS
Northumberland House
NORTHUMBERLAND ST.
Spring Gardens
Hungerford Stairs
WHITEHALL
Scotland Yard
HORSE GUARDS PARADE
Boswell's Lodgings
Whitehall Stairs
Melbourne House
Privy Garden
Plantation Office
Cockpit
DOWNING ST.
Privy Garden Stairs
(Lowth's)
DUKE ST.
PARLIAMENT ST.
Manchester Buildings
GT. GEORGE ST.
WESTMINSTER BRIDGE
Westminster Bridge Stairs
St. Margaret's Church
House of Lords
H. of Commons
Westminster Abbey
Westminster Hall
Westminster School
Cupers Garden
THE BROAD WALL
VINE STREET
NARROW WALL
ANGEL ST.
THE NEW ROAD
ST. GEORGE'S FIELDS
N
W
E
S
0
1/4
1/2 Mile
A
B
C
D
5

THE YALE EDITIONS OF THE PRIVATE PAPERS OF
JAMES BOSWELL

Boswell's London Journal, 1762–1763

Boswell in Holland, 1763–1764

Portraits, by Sir Joshua Reynolds

Boswell on the Grand Tour: Germany and Switzerland, 1764

Boswell on the Grand Tour: Italy, Corsica, and France, 1765–1766

Boswell in Search of a Wife, 1766–1769

Boswell for the Defence, 1769–1774

THE GRASSMARKET AND WEST BOW, EDINBURGH
on an execution day. Etching after a water-colour by James Skene, from an original in the Edinburgh Central Public Library

BOSWELL FOR THE DEFENCE

1769 – 1774

EDITED BY WILLIAM K. WIMSATT, JR.
Professor of English

AND FREDERICK A. POTTLE
Sterling Professor of English

Yale University

WILLIAM HEINEMANN LTD

MELBOURNE : LONDON : TORONTO

* * * * *

The Yale Editions of the Private Papers of James Boswell will consist of two independent but parallel series. One, the "research" edition, will give a complete text of Boswell's journals, diaries, and memoranda; of his correspondence; and of *The Life of Johnson* from the original manuscript: the whole running to at least thirty volumes. It will preserve the spelling and capitalisation of the original documents, and will be provided with extensive scholarly annotation. A large group of editors and a permanent office staff are engaged in this comprehensive undertaking, the first volume of which may appear in 1961. The other, the reading or "trade" edition, will select from the total mass of papers those portions that appear likely to be of general interest, and will present them in modern spelling and with appropriate annotation. The publishers may also issue limited de luxe printings of the trade volumes, with extra illustrations and special editorial matter, but in no case will the trade volumes or the de luxe printing include matter from Boswell's archives that will not also appear in the research edition.

The present volume is the seventh of the trade edition.

First Published 1960

PRINTED IN GREAT BRITAIN
BY THE WINDMILL PRESS LTD
KINGSWOOD, SURREY

EDITORIAL COMMITTEE

FREDERICK A. POTTLE, PH.D., LITT.D., LL.D,. Sterling Professor of English, Yale University; CHAIRMAN

FREDERICK W. HILLES, PH.D., L.H.D., O.B.E., Bodman Professor of English, Yale University

HERMAN W. LIEBERT, Curator, Rare Book Room, Yale University Library.

EDWARD KUHN, JR., Editor, McGraw-Hill Book Company

ROBERT F. METZDORF, PH.D., University Archivist; Research Associate, Yale University Library; Secretary to the Committee

ADVISORY COMMITTEE

C. COLLEER ABBOTT, M.A., PH.D., Emeritus Professor of English Language and Literature in the University of Durham

JAMES T. BABB, M.A., Librarian of Yale University

WALTER JACKSON BATE, PH.D., Professor of English, Harvard University

WILLIAM BEATTIE, M.A., LITT.D., Librarian, National Library of Scotland

THOMAS G. BERGIN, PH.D., LITT.D., O.B.E., Sterling Professor of Romance Languages and Master of Timothy Dwight College, Yale University

CLEANTH BROOKS, B.A., B.LITT. (OXON), Professor of English, Yale University

PAUL S. BREUNING, LITT.D., Deputy Librarian of the University of Utrecht

JAMES L. CLIFFORD, PH.D., LITT.D., L.H.D., F.R.S.L., Professor of English, Columbia University

THE RIGHT HONOURABLE THE EARL OF CRAWFORD AND BALCARRES, G.B.E., D.LITT., D.C.L., LL.D., Chairman of the Board of Trustees, National Library of Scotland

L. P. CURTIS, PH.D., Associate Professor of History, Yale University

SIR GAVIN DE BEER, F.R.S., M.A., D.SC., HON.D.-ÈS-L., Director, British Museum (Natural History)

SIR JAMES FERGUSSON OF KILKERRAN, BT., Keeper of the Records of Scotland

ARTHUR A. HOUGHTON, JR., LITT.D., L.H.D., LL.D., New York City

DONALD F. HYDE, Four Oaks Farm, Somerville, New Jersey

RONALD IRELAND, Professor of Scots Law in the University of Aberdeen

ADVISORY COMMITTEE

TABLE OF CONTENTS

LIST OF ILLUSTRATIONS

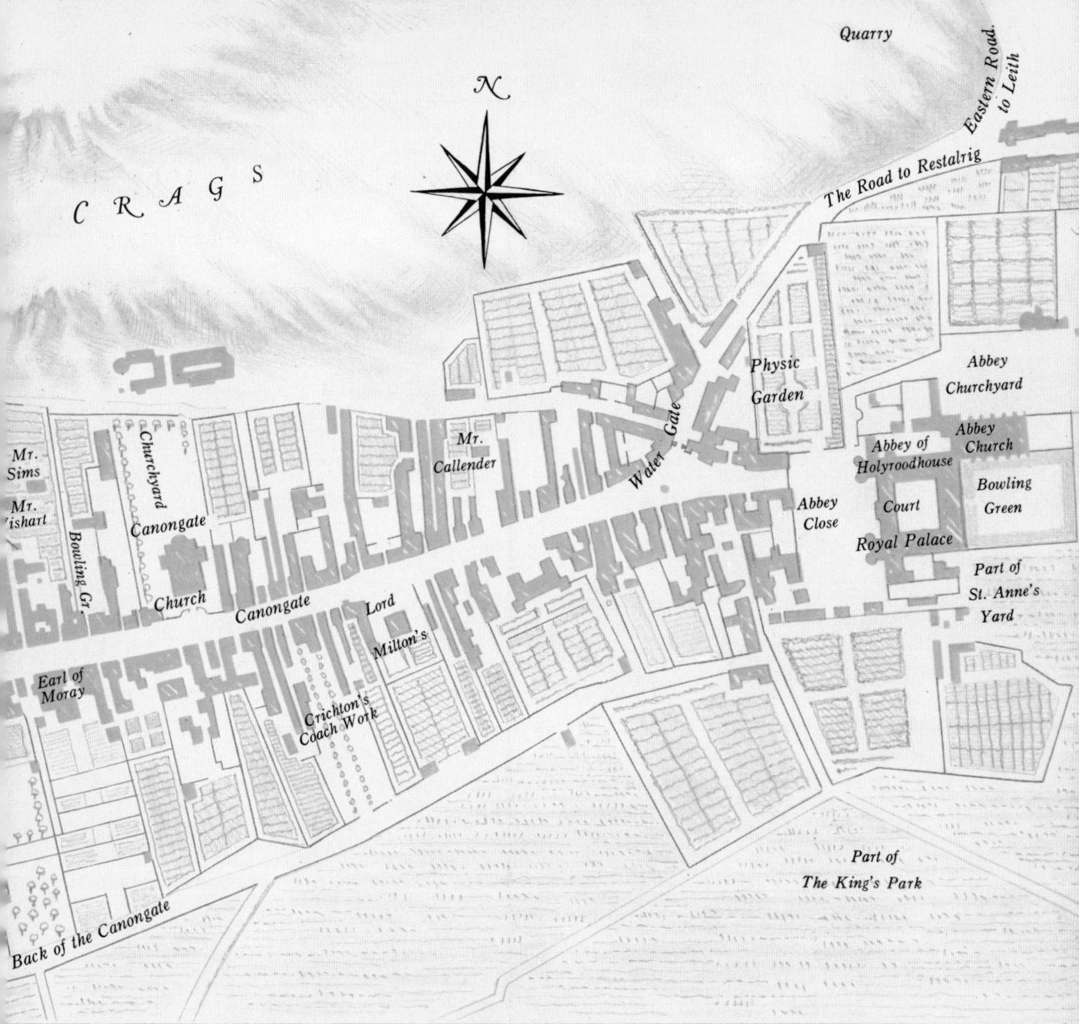

A PLAN OF THE CITY OF EDINBURGH

locating many of the places mentioned in the text

REDRAWN BY HAROLD K. FAYE FROM "THE PLAN OF THE CITY AND CASTLE OF EDINBURGH" BY WILLIAM EDGAR, 1765

LEGEND :

1. *Register Office*
2. *Theatre Royal*
3. *Methodists' Meeting*
4. *Lady Glenorchy's Chapel*
5. *Milne's Court*
6. *Writers' Court*
7. *The Royal Bank*
8. *Anchor Close*
9. *New Bank Close*
10. *Fortune's, Old Stamp Office Close*
11. *Miln's Square*
12. *Young's Street (New Street), Canongate*
13. *Webster's Close*
14. *Boswell's Court*
15. *Gordon Close*
16. *Donaldson's Close*
17. *Gosford's Close*
18. *Tolbooth*
19. *Luckenbooths*
20. *Council Chamber Close*
21. *Tolbooth Church, St. Giles*
22. *New Church, St. Giles*
23. *Blair's Land (Lord Auchinleck)*
24. *Old Assembly Close*
25. *The Market Cross (The Cross)*
26. *The Assembly (New Assembly Close)*
27. *Niddry's Wynd*
28. *Gray's Close (Mint Close)*
29. *Boyd's Close (Boyd's Inn, the White Horse)*
30. *St. John's Close (St. John's Street, or New Street)*
31. *Sir William Forbes's Bank*
32. *Back Stairs*
33. *Scot's Close*
34. *Kincaid's Close*
35. *Peter Ramsay's stable*
36. *Nicholson's Street (New Road)*

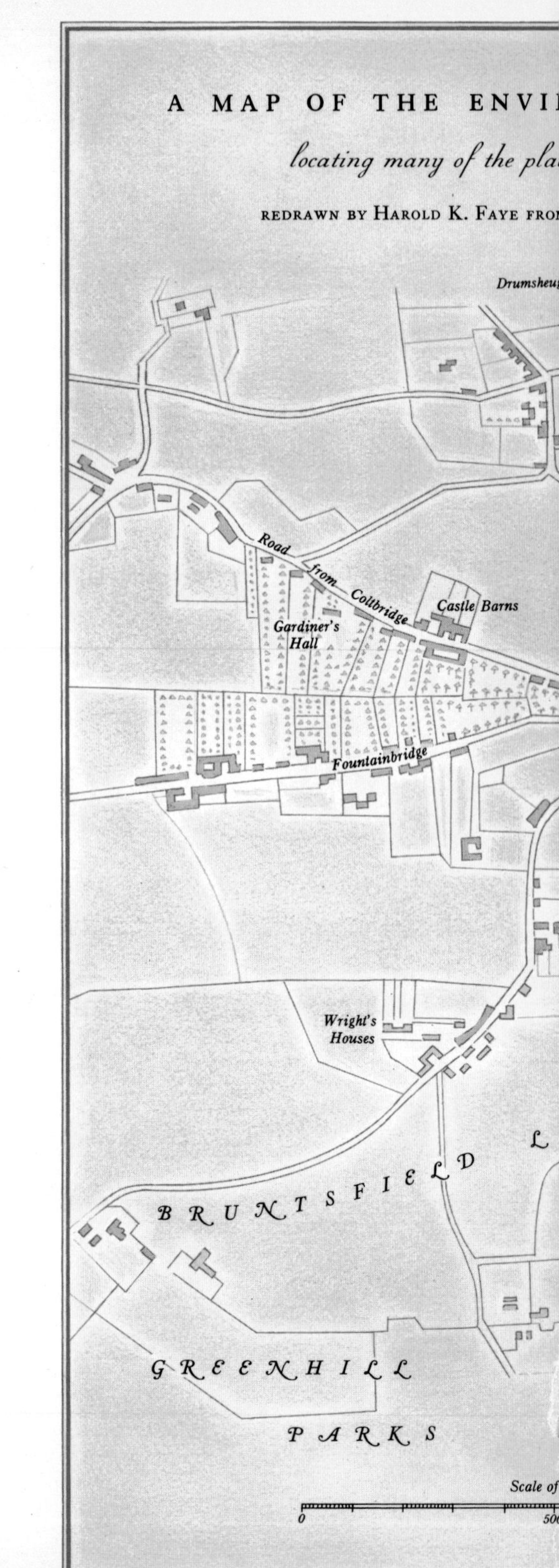

A MAP OF THE ENVI
locating many of the pla
REDRAWN BY HAROLD K. FAYE FRO
Drumsheu
Road from Coltbridge
Castle Barns
Gardiner's Hall
Fountainbridge
Wright's Houses
BRUNTSFIELD L
GREENHILL
PARKS
Scale of
0
50

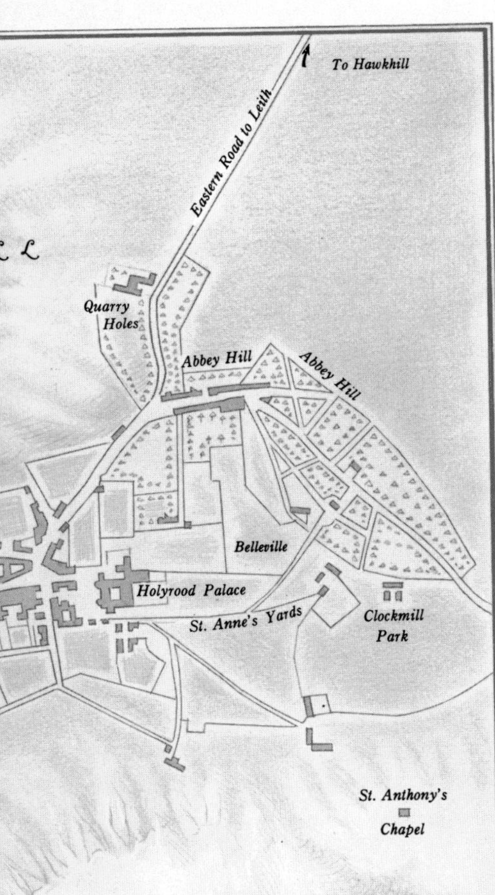
To Hawkhill
Eastern Road to Leith
C L
Quarry Holes
Abbey Hill
Abbey Hill
Belleville
Holyrood Palace
St. Anne's Yards
Clockmill Park
St. Anthony's Chapel
SALISBURY
CRAGS
ARTHUR'S
SEAT
Prestonfield

N

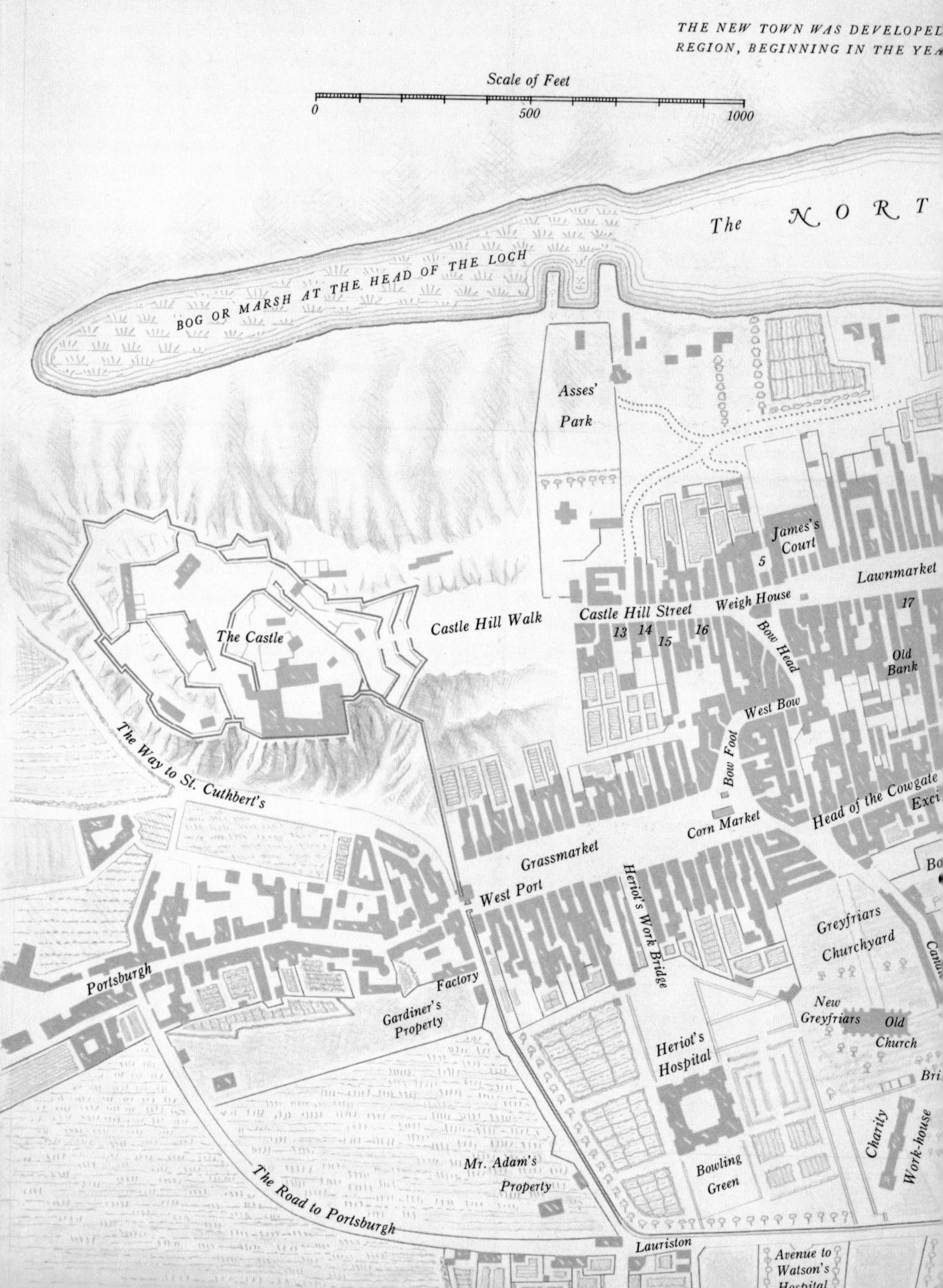
THE NEW TOWN WAS DEVELOPEL
REGION, BEGINNING IN THE YEA
Scale of Feet
0
500
1000
The NORT
BOG OR MARSH AT THE HEAD OF THE LOCH
Asses' Park
James's Court
5
Lawnmarket
Castle Hill Street
Weigh House
17
13 14 15 16
The Castle
Castle Hill Walk
Bow Head
Old Bank
West Bow
Bow Foot
The Way to St. Cuthbert's
Head of the Cowgate
Exci
Corn Market
Grassmarket
Bo
West Port
Heriot's Work Bridge
Greyfriars Churchyard
Portsburgh
Factory
Gardiner's Property
New Greyfriars
Old Church
Heriot's Hospital
Bri
Charity Work-house
Mr. Adam's Property
Bowling Green
The Road to Portsburgh
Lauriston
Avenue to Watson's Hospital

THIS
67.
Calton Burying-place
CALTON
Western Road to Leith
Orphan Hospital
College Kirk
Calton
LOCH
Bridge
Physic Garden
Paul's Work
Back of Canongate
Slaughter-house
New Port
Leith Wynd
Bridge Street
Flesh Market
Upper Market
Green Market
Canongate Flesh Market
Head of Canongate
Nether Bow Port
Exchange
The High Street
Town Guard
Tron Church
Chessel's Buildings
Marquess of Tweeddale's
Earl of Selkirk's
Poultry Market
Parliament Close
Parliament House
Doctors' Yards
The Mint
St. Mary's Wynd
Meal Market
Cowgate Port
Schoolans Tannery
Cowgate
Coal Yard
High School Yards
Tailors' Hall
Horse Wynd
College Wynd
Adam Court
Society Hall
Surgeons' Hall
Royal Infirmary
Brown Square
Argyll Square
Trades' Hospital
Bell's Brewery
Campbell's New Buildings
College
Society
Coal Yard
Coach Wrights
Potter Row Port
Row
Port
Duke of Douglas
Quakers' Burying-ground
Riding-school
Stables
Green
Bristo
Seceders' Meeting-house
Potter Row
Lady Nicolson's Park
New Road
Pleasance
George Square
1
2
3
4
6
7
8
9
10
11
12
18
19
20
21
22
23
24
25
26
27
28
29
30
31
32
33
34
35
36

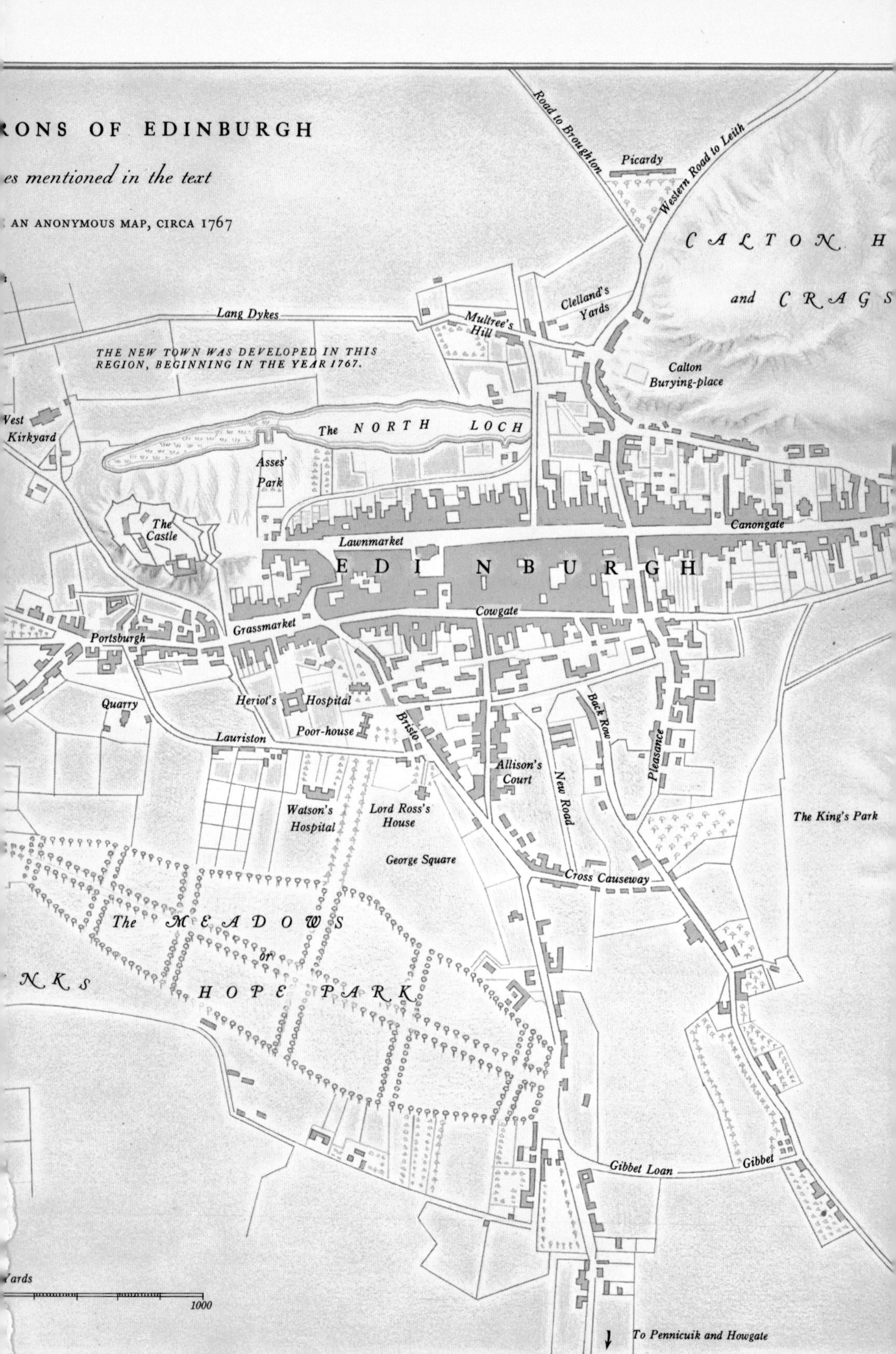
RONS OF EDINBURGH
es mentioned in the text
AN ANONYMOUS MAP, CIRCA 1767
Road to Broughton
Picardy
Western Road to Leith
CALTON H
and CRAGS
Clelland's Yards
Multree's Hill
Lang Dykes
THE NEW TOWN WAS DEVELOPED IN THIS REGION, BEGINNING IN THE YEAR 1767.
Calton Burying-place
West Kirkyard
The NORTH LOCH
Asses' Park
The Castle
Canongate
Lawnmarket
EDINBURGH
Cowgate
Grassmarket
Portsburgh
Heriot's Hospital
Quarry
Back Row
Poor-house
Bristo
Lauriston
Pleasance
Allison's Court
New Road
Watson's Hospital
Lord Ross's House
The King's Park
George Square
Cross Causeway
The MEADOWS or HOPE PARK
NKS
Gibbet Loan
Gibbet
Yards
1000
To Pennicuik and Howgate

INTRODUCTION

§ I

THE immediately preceding volume of this series ended with Boswell's happy wedding in November 1769. The present volume ends in September 1774 with the hanging of a client and his burial. The contrast in feeling between these events has a more than superficial relation to the course of Boswell's life and the evolution of his character during this period. The first five years of Boswell's married life present the spectacle of a man moving through a climacteric. The sobering and maturing effects of a prudent marriage show the first signs of giving way before the return of older, more radical impulses of extravagance and their attendant penalties. The change is not rapid or violent but it is none the less certain.

To describe the contents of the present volume in more external terms: it gives us in succession the model young husband and professional man, the adventurer returning to literary associations and the ways of the southern metropolis, and then the Scots advocate in a summer session—energetic conversationalist, steady drinker, and anguished pleader of a desperate cause. We have, in short, Boswell the "Benedict", Boswell at the Club, Boswell Agonistes.

Marriage was a good thing for Boswell. The main accent of his new life is surely that of domestic felicity. He experiences a very comfortable kind of affection for his wife, a warm glow of devotion, a degree, even, of uxoriousness. He is content with a state of relative retirement from the literary world, with a nearly uninterrupted residence in Scotland. It is a period of sustained application to professional labours. Boswell being admitted to plead in the Church Court and moving into a larger and more handsome house in Chessel's Buildings during the spring of 1770, Boswell bowling southward through the historic and scenic country-side into Northumberland with his wife on a post-chaise jaunt in August 1771, Boswell at Auchinleck in October getting lessons from his father in election law and the pruning of trees, is a picture of the solid citizen busy about his wholesome concerns—the steady "young" Laird of Auchinleck, the industrious and ambitious advocate, the attentive and companionable spouse, the dutiful son. The first two years of his married life stand out as a time of extraordinary serenity, the steadiest and most cheerful period of his whole life.

During the next three years he was to suffer certain kinds of distress; but at the same time he would have the great satisfaction of commencing father of a family. After the loss of an infant son during the summer following his marriage, in the spring of the fourth year, 1773, was born his first daughter and darling, Veronica, and in the spring of the fifth year, his scarcely less beloved second daughter, Euphemia. These little girls were to provide the brighter moments of many a Journal sequence in the years immediately ahead.

But contentment is a matter which is on the whole difficult to document. Boswell in the state of euphoria which we have been describing was such a man as for his own sake we might retrospectively wish him to have continued to be, but such as would scarcely have given us the ensuing years of his exciting Journals or the great *Life of Johnson*. One of the effects of Boswell's preoccupation with his marriage and his profession was that for a while he wrote almost nothing about himself—for about two years, scarcely more than a few pages of Journal notes. Surely there is some connexion to be noted between a degree of unhappiness, or at least of restlessness, on Boswell's part and his usual habit of self-recording. It is no doubt our good fortune that certain strains of dissonance, the effects in part of former bad habits and mistaken decisions, were never entirely suspended and were soon to grow stronger again. The difference of opinion with his father over the entail of the Auchinleck estate (really a dispute over Boswell's fitness to preserve the property and traditions of the family) had broken out as recently as the summer before his marriage. It was now somewhat intensified by his father's disappointment in the marriage and by the simultaneous appearance of a stepmother. And all along, Boswell's old discontent with the "narrow" society of the northern metropolis never entirely went to sleep. He acknowledged in himself recurrent moments of distinct uneasiness.

In the spring of 1772, with the justification of an appeal to plead before the House of Lords, he made his first return to London, and as he set out on this jaunt, he began his first fully written Journal since the month before his marriage. He had now the slightly agitating but exhilarating experience of re-exploration, re-initiation, into old favourite ways—old streets, old taverns, old friends and their homes, old habits. He recovered a way of life which had been familiar, but never so securely and habitually his own as not to be capable of such renewal and refreshment. The habit of good spirits which had prevailed during the past two years seems to have gone along with him for the space of this jaunt and even to have been heightened to a special pitch. It was with the fullest relish of which he was capable that he experienced such moments as the first meeting with his revered friend Samuel Johnson or his Easter mass at the Sardinian minister's chapel. "The sound of his feet upon the timber steps was weighty and well announced his approach. He had on an old purple cloth suit and a large whitish wig. He embraced me with a robust sincerity of friendship, saying, 'I am glad to see thee, I am glad to see thee.' " "I was . . . conducted by a person in the Ambassador's livery to a seat just before the organ and fronting the altar. The solemnity of high mass, the music, the wax lights, and the odour of the frankincense made a delightful impression upon me. I was divinely happy." Perhaps the most blissful hour of all came when he got invited to a party with Dr. Johnson and Goldsmith at General Oglethorpe's. "I felt a completion of happiness. I just sat and hugged myself in my own mind." "Nothing was wanting but my dearest wife to go home to, and a better fortune in the mean time to make her live as she deserves." During this visit to London not only did Boswell manage to avoid "deviating from fidelity" to his "valuable spouse" but, after an initially risky experiment of engaging in conversations with street-walkers, he very sensibly resolved to refrain from this indulgence, and with a minor exception he managed to keep his resolution.

On his second trip to London, during the spring of 1773, he was received into the Club of the most celebrated politicians and *littérateurs*.

In August of the same year Samuel Johnson came up to Edinburgh, and he and Boswell went off on a golden tour to the Hebrides, recorded by Boswell in a Journal that would one day be a marvellous and famous book. That book lies necessarily outside the text of the present volume, but the importance of the Hebrides episode in this phase of the mind and life of Boswell can scarcely be over-estimated. During these years Boswell's earlier connexion with London and with Johnson became a confirmed allegiance. These were the years when he formed a plan, fell into a pattern, of the yearly return to London, the regular visits which during the whole decade of the 1770s and until the death of Samuel Johnson in 1784 gave him the elaborate records of Johnson's conversation which are the glory of the *Life*. From the Journal of 1772, for example, he later pulled page after page of rich materials to be used directly as copy. Recovered only within recent years, these portions of the Journal are a special boast and revelation of the present volume.

Two London figures who chiefly share with Johnson the focus of Boswell's attention during this period are Garrick and Goldsmith. Boswell's appreciation of being admitted to the friendship of the great actor and manager had been enthusiastic and steady from the earliest encounters, through the Stratford Shakespeare Jubilee in the autumn before his marriage, and even through the quiet time while he remained at home working hard. The first awakening and exchange of literary letters, of Edinburgh and London theatrical gossip, in the spring of 1771, is with Garrick. And Boswell's chief literary exercises, the dedication of an Edinburgh edition of Shakespeare and three essays on the art of acting in *The London Magazine*, are centred upon the same glamorous figure. He cherished as one of his best memories of the London trip of 1772 a morning when he walked with Garrick along the Thames near the Adelphi and was fortunate enough to hear him burst into an animated recital of a speech from *Macbeth*. On the Hebrides tour, after Shakespearian quotations by Johnson and Boswell on the blasted heath near Forres and amid the ruins of Macbeth's castle at Inverness ("A raven perched upon one of the chimney tops"), one of the first things Boswell did was to write an account of the experience in a letter back to Garrick in London—leaving out, of course, Johnson's growls about a mere "player" and his unwillingness to get subscriptions or lend old plays.

The relation to Goldsmith is not so even. It is a striking, a somewhat disconcerting, fact that Boswell during the first years of their acquaintance had under-estimated the struggling author, had perhaps felt he could patronise him. The comic view of Goldsmith as the awkwardly over-eager and humiliated conversationalist, the habitual perpetrator of Irish bulls, continues to the very end of the record. At the same time, with Goldsmith's sudden theatrical triumph in *She Stoops to Conquer*, Boswell's enthusiasm for him had blazed. From Edinburgh, just before hurrying south at the end of March 1773, he wrote the now celebrated letter linking the new play with the birth of his own little girl Veronica and inviting the equally celebrated reply "as if in repartee". Then, a little more than a year later, the friendship is terminated by Goldsmith's death of a "fever". Boswell learns of the event, apparently from the newspapers, and sits down to memorialise his feelings and re-establish connexions with his literary friends in long-neglected letters to Langton and Garrick. A little later, in a communication to *The London Magazine*, he gives the world a song which had been dropped (because an actress could not sing) from the text of *She Stoops to Conquer*. He takes it from the only surviving copy (which thanks to his good habit as a collector he possesses), in Goldsmith's hand.

To Boswell, far away from all his London associations, kept at home that spring season by the need for attending to business and by the approaching confinement of his wife, the news of Goldsmith's death was a sad blow. But already, at least as early as November 1773, immediately after his three-months' sprint of *qui vive* during the Hebrides tour, a strong reassertion of the darker side of his mind had begun. As he saw Johnson into the coach for London and turned back towards Edinburgh and his professional duties, he had relaxed into a gradually complicating mood of depression. The habit of heavy drinking which had set in shortly after his becoming an advocate in 1766 now began to increase its hold during a year of malaise and distraction, of more than usually discouraging court-room experiences, of emerging political differences with his father. Boswell was keeping up steady convivial habits during the sessions of court. He had by now taken to rather frequent social gaming.

Above all, it was the burden of his legal undertakings which gave the distinctive shade to Boswell's returning hypochondria. We may suppose that the civil causes which formed the staple of his employment and which are noted year after year in his Consultation Book were not very exciting to him and seldom enlisted his sympathy very deeply. Even the more spectacular appeal against Hastie the ejected schoolmaster of Campbeltown, which brought Boswell to London and before Lord Mansfield in the House of Lords in the spring of 1772, seems to have been for him mainly an opportunity to travel and the occasion of his making a distinguished appearance, displaying his now fairly confident powers of legal oratory. Hastie himself must have been a coarse enough, a selfish and even brutal, fellow (perhaps Boswell had never even seen this client), and when the decision against him had been pronounced, Boswell apparently suffered no particular pang. It was off with his wig and gown and away to a party and congratulations for his effort. The great occasion, the more or less factitious reason and climax of a trip to London, had come off and served its purpose.

Boswell's emotion was always much the opposite of this in the criminal causes which he argued before the Court of Justiciary in Edinburgh. During these years he seems to have become a kind of self-appointed public defender. He acquired a distinct reputation as a man who would take on, become ardently concerned in, the causes of common criminals, the unfortunate, the desperate, the clearly guilty and imminently threatened with the pains of law. He was badly hurting his chances for professional advancement by his keenness in a kind of endeavour which was shunned by his brother advocates, those who were on their way to becoming M.P.s, Lords of Session, or Barons of Exchequer. The criminal causes of Boswell's first few years as advocate—of Hay the soldier, hanged for implication in a drunken assault and the robbery of a watch, of Raybould the forger, also duly hanged—were paralleled with increasing frequency during the bad year after the Hebrides tour. Such causes were not relatively numerous in Boswell's total practice, but they stand out in his brief Journals of the period, in extended newspaper accounts, which he himself often wrote, and in masses of legal papers which at least in a few instances he preserved. A forger who obstinately refused to confess, a pair of young scoundrels who murdered a poor rag-gatherer at night in his cottage on a heath, a half-crazed man, excited by the insults of a mob, who ran out of his house and stabbed his best friend, a sheep-stealer or a horse thief, a group of "meal" rioters, another group of burglars and arsonists, a couple of young girls, sisters, who in some kind of drunken brawl pushed over a woman shopkeeper and killed her—such were the clients, in their various degrees of guilt, who engaged Boswell's sympathy most warmly, elicited his most strenuous endeavours, his repeated visits to prison and consultations, his all-day and all-night marathon exertions in the court-room, his further visits as they awaited execution, his Bible readings with them, his exhortations to repentance.

And then we come to the summer of 1774, with its crowded activities, recorded by Boswell in a Journal which he begins on 14 June, the day of the opening of the session. For two solid months during this busy season of the Scottish metropolis, the daily affairs of the session (the court appearances, the drafting of legal papers, the appointments, the consultations) alternate and mingle with the no less regular, the feverishly regular, social engagements. Business merges with pleasure, almost daily intemperance follows hard upon recovery from the day before. We hurry along without pause through the assorted agitation of parties with his cousins and his friends, the judges, advocates, "writers", clergymen and military men, their ladies and their daughters, who make up the thronging, the bustling and talkative society of which Boswell is a part. These are the ordinary matters which fill his Journal.

But a little less than half way through the summer begins the extraordinary record of the struggle for the life of John Reid the sheep-stealer. This occupies the best part of Boswell's mind and effort for seven weeks and makes the sombre conclusion of our volume. Reid had been Boswell's first criminal client, by court appointment, in the autumn of 1766, and, with the help of his friend Andrew Crosbie, Boswell had saved Reid's life. But now Crosbie refused to be involved a second time. Against a formidable array of Crown witnesses and the suave, complacent reasoning of the Lord Advocate, Boswell adduced a single witness, a scarcely relevant forlorn hope, and threw into the balance his own flourishes of oratory. The nearly inevitable verdict and sentence led to a second phase of the episode, drawn out and agonised, as Boswell worked frantically by various means, prudent and imprudent, for a pardon or a commutation of sentence. (He gained an illusory reprieve, while the King and his advisers awaited the ruthless report of the Justice-Clerk.) At the start of the affair Boswell had said he would write of Reid only apart from his Journal, in his Register of Criminal Trials. But the uncouth tormented figure of the sheep-stealer in the Tolbooth succeeded before the end in usurping a much larger place in his sympathy and imagination than he had anticipated. No other client that he ever had came even close to filling so many pages of the Journal—with the accumulating discoveries of a story not only macabre and poignant but precise, intricate, and puzzling. The case of John Reid is much like a modern psychologically oriented detective story, especially as we are now able to fill it in with the relevant letters, petitions, and broadsides preserved in Boswell's collection. Boswell pursues the narrative, gives us the horrid picture, to the last movement on the ladder, the last words, hardly understood: "Mine is an unjust [a just?] sentence." That night he sits by his fire, with a friend and a bottle of claret, nursing himself through a misery of nervous shock.

§ II

We have Samuel Johnson's advice to Boswell on how to keep a journal, delivered in the very swim of events during Boswell's London visit of 1773. "The great thing . . . is the state of your own mind; and you ought to write down everything that you can. . . . Write immediately while the impression is fresh." (Aristotle to Menander on how to get a laugh, to the tadpole on how to become a frog.) This advice can scarcely have seemed novel to Boswell, yet one part of it was impressive enough for him to repeat it in his Journal more than a year later. "Mr. Johnson said that the great thing was to register the state of my mind."

If we wish to understand why some of Boswell's narrations, even some of the most seemingly routine or perfunctory sketches of the shape of a given day, have their own interest and carry us on easily to the next day and the next, it is because Boswell is always talking about how his days and nights felt to him. It is always a cardinal point with him to be searching for happiness, to keep testing himself to see if he is finding it, to take his own emotional temperature, to look forward to his opportunities, and backward to estimate his successes and his failures. He tries hard to state his feelings explicitly. He is busy also arranging the details of his narrative to intimate the shades of feeling. ("The state of my mind must be gathered from the little circumstances inserted in my Journal.") The great days of London life when he hugs himself for joy, certain skilfully managed Edinburgh days of just enough work, just enough sociability, just the right kind and amount of food and the warming wine carefully "sucked", and on the contrary the days of madness and rampaging, of gross boldness, of violence and intemperance in convivial life, in drinking, in making love, and the subsequent days of oppressive melancholy and desolation—these stand forth conspicuously enough in the record. At the same time he is attentive to the days of quieter tone, the intermediate values. "I rose from the table quite cool, and several of us drank tea with the ladies. This was an inoffensive day." "We three drank a bottle of claret each, which just cheered me."

Under the simple rubric of "feeling" we might be tempted to conclude that we were placing Boswell accurately as a typical man of his country and his era. Certain distinctions, however, ought to be made.

The story of Boswell is the story of man's disobedience and its fruit as that fruit grew ripe in the experience of a man who lived both marvellously in accord, and marvellously at variance, with the life of his contemporaries. Sing, terrestrial muse. . . . The literary mind of the age would have had the story, if not heavenly poetic or majestically grand, at any rate reasonably smooth and elegant or purely tender and pathetic. As a precocious Eton schoolboy, about a decade later than the events recorded in this book, would write in his Addisonian essay: the poet Chaucer "lived in a period little favourable to simplicity in poetry, and several meannesses occur throughout his work. . . . The state of equipoise between horror and laughter which the mind must here experience may be ranked among its most unpleasing sensations". There was one part of Boswell's mind which was largely in rapport with the prevailing taste of the age. "When Fancy from its bud scarce peeped, And life's sweet matins rung," he wrote in a youthful poem, and he defended the lines in his Journal: "I think them two beautiful allusions." His favourite image for what delights him in verbal composition is the edible sweet—the delicious "pineapple", the "dessert of rich flavour". Among his most frequent terms of praise for the conversation of Samuel Johnson are "majestic", "musical", "melodious".

Such expressions, however, do not bring us very close to the true imaginative principle in Boswell. For Boswell's verbal art, his actual dealing with human life and feeling, is above all realistic—and to that extent it is low rather than lofty, plain, even in a sense "ugly", rather than "beautiful". One of the books that Boswell was reading with considerable interest and taking notes from during the year 1771 was his countryman Henry Mackenzie's new novel *The Man of Feeling*. How typical of Boswell's artistic mind is his comment on a certain scene of elevated sentiment between Mackenzie's hero and a lady of the town! "Harley's behaviour to the courtesan is quite unnatural. . . . All her speech too is far beyond nature." Boswell not only knew what he was talking about—in the sense of his being an expert witness—but in this instance he was writing with critical shrewdness.

Let us observe, furthermore, that realism in the portrayal of human feelings involves, almost inevitably, a kind of impurity, a traffic with the mixed or complicated (for feelings seldom occur pure or simple). And next that there is a special kind of reflective or aesthetic feeling—an accent of realisation—which arises just out of the tension of the primary or immediate life feelings; so that paradoxically the most sensitive realism is in effect always more than realism.

It is difficult to illustrate this part of our aesthetic from Boswell's theoretical utterances. But the illustration is scarcely avoidable once we turn to his performance. Surely the most extraordinary thing about his experience and his management of feeling, in his life and in his Journals, is his capacity (defying the good taste of his age) to entertain the jostling opposites—in alternation, in conjunction: good and evil, prudence and rashness, and all their attendant range of pleasure and pain, delight and woe. One of the accents of aesthetic realisation that arises from such conflict, a major one, is the laughable. The principle of "incongruity" expounded by so many theorists of this subject applies with peculiar force to Boswell at many moments—to Boswell, in March 1772, standing before the bar of the House of Lords, Boswell recording of himself: " 'My Lords,' said I, 'I speak with warmth for this schoolmaster who is accused of too much severity. I speak from gratitude, for I am sensible that if I had not been very severely beat by my master, I should not have been able to make even the weak defence which I now make. . . ' Lord Mansfield smiled." Boswell for the defence: comic mode. A second major accent is, with Boswell, not quite the classic counterpart or full tragic opposite of the laughable, but rather a near neighbour living in certain interestingly uneasy relationships. At the level of simple transformation: almost any kind of pang at all, any internal commotion, may be enjoyable and may be deliberately sought and deliberately nursed in memory. "There is a pleasure in being to a certain degree agitated by events." Thus his repeated interviews with condemned men, his executions, and his funerals. And then—at a further depth of internality—appears his curiously flickering and detached, both complacent and assured, self-awareness on such occasions. His tortured and unselfish engagement in behalf of a doomed client merges with a quite satisfactory consciousness of his own role as eloquent defender and a prolonged exploitation of his opportunity as observer. "I was in a kind of agitation, which is not without something agreeable, in an odd way of feeling. . . . I enjoyed the applause." "I said, 'I suppose, John, you know that the executioner is down in the hall.' . . . Two o'clock struck. I said, with a solemn tone, 'There's two o'clock.' " Boswell for the defence: quasi-tragic mode.

Such are his experiences in partisanship and sympathy. But an even more central theme of the Journals is the daily endurance of his own most personal and immediate version of the human tragi-comedy. One of the most constant things that Boswell knows is the vibration between indulgence and remorse—or their near simultaneity and union. "Drinking never fails to make me ill-bred. . . . I recollect having felt much warmth of heart, fertility of fancy, and joyous complacency mingled in a sort of delirium. . . . My wife was waiting all the time, drowsy and anxious." Sometimes the awareness is more tired and casual. In those nonce reflections, incidental and effortless observations, after a day or after a supper, of which the Journals are so full, often there appears a kind of puzzled estimate of dissatisfaction, its causes, its feeble remedies. "After every enjoyment comes weariness or disgust." "Our grave reflections on the vanity of life are part of the farce—like the grave ridiculous in comedy—for, after making them, we take a jovial bottle as if we never had thought."

We ask the question, inevitably, how is this frank, this prideful, at moments even exultant, record not offensive? What is the quality or degree of Boswell's awareness of evil? Does he really understand what he is? Does he enjoy the kind of perspective needed to shape such experiences as he endures into a record that commands our serious regard?

We have to acknowledge that this record proceeds throughout upon a kind of perception which is demonstrated in the expression. It is not a record or a confession by accident. When Boswell joins with the very jury at a tavern in a species of celebration on the coffin of John Reid, there is, it is true, no embarrassment. "I was in such a frame as to think myself an Edmund Burke." Still it is Boswell himself who has acknowledged and joined these impressions for us. Another sensibility might well have screened, might well have bowdlerised and simplified—bidding for a higher degree of propriety, of the supposed tragic, pathetic, or sublime. The endless naïveté of Boswell, his profoundly childlike mentality, comes in here as a force in the self-dramatisation. If only the writer have the accuracy, the courage, to portray his childlikeness! Childlikeness directly displayed is not like what leaks out unhappily around the edges of the dishonest attempt at self-concealment. Let us add that Boswell almost never, perhaps never for any extended stretch, writes in complete ignorance or moral obtuseness. Even the exuberant whoring passages of his early Journals are likely to have their edging of apology, of rueful humour, their introspective accent, their partly foreseen and dreaded aftermath of remorse. The awareness of evil perhaps seldom or never reaches degrees of great reflective intensity. Still Boswell has a sense of evil—a feeling of it, the kind of painful impression which Johnson, after a day of fatiguing hospitality at Aberdeen, acknowledged in the words: "Sensation is sensation."

The analogy between Boswell and the sentimental hero of his day, the rake with the heart of gold in the picaresque or comic epic novel, is too striking to be resisted. Doubtless Boswell himself felt the resemblance, and he must have felt some special distress in the realisation that his own true story could not end like the fiction of *Tom Jones* ("Such a cloud of hypochondria. . . . I wish it may not press upon me in my old age.") The sentimental novels were a species of hagiography. They presented the rake as the hero of the new morality of the good heart. Boswell himself exemplifies that morality, but no author ever took less pains to glorify his hero than Boswell in his autobiography, less pains to make his readers *like* that hero.

Boswell and his Journal sometimes today do encounter the criticism that it is difficult to like Boswell. The question is hardly more relevant than a question whether we can *like* Hamlet or Heathcliff. Boswell writes a true story—beyond question—and this is one undoubted source of its peculiar power. (In real life no doubt he did care very much whether he was liked. He tried hard to be liked.) At the same time, in the detachment of his writing, in the subtle ranges and conflicts of feeling which he manages, in his firmness of detail and in the purity of his verbal style—in his general artistry as a journalist—Boswell projects himself as a figure of unique fictive significance. If we know what we are about as we read and respond to this extraordinary saga of self-portrayal, we shall hardly stop to wonder whether we do like Boswell, whether we ought to like him. (The very possibility of puzzlement is a clue to the situation.) In part no doubt we will like him. Who can fail to like the lover of Margaret Montgomerie, the patient correspondent of the neurotic Temple, the friend of Paoli, the devotee and biographer of Johnson, the desperate opponent of the Justice-Clerk, the counsel for the defence of the abandoned John Reid? At the same time there will doubtless be many respects in which we find it very difficult to like him. Why should we not admit this? What kind of purity, of whitewash, do we look for in the protagonists of our most impressive stories? The correct response to Boswell is to *value* the man through the artist, the artist in the man.

DOCUMENTATION

A. The principal documents used in their entirety to make the text of this book:

1. Manuscript Journal in London, 14 March to 20 April 1772: "Journal of my Jaunt to London, Spring 1772": bound quarto notebook with leather back and marbled board covers, 235 pages and a title page, $7\frac{1}{4}$ by 6 inches, originally numbered by Boswell 1–186, 189–237, 338–347, though continuous; but his pp. 159–164, 181–184 are missing.

2. Manuscript Journal in London, 30 March to 13 April 1773: in a wrapper endorsed by Boswell, "Journal in London, 1773," 57 numbered quarto pages, written on leaves torn from a notebook, $7\frac{7}{8}$ by $6\frac{3}{8}$ inches.

3. Manuscript Journal in Edinburgh, 14 June to 21 September 1774, in two notebooks: (1) bound octavo notebook with marbled paper back and covers, 14 June to 2 September, 147 numbered pages, 7 by $4\frac{5}{8}$ inches; the first three pages are filled by an unfinished "Review" of the period from 22 November 1773 to 14 June 1774; (2) bound octavo notebook with leather back and marbled covers, [2 September] to 26 December, 188 numbered pages, $7\frac{5}{16}$ by $4\frac{9}{16}$ inches; the text of the present volume ends with p. 72 of this notebook.

B. Other Boswellian documents quoted more or less extensively to supplement the Journals of 1772 and 1773:

1. Notes for London Journal, 22 April to 15 May 1772: 5 unpaged quarto leaves, both sides written on, loose, about 9 by $7\frac{3}{8}$ inches.

2. Notes for London Journal, [11 April] to 15 May 1773; con-

tained in the same wrapper as the Journal for 30 March to 13 April, 12 unpaged folio and quarto leaves, both sides written on, loose, ranging in size from $12\frac{9}{16}$ by $7\frac{1}{2}$ to $9\frac{1}{16}$ by $7\frac{1}{4}$ inches.

3. Manuscript of the *Life of Johnson*, passages for 30 April, 1, 7, and 10 May 1773: 12 quarto leaves, rectos numbered by Boswell 393, 398–401, 411–412, 414, 417–420, some with additions on verso, roughly $9\frac{3}{4}$ by $8\frac{1}{4}$ inches, unbound.

C. Brief Notes for Journals, mainly in Edinburgh, for the period 1772–1774, drawn upon in various ways for the editorial narratives and the annotation. These are partly in the hand of Boswell's clerk John Lawrie. They consist of seven sequences, as follows: Notes on General Paoli's visit to Scotland, 4, [9, 10, 11] September 1771; Notes for Journal in Edinburgh, 1 January to 13 March 1772; 3 August 1772 to 27 January 1773; 16 February to 29 March 1773; 15 May to 14 August 1773; 20 December 1773 to 15 March 1774; 11 April to 6 May 1774.

D. *The Journal of a Tour to the Hebrides*. The *Tour* (18 August to 11 November 1773) published in part by Boswell in 1785 was derived from a main manuscript of 314 octavo leaves, originally paged by Boswell 1–674 (78 pages are missing) and from some further leaves of notes corresponding to the beginning and end of the episode. This is another book; it is by-passed rather than embraced in the present volume; but it is drawn upon in various ways for the editorial narratives, the annotation, and the Introduction.

E. Upwards of 245 letters sent or received by Boswell between 25 November 1769 and 2 October 1774, and 14 letters sent or received by Mrs. Boswell. Boswell's letters to William Johnson Temple for this period are in the Pierpont Morgan Library. The manuscripts of his letters to Samuel Johnson for this period have not been recovered—with a single exception, that for 3 March 1772, now in the Hyde Collection, Somerville, New Jersey. Boswell's letter to Goldsmith, the only one he is known to have written to him, and his letters of 26 August 1771 and 1 March 1773 to Percy and of 22 November 1773 to Henry Thrale and of 11 April 1774 to Garrick are also in the Hyde Collection. Other letters not at Yale which have been quoted in whole or in part may be noted as follows: Boswell to

James Beattie, 27 July 1771, in King's College Library, University of Aberdeen; Lord Hailes to Boswell, c. 2 December 1771, in the possession of Sir Charles Mark Dalrymple of Newhailes, Bt.; Boswell to John Johnston of Grange, 20 October 1771 and 9 May 1772, in the possession of the Misses Carlyle of Waterbeck, Dumfriesshire; Boswell to Bennet Langton, 10 April 1774, in the British Museum; Boswell to Percy, 16 April 1773, from the collection of Roger W. Barrett; Boswell to Thrale, 13 May 1774, in the Murdock Collection in the Harvard College Library. The correspondence between Boswell and W. J. Mickle is preserved partly at Yale but mainly among the Mickle papers in the care of Professor A. J. M. Ellis; it appeared in part in *The Universal Magazine* during 1809. Unless the contrary is stated, all other letters by Boswell are printed from manuscripts in the collection at Yale; these, except for the letters to John Johnston of Grange, are copies, in several hands. Boswell's signature is added, in square brackets, to the copied letters. Letters sent and received by Boswell are quoted extensively throughout the editorial narratives. Nine letters by him and fourteen to him are presented in their entirety. Of these the most important are: Boswell to Johnson, 3 March 1772; Johnson to Boswell, 15 March 1772; Boswell to Garrick, 10 September 1772; Boswell to Goldsmith, 29 March 1773; Goldsmith to Boswell, 4 April 1773. Boswell's Register of Letters, now at Yale, is useful for fixing dates when Boswell sent and received letters and for its listing of letters now lost.

F. Upwards of 50 miscellaneous documents, 20 December 1769 to 10 October 1774. These include such items as letters between other persons, Boswell's reading notes, verses by Boswell. They have been used in various ways in the editorial narratives and the annotation; and 5 letters, all having to do with the John Reid case of 1774, have been presented in their entirety.

G. Legal papers relating to the trial, sentencing, reprieve, and execution of John Reid for sheep-stealing, 1 August to 21 September 1774, in three groups:

1. Those relating to the trial and sentencing preserved in Boswell's own archives: (a) report of the trial, 1 August 1774: 14 folio leaves, 28 sides written on; in Boswell's hand to the bottom of p. 27,

where, after the heading, "My Charge", the remainder is written by John Lawrie; (b) "Copy. Declaration of John Reid, 23 March 1774": 2 folio leaves, 3 sides written on, in an unidentified hand; (c) report of a portion of Boswell's opening plea for Reid: 2 folio leaves, 2 sides written on, in Lawrie's hand; (d) "Defences for John Reid": 2 folio leaves, 2 sides written on, in Lawrie's hand; (e) indictment of John Reid, with list of witnesses and list of names from which the jury was to be chosen: 6 printed quarto pages; (f) "On John Reid's Verdict": marginal notes, in Boswell's hand, on 5 of 6 printed pages of a legal petition dated 26 July 1774.

2. Official records of the trial: the Indictment, Declaration, Verdict, Sentence, and other documents relating to the trial preserved in the Scottish Record Office—Justiciary Records, Books of Adjournal 1773–1774, Series D, vol. 38, 1 August 1774; and Processes 1774, Trial of John Reid.

3. Papers relating to the reprieve, preserved in the Public Record Office, Scottish Entry book, Criminal, H.O. 104/1, pp. 140–142: three letters.

Extensive quotations from these three sets of papers are inserted in the editorial narratives and the annotation under the dates in question; and two documents, the Indictment of Reid and his Declaration, are quoted in their entirety.

Boswell's collection concerning Reid contains also four printed broadsides, two of which (including one written by Boswell himself) are presented in their entirety.

H. Published works of James Boswell: A few miscellaneous publications, chiefly essays and communications appearing in *The London Chronicle* and *The London Magazine* for the period 1769–1774, are drawn upon in various ways in the editorial narratives and the annotation; and one letter by Boswell, signed "A Royalist" and published in *The London Chronicle* for 17–20 September 1774, is presented in its entirety.

Two of the Journals published in the present volume (those for 14 March to 20 April 1772 and 14 June to 21 September 1774) and the Journal Notes and Condensed Journals for 1 January to 13 March 1772, 22 April to 11 May 1772, and 16 February to 29 March 1773 were published in 1930 by Frederick A. Pottle in the ninth volume of the *Private Papers of James Boswell from Malahide Castle in the Collection of Lt.-Colonel Ralph Heyward Isham*, a limited edition of 570 copies. The third Journal published in the present volume (that for 30 March to 13 April 1773) and the Condensed Journal for 11 April to 15 May 1773 were published by Geoffrey Scott in 1929 in the sixth volume of the same edition of the *Private Papers*. Mrs. Boswell's letter to her husband of 7 February 1770 was published by Professor Pottle in 1930 in the eighth volume of the same edition. Boswell's letters to Temple and some of his other letters were published in Professor C. B. Tinker's *Letters of James Boswell*, Clarendon Press, 1924; and most of Boswell's letters to Temple had been published even earlier in *Letters of James Boswell Addressed to the Rev. W. J. Temple* [ed. Sir Philip Francis], 1857, reprinted by Thomas Seccombe in 1908. Boswell's letters to Johnson (in part) and Johnson's to Boswell were first published by Boswell himself in his *Life of Johnson*, 1791, the most authoritative edition of which is that of G. B. Hill (1887), revised by L. F. Powell, 1934–1950. The most recent and authoritative edition of Johnson's letters is *The Letters of Samuel Johnson*, by R. W. Chapman, Oxford, 1952. The greater part of the manuscript of Boswell's *Journal of a Tour to the Hebrides* was published by Frederick A. Pottle and Charles H. Bennett in 1936. Boswell's Notes on Dr. Johnson's visit in Edinburgh, 14 to 17 August 1773, on which the first part of his *Tour* is partly based, were published by Geoffrey Scott and Professor Pottle in the sixth and ninth volumes of the *Private Papers of James Boswell*.

The spelling, capitalisation, and punctuation of both manuscripts and previously printed material have been brought close to modern norms. (Boswell has been allowed to retain certain idiosyncrasies.) Abbreviations and contractions have been expanded. All quotations have been standardised in the same fashion. The standard of spelling for all but proper names is *The Concise Oxford Dictionary* (1956). For place names F. H. Groome's *Ordnance Gazetteer of Scotland*, J. G. Bartholomew's *Survey Gazetteer of the British Isles*, and *London Past and Present* by Peter Cunningham and H. B. Wheatley have been followed. Family names have been brought into conformity with the usage of *The Dictionary of National Biography*, Mrs. Margaret Stuart's *Scottish*

Family History, G. E. Cokayne's *Complete Baronetage* and *Complete Peerage*, Sir James Balfour Paul's *Scots Peerage*, and various other special books of reference. Names of speakers in conversations cast dramatically, whether supplied by Boswell or by the editors, are put in small capitals without distinction. A few clear inadvertencies have been put right without notice. Square brackets indicate words added where the manuscript shows no defect, but where for one reason or another the editors have made an insertion; angular brackets indicate reconstruction of words lost through defects in the manuscript, where the reconstruction is not entirely certain.

The editorial narratives of this volume draw upon the correspondence of Boswell, his Condensed Journals and Journal Notes, his publications, and various other minor sources to tell the story of his life for the period that comes between his marriage in November 1769 and his first return to London in the spring of 1772, and thereafter for the extended periods which come between the London Journals of 1772 and 1773 and between the second of these and the Edinburgh Journal for the summer of 1774. Shorter editorial summaries help to complete the London Journals of 1772 and 1773 and appear also at various places in the account of the case of John Reid. The annotation of the Journals and letters attempts to provide essential information when it is available and occasionally to add sidelights upon the character of a person or event. But complete annotation has been reserved for the research edition. The index of the volume is intended not only as a finding tool but as a supplement to the annotation; we have sometimes reserved for the index the Christian names, professions, and titles of persons mentioned by Boswell only casually.

Both the textual editing and the annotation of this volume owe much to earlier works of scholarship already mentioned: the edition of the *Private Papers of James Boswell* by Geoffrey Scott and F. A. Pottle, that of the *Tour to the Hebrides* by F. A. Pottle and C. H. Bennett, that of Boswell's *Letters* by C. B. Tinker, the great edition of the *Life of Johnson* by G. B. Hill as revised by L. F. Powell, and the edition of the *Letters of Samuel Johnson* by R. W. Chapman. To these titles should be added Professor Pottle's *The Literary Career of James Boswell, Esq.*, 1929, the catalogue of the *Private Papers of James Boswell* by F. A. Pottle and

Marion S. Pottle, 1931, and *A Catalogue of Papers relating to Boswell . . . found at Fettercairn House*, by Claude Colleer Abbott, 1936. A considerable amount of unpublished preliminary work has also been available. More than twenty years ago (1936–1937) the writer of this Introduction prepared in two typescript volumes, as a class exercise in the Yale Graduate School, an editing of Boswell's London Journal and Notes, 14 March to 15 May 1772. At the same time A. Stuart Pitt prepared a similar editing of Boswell's London Journal and Notes, 13 March to 15 May 1773. And in 1939 John Murray presented to the Faculty of the Yale Graduate School his doctoral dissertation in four typescript volumes, *James Boswell in Edinburgh*, an editing of Boswell's Journal Notes in Edinburgh for the years 1771–1774, with elaborate attention to the institutions and customs of the city and to Boswell's literary and legal career. In 1955 Mary E. Dukeshire presented as her doctoral dissertation an editing of *Selected Correspondence of James Boswell, 1770–1773*. In 1952 Charles McC. Weis presented as his doctoral dissertation *The Correspondence of James Boswell and Sir David Dalrymple*, and in the same year Frank Brady presented *The Political Career of James Boswell, Esq*. In 1954 Charles N. Fifer presented in two volumes *Letters between James Boswell and Six Members of the Club*. In 1953 Marshall Waingrow began the task of transcribing and editing the manuscript of Boswell's *Life of Johnson*. Meanwhile, Dr. Charles H. Bennett had gone ahead with a systematic and nearly exhaustive annotation of Boswell's Journals from the point (June 1774) where John Murray's dissertation had left off. Using such of the foregoing materials as were available and others resulting from his own researches, Professor Pottle more than eighteen years ago completed a text and a set of notes for a reading edition of the three Journals printed in this volume. Then the recovery of further papers from Malahide Castle and of other documents and the release of those that had been recovered at Fettercairn House necessitated the planning of a quite different series of volumes, with extensive revision of the earlier editing.

ACKNOWLEDGMENTS

The plan of this volume, though the editors themselves are responsible for the general layout and the details, has benefited considerably from the advice of the Editorial Committee. Mr. Herman W. Liebert assumed the special responsibility of providing the artist with material for the maps, and Dr. Robert F. Metzdorf was not only chief technical assistant at every stage but also the principal collector of the illustrations. Mr. John Oates, special assistant in the Boswell Office during the summer of 1958, typed almost the entire manuscript and executed a number of assignments in research; Mr. Anthony Moore, '59, Bursary aide in the Boswell Office, 1957–1959, helped in various ways. Miss Harriet Chidester, principal secretary in the Boswell Office during the period of the book's production, not only typed parts of the manuscript but verified the normalising and preparation of the whole for the printer and in addition made numerous special contributions through her skill in the transcription of Boswellian documents and her mastery of the files. Mr. Norman Chodikoff Charles, '59, assistant in the Boswell Office during the summer of 1959, performed tasks of research and helped in proof-reading the book. The index was compiled by Miss Delight Ansley.

Proof for this volume was read not only by the members of the Editorial Committee and the office staff but by several members of the Advisory Committee—Professor Bergin, Professor Brooks, Professor Clifford, Sir James Fergusson, Professor Ireland, Dr. Malcolm, and Dr. Powell.

We gratefully acknowledge various kinds of learned assistance from the following friends: David Baxandall, William Beattie, Frank Brady, James L. Clifford, N. S. Curnow, P. B. Daghlian, Christopher S. A. Dobson, the Edinburgh Central Library, Olof von Feilitzen, Sir James Fergusson, C. Beecher Hogan, Mrs. Henry W. Howell, R. E. Hutchison, Mr. and Mrs. Donald F. Hyde, Ronald Ireland, George M. Kahrl, Helge Kökeritz, George Lam, W. S. Lewis, Mrs. Joyce T. McCombe (formerly Lady Talbot de Malahide), C. A. Malcolm, Roy M. Mersky, Charles S. Minto, Ernest C. Mossner, Henri Peyre, Mrs.

Marion S. Pottle, Konstantin Reichardt, Philip Ritterbush, L. W. Sharp, Brooks Shepard, Robert Smith, Warren H. Smith, G. H. Spencer, G. W. Stone, T. W. Strachan, Alexander Vietor, Marshall Waingrow, Ralph Walker, René Wellek, Robert Williams.

This edition of *Boswell for the Defence* was seen through the press by Dr. Metzdorf.

W.K.W., Jr.

Yale University, New Haven, 18 May 1959

BOSWELL FOR THE DEFENCE

1769 – 1774

I felt a completion of happiness. I just sat and hugged myself in my own mind. Here I am in London, at the house of General Oglethorpe, who introduced himself to me just because I had distinguished myself; and here is Mr. Johnson, whose character is so vast; here is Dr. Goldsmith, so distinguished in literature. Words cannot describe our feelings. The finer parts are lost, as the down upon a plum; the radiance of light cannot be painted. [10 APRIL 1772]

It was now about eight in the evening, and gloom came upon me. I went home and found my wife no comforter, as she thought I had carried my zeal for John too far, might hurt my own character and interest by it, and as she thought him guilty. I was so affrighted that I started every now and then and durst hardly rise from my chair at the fireside. [21 SEPTEMBER 1774]

BOSWELL FOR THE DEFENCE

1769–1774

Calendar of Boswell's Life to November 1769. 1740. Boswell was born at Edinburgh on 29 October, eldest son of Alexander Boswell, the head of an ancient landed family in the shire of Ayr, and a judge in the Supreme Courts of Session and of Justiciary in Scotland, enjoying by virtue of this position the title Lord Auchinleck. Boswell's mother, Euphemia Erskine, was descended from the Earls of Mar and the Earls of Lennox and through the latter from James II of Scotland.

1753–1759. Boswell went through the regular arts course at the College of Edinburgh and then studied law at the University during the session of 1758–1759. About that time, however, he began to show a special interest in the literary and theatrical life of the city and was, apparently for that reason, in 1759 removed by his father to the University of Glasgow—where he again very quickly succeeded in forming theatrical friendships.

1760. In the spring Boswell ran away to London and made the experiment, exceedingly dangerous to his legal and political prospects, of becoming for a short time a Roman Catholic. He was reconverted under the tutelage of his father's Ayrshire neighbour the Earl of Eglinton and systematically introduced "into the circles of the great, the gay, and the ingenious".

1762. In July he passed the civil law examination at Edinburgh. In the autumn he returned with his father's permission to London and attempted by influence to obtain the commission in the Foot Guards which his father refused to purchase. During the months of this first extended stay in London, Boswell wrote his first long stretch of Journal. Towards the end, he met and became a friend of Samuel Johnson. (Boswell's Journal was discovered in 1930 by Professor C.

Colleer Abbott at Fettercairn House and in 1950 published under the title *Boswell's London Journal*, 1762–1763, the first volume of the present series, by the McGraw-Hill Book Company, Inc., of New York and William Heinemann, Ltd., in London.)

1763. Having failed to secure his commission, Boswell now yielded to his father's desire and agreed to become a lawyer; he crossed the Channel to Utrecht in August and spent an unhappily ascetic year in Holland applying himself to the study of civil law. Near the end, a relaxation of moral rigour and an interest in a Dutch girl of noble family, Belle de Zuylen (Zélide), revived his spirits. (His Journal for the period was in large part lost soon after, but the story, constructed from his memoranda and letters, has been published as the second volume of the present series, *Boswell in Holland*, 1763–1764, 1952, by the same publishers.)

1764. In June Boswell started on his Grand Tour, the reward extorted from his father for the completion of his legal studies. His first travelling companion was the veteran Scots Jacobite and diplomat in the service of Prussia, George Keith, Earl Marischal of Scotland. After visiting a number of the German courts but failing to meet Frederick the Great, Boswell entered Switzerland, where he enjoyed the triumph of intimate conversations with Rousseau and Voltaire. (*Boswell on the Grand Tour: Germany and Switzerland*, 1764, appeared in 1954, the fourth[1] volume in the present series.)

1765. In January Boswell went over the Alps to Italy, where he continued with equal zest his usual pursuit of women and of important personalities. He hob-nobbed with the English political exile John Wilkes, and he travelled with the Earl of Bute's eldest son, Lord Mountstuart. The most serious amour of his continental sojourn occurred in Siena, with the wife of the "Capitano", or mayor, of the city, Girolama Piccolomini. In October and November he visited revolutionary Corsica and achieved the friendship of the warrior leader Pasquale de Paoli. From Corsica he travelled to Genoa and then through France to Paris. (*Boswell on the Ground Tour: Italy, Corsica, and France*, 1765–1766, appeared in 1955, the fifth volume of this series.)

[1] The third was *Portraits, by Sir Joshua Reynolds*, published in 1952.

1766. In January at Paris Boswell read in a newspaper that his mother had died. He hurried homeward, stopping briefly at London, and arrived in Edinburgh about 7 March. During the next few months his experiments in gallantry became even more complicated than before, while at the same time he began to look more and more seriously towards marriage. A feverish interest in a gardener's daughter at Auchinleck soon gave way to a much deeper entanglement with a "dark" mistress, a "Circe", Mrs. Dodds, first encountered during a visit in May to the watering village of Moffat. At Edinburgh in late July he printed his Latin thesis on a title of the Roman Civil Law, *Concerning Legacies of Household Furniture* (*De supellectile legata*), and, having gone through the formality of defending it before the Faculty of Advocates, he was admitted advocate. Before the autumn Circuit Court at Glasgow, and then at Edinburgh with his friend Andrew Crosbie, Boswell successfully, if precariously, defended his first criminal client, John Reid, in a trial on the capital charge of sheep-stealing. He settled in now to spending busy winters and summers at Edinburgh during the sessions of court. He enjoyed a professional success which he realised, uncomfortably, was due in some measure to the presence of his father on the Bench.

1767. The year was marked by the continuation, rupture, and renewal of his affair with Mrs. Dodds, by the respectable courtship of Catherine Blair, an Ayrshire "Heiress" or "Princess", his father's candidate, and by his spectacular participation as publicist and volunteer advocate in the celebrated "cause" concerning the succession to the estate of Douglas. Boswell published a poem, an allegorical fiction (*Dorando*), two polemical pamphlets, and an edition of Lady Jane Douglas's *Letters* in support of young Douglas, who suffered a temporary defeat in July of this year by a decision of the Court of Session. In December Mrs. Dodds presented him with a daughter, Sally.

1768. Early in February Boswell renewed relations with Mrs. Dodds, was a few days later (though without connexion between the events) formally rejected by Miss Blair, and about the middle of the month published through Messrs. Dilly in London his first widely successful book, begun about a year earlier, his *Account of Corsica*.

Having thus established his position as a man of letters, he set out in March on a three-months' trip to London, complicated by a brief excursion to Oxford for the purpose of seeing Samuel Johnson. In August a new marital prospect appeared, an Irish heiress sixteen years old, Mary Ann Boyd, visiting in Ayrshire at the home of Boswell's cousin Margaret Montgomerie.

1769. The year began auspiciously when in February the House of Lords reversed the decision of the Court of Session against Douglas, and Boswell led the Edinburgh mob which broke windows in the houses of his father and other judges who refused to acknowledge the event by "illumination". At the end of April Boswell in company with Miss Montgomerie went on a trip of conquest to Dublin, the home of the Irish heiress. The result was a new revelation or the confirmation of an old suspicion, a conquest by his travelling companion: by 25 July he and Margaret Montgomerie were formally engaged. At the end of August he set out for a last bachelor jaunt, partly in order that the London doctors might "clear his constitution". The trip included a sortie in September to Garrick's Shakespeare Jubilee at Stratford-on-Avon, where he made his celebrated appearance at the masked ball as an armed Corsican Chief. On 10 November Samuel Johnson came in from Streatham to London with him and saw him into the post-chaise which was to carry him on his road to Scotland and his marriage a fortnight later. (The events of the three and a half years between Boswell's return to Scotland from Paris in the winter of 1766 and his marriage in the autumn of 1769 are told in *Boswell in Search of a Wife, 1766–1769*, which appeared in 1956, the sixth volume in the present series.)

1769–1772

Boswell's Life from his Marriage to his Jaunt to London in 1772. Boswell was married to his cousin Margaret Montgomerie, his "valuable friend", his "lady", the woman whom he had "preferred to all others for her real merit", on Saturday 25 November 1769, at the seat of her family, Lainshaw, in the shire of Ayr. On the same day, or a few days earlier, at Edinburgh, Boswell's father, nearly four years a widower, was married again, to another cousin, Elizabeth Boswell of Balmuto.

The younger Boswell's bride wore a white (or silver) dress which he had apparently brought up from London, and from Edinburgh to Lainshaw on the day of the wedding. At a late dinner that afternoon, not only the bride but Boswell himself was dressed in white. The wedding-ring was a plain gold band, for a slender finger. Boswell's distinguished client and friend Douglas of Douglas was present and put his name as witness to the marriage contract, which had been witnessed in London by Samuel Johnson and Pasquale de Paoli.

"I wish you could steal out of Edinburgh when nobody can suspect where you are going," Peggie Montgomerie had written, "and let the ceremony be put over as privately as possible, as I would like to remain in the country till you thought it necessary for me to come to town." Court was in session at Edinburgh; it is likely that his wife came back with him immediately—in a letter three days before the marriage she had written: "Be you positive to take me with you." Lord Auchinleck's grudging acceptance of his niece (neither richly dowered nor brilliantly connected), his habitual loggerheads with his son, his severe, sarcastic, and chilling manner, the passionate resentment of Boswell at the second marriage and all it might threaten for the family succession, made it unthinkable that Boswell could resume residence under his father's roof. In London, Samuel Johnson had strongly advised against this. In his last letter to his sweetheart "as a young lady", two days before the marriage, Boswell wrote: "I cannot think of our coming to my father's house. It would be mixing gall with my honey. We shall concert what to do when we meet." The first two months of his domestic life remain almost invisible to us. He receives congratulations, both serious and jocular. The friends of his early days, Erskine and Temple, add expressions of commiseration on the marriage of his father. "I was very sorry that your father had felt a tingling in his veins and had done the most foolish thing that an old man can do." "Do not allow your father's marriage to affect your spirits. . . . Cultivate your stepmother's good opinion. . . . If your father should be provoked or inveigled to leave his estate past you, think what would be your situation, what would be Mrs. Boswell's, what would be your children's!"

The first letter known to survive from the hand of Boswell after his marriage is one addressed to his wife early in February of the new year. A brother-in-law of Mrs. Boswell's died, and after the visit to Lainshaw for the funeral, Boswell returned alone to Edinburgh a week ahead of his wife.

"I am anxious on account of the cold which you had when I left you. I am afraid your rising so early and taking so kind a charge of me, when setting out, may have done you harm. Pray take care of yourself. You have always been my steady friend. Consider that your being well and happy is absolutely necessary to make me so. . . . Believe me, my dearest, the short absence which I have now suffered has convinced me still more feelingly than before how much I love you, what real happiness it is to me to enjoy your company, and how ill I can do without you. . . . It is a common observation that we never value sufficiently any happiness till we are deprived of it. It is lucky if a short separation has the same effect on both our minds that the long and melancholy parting by death has on the survivor. . . .

"Tomorrow I dine with Mr. Hugh Maxwell[1] in our new house. I shall please myself with the prospect of our happiness in it. . . . My family affairs go on very well. I keep an exact account, as I know you

[1] A cousin of Boswell's, a "writer", that is to say, a law-agent or solicitor. Many of Boswell's acquaintances to be encountered in this volume will be writers,

will make a strict inquiry into my administration."

And she wrote on the same day, answering another letter he had written the day before:

"How much am I indebted to my kindest, dearest friend for the relief his friendly letter gave me! I dare say you can figure my distress, and may therefore judge how agreeable it was to receive good accounts when I was so apprehensive of the contrary. I thank God for his goodness to me and pray for his friendship and protection to My Dearest Life. . . . I am sorry your father has been indisposed. Is it the cold or his old complaint?"[1]

The new house is no doubt the "house in the Cowgate near the Excise office", at which Boswell receives letters during March and April. No doubt a modest house, in that modest neighbourhood. They did not stay there long, but moved, the last week in May, to a more commodious place in the newest and finest residential development in Edinburgh, Chessel's Land, or Chessel's Buildings, in the Canongate. In the same month Boswell became a church lawyer, being admitted to practice at the Bar of the General Assembly. One of his closest professional friends, John MacLaurin,[2] lay reader of the popular party in the Assembly, sent him a witty celebration of the event in verse: *The Moderator's Advice to James Boswell Esq. . . . to the tune of "A Bumper, Squire Jones" in "The Provoked Wife"*.

Sure great is the folly
In him whom Paoli
His friendship permitted to share
  To go for a guinea
  (Dear Boswell, what mean ye?)
To plead at so scurvy a bar. . . .

[1] A suppression of urine, probably due to an enlarged prostate. The affliction had first appeared about four years earlier, when at the Ogilvy murder trial (see below, p. 305 *n.* 2) Lord Auchinleck had sat nine hours without rising. One severe attack had occurred on the second day of January 1768. On the present occasion he had a cold.

[2] See below, p. 219 *n.* 2.

 B*

Boswell had been able to clear over eighty guineas during a winter term even in his first year at the bar (1766–1767). He had his clerk come to him every morning at six and could dictate to him at a pinch forty folio pages in a day. We can fill in without much trouble a picture of the young advocate during his first winter of married life as a man "kept very throng", a man of affairs, thriving, extremely busy—very much absorbed also in domestic felicity. He passes through a phase of his career marked so successfully by marital devotion, sobriety, and business that the record all but completely escapes being written.

One legal cause in which Boswell was engaged at this time was characteristic of involvements which during the next few years would become both more frequent and more intense. A merchant in Ayr named William Harris had been arrested in the summer of 1768 on a charge of wholesale forging of the notes of the Thistle Banking Company in Glasgow. After lying in prison at Ayr and Edinburgh for about fifteen months, he had shortly before Boswell's marriage escaped from the Edinburgh Tolbooth but had been recaptured and put in irons. A statement by the gaoler concerning this phase of his imprisonment records that Boswell visited him and gave him a guinea. In February he attempted to strangle himself. The "Petition and Complaint" brought against Harris early in 1769 by the Glasgow bankers in conjunction with the Lord Advocate resulted in an extended trial during February 1770 before the Court of Session. He was found guilty by a decree of 10 March and remitted to the Court of Justiciary. He feigned madness at his criminal trial on 24 April but was pronounced sane and again found guilty. In a letter of 31 May to his close friend the philosophic Edinburgh writer and "worthy country gentleman" John Johnston of Grange, Boswell describes the final scenes:

"I visited Harris the evening before he was executed, and insisted to know from him as a dying man the truth as to his accomplices. He persisted in what I told you and added something stronger. . . . I can hardly believe him. I saw him hanged yesterday. He seemed very penitent and not at all frightened. He suffered great pain to all appearance. I was much shocked and am still gloomy."

We get other glimpses of Boswell's mind during this period through his correspondence with Temple, his old classmate at the University of Edinburgh and his closest friend, now rector of the small parish of Mamhead in Devonshire. Boswell had paid a visit there, going down from London, during the autumn before his marriage, had formed or at least had expressed in his Journal a better opinion of Mrs. Temple than he had earlier entertained, and had stood godfather to Temple's first son. Temple was the correspondent to whom Boswell had spread out the most unexpurgated pageant of his adventurous heart during his years in search of a wife. It will be readily conceived that the new Boswell no longer had quite so much to say to Temple, nor so much gusto of introspection and lover's torment to say it with. Temple himself during these years is increasingly a doleful and verbose correspondent, full to the brim with his own frustrations, his provincial seclusion, his poverty, his growing family, his abortive literary hopes and projects (to write a history of Venice, of Florence, of Rome, to translate some Italian book of travels). He sends frequent requests to Boswell, or to David Hume through Boswell, for advice on what books he ought to read, in what order, what he ought to try to write. He sends other requests, unhappy pleas, to Boswell to use influence with somebody to get him a better place, a chaplainship at Turin, Venice, or Florence. Nevertheless, Temple stands always high in Boswell's esteem, and he succeeds in writing paragraphs of kindly, if sometimes rather officious, insight into Boswell's affairs, of warm friendly and "sacerdotal" advice. On 15 December, the same day that he wrote his letter of congratulation to Boswell, Temple had written also to Mrs. Boswell:

"My dear Madam,—I hope you will pardon the liberty I take in addressing you in this familiar and affectionate manner. . . . Indeed I do not know a more valuable man than Mr. Boswell. No man has a better heart, no man has better principles, no man has a nicer sense of honour. . . . If anybody can make my friend happy, I think you must be the person. Your easiness of temper and equal flow of spirits will keep him in good humour, check his flights when he soars too high, and gently agitate and exhilarate him when he inclines towards melancholy and gloomy reflections. Your own prudence will tell you how necessary it is that he should live upon a friendly footing with his father and even his stepmother."

When Boswell resumes his correspondence with Temple during the spring of 1770, such messages, such themes (mingled with much more about Hume on studying history, about Temple's own dilemma and discontent) pass repeatedly back and forth.

"Why do you still distress yourself about your father's marriage? You know at all adventures you would not have lived with him, his wife can have no children, and I suppose he will leave her a very moderate jointure. Take my advice then, live in a friendly and familiar manner with them and make yourself easy."—TEMPLE, 26 April.

"Well do I know that I have the seeds of the same discontent. But I strive to bury them."—BOSWELL, 7 May.

"Women at forty seldom conceive; if they do, it is often fatal to them. . . . Does Mrs. Boswell engross you entirely? Can the gay, the volatile Boswell, whom hardly variety itself could satiate, confine himself to one object? Have you no expedition in your head, no essay in prose, no epistle in verse? or do you begin to think it your chief merit to be a good husband and a good lawyer? Throw yourself out upon paper, let me know all the movements of your heart!"—TEMPLE, c. 26 May.

"My father is come to town and never looked better in his life. Honest man, he really is, I believe, very fond of me; and we are at present on very good terms. I behave with prudence towards the person who has occasioned so much uneasiness. I do not as yet see any appearance of her multiplying."—BOSWELL, 19 June.

Both Temple and Boswell were approaching fatherhood that summer, Boswell for the first time (legitimately), Temple for the second, and Temple strained at the leash towards the moment of escape when he could contrive a trip to the North—first to Gainslaw, near Berwick, where he felt he had family business to superintend ("Good God! how my father has managed my little fortune!") and then, in a bolder dash, even farther. "As soon as my wife is a week delivered, I set out for the North; I hope the first or second Sunday in August. I trust soon after to see you at Edinburgh. . . ." Temple's wife was safely delivered of a son on the 20th of July, and on the 6th of August Temple set out. On the 30th he wrote: "Pray tell me how Mrs. Boswell is and when you wish me to come. Are you a father yet?"

But Boswell had been less fortunate. His son, born on 28 August, after Mrs. Boswell had suffered two days of "illness and real danger", died within two hours. We have his note the next day to Johnston of Grange ("Pray come to me directly") and a letter to Temple: "I am very glad you are so near me. . . . I have much need of your comfort." And this is followed by an exchange in which incidental references to a certain philosopher of Edinburgh chime appropriately enough with an inquiry into the origins of parental feeling.

"You ought not, you cannot feel much for what you have lost. People of reflection love their children not so much from instinct as from a knowledge and esteem of their good and amiable qualities. Think then no more of your misfortune and trust that Providence will be more favourable to you upon another occasion. . . . Is Mr. Hume now at Edinburgh?"—TEMPLE, 4 September.

"The consolation of hearing from you and the prospect of seeing you soon do me more good than your philosophical consideration on the death of my child. I grant you that there is no *reason* for our having an affection for an infant which, as it is not properly a rational being, can have no qualities to engage us; yet Nature has given us such an instinctive fondness that being deprived of an infant gives us real distress. I have experienced this; and there is no arguing against it. . . .

"Mr. Hume is just now at Sir Gilbert Elliot's country seat. He will be here again in ten days. . . . My wife will be in her drawing-room next week, if it please God to continue to favour her. My dear friend! how happy will it make me to have you under my roof and enjoy with you some invaluable hours of elegant friendship and classical sociality." —BOSWELL, 6 September.

Temple came during the third week of September and stayed about a week. As he retreated again to the South, he and Boswell wrote echoing portraits of Boswell's felicity in his wife:

"How can I express with what regret I parted from you! I had not passed a week so happily a long time. I shall always remember with pleasure and gratitude the sensible, the lively conversation of Mrs. Boswell (let me call her your *excellent wife*), and her tender attention about me. *O fortunate nimium si bona, etc.*[1] If you are not the happiest of mortals, it will be your own fault. Never did I see such a command of temper, such amiable sensibility. It is absolute cruelty and tyranny to give that woman the least room for uneasiness. Depend upon it, you will always be in the wrong; she loves you too well ever to give you unnecessary pain. Continue to love her, to respect her, and thank God daily for having given you, for preserving to you, so excellent a wife. Tell her I wish her every satisfaction this world can afford. . . .

"Make my respectful compliments to Mr. Hume."—TEMPLE, 30 September.

"You cannot say too much to me of my wife. How dare you quote to me *sua si bona norint?* I am fully sensible of my happiness in being married to so excellent a woman, so sensible a mistress of a family, so agreeable a companion, and above all so affectionate and peculiarly proper helpmate for me. I own I am not so much on my guard against fits of passion or gloom as I ought to be; but that is really owing to her great goodness. There is something childish in it I confess. I ought not to indulge such fits. It is like a child that lets itself fall purposely, to have the pleasure of being tenderly raised up again by those who are

[1] "O happy farmers! did they but know their blessings!" (*O fortunatos nimium, sua si bona norint, agricolas!* Virgil, *Georgics* II, 458–459).

fond of it. I shall endeavour to be better. Upon the whole, I do believe I make her very happy. God bless and preserve her."—BOSWELL, 6 October.

And Boswell announces that they intend to set out on Monday for Ayrshire. They would stay part of the time with her sister at Lainshaw, and part at Auchinleck. It would be their second return to Lainshaw since the marriage, their first to Auchinleck, to Boswell's father and the other person.

In spite of the loss of their first child, in spite of strained relations with the household of Lord Auchinleck, in spite of Mrs. Boswell's uncertain health during the next year, this period must have been a very successful and happy one in the lives of Boswell and his wife. There is little to indicate that the tenor of their existence did not remain relatively unruffled for another year and a half. During the winter of 1771 they moved once more, this time into a smallish flat which belonged to the philosopher David Hume and had formerly been his home, in James's Court, in the Lawnmarket. It is perhaps significant that the letters of Temple during this year, though they continue in frequency and length and are increasingly full of his own literary and domestic problems ("My wife's questions indeed and the petulance and squalls of my children often interrupt me and distract my attention"), at the same time tell us somewhat less than before about the troubles of Boswell. Boswell's side of the correspondence for this period is lost. And he was keeping no Journal. A few happy and sunlit pictures of the Boswells on vacation are preserved in letters from Boswell to Johnston of Grange. Immediately after a swing into Ayrshire, on 22 May 1771:

"My wife and I had a very good journey west. I left her at Treesbank with her sister[1] and went by myself to Auchinleck, where I was four nights. I then accompanied my father on the Western Circuit. I passed six days at Inveraray, without seeing a shower; and being in perfect good health I fully saw the whole of that place, which is truly a

[1] Mary Montgomerie. She was the second wife of James Campbell of Treesbank, an elderly cousin of Boswell's.

magnificent seat. It has all the highland wild grandeur, and a vast addition from art. I have written a pretty good description of it, which you shall see. I then came on the Circuit to Glasgow, where I passed two days, and then returned to Treesbank, where I remained two nights comfortably and quietly; and then my wife and I, with a little daughter of Treesbank, came into Edinburgh.

"I am now in my house in James's Court, which we find large enough for us, very convenient, and exceedingly healthful and pleasant. My wife is very fond of it. Her jaunt to the country has done her great good, made her fatter, and given her a much stronger look than when we parted. . . .

"I am immersed in General Assembly business, having no less than five causes before that venerable court and being in expectation of a sixth. I am engaged on different sides both for and against patronage. But you know I am to have no opinion. I am only to speak in the person of others. So that the judgments of the Assembly do not affect me.

"But let them say or let them do,
It's aw ane to me,
If I but get into my pouch
A braw swingeing fee, etc."

Again, in late August, Boswell took his wife for a week's jaunt to the South—writing a journal-style letter which he put into Grange's hand on his return to Edinburgh. "We dined at Norton and got to Cornhill at night, so that we slept the very first night in old England." Onward, the next day, past country-seat and castle, they drove pleasantly, past

" . . . the bridge at Coldstream, the ancient castle on the English side . . . Flodden Field, Milford Plain, the finest sheep-ground and hunting-ground that can be imagined, and several seats whose names the post-boys could not tell. We had fine weather, and my travelling companion was delighted with the quick, lively motion of driving post."

In September and October Boswell made another pilgrimage and a retreat with his father at Auchinleck. His purposes were bucolic and legal education—that is, to allow his father to instruct him in the care of the estate and in Scots law and antiquities. Lord Hailes's letter of 23 September, forwarded by Mrs. Boswell from Edinburgh, urges Boswell to attend carefully to all that his father has to say about the law. "Everything that you hear you ought to commit to writing." Boswell's letter to Grange (20 October 1771) describes the sober and diligent life of the pupil.

"The complaint[1] which I had is quite removed by sober regular living, country air, and exercise. I have been serving an apprenticeship with my father in the art of pruning, and I hope in time to be a skilful and diligent guardian of the trees here. My father has been as good as his word in giving me a college upon the election law of Scotland, mixed with its antiquities, which illustrate it in an entertaining manner, and without which one cannot have a full and clear knowledge of it. My father just dictated to me a system, which I took down in writing, and which will be a valuable collection.[2] I can say with truth that I have been employing my time to good purpose."

Still, this stay at his father's house *was* a retreat, a separation and privation. Apparently his wife had come with him on the visit to Auchinleck in October of 1770, but on the second visit to the West, in May of this year, she had pointedly remained with her sister at Treesbank. And now:

"I must tell you that I have suffered much more than anybody would imagine, on account of so long a separation from my wife. You know, my worthy friend, with what uncommon affection and true happiness she and I live together. To be deprived of that inestimable

[1] Possibly a return of the malaria which he had contracted in Corsica and had suffered from again in the autumn of 1766.

[2] Boswell's manuscript of his father's *Observations on the Election Law of Scotland* is owned by Mrs. Joyce T. McCombe (formerly Lady Talbot de Malahide); it is deposited in the National Library of Scotland. The text was privately printed at Edinburgh in 1825.

blessing for day after day and week after week (for so I have counted the time though it is not four weeks yet since I left her) has seriously distressed me. I have been seized with fits of impatience and my heart has fluttered like a bird confined in a cage, and I have had the most anxious apprehensions about her, while my strong imagination has in the silence and solitude of night presented to me such dreary thoughts as are the more afflicting that we can have no certainty but they may be realised. Thank God, she is in much better health than when I left her."

Boswell's parallel account to Temple is lost, but we have Temple's commentary:

"I think you were very right in passing part of your vacation with your father, but am sorry my prudent friend did not accompany you. So manifest a proof of dislike and irreverence cannot serve any good purpose. . . . Pray desire her to learn a little dissimulation, or to give it a more honourable name, a little Christian charity and forgiveness. . . . If you think I have said too much, do not show this part of my letter."

We may suppose that the effect of these words upon Boswell was somewhat muffled by the volume of Temple's own complaints: "It grieves me, my dear friend, to say it, but in my desponding hours I am sometimes inclined to suspect that you do not feel for me as I think I would for you in my situation. . . . Indeed, I begin to experience some of the symptoms of age before I am well a man. My nerves already tremble, as you must perceive by my handwriting."

And all this while, what of Boswell the man of letters, the man of travels, the friend of Johnson, of Garrick, of Goldsmith, of Paoli? What of Corsica Boswell? Boswell's inevitable return to the world of these associations would not of course be an entirely unprepared eruption. It would have been difficult for him to cease altogether at this stage of his career to be the public figure. *Corsica* alone would carry him a long way. Already he was on the Continent one of the best known English authors—better known perhaps than Samuel Johnson. In addition to the three London editions of *Corsica* and the three editions printed in Ireland, there had been, as Boswell was later to point out proudly, translations into Dutch, German, and Italian, and two into French. What prevented an appearance in Russian seems to have been mainly the fact that a writer hard at work during the spring of 1771 fell dead one evening in the very act of translation.[1] It would have been exceedingly difficult now for Boswell to change his habits so radically as to refrain from contributions to the periodical press. His marked file of *The London Chronicle* shows us during the first half of 1770 alone no fewer than nine communications on political, civic, legal, and literary topics. (This newspaper was sent to Boswell "as a present from the proprietors".) More ambitious essays appear during these years in *The London Magazine*, of which in fact Boswell had become one of the proprietors while in London during the autumn of 1769.[2] From London, Boswell's words in both *Magazine* and *Chronicle* were as likely as not to be echoed back to Edinburgh in *The Scots Magazine*.

One of the most conspicuous themes is the theatrical. Boswell's early and eager resort to the world of the theatre had given him a habit which did not wear off easily. After his return from the Continent, one of his most widely publicised theatrical feats had been the Prologue which he wrote for the London actor David Ross on his opening of a Theatre Royal at Edinburgh, against strong local opposition, in December 1767. ("This night loved GEORGE's free enlightened age Bids ROYAL FAVOUR shield the Scottish stage. . . . I wish to hold no RIGHT but by YOUR *choice*; I'll trust my *patent* to the PUBLIC VOICE.") Two years later, in the month after Boswell's marriage, the Prologue for the opening of the new season was both written and spoken by Ross, but Boswell participated by sending an account to *The London Chronicle*—shortly after a "Notice" of his own marriage. Congratulations on his marriage came to Boswell from Ross in the same month, and in February another old theatrical companion, the author-actor Francis Gentleman (dedicator to Boswell of an edition of the

[1] As Boswell's correspondent in St. Petersburg put it, death "translated" him.

[2] Boswell seems to have held a sixth part of the ownership, worth in 1777 £240. The yearly dividend was in 1774 £15 (see below, p. 284) and in 1778 £12. 11. 4.

tragedy *Oroonoko* in 1760), wrote from London, combining flowery congratulations with announcement of a new tragedy of his own, just published. During the first year after his marriage (August, September, and October 1770) Boswell came out in *The London Magazine* with three essays "On the Profession of a Player"—the first two being in part an encomium on the acting of David Garrick, in part a shrewd self-revelation concerning Boswell's own affinity for the stage.

"Mr. Garrick exhibits in his own person such a variety of characters, with such propriety and excellence, as not only to catch the immediate applause of the multitude, but to be the delight and admiration of the judicious, enlightened, and philosophical spectators."—August 1770.

"If I may be allowed to conjecture what is the nature of that mysterious power by which a player really is the character which he represents, my notion is that he must have a kind of double feeling. He must assume in a strong degree the character which he represents, while he at the same time retains the consciousness of his own character. The feelings and passions of the character which he represents must take full possession as it were of the antechamber of his mind, while his own character remains in the innermost recess. This is experienced in some measure by the barrister who enters warmly into the cause of his client, while at the same time, when he examines himself coolly, he knows that he is much in the wrong, and does not even wish to prevail."—September 1770.

Early in the year 1771, Boswell's friend Alexander Donaldson, the Edinburgh publisher, brought out an eight-volume duodecimo edition of Shakespeare. To this he prefixed a dedication to Garrick, the eloquence of which may well have aroused in the right readers a certain kind of suspicion.

"An edition of Shakespeare is inscribed to you with such peculiar propriety that it cannot fail of meeting with universal approbation. You, Sir, by animating his characters on the stage, have shown the

British nation the astonishing treasures of the Father of their Drama: and I even question if ever his genius was sufficiently acknowledged by the general voice till you appeared."

In a letter written to Garrick on 30 March, Boswell apologises for long silence ("I married a few weeks after I left you. . . . I am . . . comfortably settled. . . . *Tempora mutantur*") and then quickly stakes out a claim:

"Mr. Donaldson tells me he has sent you a copy of his edition of Shakespeare. You must know the dedication is written by your humble servant. I should be glad to know how you like it."

That year the Edinburgh Theatre was leased by one of Garrick's most formidable rivals, the English Aristophanes, the mimic-actor and manager Samuel Foote. One of the incidents which Boswell remembered years later, in writing his *Life of Johnson*, was that in a "numerous Scotch company" Foote undertook to entertain "with a great deal of coarse jocularity" at the expense of Johnson. "I felt this," says Boswell, "as not civil to me, but sat very patiently till he had exhausted his merriment on that subject, and then observed that surely Johnson must be allowed to have some sterling wit, and that I had heard him say a very good thing of Mr. Foote himself." With Foote all eagerness to hear, Boswell then related a piece of conversation which he had recorded in his London Journal of October 1769:

BOSWELL. "Pray, Sir, is not Foote an infidel?" JOHNSON. "I do not know, Sir, that he is an infidel. But if he be an infidel, he is an infidel as a dog is an infidel; that is to say, he has never thought upon the subject."

In the letter to Garrick, Boswell says that Foote is making a "very good campaign of it", that he has along with him in his troupe Henry Woodward, who has been a "great support", and also "his favourite Mrs. Jewell", who, however, has "not taken". "Her poorness of figure and awkward inanimate action disgust us much." (At about the same date, Boswell receives a facetious invitation from Woodward in the character of a Jonsonian braggart: "Captain Bobadil kisses Master Boswell's hilts; does not command, but entreats him to a taste of his Trinidado. . . .") Garrick's reply to Boswell reveals how theatrical success, like other kinds, may depend much upon point of view: "Our friend Foote has convinced me that he has brought from Scotland a balance of above one thousand pounds—but his account of the theatrical matters there differs widely from yours. He tells me (this is between ourselves) that he was much followed and that Woodward was deserted, and likewise that Mrs. Jewell was much approved of."

It is possible that Boswell had entered upon his married life with something like a conscious resolution to keep his back turned for a good while upon the attractions of his former ways. Or, more likely, a spontaneous absorption in domestic duties, in domestic felicity, and in his freshly realised powers as an advocate had kept him for a while simply unmindful of his important friends in the South. But an equally spontaneous motive or concurrence of motives turned his mind once again, during the spring of 1771, in the old direction. The letter to Garrick of 30 March was followed on 18 April by one to Johnson. Of this unhappily we know only the beginning, inserted by Boswell later in the *Life of Johnson*.

"My dear Sir,—I can now fully understand those intervals of silence in your correspondence with me which have often given me anxiety and uneasiness; for although I am conscious that my veneration and love for Mr. Johnson have never in the least abated, yet I have deferred for almost a year and a half to write to him."

Johnson waited about two months and then wrote (20 June):

"Dear Sir . . . I wished for your letter a long time, and when it came it amply recompensed the delay. I never was so much pleased as now with your account of yourself and sincerely hope that between public business, improving studies, and domestic pleasures, neither melancholy nor caprice will find any place for entrance. Whatever philosophy may determine of material nature, it is certainly true of intellectual nature that it *abhors a vacuum*; our minds cannot be empty; and evil will break in upon them if they are not preoccupied by good. My dear Sir, mind your studies, mind your business, make your lady happy, and be a good Christian."

During the summer, the Professor of Moral Philosophy at Aberdeen and author of a notable anti-Humean *Essay on Truth* published early in 1770,[1] Mr. James Beattie, was on his way to London and carried with him from Boswell a note of recommendation to Johnson. "His genius and learning, and labours in the service of virtue and religion" rendered him very worthy of it. The best time to find Johnson "at home," wrote Boswell to Beattie himself, "is about eleven o'clock in the forenoon."

"Although you may not find him the first time you call, do not give up your purpose of waiting upon him. It was by much perseverance that I attained to that acquaintance with him which improved into an intimacy that I value very highly. . . . I would suggest to you that it may be necessary for you to exert yourself when with Mr. Johnson to lead him to talk of such subjects as are agreeable. You must not be discouraged though he should appear reserved and wanting in some of the commonplace modes of making a stranger easy. Bring him upon something worthy of his abilities as soon as you can, and I will venture to promise you conversation superior to any you have ever heard."

On the 30th of July this summer the poet Gray died, and Temple, who had known Gray well at Cambridge, concluded a letter of 3 September to Boswell with a character of Gray which Boswell liked so well that he sent it to *The London Magazine*, where it was published without Temple's name in March 1772. (Later this was picked up by William Mason for the conclusion of his *Life of Gray*—his "Peroration," as Boswell said, an "apex upon the top of the monument of Gray.")

[1] Boswell appears as yet to be unaware of Beattie's Spenserian poem, *The Minstrel*, which had appeared earlier this year and is today his principal claim on posterity. See below, p. 151.

Another event of the summer, Boswell's excursion with his wife to Newcastle in August, was not without its special literary opportunity. On the way home, they stopped at Alnwick, and Boswell sent over to the Castle a note to the "Rev. Mr. Percy who published the *Reliques of Ancient English Poetry*."[1] ("Reverend Sir, I have been taking a little jaunt in the north of England with my wife for her health, and am just arrived at Alnwick, where I am informed you now are. If you are at leisure, I should be very happy to have the pleasure of your company at the White Hart.") Percy came and "sat an hour"[2] with them, giving Boswell "good accounts" of Johnson.

The summer reached a climax when the hero of the Corsicans, General Pasquale de Paoli, visited Scotland in company with the Polish Ambassador, Count Burzynski. From Tuesday 3 to Wednesday 11 September, Boswell showed them Edinburgh and conducted them on a triumphal progress of the West: to the Carron Iron Works, to Glasgow and the University, to Auchinleck, to Treesbank, to Loch Lomond. He kept hasty notes of a few conversations during this visit. He sent a flourished account to *The London Magazine*. Early in this year Mr. Charles Gascoigne of the Carron Works had been dunning Boswell and his friend Crosbie for a sum of £514. 11. 1 which was still owed by a group of Scottish gentlemen who had sent cannon to the brave Corsicans a few years past. In Boswell's *London Magazine* account of Paoli's visit:

[1] Not the direction on the letter but Boswell's explanation in his letter to Grange.

[2] Percy's diary in the British Museum, 26 August, has inserted in a smaller handwriting than the rest (perhaps at a later date): "I saw Mr. and Mrs. Boswell at the Swan." His Royal Highness the Duke of Cumberland had been visiting at Alnwick Castle for several days, making various trips around the country. This evening there was a "grand dinner, cards, etc." at the Castle, and Percy had to hurry back. On the morning of 27 August Percy set out with the Prince and others in ten carriages for Berwick-upon-Tweed, where the Corporation was to give a dinner and the Duke of Northumberland a ball. The Boswells were invited to the latter. But Boswell, sitting at the inn writing to Grange, decided to "shun" the crowd and confusion and shortage of horses and go home a quieter way. Meanwhile: "Monsieur Dutens, formerly resident at Turin and now an English clergyman, who has been making the tour of Europe with Lord Algernon Percy, is left in the Castle. He showed us the inside of it, and an old porter showed us the outside."

"They . . . proceeded on the Falkirk road and viewed the great canal of communication between the eastern and western seas, which is without question one of the greatest works in modern times. They then viewed the iron works at Carron, which are carried on at so prodigious an expense and have diffused so much opulence and such a spirit of improvement in that part of the country. General Paoli had a peculiar pleasure in viewing the forge where were formed the cannon and warlike stores which a society of gentlemen in Scotland sent to the aid of the brave Corsicans. They were elegantly entertained at dinner by Charles Gascoigne, Esq., of the Carron company, and while they sat at table all the vessels at Carron-shore, which were just in their view, had their flags displayed, a circumstance which led the General to speak with his usual esteem of the British *hearts of oak*."

In a letter to Garrick, Boswell alludes to the Auchinleck stage of the tour. "I have just been enjoying the very great happiness of a visit from my illustrious friend Pascal Paoli. He was two nights at Auchinleck, and you may figure the joy of my worthy father and me at seeing the Corsican Hero in our romantic groves." (Lord Auchinleck's well-enough-known characterisation of Paoli as a "landlouping scoundrel of a Corsican" was later set down—or invented—by Sir Walter Scott.) General Paoli spent his last night in Scotland at Boswell's house in Edinburgh, and on his departure next day Mrs. Boswell herself gave him "a convoy as far as Haddington".

Another part of Boswell's letter to Garrick calls attention to the three essays "On the Profession of a Player" in *The London Magazine* last year ("Pray have you read them?"). And Boswell makes the following pregnant announcement: "I intend being in London next March, and promise myself much happiness with you and my other friends there."

It seems characteristic of the complicated life which Boswell always led that even so agreeable an event as the visit of Paoli could have uncomfortable consequences. Sir David Dalrymple, Lord Hailes, colleague of Boswell's father in the Court of Session, avuncular friend and antiquarian correspondent of Boswell, had a brother who was Lord Provost of the City of Edinburgh. This Lord Provost for some reason failed to confer upon Paoli and the Polish Ambassador the freedom of the city and failed also to entertain them. Boswell, in the generously indignant but somewhat indirect manner which he often enough displayed, published two anonymous attacks upon the Provost in letters to the printer of *The London Chronicle* (24 October and 28 November), the second of these being an ironically pretended refutation of the first:

"I see, Sir, you do not know that our Provost is what is called a *Luckenbooths Merchant*, that is to say, is one who keeps a shop for retailing cloths, silks, and other materials for dress. Now, Sir, I desire to know what chance he could have of *selling any goods* either to General Paoli or the Polish Ambassador? . . . As to the *expense* of entertaining the strangers . . . as they are both Roman Catholics, he could have invited them on a *meagre* day. . . . Your correspondent says he has heard abundance of *personal* reflections! Our Provost's *person*, I am sure, cannot be reflected upon with any justice, unless being *fat* is to be held as a reflection."

Boswell's reward was a peppery letter from the Lord of Session:

"DEAR SIR,—Having long taken a sort of charge of you in various circumstances of life, I think it necessary to explain to you the reason of my putting a memorandum into your hands this morning. . . .

"I hope that because you was dissatisfied with his conduct in one particular, *you* did not insinuate that there were other *unnamed* circumstances in his conduct which you *could* mention as blameworthy. I hope that while you *attacked* with a *charge* you did not stab with an *insinuation*. . . . in other words, I hope *you* are *not* the author of the two articles in the London newspapers."

Hailes docketed his copy of the letter: "No answer made to this: but he visited me no longer."

Along with this letter from Hailes, we may note an exchange that had taken place between Boswell and another judge, Lord Kames, about a year earlier (6 and 13 October 1770). He wrote to Lord

Kames putting a combined question of law and conscience. "You know it has been questioned by some nice philosophers whether the practice of the law be consistent with strict moral rectitude." This question had come home with peculiar force on Boswell's looking up a principle in Kames's *Dictionary of Decisions* and then going down to the Advocates' Library to consult the original manuscript report on the sixteenth-century case cited in the *Dictionary*. He found that the latter was "totally different" from what the *Dictionary* said. "Now, my good Lord, what ought I to do? The *Dictionary of Decisions* is a book of authority in our court. . . . I know your Lordship is not answerable for the exactness of every decision in the *Dictionary*, as you have told me a part of it was done by another hand." "Friend Boswell," wrote Kames in reply, "I have not been much accustomed to answer casuistical queries, especially of such a squeamish nature. What business has your officious Honour to pry into secrets—was not the *Dictionary* sufficient authority without going farther? Take what you have got for your peeping." Then, relaxing, he went on to give Boswell some very good legal advice (perhaps what Boswell was in part angling for) and ended, "Yours affectionately, Henry Home. My hearty good wishes to your spouse, not forgetting, as the phrase is, my good brother and his lady."

On the first day of the new year, 1772, Boswell began again to keep a condensed Journal, mainly notes of social engagements and law cases, with a gradual increase of miscellaneous comment as the Journal lengthened into the month of March. We learn that he was deeply absorbed in professional duties. On 7 February, for instance, "hard, hard work". One entry, that for 21 February, shows that relations with the stepmother were not entirely ruptured. "My father and Lady Auchinleck . . . dined. Comfortable."

Other entries in February allude to Boswell's participation as counsel for the defence in a criminal trial. A certain George Macdonald, alias Baddinoch, indicted at the instance of His Majesty's Advocate for stealing an ox during the past summer in the county of Perth, and also for stealing seventeen sheep, and accused of "being habit and repute a thief", was tried before the Court of Justiciary on 17 February. The examination of witnesses took all day, until eight o'clock at night, when the Solicitor-General, Henry Dundas, summed up for the Crown and Boswell for the accused—"very ably". The jury next day found the sheep proved (though not the ox) and Macdonald a person of suspicious character, even if not a thief by "habit and repute". He was sentenced to transportation for life, the first seven years of his service to be given to the contractor for carrying convicts. Boswell's record of the trial day shows him well enough content.

[MONDAY] 17 [FEBRUARY]. Up by four, busy preparing charge to jury for Macdonald. Fine and solemn. In court all day, felt manly and calm and bold. Home fine.

Boswell's return to London for the first time after his marriage was now close at hand. Certain letters to and from London immediately preceded it. An exchange with Garrick at the end of February turned on the fact that word had come to Boswell that Garrick, perhaps through the carelessness of his maid, had lost Boswell's letter of the preceding October. "I ought in law and justice to prevail in an action of damages against her, and should be allowed to make oath as to the *pretium affectionis* which I put upon a letter from Mr. Garrick. I need not tell you that I could very honestly swear to a very high value; probably to more than your maid could well spare. If your maid be handsome and I were not a married man, I would move that she should give satisfaction by delivery of her person to the plaintiff according to the maxim of the civil law, *Qui non habet in aere luat in pelle*."[1] And Garrick: "It gives me great pleasure with the rest of your friends to hear that you are so happy; it is an old observation, and may be a true one, that rakes make the best husbands; however, between you and me, I think there is some risk in the experiment, and I most sincerely wish your lady joy of her success in the trial."

The proposed trip to London had a comfortable enough professional excuse. This was the principal theme of an exchange between Boswell and Johnson.

1 "He who does not have the price in coin shall have it taken out of his hide."

[Boswell to Samuel Johnson]

Edinburgh, 3 March 1772

My dear Sir,—It is hard that I cannot prevail with you to write to me oftener. But I am convinced that it is in vain to push you for a private correspondence with any regularity. I must therefore look upon you as a fountain of wisdom from whence few rills are communicated to a distance, and which must be approached at its source to partake fully of its virtues.

I fairly own that after an absence from you for any length of time I feel that I require a renewal of that spirit which your presence always gives me, and which makes me a better and a happier man than I imagined I could be before I was introduced to your acquaintance.

I am coming to London for some weeks this spring and hope to find you there and at length to fix our voyage to the Hebrides, or at least our journey through the Highlands of Scotland. I am to appear in an appeal from the Court of Session in the House of Lords. A schoolmaster in Scotland was deprived of his office for being somewhat severe in the chastisement of his scholars. The Court of Session considered it to be a very delicate matter to interfere between a master and his boys, and rather dangerous to the interests of learning and education in general to lessen the dignity of teachers and make them afraid of the resentment of too indulgent parents, instigated by the complaints of their children, and therefore restored him to his office. His enemies have appealed to the House of Lords, though the salary is only £20 a year. I was counsel for him here and am also to be so in the Supreme Judicature. I hope there will be little fear of a reversal. But I must beg leave to have your aid in my plan of supporting the decree. It is a general question and not a point of particular law.

Lord Elibank[1] remembers you always with great respect. I believe he will be with us this spring in London. We must have some select meetings with him.

[1] Patrick Murray, fifth Lord Elibank, advocate, soldier, and *littérateur*; patron and encourager of Scots men of letters. His country-seat was at Ballencrieff, near Haddington. He was some six years older than Johnson, who once assured him in a letter that he never met him without going away a wiser man.

I beg you may make my best compliments to Mr. Thrale's family,[1] and put my other friends in kind remembrance of me; and if you can without much trouble write me a few lines when you receive these, it will make me very happy. I ever am with unalterable respect and affection, my dear Sir, your much obliged humble servant,

JAMES BOSWELL.

[Received c. 22 March, Johnson to Boswell]

[London] 15 March 1772

DEAR SIR,—That you are coming so soon to town I am very glad; and still more glad that you are coming as an advocate. I think nothing more likely to make your life pass happily away than that consciousness of your own value which eminence in your profession will certainly confer. If I can give you any collateral help, I hope you do not suspect that it will be wanting. My kindness for you has neither the merit of singular virtue nor the reproach of singular prejudice. Whether to love you be right or wrong, I have many on my side: Mrs. Thrale loves you, and Mrs. Williams[2] loves you, and what would have inclined me to love you, if I had been neutral before, you are a great favourite of Dr. Beattie.

Of Dr. Beattie I should have thought much, but that his lady puts him out of my head: she is a very lovely woman.

The ejection which you come hither to oppose appears very cruel, unreasonable, and oppressive. I should think there could not be much doubt of your success.

My health grows better, yet I am not fully recovered. I believe it is held that men do not recover very fast after threescore. I hope yet to see Beattie's College and have not given up the western voyage. But however all this may be or not, let us try to make each other happy when we meet, and not refer our pleasure to distant times or distant places.

[1] Henry Thrale, wealthy brewer and M.P. for Southwark, and his wife Hester Lynch (later celebrated as Mrs. Piozzi). At their hospitable houses in Southwark and Streatham Johnson found the favourite havens of his later years.

[2] Anna Williams, the blind poetess, had been a friend of Johnson's wife and was now an inmate of Johnson's household.

How comes it that you tell me nothing of your lady? I hope to see her some time and till then shall be glad to hear of her. I am, dear Sir, etc.,

SAM. JOHNSON.

Three entries near the end of Boswell's brief Journal for the winter contain references to his wife and record a crisis. (The character Π stands for "Peggie".)

SATURDAY 28 FEBRUARY. Breakfasted with Grange between 10 and 11 most comfortably. Π ill.

TUESDAY 3 MARCH. Π very ill. Loss sustained. Digges dined with me tête-à-tête. Thought of old days. . . . [Letters from Temple of 26 March and 3 April confirm the meaning. "It gives me much pain to hear so indifferent an account of Mrs. Boswell's health. Miscarriages are disagreeable circumstances. . . . "]

FRIDAY 13 MARCH. . . . Dined father's. . . . Home and romping like to have been fatal. Π to part. I looked it in the face calm a little but soon grew uneasy. Made up again.

He departed for London on the morning of 14 March, a day which he signalised by resuming his fully written Journal.

JOURNAL OF MY JAUNT TO LONDON

SPRING 1772

SATURDAY 14 MARCH. I was in a flutter to a certain degree at the thoughts of setting out for London, for which I have always had an enthusiastic fondness. I was at the same time seriously concerned at parting with my wife. Everything depends upon our ideas; and I could with truth describe what passed in my mind this day in such a manner as to furnish out a narrative like that of the Londoner in the *Idler* who gives a dreadful detail of the disasters which befell him on a jaunt into the country, such as rain falling upon him from the heavens and many other circumstances.[1] My parting with my wife this day would make just such a figure should I describe it as I really felt it; for to part with a valuable friend and constant companion and go four hundred miles from her, though but for two months, is something considerable to a domestic man who has any turn to anxiety of mind.

I set out about four o'clock in the afternoon. Mr. William Wilson, Writer to the Signet, was my travelling companion. He gave me my first fee, which has made me ever since look upon him with particular regard.[2] He has indeed given me a great many more fees, which has served to keep alive the first impression made upon my—*hand*, which, as a lawyer, is equivalent to making an impression on my *heart*. He will be sixty-two the 25 of April next but has nothing of an old man about him except experience, being healthy and cheerful though

[1] Will Marvel in *Idler* No. 49.

[2] A fee of one guinea, received for a cause argued before the Justice-Clerk (Thomas Miller) on 29 July 1766, the day that Boswell put on the gown. On 27 January 1786, Boswell, setting out for London in company with William Wilson's son John, recalled once more that the father had given him his first fee.

most laborious in his profession. We had along with us in another chaise Mr. Home the coachmaker's son and a son of Mr. Callander of Craigforth's. The first, being bred to his father's business, was going to London for his improvement. The latter, a fine smart little fellow about seventeen who had already been three years in America, was going out to the East Indies. The country was deeply covered with snow, and we were told we could not take the Blackshiels road; so we went by Haddington. We got to Dunbar at night. The house was dirty and confused. We were served by a *lass* who was both ugly and stupid. When Mr. Wilson asked if she could get him some oatmeal porridge, she answered, "Some oatmeal punch?" Had one of your Englishmen, well prepared to form strange notions of Scotland, heard this, it would have been enough for him to represent us as so devoted to oatmeal that we make our very punch with it.

SUNDAY 15 MARCH. We went on very well, considering the deep roads. We resolved never to dine but only to take some cold meat at midday, which we did very heartily. We got at night to Alnwick.

MONDAY 16 MARCH. Mr. Wilson and I studied law papers sometimes during this our journey, and sometimes sang. It was curious to hear him sing the songs in *The Beggar's Opera*. He had a various reading of the line, "And turns our lead to gold." He sang: "And turns *all* our lead to gold," believing it to be the genuine text; and he insisted very strongly on the justice of the preference given to the highwayman's fire over that of the chemist, in this view: because the chemist's fire turns only a small proportion to gold.[1] I gave him my explanation of a line which is by no means clear in its meaning to most people and may perhaps be mistaken by me. The line I mean is, "As men should serve a cucumber." It refers to the expression in the next line: "She flings herself away." Now the question is, why should men fling away a cucumber? My explanation is this. It is a common saying, "As cool as a cucumber," so that a cucumber is a cooling thing. Now Mrs. Peachum who sings the song was a woman of that genius that did not like men should be cool but on the contrary; and there-

[1] He was right as to the text (*Beggar's Opera* II, ii, Air XX), but not necessarily so in his explanation.

fore she would have them fling away such frigorific stuff.[1] We got at night to Darlington. I stopped about a quarter of an hour with my brother at Newcastle;[2] and we were stopped a while by boating the river. It was terrible to see the ruins of the bridge.[3]

TUESDAY 17 MARCH. Nothing material happened. We got at night to Doncaster. (I should have observed[4] that I paid a visit at Morpeth to Mrs. Collingwood, a widow lady, mother to a gentleman of a good estate in the neighbourhood, and aunt to my friend Temple's wife. I always pay her that compliment, unless when I pass through Morpeth in the night-time. She takes it very kind. Upon this occasion she said I showed her "such unparalleled attention".)

I this day[5] paid a visit at Grantham to the Reverend Mr. Palmer, a clergyman who has a good living there. He was chaplain to Sir John Cust when Speaker of the House of Commons. He carried me upstairs to an elegant room ornamented with some fine prints, and as it was a beautiful forenoon, the sun shone brightly upon them. But I saw what I had never seen before: his spouse, a comely Vandyck figure, and his daughter, one of the loveliest figures I ever beheld. I cannot help being instantaneously affected by the sight of beauty. Mr. Palmer is a man of learning and worth, hospitable and decently social. He has a jolly appearance, not plump and sleek, but a fair well-kept skin, easy and happy. My being accustomed to the bar has made me callous to the most attentive looks of the ablest men. But a glance from a fine eye can yet affect my assurance. I felt this today. I compared myself to

[1] *Beggar's Opera* I, viii, Air VII. In the Hebrides, 5 October 1773, Johnson would give Boswell the correct explanation: "It has been a common saying in England of every great physician, that he prescribed that a cucumber should be well sliced and dressed with vinegar, and then thrown out, as good for nothing."

[2] Boswell's brother John, a half-pay lieutenant in the Army, had for ten years been subject to recurring attacks of insanity, and was now under the care of a Dr. Wilson at Newcastle.

[3] The ancient stone bridge across the Tyne, dating from 1250, had been destroyed by a flood four months earlier.

[4] Under Monday 16 March.

[5] Rather, on Wednesday 18 March, for Grantham is fifty-two miles south of Doncaster. The manuscript shows a complicated confusion in the dating at this point.

one of those animals who by their strong scales or tough skins are invulnerable by a bullet but may be wounded by the sharp point of a sword, which can pierce between the scales or hit some weak point of the skin.

We got at night to Doncaster. The English inns are indeed most admirable; and whenever a man has been some time without seeing them, he must be agreeably struck.

WEDNESDAY 18 MARCH. Nothing worth recording was either said or done. But I shall here put down a simile which I made at Alnwick on Sunday night. Mr. Wilson was observing what an advantage it was to a lawyer to have much practice. "Ay," said I, "he never knows law well till he has had it connected in his mind with facts, with particular causes. They are to principles of law like sticks to peas in a garden. Principles will lie sluggish in the mind by themselves. They will not rise vigorous unless supported by real causes." This is a good idea; and upon some occasion when my imagination is warmer and my expression more fluent I may expand it. It is a bud which would have an excellent appearance if fully and beautifully blown. We got at night to Buckden.

THURSDAY 19 MARCH. We breakfasted at Stevenage, where we shaved and dressed. Wilson, our barber there, had married a woman of Welwyn in Hertfordshire, six miles from this place, so knew or pretended to know the celebrated Dr. Young. He gave us a strange account of him. He said his son had somehow offended him, and the Doctor would never be reconciled to him and would not so much as see him when on death-bed; that he put everything past him that he could; but that the son succeeded him in a pretty estate and then married the daughter of a clergyman in whose house he had lived and been supported during his father's displeasure. This implacability was not improbable in the dark and forcible spirit of the author of *Night Thoughts*.[1] But our barber gave us a more extraordinary

[1] Edward Young's *The Complaint, or Night Thoughts on Life, Death, and Immortality*, a sombre poem of nine books in blank verse, appeared from 1742 to 1745 and was widely known both in England and on the Continent. It is remembered today most often in the line (I. 392): "Procrastination is the thief of time."

anecdote. He said the Doctor kept a mistress, a likely woman who lived with him till he died; that he left this woman all he could, and that their connexion was well known. I think it is Ranger who says, "Your grave men are always the greatest whoremasters."[1] The observation may be true. But Doctor Young was much more than a grave man; he was a gloomy, a melancholy, a miserable man; a man to whom all Nature appeared under the darkest shade, a man of the deepest theology and most sublime ideas of futurity. That such a man should keep a mistress seems hardly credible.[2] Our barber however was very confident in his assertion. I humoured the fellow, and when a very pretty maid came into the room, "That," said I, "would do for Dr. Young." I have for some time thought of writing an essay on the genius and writings of Dr. Young. It seems his son now lives at Welwyn. I may contrive to get some authentic information with regard to his private life.[3]

The snow was now very thin and we found ourselves in a milder and more benign climate. I looked back on former parts of my life, and my present firmness and cheerfulness of mind had full value by comparison with the weakness and gloominess which I recollected. The very driving in the post-chaise was a considerable pleasure. We arrived in London about five o'clock, having just taken about five days to the journey, and indeed it cannot be performed in less with comfort; that is to say, taking a moderate degree of the refreshments of eating, drinking, and sleeping, which one ought surely to do unless when some necessity obliges to hurry. There was a thick fog over

[1] Ranger is the principal character in Benjamin Hoadly's *Suspicious Husband*, a favourite role of actors in the eighteenth century. The quotation, slightly inaccurate, is from Act II, Scene iv.

[2] See below, p. 66. Johnson also rejected the story. "I asked him if there was any improper connexion between them. 'No, Sir, no more than between two statues' " (*Hebrides*, 30 September 1773). Miss Mary Hallows, daughter of a clerical friend of Young's, was about thirty-eight years old when she came to live with him as his housekeeper in 1748. On his death in 1765 at the age of eighty-two he left her £600.

[3] Boswell, in Johnson's company, did visit Frederick Young at Welwyn, 2 June 1781, and did succeed in obtaining from him some interesting details about the author of *Night Thoughts*, but the projected essay was never written.

London today, so that I did not get the view of it from Highgate Hill which used to elate me so highly. We stopped at the Lemon-tree Inn at the top of the Haymarket, a true Scots house, where Colin Donaldson lived many years and made much money. He gave up business some time ago and was succeeded by one Armstrong, who was just dead; so the house was in a state of viduity. It was as dirty and confused as any Scots inn can be, though in the middle of London. As it was the first house I was in when I came first to London, there was a certain curious pleasure in finding myself in it again.

We eat a beefsteak and drank a glass of port and then every man went to his proper destination. General Paoli had invited me to come and lodge at his house, and I indeed reckoned upon being there. I immediately went to his house in Albemarle Street. I asked a chairman which was General Paoli's. "What," said he, "the General who is married to Lady———?" (I did not hear what.) "No," said his companion, "the foreign gentleman." So little is the great Paoli known by some. I immediately after this dialogue perceived Giuseppe, the General's little Corsican servant, just before me. I called; he came running up and seized me by the hand, then hurried along to his master's.

Paoli embraced me with all welcome. Count Gentili was with him, a Corsican count long in the Austrian service, and who gave up his commission to go home and fight along with his countrymen, and then accompanied the General to England. The Count is a thin creature with a sharp hooked nose and a voice like a *fugie cock*,[1] like a crow screaming when pursued by a hawk. He was very happy to meet me again, but was rather a little troublesome, for it seems he had lodged eighteen months with two Miss Carnegies from Scotland settled in London and was very keen to speak Scots; and indeed he had made a good proficiency in it, though I had no pleasure in hearing him cry, "How's aw wi' ye? Will you sit into the fire?" And then he told that when the King asked the Duchess of Gordon how she liked London, she said, "It's frizzle-frizzling aw the morning and knock-knocking aw the neght" (night).[2] This was natural enough for Jeanie

[1] A cock that runs away and will not fight.

[2] "You spend all the morning getting your hair dressed and all the evening bustling about."

Maxwell. But the Count's figure and sharp key of speaking and a broadness High German could not but disgust me. There was also here Signor Martinelli, an Italian *letterato*, an old man. He has written a history of England which the General praised. There was lying on one of the tables in the room a fine edition of Boccaccio, published by him with notes, at London, some years ago. He said he had lost £400 sterling by it. I took this to be excessive exaggeration, to which such foreigners are much given. I was glad he had no *Proposals* to offer. In a little came in a Corsican abbé, the Abbate———.[1] He had been of the party for the Genoese;[2] but having gone to Venice and studied, his mind opened and he became a zealous patriot. The conversation was of a political and literary kind; but as I had not yet recovered a readiness at following people speaking Italian, I made little of it.

When I made a motion to go away and told the General that I had not fixed my lodgings, he asked me to take a room in his house; but I could see that he did not think he had one sufficiently good, and besides that, as Count Gentili was now lodged with him, it would not be convenient that I should be with him too. I considered also that my being lodged there might give the Grub-street writers an opportunity of throwing out low abuse, and saying that he was pensioned by British generosity and kept a Scotsman gratis in his house.[3] I therefore begged leave to decline accepting his invitation but said I should take lodgings near him. I then took my leave for that night and got into the street in a disagreeable uncertainty where I should sleep. I did not know but Mr. Dilly's house might be full; and it was a great distance from me now.[4] I had no small repugnance at the thought of sleeping at the Lemon-tree, but imagined I might be obliged to land there. As I walked up the Strand and passed through a variety of fine girls, genteelly dressed, all wearing Venus's girdle, all inviting me to

[1] Probably Andrei, whom Boswell meets, as a former acquaintance, at Paoli's 3 April 1775.

[2] The power against which the Corsicans under Paoli's leadership revolted. See *Boswell on the Grand Tour: Italy, Corsica, and France, 1765–1766*, p. 155.

[3] Paoli had received a large pension (£1200 a year) from the Civil List. For this there can be little doubt that Boswell's book had been largely responsible.

[4] "Mr. Dilly" was Edward, senior member of the firm of Edward and Charles Dilly, who had published Boswell's *Account of Corsica* in 1768.

amorous intercourse, I confess I was a good deal uneasy. My ideas naturally run into their old channels, which were pretty deeply worn, and I was indulging speculations about polygamy and the concubines of the patriarchs and the harmlessness of temporary likings unconnected with mental attachment. I was really in a disagreeable state and yet would not free myself from it by taking a coach. I resolved never again to come to London without bringing my wife along with me.

I called and sat a few minutes with Mr. William Wilson, who had taken up his quarters at a friend's house, Mr. Murray's, bookseller in Fleet Street.[1] I then called in Johnson's Court for my revered friend, Mr. Samuel Johnson. But he was at Mr. Thrale's in the Borough, and was not to be home till next day; and Mrs. Williams was out upon a visit. I proceeded to the Poultry to Mr. Dilly's. Mr. Charles was at home and gave me a hearty welcome. I was pleased to find Mrs. Judd the housekeeper and James the servant both there. Mr. Charles was full of the history of Bolland, the sheriff's officer who had been hanged the day before at Tyburn,[2] and our conversation was quite the London style—the City style.[3] We sat down to a cold fowl and ham and tarts, and I also got a basin of excellent soup and felt myself quite comfortable. In a little in came my friend Mr. Edward Dilly, as lively, as quick-speaking, and as cordial as ever, and much happiness did he show on seeing me. Along with him was Mrs. Knowles, famous for needlework. She did a head of the King for which the Queen made her a *present* of £800, but said her work was invaluable. Her husband was an apothecary; but upon his wife's getting thus a kind of interest at Court, bethought himself of commencing physician and is now actually studying at Edinburgh in order to take his degrees. She was

[1] Founder of the house of John Murray, Ltd. Byron's publisher was his son.

[2] James Bolland had started life as a short-weight butcher. He later turned sheriff's officer and blackmailed young men whom he arrested into securing on account from tradesmen large quantities of goods, to be brought to his house and sold. He was finally hanged for forging an endorsement on a note. *The Gentleman's Magazine* for this month lists two book-length biographies of him.

[3] Boswell is distinguishing the mercantile style of the old City of London (the portion east of Temple Bar) from the fashionable or West End style of Albemarle Street.

formerly a distinguished beauty and still looked very well, and was a clever agreeable woman. Mr. Dilly insisted on my lodging there. He wanted to have me altogether, but at any rate insisted I should stay that night, and whenever I was late in the City end of the town, should always come to my room there and consider it as my home. I felt myself truly well, and only regretted that my dearest companion was not with me.

FRIDAY 20 MARCH. While we were sitting at breakfast, in came my old friend Captain Hoggan,[1] one who under an external appearance of being very delicate and even a little foppish is a man of steady and generous friendship and has uncommon prudence and knowledge in the common affairs of life. He kindly offered to assist me in getting lodgings; and very luckily a Captain Boothby of his regiment, an acquaintance of ours, had that very morning left very good lodgings at Mr. King's, glover, corner of Conduit Street. We drove immediately in a hackney-coach to look at them, and they pleased me much; and not the less so that they were only a guinea a week, which, for a first floor in a centrical part of the town, is very reasonable. Laird Heron occupied them last year. I therefore without hesitation hired them, and was glad to be fixed in a home at once, without having any time to pass in a disagreeable state of doubt, like a bachelor who is determined to marry but knows not on whom to fix. Lodgings are still more difficult to choose than wives; because it does not often happen that a man conceives a particular affection for one lodging more than another till he has lived a while in one and takes a kind of regard for it from habit.

I then went and called for the Duke of Queensberry.[2] Old Quan, the porter, shook me by the hand and most cordially ushered me in. The Duke received me very civilly, and we had some conversation on the common topics of the times, when in came Captain Douglas of

[1] It is not known when Boswell formed an intimacy with Captain James Hoggan, but they were already "old companions" when they met in Ireland in May 1769.

[2] The patron of letters in the generation of Pope and Gay was now Keeper of the Great Seal of Scotland (since 1760) and Lord Justice-General (since 1763).

Kelhead.[1] After sitting a little, he and I went and called for DOUGLAS (the Laird),[2] but he was not at home. I found David Kennedy at home and had a laugh with him.[3]

I find it would be very tedious and idle to put down every visit which I made, so I shall mark only what is of some consequence and not tell that I called at doors and did not find people at home. My views in coming to London this spring were: to refresh my mind by the variety and spirit of the metropolis, the conversation of my revered friend Mr. Samuel Johnson and that of other men of genius and learning; to try if I could get something for myself, or be of service to any of my friends by means of the Duke of Queensberry, Lord Mountstuart,[4] or Douglas, all of whom had given me reason to expect their assistance; to be employed in Scotch appeals in the House of Lords, and also see how the land might lie for me at the English bar; and to endeavour to get my brother David well settled as a merchant in London.[5] There is business enough.

I dined this day with General Paoli. Brompton the painter was there. He seemed to be a genteel, sensible man, and spoke Italian remarkably well. Our conversation was just on ordinary topics. In the afternoon I called on my friend Sir Alexander Macdonald and found him and my beautiful cousin, my Lady,[6] sitting by themselves in

[1] Capt. (later Sir) William Douglas of Kelhead was a fairly close relation of Boswell's, his grandmother and Boswell's mother being half-sisters. He was much more distantly related to the Duke, but was none the less in line for the Queensberry marquessate and earldom, to which his son succeeded in 1810.

[2] Boswell's client and the victor in the celebrated Douglas cause in 1769, Archibald James Edward Douglas; he became first Baron Douglas in 1790. Boswell frequently writes GOD and DOUGLAS in large characters.

[3] David Kennedy, advocate and M.P., later tenth Earl of Cassillis, was a joker, as Boswell explains below (5 April 1773).

[4] Boswell's companion of the Italian tour, son and heir of the great Lord Bute, would fail to justify present hopes.

[5] David, under the more acceptable name of Thomas (the name David aroused anti-Semitic responses among the Spaniards), was now a merchant at Valencia and through the efforts of Boswell's friend the Earl Marischal held a patent as consul.

[6] Sir Alexander Macdonald of Sleat was a Highland laird with an Eton education. Lady Macdonald was daughter to Godfrey Bosville of Gunthwaite and

a very tolerable house in Cavendish Square, not magnificent but very well. They were in great spirits at seeing me. I should have mentioned that I met his brother Archie in the forenoon and walked with him to his chambers in Lincoln's Inn, and was told by him that Sir Alexander was thinking to stand for Member of Parliament for the shire of Inverness. I also should have mentioned that I called at my old friend Mr. Love's of Drury Lane Theatre, whom I found very ill of a severe cough and looking as ill as ever he had pretended to do in any character upon the stage. I promised to see him sometimes. Sir Alexander Macdonald and I are always merry when we meet and always get into the humour of punning and playing upon words, which I cannot help thinking very good amusement. Lady Macdonald said she was just going abroad to visit a lady who was lying in, and who was a great wit. "Ay," said I, "it seems she is a lady of a *pregnant* genius." The Knight and I went in his coach and called for my kinsman Mr. Bosville and for Mr. Dempster, but found neither. He went to a rout; and I strolled about awhile and then went home.

The maid of the house was a pretty little black-eyed girl, and I was informed (as a secret) by Hoggan that Captain Boothby had found her to be very complaisant. This was rather a bad circumstance for me. Before I went to bed the gipsy came, and with a sweet English voice asked, "Do you want anything more tonight, Sir?"

SATURDAY 21 MARCH. Captain Hoggan breakfasted with me. Joseph, my servant, whom I had left at Newcastle to come by sea if the wind was fair, and if not, by the fly, had arrived last night, but having forgotten the street where General Paoli lives, did not find me out till this morning. I was glad to see him; for I found myself not at my ease without him.

I went to Johnson's Court, Fleet Street, and was happy enough to find Mr. Johnson at home. Frank, his black, who had left him for some years, was returned to him, and showed me up to his study. Frank and I were pleased to renew our old acquaintance. I waited a

---

Thorpe, the Yorkshire squire whom Boswell, on very tenuous evidence, accepted as his chief. She had at one time been on Boswell's own list of matrimonial possibilities.

little and then heard the great man coming upstairs. The sound of his feet upon the timber steps was weighty and well announced his approach. He had on an old purple cloth suit and a large whitish wig. He embraced me with a robust sincerity of friendship, saying, "I am glad to see thee, I am glad to see thee. Come sit you down. You have not had my letter?"[1] "No, Sir." (I shall give what passed, as much as I can, in the way of dialogue.) "Well, I am glad you are come, and glad you are come upon such an errand" (meaning, to support the schoolmaster of Campbeltown in the House of Lords).[2] "I hope, Sir, there will be no fear of him. It is a very delicate matter to interfere between a master and his scholars; nor do I see how you can fix the degree of severity that a master may use." JOHNSON. "No, Sir. Till you fix the degree of negligence and obstinacy of the scholars, you cannot fix the degree of severity of the master. Severity must be continued until obstinacy be subdued and negligence cured." BOSWELL. "To speak candidly, Sir, this man was rather too severe." JOHNSON. "Has he broke any bones?" BOSWELL. "No." JOHNSON. "Has he fractured any skulls?" BOSWELL. "No."[3] JOHNSON. "Then, Sir, he is safe enough. My master at Lichfield, Hunter, used to beat us unmercifully. He erred in not making a distinction between mistake and negligence; for he would beat a boy equally for not knowing a thing as for neglecting to know it. He would have asked a boy a question, and if he did not answer it, he beat him, without considering whether he had an opportunity of knowing how to answer it. Now, Sir, if a boy could

[1] See above, p. 28. Boswell's Register of Letters fails to record the receipt of this letter.

[2] See above, p. 27. The schoolmaster's name was John Hastie. Though the principal charge against him was brutality, the magistrates and council also alleged irregular attendance. He maintained that his office was not a public one and that the magistrates had no jurisdiction; furthermore that there was no reasonable cause for his dismissal.

[3] He at least came close to it. "Scarce a day passed without some of the scholars coming home . . with their heads cut and their bodies discoloured. . . . He beat the pupils with wooden squares . . . and sometimes with his fists, and used his feet by kicking them. . . . dragging them by the hair of the head." (Paton's *Reports of Cases upon Appeal from Scotland*, ii. 277, quoted by G. B. Hill, *Life of Johnson*, ii. 186 *n*.).

answer every question, there would be no need of a master to teach him."

By this time his levée was attended by the Reverend Mr. Stockdale, a strange mortal born at Berwick-upon-Tweed and an acquaintance of my worthy friend Temple's, by whose recommendation I had him once to breakfast with me as I passed through Berwick. He was once an officer in the Army; then turned clergyman; then was guilty of irregularities, left an old woman whom he had married for money, and ran away to France with a young lady. The old woman having died, he came to London, married the young lady, commenced translator and author, and is now curate of Ludgate and chaplain to the Fleet Prison. He is a profound admirer of Mr. Johnson's, who is very good to him.[1] The other attendant on the levée this morning was a Mrs. Desmoulins, the wife of a writing-master, who seemed to be an old acquaintance of Mr. Johnson's, having been intimate with his wife. Stockdale and she did not much interrupt our conversation.

I said, "Hunter is a Scotch name. So this master who beat you so severely has been a Scotsman. I can now account for your prejudice against Scotsmen." JOHNSON. "No, Sir, he was not Scotch; and, abstracting from his brutality, he was a very good master."

We had before this when by ourselves talked of his[2] two political pamphlets *The False Alarm* and *Thoughts respecting the Transactions*

[1] The Reverend Percival Stockdale (1736–1811), miscellaneous journalist, poet, and eccentric, later thought himself badly used by the booksellers when they passed him over and chose Johnson to write the *Lives of the Poets*. In the *Life of Johnson* Boswell refers to a poem by Stockdale entitled *The Remonstrance*, published in 1770. This contains the memorable couplet (p. 31):

> The frantic mother, and the weeping sire,
> Virgins deflowered, and property on fire!

Stockdale had also written, in 1764, an *Elegy on the Death of Dr. Johnson's Favourite Cat* (Hodge).

[2] Boswell pillaged this Journal extensively when he came to write the *Life of Johnson*, removing for copy most of the leaves which contained Johnsonian conversations. All but one of the missing fragments having turned up when Boswell's manuscript of the *Life* was unearthed at Malahide Castle in 1940, they are now printed for the first time as Boswell originally wrote them. The first of the recovered portions (eight pages of the manuscript) begins at this point.

concerning Falkland's Islands. JOHNSON. "Well, Sir, which of 'em did you think the best?" BOSWELL. "I liked the second best." JOHNSON. "Why, Sir, I liked the first best; and Beattie liked the first best. Sir, there is a subtlety of disquisition in the first that is worth all of the fire of the second." BOSWELL. "Pray, Sir, is it true that Lord North paid you a visit, and that you got £200 a year of addition to your pension?" JOHNSON. "No, Sir. Except what I had from the bookseller, I did not get a farthing by them. And between you and me, I believe Lord North is no friend to me."[1] BOSWELL. "How so, Sir?" JOHNSON. "Why, Sir, you cannot account for the fancies of men." BOSWELL. "But, Sir, don't you think him an able minister?" JOHNSON. "Yes, indeed, Sir.—Well, how does Lord Elibank? and how does Lord Monboddo?" BOSWELL. "Very well, Sir. Lord Monboddo[2] still maintains the superiority of the savage life." JOHNSON. "What strange narrowness of mind now is that to think the things we have not [known] are better than the things which we have known." BOSWELL. "Why, Sir, that is a common prejudice." JOHNSON. "Yes, Sir. But a common prejudice should not be found in one whose trade it is to rectify error."

Then came in a Mr. ——— who was to go out mate in the ship along with Mr. Banks and Dr. Solander.[3] Mr. Johnson asked what were the names of the ships which were to go upon the expedition. Mr. ——— said they were once to be called the *Drake* and the *Raleigh*, but now they were to be called the *Resolution* and the *Adventure*. JOHNSON. "Much better; for had the *Raleigh*[4] returned without going round the world, it would have been ridiculous. To give them the names of the *Drake* and the *Raleigh* was laying a trap for satire." BOSWELL. "Had not you some desire to go upon this expedition, Sir?" JOHNSON. "Why, yes; but I soon laid it aside. Sir, there is very little

[1] It is difficult to arrive at a confident interpretation of the fact that shortly after the publication of Johnson's *Taxation No Tyranny* in 1775, Lord North as Chancellor of the University of Oxford proposed the degree of Doctor of Civil Law for Johnson.

[2] See below, p. 146.

[3] On Cook's second expedition, which sailed on 13 July 1772. Banks and Solander later changed their minds and made a tour to Iceland instead.

[4] As Croker pointed out, Boswell should have written "*Drake*".

intellectual in the course. Besides, I see but at a little distance. So it was not worth my while to go to see birds fly which I should not have seen fly, and fishes swim which I should not have seen swim."

Mr. ——— went away and Mr. Johnson left us for a little; when Stockdale and Mrs. Desmoulins (or Dem*ull*ins as they call her in English) began to open a little with me. I said I thought there was glory in Banks, a fine young fellow of £5000 a year, going out on so dangerous an expedition from a thirst of knowledge. Stockdale contested this and said it was no more in Banks than a gratification of his particular passion instead of going to Newmarket or the like; that he thought it would be much more glorious for him to stay at home and employ his fortune in relieving indigent merit and doing good to numbers. That he thought a man's going on a dangerous expedition in order to make himself independent rather than lounge at home was glorious. Mrs. Desmoulins said she could not see how it was glorious in a man to do what he was driven to by necessity. I said, "I indeed cannot see that if the one is not glorious, the other should be it. There is surely no glory in a man's going out on an expedition to get his dinner. I know not but Mr. Banks may have been partly actuated by public spirit. But at any rate I think it is glorious for a young man of great fortune to have so noble a passion instead of those mean passions by which most of them are actuated."

We talked of Dr. Hawkesworth's[1] being employed in writing an account of the expedition which Mr. Banks and Dr. Solander have already made, and that he would do it well. "Ay," said I, "he has formed himself upon the great model" (meaning Dr. Johnson). Stockdale said, "I have observed that Dr. Johnson's friends are like Alexander's courtiers, who imitated his wry neck. They imitate Dr.

[1] John Hawkesworth, LL.D. (c. 1715–1773) had been the editor and one of the authors, along with Samuel Johnson, of *The Adventurer*, 1752–1754. In 1771 upon Garrick's recommendation he had been appointed by the Admiralty to publish *An Account of the Voyages Undertaken by the Order of His Present Majesty for Making Discoveries in the Southern Hemisphere . . . Drawn up from the Journals Which Were Kept by the Several Commanders, and from the Papers of Joseph Banks, Esq*. This work appeared in three volumes in 1773 and met with such severe criticism for inaccuracies and indecencies that Hawkesworth's health was thought to have been affected and his end hastened. He died in November of that year.

Johnson's weaknesses, if I may [say] so, or oddities." "Particularities if you please, Sir," said Mrs. Desmoulins.

When Mr. Johnson returned to us, I told him we had been disputing whether Banks and Solander could be allowed to have glory from this expedition.[1] He said, "Why, Sir, it was properly for botany that they went out. I believe they thought only of culling of simples."[2]

I had thanked him for showing civilities to Beattie. "Sir," said he, "I should thank you. He's a fine fellow, Beattie. Mrs. Thrale says if ever she has another husband, she'll have Beattie. He sunk upon us[3] that he was married; else we should have shown his lady more civilities. She is a very fine woman. But how can you show civilities to a nonentity? I did not think he had been married. Nay, I did not think about it, one way or other; but he did not tell us of his lady till late."

He then spoke of St. Kilda.[4] I told him I thought of buying it. "Pray do," said he. "We shall go and pass a winter amid the blasts there. We shall have fine fish, and we shall take some dried tongues with us and some books. We shall have a strong-built vessel and some Orkney men to navigate her. We must build a tolerable house. But we may carry with us a wooden house ready made and nothing to do but to put it up. I remember there was a gentleman going to North America who had a curiosity to see me, and I gave him that advice, as he was going to a country where they cut down wood only to get rid of it. Consider, Sir, by buying St. Kilda you may keep the people from

[1] That is, from Cook's *first* expedition, 1768–1771. The question is whether the scientific observers should share the glory of what was popularly thought of as a great feat of navigation.

[2] *Romeo and Juliet*, V, i, 40.

[3] "Suppressed the fact". Beattie was offended by this remark when it appeared in the *Life of Johnson*, and wrote a letter to Boswell which was printed as a note in the second edition.

[4] The chief islet of a rocky group lying in the Atlantic forty miles north-west of the north-west extremity of North Uist in the Outer Hebrides. Long the only inhabited island of the group, it has in recent years been evacuated. Johnson and Boswell had talked about St. Kilda in the spring of 1768 and in July 1763. Its remoteness and mystery may be taken as a symbol of what they will seek in the Hebrides on their tour in the following year.

falling into worse hands. We must give them a clergyman, and he shall be one of Beattie's choosing. I'll be your Lord Chancellor or what you please." BOSWELL. "Are you serious, Sir, in advising me to buy St. Kilda? for if you should advise me to go to Japan, I believe I should do it." JOHNSON. "Why, yes, I am serious." BOSWELL. "Why, then I'll try it."

I gave him an account of the two parties in the Church of Scotland, those for patronage and those against it.[1] He said it should be settled one way or other. He said he could not be for a popular election when he considered that it occasioned such unworthy courting of the people, such slandering by one party against the other, and other such disadvantages; and that it was enough to allow the people to insist against the settlement of a minister for solid reasons (either of heresy or immorality I suppose he meant).

He was engaged[2] to dine with Sir Joshua Reynolds; so I left him, and he bid me come again at nine in the evening. I called on Mrs. Williams for a little, and then went to Dolly's beefsteak house, where I dined very comfortably, meditating on old times when I used to dine there frequently[3] and was in a most dissipated and sickly state of mind, without any fixed rational purpose and being hardly able to observe common decency of conduct.

I entered into conversation with some gentlemen at the same table. One of them showed me a pair of shoes he had on which he said cost him eleven shillings, having double soles made of the very choice part of the hide. Another had on a very handsome wig. I asked him who made it. "For," said I, "Sir, I have a wife who was very angry at me for cutting off my hair, and wants much I should at least have a genteel wig." He told me it was made by Howard in Leicester Fields. "Thank you, Sir," said I; "you will enable me to establish domestic tranquillity." There is an immense satisfaction in talking away freely, where one is not known. I observed that the greatest disadvantage of

[1] On 17 April Boswell wrote an essay on this subject for *The London Magazine*. See below, pp. 131, 132.

[2] Here the first newly recovered portion of the text ends. See above, p. 42 *n*. 2.

[3] See, for example, *Boswell's London Journal, 1762–1763*, the entry for 15 December 1762.

Dolly's was that a man had for most part no society but just eat his dinner by himself. The gentleman with the eleven-shillings shoes said that was not the case here. But, besides, he had often heard it observed that a man could not eat his dinner alone, but that he could not say he had ever experienced this. That it depended very much on a man's manner of life. That he (who it seems was an attorney), when tired with a long day's business in Westminster Hall, would have thought it a fatigue to have had anybody along with him at dinner; but would go home and sit down by himself and eat his dinner most heartily and comfortable. There was a true specimen of John Bull here. But I know not if in certain states of mind the doctrine may not be just.

I called at Dempster's.[1] He had an Indian lad and an Indian boy for his servants; and while I was writing a note to him in his room, as he was abroad, I was attended by a grave, decent-looking man whose office in the household I could not divine. He turned out to be a master who came in to instruct the two Indians.

I strolled about and at half an hour past nine returned to Mr. Johnson's. We drank tea with Mrs. Williams. She told us a story of second sight which happened in Wales, her country. Mr. Johnson said he should like to have some stories as to that well authenticated. I told him the story of this Lord Eglinton and another officer having seen what we in Scotland call the *wraith*, that is to say, the appearance, before he died, of a Captain Veal upon the Inch[2] at Perth at a time when Captain Veal was on his death-bed. I had the story from the late Lord. But as one should always go to the fountain-head, I shall try to get this Lord to tell me it.[3] Mr. Johnson observed that in all supernatural appearances we could have no certainty of their truth unless something was told us which we could not otherwise know or some-

[1] George Dempster of Dunnichen, M.P., devoted himself to the improvement of Scots agriculture and fisheries, and was from 1769 to 1773 a Director of the East India Company. Though eight years older than Boswell, he had been one of his closer associates in the year preceding his marriage.

[2] Two public meadows or parks at Perth are called the North Inch (i.e. island) and the South Inch, from the fact that they were at one time insulated by the river Tay. The point is that Eglinton saw the wraith, not under extraordinary circumstances, but in a place of public resort.

[3] Boswell records doing so in his Journal for 24 September 1778.

thing done which could not be done but by supernatural power; that Pharaoh, in reason and justice, required such evidence. Nay, that[1] our Saviour said, "Unless I had done the things which never man did, you would not have had sin." (He gave the very words. I shall look them out.)[2] He had said in the forenoon that Macaulay's *History of St. Kilda* was very well written except some foppery about liberty and slavery. I told him that Macaulay told me he was advised to keep out of his book the wonderful story that upon the approach of a stranger all the inhabitants catch cold; but that he had it so well authenticated he determined to keep it in. "Sir," said Mr. Johnson, "to keep things out of a book merely because people tell you they will not be believed is meanness. Macaulay acted with more magnanimity."[3]

We talked of the Roman Catholic religion and how little difference there was in essential matters between ours and it. "True," said he. "All denominations of Christians have really little difference in point of doctrine, though they may differ widely in external forms. There is a prodigious difference between the external form of one of your Presbyterian churches in Scotland and a church in Italy; yet the doctrine taught is essentially the same."

I mentioned Purgatory, being very desirous to hear his ideas as to the particular state of souls after death. Lady Colville[4] bid me try to

[1] Ten more pages, removed by Boswell as copy for the *Life*, are here restored. See above, p. 42 *n.* 2.

[2] John xv, 24 (King James version): "If I had not done among them the works which none other man did, they had not had sin: but now have they both seen and hated both me and my Father."

[3] The Rev. Kenneth Macaulay's *History of St. Kilda* appeared in 1764; his account of the inhabitants' catching cold whenever a ship arrived had been discussed by Johnson and Boswell in the spring of 1768. Johnson and Boswell visited Macaulay at Cawdor 27 August 1773, and Johnson was persuaded from his conversation "that he had not written the book which goes under his name". Actually it had been revised and enlarged by a friend, Dr. John Macpherson. Macaulay was the great-uncle of the historian Thomas Babington Macaulay.

[4] Lady Elizabeth Erskine, by her second marriage Lady Colville of Culross, was eldest daughter of the Earl of Kellie and a sister of Boswell's early friend and correspondent Lieutenant Andrew Erskine. He had once thought of proposing marriage to her; she was now one of his favourite Edinburgh hostesses. See below, p. 226.

learn from him what I could upon that subject. He avoided it. I must try at another time.[1] I mentioned the petition for removing the subscription to the Thirty-nine Articles. Said he, "It was soon thrown out.[2] Sir, they talk of not making boys at the University subscribe to what they do not understand. But they ought to consider that our universities were founded to bring up members to the Church of England and we must not supply our enemies with arms from our arsenal. No, Sir, the meaning of subscribing is not that they fully understand all the articles but that they will adhere to the Church of England. Now take it in this way, that they should only subscribe their adherence to the Church of England, there would be still the same difficulty, for still the young men would be subscribing to what they do not understand. For if you should ask them, 'What do you mean by the Church of England? Do you know in what it differs from the Presbyterian Church? from the Romish Church? from the Greek Church? from the Coptic Church?' they could not tell you. So, Sir, it comes to the same thing." BOSWELL. "But, Sir, would it not do to subscribe the Bible?" JOHNSON. "Why, no, Sir; for all sects will subscribe the Bible. Nay, the Mahometans will subscribe the Bible; for the Mahometans acknowledge Jesus Christ as well as Moses, but maintain that God sent Mahomet as a still greater prophet than either."

I mentioned the motion to abolish the fast of the 30 of January.[3] "Why, Sir," said he, "I could have wished that it had been a temporary act, perhaps to have expired with the century. I am against abolishing it because that would be declaring that it was wrong to establish

[1] Boswell had raised this topic with Johnson on 26 October 1769, and he returned to it again this year, on 28 March (see below, p. 75). Lady Colville, as a Scots Episcopalian, was probably sympathetic to the doctrine of Purgatory. In a codicil to his will, dated 30 May 1785, Boswell himself wrote: "Finally I request the prayers of all my pious friends for my departed soul, considering how reasonable it is to suppose that it may be detained some time in a middle state."

[2] The petition was presented in Parliament on 6 February of this year. By a majority of 217 to 71 leave was refused for it to be brought up.

[3] The anniversary of the execution of Charles I. Dr. Nowell, the preacher of the fast sermon for this year, had offended the House of Commons by comparing its Members to the opponents of Charles I.

it; but I should have no objection to make an act continuing it for another century and then letting it go out." He disapproved of the Royal Marriage Bill; "because," said he, "I would not have the people think that the validity of marriage depends on the will of man, or that the right of a king depends on the will of man. I would not have been against making a royal marriage without the approbation of King and Parliament highly criminal."[1]

In the forenoon we had talked of old families and the respect due to them. "Sir," said he, "you have a right to that kind of respect and are arguing for yourself. I am for supporting the principle and am disinterested in doing it, as I have no such right." BOSWELL. "Why, Sir, it is one more incitement to a man to do well." JOHNSON. "Yes, Sir, and it is a matter of opinion very necessary to keep society together. What is it but opinion by which we have a respect for authority that prevents us who are the rabble from rising up and pulling down you who are gentlemen from your places and saying, 'We will be gentlemen in our turn'? Now, Sir, that respect for authority is much more easily granted to a man whose father has had it than to an upstart, and so society is more easily supported." BOSWELL. "Perhaps, Sir, it might be done by the opinion of office, as among the Romans, where the dress, the *toga*, inspired reverence." JOHNSON. "Why, Sir, we know very little about the Romans. But surely it is much easier to respect a man who has always had respect than to respect a man who we know was last year no better than ourselves and will be no better next year. In republics there is not a respect for authority but a fear of power." BOSWELL. "At present what seems to gain most respect is having riches." JOHNSON. "No, Sir, riches do not gain respect. They procure court being paid. A very rich man from low beginnings may buy the election of a borough. But *cæteris paribus* a man of family will be preferred. People will prefer one for whose father their fathers

[1] This bill gave the King complete control over the marriages of members of the royal family under twenty-five and partial control over the marriages of those above that age. It had been introduced because of the marriage of two of the King's brothers (the Dukes of Gloucester and Cumberland) to ladies not of royal blood, and was at this moment the subject of lively debate in Parliament. The King gave his assent on 1 April.

have voted, though they should get no more money or even less. This shows the opinion to be real. If gentlemen of family would allow the rich upstarts to spend their money profusely, which they are ready enough to do, and not vie with them in expense, the upstarts would soon be at an end and the gentlemen would remain. But if the gentlemen will vie in expense with the upstarts, which is very foolish, they must be ruined."

He said Dr. Burney was a very pretty kind of man; but he could not read through his book.[1] I asked him why. He said, "Because I could not read about fiddles and fiddlestrings." I mentioned Foote's taking him off. " I thought," said he, "I had cured Foote of that."[2] I gave him an account of Cullen's mimicry.[3] I said, "Don't you think, Sir, it is a very mean thing?" JOHNSON. "Why, Sir, it is making a very mean use of one's powers. But to be a good mimic requires great powers, great acuteness of observation, great retention of what is observed, and great pliancy of organs, to represent what is observed. I remember a lady in this town, Lady Amelia Hervey,[4] who was a wonderful mimic and used to make me laugh immoderately. I have heard she is now gone mad." BOSWELL. "It is amazing how a mimic can

[1] *The Present State of Music in France and Italy*, 1771, a report on his travels, much of which Burney would subsequently repeat in his *History of Music*. In preparing the copy for the *Life* Boswell deleted this reference to Burney entirely.

[2] Johnson, on hearing that Foote intended to take him off, had let it be known he was ready to purchase an oak stick. "Sir, fear restrained him; he knew I would have broken his bones" (19 October 1769).

[3] Robert Cullen, a son of the famous Scots physician William Cullen, was an advocate who later became Lord of Session with the title Lord Cullen. In the *Life* at this point he appears merely as "a friend of mine in Scotland". During Foote's visit to Edinburgh for the winter season of 1771, he had apparently been pitted against Cullen in some kind of contest of mimicry. "There is one of the most serious affairs to be decided this night here that ever happened in any country, between the Great Northern and Southern Potentates, Cullen and Foote . . ." (Thomas Alexander Erskine, sixth Earl of Kellie, to Boswell, from Fortune's, Saturday evening, no date).

[4] The name is left blank in the *Life* but was correctly identified by Mrs. Piozzi in a marginal note to the 1816 edition. Lady Emily (Amelia Caroline Nassau) Hervey was a daughter of Pope's opponent Baron Hervey of Ickworth. Mrs. Piozzi adds: "She was never mad as I know of."

not only give you the gestures and voice of a person whom he represents, but will even give you what a person would say on any particular subject." JOHNSON. "Why, Sir, you are to consider that the manner and some particular phrases of a person do much to impress you with an idea of him, and you are not sure that he would say what the mimic says in his character." BOSWELL. "I don't think Foote a good mimic." JOHNSON. "No, Sir, his imitations are not like. He gives you something different from himself but not the character which he means to assume. He goes out of himself without going into other people. He cannot take off any person but who is very strongly marked, such as George Faulkner. He is like a painter who can paint a man who has a wen upon his face and who therefore is easily known. If a man hops upon one leg, Foote can hop upon one leg.[1] But he has not that nice discrimination which your friend Cullen seems to possess. Foote is however very entertaining, with a kind of conversation between wit and buffoonery."

I told him of the renunciation which I granted to my father of my right to the family estate by my mother's contract of marriage, which I did about the time I became major from a generous principle of preserving the family, as my father threatened, while I was very dissipated and licentious, that he would sell Auchinleck.[2] JOHNSON. "Why, Sir, you did a very foolish thing." BOSWELL. "Last winter, Sir, I had the paper in my hand, my father having left open the bookcase in which it was lying; and I once thought of putting it into the fire, as it

[1] The Dublin publisher George Faulkner had lost a leg; in 1766, Foote, who had long been mimicking him, lost one too. "Now," he exclaimed, "I shall take off old Faulkner indeed to the life!"

[2] There is among the Boswell papers at Yale a deed executed in the spring of 1762 in which, in return for an unconditional grant of an allowance of £100 a year, Boswell consents to be put under trustees of his father's choosing in case he succeeds to Auchinleck. This, however, makes no mention of rights conferred by his mother's contract of marriage, and can therefore hardly be the renunciation here referred to. Presumably Lord Auchinleck, having concluded that his son would turn out a hopeless wastrel, had previously extorted a more extreme concession from him, and still continued to hold it over his head. Boswell later became convinced that his father had never had the power to pass him over as heir, and suspected that he had known it all along.

was a thing to which he had no right. However, as I had once granted it to him, I had a scruple, and so laid it back again into its place." JOHNSON. "You did right, Sir. To take it and burn it would have been destroying a deed. We should have had you hanged, ha! ha! ha! No. You would not have been hanged, but you[1] might have been whipped, or transported, ha! ha! ha! However, Sir, your father did wrong to take it from you, and he ought to give it up to you. If you do not tease him, he will make no use of it and it can do you no harm; for a renunciation granted to him can avail no one else." BOSWELL. "He talks, Sir, of entailing his estate; but he carries on the representation of heirs male only to a certain length. Now, I have no idea of any representation of a family but by males. Don't you think it the true representation, Sir?" JOHNSON. "Why, yes, Sir." BOSWELL. "What makes me more anxious with regard to it in our family is a principle of good faith to one of my ancestors who gave the estate to his nephew, passing by his own daughters; and I therefore think that as we received it in trust as a male fee we are bound to continue it as a male fee. I am therefore determined to sign no more papers or give any consent to female succession." JOHNSON. "Why, Sir, from what you have stated, your case is stronger than usual, and since you think it wrong to consent to such an entail as your father talks of making, you should not do it. But let him alone and he'll die without making any."[2] BOSWELL.

[1] Here the second newly recovered portion of the text ends. See above, p. 42 *n.* 2.

[2] The long and impassioned dispute between Boswell and his father over the entail of Auchinleck (expounded by Boswell himself at length in the *Life of Johnson* under 1776) had broken out first during the summer before Boswell's marriage. The purpose of an entail was to make an estate permanently unsaleable and unattachable for debt and hence to protect family ownership against profligacy of the sort which now seemed to Lord Auchinleck all too likely if his son should succeed him. But Lord Auchinleck wished to entail the estate upon heirs whatsoever of his own body, "males and females indiscriminately". Boswell on the other hand defended a kind of feudal mystique, a "Gothic, Salic" faith in the transmission of family blood through males only. He had a "zealous partiality for heirs male, however remote" of the original Thomas Boswell, who had fallen along with his Sovereign at the Field of Flodden in 1513. An entail on these lines would of course have extended the remote possibility of inheritance to some undistinguished branches of the family (such as that headed by a dancing-master named David

"Don't you think, Sir, that the deed which I granted might be set aside as granted by a young man under fear of his father, and to his very great prejudice?" JOHNSON. "Why, I don't know but it might."

Thus have I collected this day's conversation, excepting only that I now recollect he advised me to go and see Cox's Museum, which he said for power of mechanism and splendour of show was a very fine exhibition.[1] He seemed happier to see me than ever. He said, "I do love thee. I do love thee"; and when I left him he said, "Good-night, dear Sir. I am glad to see you again, very glad to see you again."

SUNDAY 22 MARCH. I breakfasted with Dempster, whom I found as agreeable and as friendly as ever, improved much in speaking English, and appearing to be as happy as I could wish him. Parliament and the East India Company had accustomed him to manly employment, and I could see that he was really satisfied with his situation. He is conscious of acting with honour and fidelity and spirit, and he feels himself happy in having a share in the great deliberations both as to this nation and the empire in India. He said he would not give up the enjoyment of the two sessions which he had sat in Parliament for any consideration. I gave him some account of his old friends in Scotland. He said he thought with a pleasing regret of our parties with the Ladies

---

Boswell). After a series of feverish changes of heart and belated qualms at the prospect of excluding his own daughters, Boswell on 7 August 1776 went to his father's house and signed a compromise entail preferring all males descended from Lord Auchinleck's grandfather. (The dancing-master was still excluded.) And two years later Boswell succeeded in getting a sight of his mother's marriage contract and found that it had never been in his father's power ("even with my consent") to alter the destination to heirs male of his body.

[1] "The objects that first strike the eye are two-and-twenty pieces of mechanism, some nine, some ten, some twelve, and some sixteen feet high, each blazing with a profusion of the most costly gems. . . . An elephant, richly caparisoned, supports a pedestal on which is a triumphal car, drawn by four golden self-moving horses. . . . Another car is drawn by doves round a magnificent temple of mother-of-pearl. . . . Pagodas, pouring all Golconda upon the sight of the beholder, rise to the music of their own chimes. . . . The various flowers of the year bloom in jewels. . . . Storks, dragons, lizards, dolphins . . . present themselves . . . in gold, silver, agate, amber, lapis lazuli, and aventurine . . ." (*Gentleman's Magazine*, March 1772). The Museum was in Spring Gardens, Charing Cross, admission half a guinea.

of Kellie in which we were so happy. He said some good things, which go down into my *Boswelliana*. Dempster said it would be the greatest treasure of this age. Indeed it will contain a rich collection of good things. I said I should have riders to go about and pick up good things for me, or have correspondents established in all the country towns. He kept out all company till we had taken a hearty draught of free and friendly conversation. But then I saw a specimen of his inconveniences; for in came Angus lairds, speaking with a most uncouth tone, and beings of other disagreeable kinds, to all of whom he was obliged to be very courteous.

I then called on Sir Alexander Macdonald, and found him and my Lady by themselves; then paid a visit to Lady Margaret Macdonald, with whom I sat a good while. She revived in my mind lively ideas of the Eglinton family; and, by an association of ideas, had a kind of connexion with my dear cousin, now my wife, being a Margaret Montgomerie and properly of the same family.[1] I returned to Sir Alexander, and he and I walked about together, looking at Portman Square and other new buildings. The increase of London is prodigious. It is really become too large. The consequence is that people live at such a distance from each other that it is very inconvenient for them to meet, and are so crowded that they confuse one another; and it is easier for people who live ten or twelve miles from each other in the country to meet than it is for people who live a few streets from each other in London.

I went to dine by invitation at my cousin or kinsman Mr. Bosville's in Great Russell Street, Bloomsbury. It was a very bad day. There fell a very heavy rain and there was the loudest thunder I ever heard. As I was going along Great Russell Street it seemed to be just over my head. It was indeed very near; for not very far from where I then was it broke upon Tottenham Court Road Chapel and killed a man in the midst of Mr. Wesley's congregation.[2] Honest Mr. Bosville received

[1] Lady Margaret Macdonald, before her marriage Lady Margaret Montgomerie, was Sir Alexander's mother, and sister to the tenth and eleventh Earls of Eglinton. A dowager well loved in the Isle of Skye, she had helped to harbour Prince Charles in the Isle after the battle of Culloden.

[2] "Mr. Goodson, a master tailor in Craven Buildings, being at the late Mr.

me with his usual cordiality and his lady with her usual civil formality. His daughter Miss Julia was grown the finest British woman I ever beheld, and his son Tommy was grown a stout young fellow, and was now entered to the business of a merchant in the city. There were with us his sister Mrs. Place, a widow lady, and her sister Miss Wentworth, and a Miss Jenkins, a little old crooked creature of great fortune. Nothing worthy of remark passed at dinner. After dinner Mr. Bosville read me some letters from his eldest son, the Captain,[1] who was now on his travels in Italy. I was pleased with his remarks, which were sensible, short, and humorous. Mr. Bosville himself has a good deal of humour of a certain kind. Sir Alexander Macdonald told me that Mr. Bosville was reading one of his son's letters to a company, and when it was done, a person present asked, "What, is there no more, Sir?" "O yes," said he: " 'I am your dutiful son, William Bosville.' " Sir Alexander came and drank coffee with us.

I then went to Sir John Pringle's,[2] who had asked me to dine with him. When I was last in London he was a little offended at something about me, and we parted rather drily. I was anxious to meet him again, as he is a worthy, sensible, knowing man, an old friend of my father's, and has always been very kind to me. He received me with great affection, and I saw that any former dryness was at an end. He had with him Lord Lyttelton and several more gentlemen, in particular the famous Mr. Banks and Dr. Solander, whom I had a great curiosity to see. Mr. Banks was a genteel young man, very black, and of an agreeable countenance, easy and communicative, without any affectation or appearance of assuming. Dr. Solander, though a Swede, spoke English with more fluency and propriety than most natives.

I then called at General Paoli's for a little; Count Gentili and the Corsican Abbé ——— were with him. I should have mentioned that the day after I came last to London, I resumed to him his observation on painting, which he made to me while we were travelling on the

Whitefield's chapel in Tottenham Court Road, was struck dead by a flash of lightning" (*London Chronicle*, 24 March 1772).

[1] Of the Coldstream Guards, celebrated *bon vivant* and traveller.

[2] Scotsman; physician to the Queen and (in 1774) to the King; President of the Royal Society. His house was in Pall Mall.

banks of Loch Lomond: viz, that we seldom or never can know what is meant by an emblematical or historical picture unless we have some previous instruction to direct us. I gave him an excellent instance in confirmation of this. We all know immediately when we see a female figure holding a balance painted that it is Justice, because we are told beforehand that Justice is so represented. But my little niece Jeanie Campbell,[1] who as yet knows nothing of emblems, when she saw a print of Justice with the scales, cried out, "Eh! there a wife selling sweeties"; i.e. "There's a woman selling sweetmeats." The General was delighted with this instance. I was so sleepy from having sitten up so late with Mr. Johnson the night before that I hastened home and went to bed. I am sorry that I have not been at church today.

MONDAY 23 MARCH. I breakfasted with Captain Hoggan, and then went to Mr. Johnson's, with whom I had an appointment to spend this day and consider the cause of the Campbeltown schoolmaster. When I came into his study, he was busy preparing a new edition of his folio Dictionary, and had one Mr. Peyton writing to him and picking out words from Ainsworth.[2] I gave him a meaning of the word *side* which he had omitted; viz., father's or mother's side. He said he would put it in. I asked if *civilisation* was a word; he said no, but *civility* was. I suggested *humiliating*. He said he had seen it frequently used but he did not know if it could be allowed to be English. With great deference to him, I should think *civilisation*, from to *civilise*, a good word and better than *civility* in that sense, as it is better to have a distinct word for each sense[3] than one word with two senses, which *civility* is, in his way of using it.[4]

A Mr. ———, a tall gentleman like a clergyman, just went out as I

[1] Mrs. Boswell's sister's step-daughter: Treesbank's daughter by his first wife.

[2] Robert Ainsworth, *A Compendious Dictionary of the Latin Tongue*, 1736.

[3] Here four pages, removed as copy for the *Life*, are restored. See above, p. 42 *n.* 2.

[4] Boswell's meaning of *side*, with an illustration from the poet Parnell, appears as the eighth and last meaning of *side* in the fourth edition of Johnson's *Dictionary*, folio, 1773, but not in earlier editions. The *Oxford English Dictionary* quotes the passage of Boswell's *Life of Johnson* corresponding to the present Journal passage for the earliest occurrence of *civilisation* in Boswell's sense. The same authority quotes *humiliating* from a newspaper passage of 1757.

came in. He seemed busy about some sort of chemical operations. I was entertained to see how he sent Mr. Peyton an errand. "Mr. Peyton, Mr. Peyton, will you be so good as take a walk to Temple Bar? You will there see a chemist's shop; buy for me an ounce of oil of vitriol; not spirit of vitriol but oil of vitriol.[1] It will cost you three half-pence." Away went Peyton and returned with it, and told it cost but a penny.

I then took out the Session papers in the schoolmaster's cause. I asked if I should read. "No, Sir," said he. "I can read quicker than I can hear." So he read to himself.

After he had gone on a little way, in came a little brisk man, Mr. Kristrom or Christian, a Swede, who was tutor to some young gentlemen in the city.[2] He told me that there was a very good history of Sweden by Dalin. I asked Mr. Johnson if one might write a history of Sweden without going thither. He said, "Yes, one for common use."

We talked of languages. Mr. Johnson observed that M. Leibnitz had made some progress in a work tracing them all up to the Hebrew. "Why, Sir," said he, "you would not imagine that the French *jour*, day, is derived from the Latin *dies*, and yet nothing is more certain, and the intermediate steps are very clear. From *dies* comes *diurnus*. *Diu* is, by inaccurate ears or inaccurate pronunciation, easily confounded with *giu*; then the Italians form a substantive of the ablative of an adjective and thence *giurno*, or as they make it *giorno*, which is readily contracted into *giour* or *jour*."[3] He observed that the Bohemian[4] language was true Slavonic. The Swede said it had some similarity with the German. "Why, Sir, to be sure," said he. "Such parts of Slavonia as confine with Germany will borrow German words, and such parts as confine with Tartary will borrow Tartar words."

[1] In modern nomenclature, concentrated (not dilute) sulphuric acid.

[2] Pehr Chriström, mathematician and philologist, at this time sixty-six years old. He had been travelling tutor to the sons of a rich Jewish family named Salvador, and was now retired on a pension of £100 a year.

[3] Even for his time, Johnson was not a good etymologist, but he is here reasonably near the facts as at present understood. *Giorno* and *jour* are independent developments from the accusative (not ablative) *diurnum*, of which the final *m* was lost at an early period.

[4] We would say Czech.

He said he never had it properly ascertained that the Scotch Highlanders and the Irish understand each other. I told him that my cousin Colonel Graham of the Royal Highlanders, whom I met at Drogheda, told me they did. He said if the Highlanders understood Irish, why translate the New Testament into Erse, as was done lately at Edinburgh?[1] I said that although the Erse and Irish were both dialects of the same language, there might be a good deal of diversity between them, as between the different dialects in Italy.

The Swede went away, and Mr. Johnson continued his reading of the Session papers. It was curious to see Mr. Samuel Johnson reading his papers like a Lord of Session. As he read Ilay Campbell's Information, he said, "This is a bloody charge against us," and really took a strong interest for the schoolmaster. He laboured very patiently. I said, "I am afraid, Sir, it is troublesome to you." "Why, Sir," said he, "I do not take much delight in it; but I'll go through with it." He read Crosbie's and Ilay Campbell's Informations, and my Reclaiming Petition.

We went over to the Mitre and dined in the room where he and I first supped together, about ten years ago. He ordered some cod and some smelts and some roasted lamb. He eat heartily but drank only negus. He gave me great hopes of my schoolmaster. "Sir," said he, "the government of a schoolmaster is somewhat of the nature of military government; that is to say, it must be arbitrary according to particular circumstances. You must show some learning upon this occasion. You must show that a schoolmaster has a prescriptive right to beat, and that an action of assault and battery cannot be admitted against him unless there is some great excess, some barbarity. This man has maimed none of his boys. They are all[2] left the full exercise of their corporeal faculties. In our schools in England many boys have been maimed. Yet I never heard of an action against a schoolmaster. Pufendorf, I think, maintains the right of a schoolmaster to beat his scholars. Besides, Sir, we know not how ill the boys have behaved in

[1] The Reverend James Stuart's Gaelic translation of the New Testament appeared in Edinburgh in 1767.

[2] Here the third newly recovered portion of the Journal ends. See above, p. 42 *n.* 2.

this case, so cannot judge whether the degree of severity was proper or not." He promised to assist me by putting down some thoughts upon the subject.

I had read in his library this forenoon the Dedication to Kennedy's *Scripture Chronology*, which I immediately knew to be his. I said, "You cannot deny it." He answered, "Why, I don't deny it."[1] We went home to his house and Mrs. Williams gave us some tea. This was his Club night. So I left him.

I called at General Paoli's. He had with him M. Dunant, a Swiss, formerly an officer in the Sardinian service and now seeking his fortune in London, and Signor Poggi, a young painter, the son of a Corsican, of distinguished talents but little application.

TUESDAY 24 MARCH. I called on Sir John Pringle for a little, and he asked me to come and sit with him in the evening. I then found DOUGLAS at home. His house, late Lord Egmont's in Pall Mall, was truly magnificent. He received me as usual, and presented me to Lady Lucy, whom I thought a pretty little smart lady. I was hurt to see her have that disagreeable distance, reserve, and, I cannot help thinking, absolute want of civility which your English women of fashion in general have. When I was introduced to her she should certainly have expressed some satisfaction at seeing so great a friend of her husband's; in place of which she just rose, curtsied, and said not a word. However, I made way for myself, took a most hearty breakfast and talked away, and forced her Ladyship to speak by asking her questions. Charles Greville, Lord Warwick's son, was there. Douglas showed me his house, which is indeed magnificent; and so it may, for it cost him £13,000. I told him, "This will not do. You must come among us. It cost us too much trouble to make you a Scotsman to let you be an Englishman." He assured me he would be six months in Scotland next summer and have Lady Lucy along with him.

I then went to Lord Mountstuart, who was living at his mother-in-law Lady Windsor's, his own house not being yet ready for him. He

[1] Boswell apparently confuses the Reverend John Kennedy's *Scripture Chronology* with the same author's *Complete System of Astronomical Chronology*, 1763, for which Johnson wrote the Dedication and the final paragraph of the text.

received me as if we had not been a day separated, showed me his eldest son, a fine boy, and told me he was always at home in the evening when Parliament was not sitting, and would be happy to see me. John Ross Mackye[1] came in. I told my Lord about my schoolmaster. I said I was keen for him because I was sensible how much the better I myself had been of being heartily licked. My Lord, who has a talent for saying sly things, by the by answered, "I wish you had got a little more of it." I went down and saw a committee of the House of Commons sitting on a Merse Road Bill.[2] Rae[3] and Wight spoke as counsel while I was there. I was surprised to find a committee, of which I had heard so much, a very simple matter.

I dined at General Paoli's, just he and I and the Count. I shall always mention them if there are any more. The General spoke much of Scotland; and, what gave me much pleasure, he commended highly my dearest wife, said she had something of the Italian manner, a frankness, an attention, and a politeness; and particularly remembered her giving him a convoy as far as Haddington.

In the evening I went to Sir John Pringle's and found him alone with his nightcap, quite at ease. We had a little bowl of punch and some biscuits and were most comfortable. He told me he had a letter from my father in which my father expressed much satisfaction with me. I was sincerely happy at this; and I felt a manly consciousness of being improved when I felt that I could talk on a tolerable equality with Sir John Pringle, of whom I used to stand so much in awe. He agreed with me as to my notions of succession in our family and said, "No, no, the dancing-master must not be cut off, though his profession need not be named."[4] I had told him that my father had in the

[1] M.P. for Lanark and the Stewartry of Kirkcudbright, 1741–1768. His sociability at an advanced age is recorded by Boswell in his Journal for 23 November 1793.

[2] See below, p. 135 *n.* 2.

[3] See below, p. 99.

[4] David Boswell at Leith, representative of the Craigston Boswells, first cousin of John Boswell (married to the heiress of Knockroon), and Lord Auchinleck's cousin in the sixth degree. Considering the number of nearer male lines, Lord Auchinleck's caution seems pedantic. But the real reason for the exclusion, as Boswell proceeds to say, was pride. If Lord Auchinleck had included the Craigston

main the same notions with me and wished to entail his estate in the male line for many generations; but stopped at one of the branches of our family, who is a dancing-master, because his pride cannot bear it: without considering that it is a family's fault when their connexions fall low, and besides, that by the time the succession may open to them, the dancing-master's descendants may be greater than any of us.[1] Sir John however would not allow that there was any obligation upon us to prefer the male line because one of our predecessors did it; for he pleased his fancy, and so may another man please his. Said he: "Suppose a man should take a fancy to leave me an estate because I am marked with the smallpox; that would lay no obligation upon me to leave it to another man marked with the smallpox, in preference to my own near relations." I answered that his supposition was mere whim. But the preference given to male succession was a principle.

Sir John, I saw, had taken somewhat of a liking to your dissenters and what are called more rational Christians. He gave me a little penny pamphlet containing the trial of one Mr. Elwall for heresy and blasphemy, for denying the Trinity and several other orthodox principles, with remarks.[2] And he seemed to approve of a late publication attempting to prove the two first chapters of Matthew's Gospel spurious.[3] He said, "You know the castor, the beaver, when he is pursued bites off and throws from him what he knows the hunters pursue him for. So this dissenting divine throws off those two chapters on which the Deists found so many of their objections." He said he was now come to give little faith to history, because he knew

line in the entail, he would have had to recognise the dancing-master socially; and this he was determined not to do.

[1] It is not on record that the dancing-master's descendants did come up in the world, but it is a pleasantly ironical circumstance that when Lord Auchinleck's heir of line sold the estate, Auchinleck House was purchased by the representative of John Boswell of Knockroon, whose father was a Craigston Boswell.

[2] Edward Elwall (1676–1744) published his *True Testimony for God . . . against All the Trinitarians under Heaven* in 1720 and was tried for heresy in 1726. The pamphlet was reprinted by Joseph Priestley in 1772 and became a stock tract with the Unitarians. See below, p. 77.

[3] John Williams's *Free Enquiry into the Authenticity of the First and Second Chapters of St. Matthew's Gospel*, 1771.

for certain that the Princess Dowager of Wales[1] had for these many years taken no share in politics and never had any improper connexion with Lord Bute; and yet she would go down to posterity as having managed all the affairs of this nation till her death and been concerned in a criminal intercourse with Lord Bute. He said it would not be proper for him to mention them, but that his situation about the royal family gave him an opportunity of knowing circumstances that made it certain that the Princess was altogether free of both these concerns. He said that when it was imagined there would be a long minority, the late King being very old and his grandson very young, a party of the great people about Court, apprehending that Lord Bute's intimacy with Frederick Prince of Wales might give him a great ascendancy over this King, formed the plan to raise a report of scandal between the Princess Dowager and Lord Bute; and he would do Mr. Fox, afterwards Lord Holland, the justice to say that he alone struck out against it. It was, however, put in execution, and was asserted with such effrontery that many who had occasion to know better believed it. He therefore could not regard history farther than just as chronology and relating certain facts which could admit of no falsifying, such as that a king reigned so long, a battle was fought, or such things. But as to accounts of characters, or the secret springs and motives of actions and events, he could not credit historians. This was really a good evening with my father's old friend.

WEDNESDAY 25 MARCH. I breakfasted with Mr. Samuel Mitchelson, Junior,[2] who was come up upon the Peerage of Caithness, and with him I kept myself in mind of business. I then called on Dempster and walked out with him. I observed that when a man comes to London as a stranger, he is confused and knows not well how to do; like one at a great table who is unaccustomed to it and whose attention is distracted by the variety of dishes. Whereas one settled in London is like a man accustomed to a great table, upon whom the variety of

[1] Augusta, daughter of Frederick II, Duke of Saxe-Gotha, married Frederick Louis, Prince of Wales, in 1736 and was the mother of George III. She died 8 February 1772. See below, p. 89 *n*.2.

[2] A Writer to the Signet. Boswell's Fee Book often enters "S. Mitchelson Jun." as agent in cases where Boswell was advocate.

dishes makes no impression, and who singles out his piece of beef or mutton or any other particular dish which he likes without being in the least disturbed.

I called on Sir Alexander Macdonald, who walked down with me to Westminster and showed me several committees of the House of Commons; and, as he knows almost every man of rank or distinction by face, pointed out to me Sir George Savile, Commodore Saunders, and many more of whom I had heard and whom I was curious to see.[1] We then went into the House of Lords and heard an appeal from the Exchequer of England, Dunbar against Lem. We heard only one side. Mr. Thurlow, the Attorney-General,[2] spoke in a deliberate, distinct, manly method, and Counsellor Ambler spoke with fluency and propriety. I was very curious to see the form of proceeding in the House of Lords in hearing causes, which I had never done before, having never been in London when the Parliament was sitting except when I had an aversion at everything that had the appearance of business. I went home with Sir Alexander to dinner. We had with us Captain MacLeod, late of the *Lord Mansfield* East Indiaman, his lady and daughter, Major Chisholm of Chisholm, and Archie Macdonald. We did very well.

At night I went to Lord Mountstuart's. Lord Denbigh and John Ross Mackye were with him. Lord Denbigh is a droll genius.[3] He had in his pocket a petition to bring in my schoolmaster's cause on an early day. "Come," said he, "tell me about this schoolmaster's cause; for curse me if I judge of it." I gave him some account of it, and he swore and raved, but I do not remember in what terms. After he and Ross Mackye went away, my Lord and I chatted admirably. But I

[1] Sir George Savile, one of the most respected of the Whig leaders, in the previous month had made an eloquent speech supporting the petition for relief from subscription to the Thirty-nine Articles. Johnson called him "a little dirty scoundrel" (Journal, 23 September 1777). Admiral Sir Charles Saunders was commander-in-chief of the fleet which supported Wolfe at Quebec.

[2] Later Lord Chancellor. He had made his reputation on the side of Douglas in the appeal before the House of Lords in February 1769.

[3] Basil Feilding, sixth Earl of Denbigh (1719–1800), was Lord of the Bedchamber from 1763 to his death. He earned a reputation as a "droll genius" when under the influence of the bottle.

found that as when he knew me first in Italy I was very odd and extravagant, he could not yet have an idea of my being altered; so was playing foolishly as we used to do. This was a little troublesome. But I considered it would wear off. He said it was impossible to get any survivancy.[1] But he promised he would get me a gown in the Court of Session. He is truly an amiable young nobleman with very good parts, and is only too indolent and cool till pushed.

THURSDAY 26 MARCH. I breakfasted with Crosbie,[2] who told me that he had full powers from the Laird of MacLeod to sell the barony of Harris; but that St. Kilda was to be excepted, as it was so curious a piece of property.[3] I called on Dr. Percy at Northumberland House. I had left cards for the Duke and Duchess, but had received neither visit nor message from them. It was agreeable to find Percy in a large room looking into the Strand, and at the same time his room as much a library—as crowded and even confused with books and papers—as any room in a college. He showed me many curiosities; in particular, a collection of all the Spanish authors mentioned in *Don Quixote*; and he told me that a clergyman[4] down in the country, who has probably more Spanish learning than any Spaniard, was assisting him in finding out the various passages mentioned or alluded to, that he may make a kind of key to *Don Quixote*. This will be a work of universal curiosity. He showed me a very good translation of Homer into Latin verse by ———,[5] a Hessian who lived in Erasmus's time,

[1] Nomination to an office to which Boswell would succeed upon the death of the holder.

[2] Andrew Crosbie had assisted Boswell in his first criminal case (that of John Reid the sheep-stealer in 1766) and had become one of his closest friends; he was also joined with Boswell in the defence of Hastie the schoolmaster. He was generally granted brilliant parts, and no member of the Faculty had warmer friends, but his advocacy of unprofitable causes was winning him a reputation for being quixotic and erratic.

[3] In 1779 Captain Alexander MacLeod (with whom Boswell had dined on the day preceding this) purchased from the commissioners of the next Laird of MacLeod for £15,000 the barony of Harris, including Bernera, St. Kilda, and other small isles.

[4] The Reverend John Bowle, vicar of Idmiston in Wiltshire, whose edition of *Don Quixote* appeared in 1781.

[5] Helius Eobanus Hessus (1488–1540).

and on a blank leaf of it he had transcribed a very high character of this ——— by Erasmus, saying that he alone was sufficient to give fame to all Germany. I observed how humbling it was to literary ambition that this man who had so much merit and was so high in fame should now hardly be known. He showed me also a book which had belonged to the famous but foolish Earl of Pembroke, who had a custom of writing upon the margins of his books, not things which had any connexion with the text, but all sorts of things as they came into his head. This book was scribbled over with the strangest nonsense, as thus: "Take away the Castle and take away the Haven, and then where is my Lord of Castlehaven? Take away the Bridge and take away the Water, and then where is my Lord of Bridgewater?"[1] It is hardly possible to conceive the variety of nonsense thus written. There are several of his Lordship's books in the British Museum. I told Dr. Percy of my barber at Stevenage's story of Dr. Young's keeping a mistress. He said it was mere scandal, just as one should say that Mr. Johnson keeps Mrs. Williams. He said he had just begun to form an acquaintance with Dr. Young; that he could not so much as say, *Virgilium tantum vidi*,[2] for that he had not seen him, but had one letter from him.

Mr. Percy and I went together to General Paoli's. A curious circumstance occurred. The General had read in a foreign journal that the late Dr. Brown had written a memorial in favour of the Corsicans. The journal said, "This famous scholar's death was a blow to the republic of letters in general, and especially to the brave Corsicans, in whose favour he had written a memorial of such force that it would

[1] Philip Herbert, fourth Earl of Pembroke (1584–1650), one of the "incomparable pair of brethren" to whom the first folio of Shakespeare is inscribed, was Lord Chamberlain of the household of Charles I and Chancellor of Oxford University. He was famous and eccentric but apparently not foolish, even though he is well known to have had the habit of writing mysterious remarks in the margins of his books. It is possible that the scribblings on Lord Castlehaven, at least, had a definite enough meaning. Castlehaven (the second Earl, 1593–1631) and Bridgewater were brothers-in-law, and Pembroke also was connected with them by marriage. Castlehaven, having been found guilty of sodomy and assisting at the rape of his own wife, was attainted of felony and on 14 March 1631 beheaded on Tower Hill.

[2] "I no more than saw Virgil": Ovid, *Tristia*, IV, x, 51.

undoubtedly have made a great impression on all the ministries of Europe,"[1] or words to that purpose. The General was very anxious to see this memorial, and Dr. Percy had been doing all in his power to get it from the Doctor's executors, but in vain; though he concluded that as he had heard it mentioned in England, and the General had read of it in a foreign journal, it must have existed, and he did not despair of finding it. While they were talking, I recollected that in the time of the Corsican war, when I used to keep the newspapers constantly warm with paragraphs about the brave islanders, I had among other things mentioned that "the late Dr. Brown had, before his death, written a memorial in behalf of the brave Corsicans, which was to have been published at Petersburg under the auspices of the Empress of Russia; and that it showed a wonderful political revolution when the strongest memorial in favour of Liberty was to have been published in the capital of Russia."[2] This was enough to make it be talked of in England; and the foreign journal had copied it from the newspaper. My telling this put an end to the search; and it made me have less literary faith, as Sir John Pringle has less historical faith; for this invention of mine will be handed down on the Continent wherever Dr. Brown is mentioned, unless I correct it in some publication.

I dined by Sir John Pringle's invitation with the Club at the Mitre Tavern, all the original members of which are Fellows of the Royal Society. Burrow, who publishes the *Reports*,[3] sat at the head of the table as vice-president. Mr. Banks and Dr. Solander and Mr. Whitaker, the author of the *History of Manchester*, were there. There was little conversation that I could learn, from the company being numerous. I then went to Drury Lane to see Garrick play Bayes. In my way I called at Donaldson's shop.[4] He carried me upstairs, where

[1] Boswell actually writes this sentence in French.

[2] *London Chronicle*, 9–11 October 1766, p. 360. (John Brown, author of *An Estimate of the Manners and Principles of the Times*, 1757, had committed suicide on 22 September 1766.) Boswell (who is quoting from memory) gives the substance but does not reproduce closely the language of his own newspaper paragraph.

[3] Sir James Burrow. He compiled *Reports of Cases Argued and Determined in the Court of King's Bench during the Time of Lord Mansfield's Presiding, 1756–1772.*

[4] Boswell's friend and client Alexander Donaldson, the Edinburgh bookseller, was in partnership with his brother John at No. 195 in the Strand.

he had Mr. Elphinston, who keeps an academy at Kensington, and translates many of the mottoes of *The Rambler*, with him, and Mrs. Elphinston, and another gentleman. Mr. Elphinston it seems had a very great desire to be acquainted with me, and gave me more praise than even I could well take. However, it went down with me. I engaged to dine with him on Saturday sennight. By the time I got to the playhouse, the crowd was such that after trying boxes, pit, and middle gallery, I found I could not get any kind of place. I then tried the one-shilling gallery, into which I just squeezed myself a little. The heat was intolerable and I was quite tantalised; for I saw very ill and could hardly hear at all, and yet I heard constant peals of laughter. I stayed three acts.

I then went to the London Coffee-house on Ludgate Hill, to which the master of the late coffee-house in St. Paul's Churchyard, where a club of which I was admitted a member met every other Thursday, was removed. Dr. Franklin[1] had promised to meet me there tonight. But when I got thither, neither he nor anyone else whom I knew was there. One of the members came out but could recollect nothing of me. This was very awkward. He however went in again to see if anyone else could recollect me; and Dr. Kippis, a dissenting clergyman, did.[2] So in I went. There were very few there. The club is composed principally of physicians, dissenting clergy, and masters of academies. Dr. Priestley[3] was there this night. I should not have known him by his works of religious controversy. *They* are in my opinion insolent; and *he* appeared to be very civil. He seemed happy in a story that a Methodist sailor who was along with Mr. Banks and Dr. Solander had brought several of the wild men to be pretty well disposed to

[1] Benjamin Franklin, Colonial Agent in England for Pennsylvania, visited Sir Alexander Dick at Prestonfield about 1759 and if he did not meet Boswell then, had met him by 4 May 1768, when Sir John Pringle brought him to Boswell's lodgings in London.

[2] Andrew Kippis was the editor of the second edition of *Biographia Britannica*, 1778–1793.

[3] Joseph Priestley, scientist and Unitarian theologian, first described oxygen ("dephlogisticated air") in a letter of 1772 addressed to Sir John Pringle and read before the Royal Society. In this year also he issued a reprint of the *Trial* of Edward Elwall referred to by Pringle (above, p. 62).

Christianity; but whenever he showed them a print of Christ on the cross in his prayer-book and attempted to explain to them the doctrine of the Trinity, they all left him. Perhaps the story is not true. But suppose it true, it only proves that the Methodist sailor was a bad explainer of a mystery, or that the savages had not patience and humility sufficient. I entertained the club with my schoolmaster's cause. We broke up between eleven and twelve.

I must now remark that since I came last to London I have indulged myself with several interviews with women of the town, from a kind of inclination to entertain my curiosity, without deviating from my fidelity to my valuable spouse. This night completing a week in London, I solemnly resolved to indulge myself so no more; because I could learn nothing but what I had formerly heard over and over again, their stories being mostly the same; and because there was a degree of depravity in associating with them, and, as the idea of the distance between me and them now was lessened by my seeing them familiarly, I might fall into an infidelity which would make me very miserable. The heat of the theatre, eating and drinking a variety of things some of which had not suited my constitution, and the cold of the streets had made me ill, and when I got home I was very uneasy.

FRIDAY 27 MARCH. I awaked exceedingly distressed. Captain Hoggan came in upon me before I got up. I rose but could hardly hold up my head. The day was dark and rainy, which made me worse. Honest Hoggan truly sympathised with me. I sent to General Paoli for his coach and Hoggan and I took a drive in Hyde Park. This did me good. But I was still in a sad state. I set Hoggan down at his lodgings and then drove to the House of Peers. I heard Lord Advocate[1] and Mr. Rae plead in the appeal, Willock, etc., against Ouchterlony.[2] It was encouraging to me to see the civility and mild attention with which

[1] James William Montgomery (created a baronet in 1801) was Lord Advocate of Scotland, 1766–1775. He will figure prominently in Boswell's Journal for the summer of 1774.

[2] Like the cause of the Caithness Peerage mentioned above, p. 63, and like the appeals of Bruce of Kinross and of the Earl of Home which Boswell hears later this spring (below, pp. 95, 99, 103, 104, 106), Willock, etc., against Ouchterlony was a case which illustrated and tested the laws of succession and inheritance.

the Chancellor[1] and Lord Mansfield behaved. I thought I should be under no uneasiness in pleading at that bar. I dined at General Paoli's, but was not yet recovered. I was invited to a rout at Mrs. Bosville's this evening; but Joseph not having come in to get me things for dressing till it was rather too late concurred with my indisposition, and I stayed quietly at home writing this my Journal.

SATURDAY 28 MARCH. Mr. John Wright came to me in the morning by appointment to settle his father's case in the appeal, Wright against Ure.[2] After so much variety, though I can hardly call it dissipation, I felt the force of Shakespeare's observation that "if all the year were holidays, to work would be to play."[3] Working at this case solaced me. As we were going on, in came Sir Alexander Macdonald and Major Craufurd of Craufurdland,[4] and they all breakfasted with[5] me, I sitting in my nightcap, and they observing that I was like my father. I indeed felt myself very steady and very composed. The Major made me a very genteel offer. He said if I would stand candidate for the shire of Ayr at next election, he would pass a charter[6]

[1] Lord Apsley, later Earl Bathurst; he has been called the least competent Lord Chancellor of the century.

[2] This is probably John Wright, a teacher of law and mathematics in Edinburgh, a man of "low origin", whom Boswell in 1781 supported in his getting admission to the Faculty of Advocates. On 1 May 1772 the House of Lords affirmed the decision of the Court of Session against Wright's father, Thomas, of Easter Glins, the appellant. He was ordered to pay the respondents £80 for costs.

[3] *1 Henry IV*, I, ii, 228–229:

If all the year were playing holidays,
To sport would be as tedious as to work.

[4] A veteran of Dettingen, Fontenoy, and Quebec, promoted lieutenant-colonel later in this year. He is said to have been put at the bottom of the Army list for having held one corner of the cloth that received the head of the Earl of Kilmarnock at his execution after the '45.

[5] Eight pages, removed for the *Life of Johnson*, are restored. See above, p. 42 *n*. 2.

[6] Would take legal steps to qualify as a voter, which he had hitherto neglected to do. See below, p. 211. In consequence of the severe limitation of the franchise, there were at this time only about one hundred registered voters in Ayrshire. How Boswell would have qualified as a candidate is not clear. His lands of Dalblair (purchased in 1767) did not carry a vote.

and give me his vote. He went away. Sir Alexander sat a little with Wright and me while we settled our case, and he helped us in correcting the English. He went away for a while. We finished it, and he returned and then he and I walked up to Mr. Johnson's. Mr. Johnson had said to me, "I should wish to be acquainted with Sir Alexander Macdonald." Every wish of Mr. Johnson's is watched by me, and my friend Sir Alexander was happy to be introduced to him. So away we went.

Mr. Johnson received him very courteously. Sir Alexander, eager to show himself, began. SIR ALEXANDER. "I think, Sir, our chancellors in England are chosen from views much inferior to the office. They are chosen from temporary political views." JOHNSON. "Why, Sir, in such a government as ours no man is appointed to an office because he is the fittest for it. Nor hardly in any other government; because there are so many connexions and dependencies to be studied. A despotic prince may choose a man to an office because he is the fittest for it. The King of Prussia may do it." SIR ALEXANDER. "I mean, Sir, that chancellors must be subservient to the Court, and will be turned out if they do not acquiesce in everything." JOHNSON. "No, Sir. What chancellors were turned out?" BOSWELL. "Why, Lord Camden, Sir." JOHNSON. "Lord Camden, Sir, is but a single instance; and besides, a more worthless fellow, take him out of his legal capacity, the earth does not bear. I believe he is a man of parts; but he is a man who courted the rabble to get into office, and when in office opposed the King. He did ill to get into office, and did ill after he was in office." SIR ALEXANDER. "I think it was wrong in him to sit to his picture, and have it put up in Guildhall." BOSWELL. "It was wrong in him to accept of applause for having given judgement in a manner agreeable to the people. Applause ought only to be received for something which depends on the will. Now a judge ought to have no will in determining a cause. It is only a matter of judgement."[1] JOHNSON. "Sir, you under-

[1] Charles Pratt, Lord Camden, was a Whig, who before his first government appointment had argued that juries were competent to determine law as well as facts in cases of seditious libel; while Attorney-General he carried through the House of Commons a Bill for extending the Habeas Corpus Act to civil cases. As Chief Justice of the Common Pleas he ruled, in the case of John Wilkes and others,

stand the thing very well." SIR ALEXANDER. "I think, Sir, almost all great lawyers, such now as have written upon law, have known only law and nothing else." JOHNSON. "Why, no, Sir. Judge Hale was a great lawyer and wrote upon law; and yet he knew a great many other things and has written upon other things. Selden too." SIR ALEXANDER. "Very true, Sir. And Lord Bacon. But was not Lord Coke a mere lawyer?" JOHNSON. "Why, I'm afraid he was. But he'd have taken it very ill if you had told him so. He would have prosecuted you for scandal." BOSWELL. "Pray, Sir, whether do you pronounce it Lord Coke or Lord Cooke?" JOHNSON. "Why, Sir, we pronounce it Lord Cooke."[1] BOSWELL. "Lord Mansfield is not a mere lawyer." JOHNSON. "No, Sir. I never was in Lord Mansfield's company. But, Sir, Lord Mansfield was distinguished at the University. Lord Mansfield when he came first to town 'drank champagne with the wits,' as Prior says. He was the friend of Pope." SIR ALEXANDER. "The bar is not so abusive as it was formerly. I fancy they had less law long ago, and so were obliged to take to abuse to fill up the time. Now they have such a number of precedents, they have no occasion for abuse." JOHNSON. "Nay, Sir, they had more law long ago than they have now. As to precedents, to be sure, they will increase in course of time. But the more precedents there are, the less occasion is there for law; that is to say, the less occasion is there for investigating principles. Is it not so, Bozzy?" BOSWELL. "Certainly, Sir." SIR ALEXANDER. "I have been correcting several Scotch accents in my friend Boswell. I doubt, Sir, if any Scotchman ever attains to a perfect English pronunciation." JOHNSON. "Why, Sir, few of 'em do; because they do not persevere after attaining to a certain degree of perfection. But, Sir, there can be

---

that the Government's use of general warrants was unconstitutional, and when raised to the peerage spoke in the House of Lords against the Stamp Act and taxation without representation. He became almost as popular with the people as Wilkes himself. The Mayor and Corporation of London gave him the freedom of the City in a gold box and commissioned Reynolds to paint his portrait. He became Lord Chancellor in 1766 on the formation of Chatham's second administration, and was turned out in 1770.—Johnson's vigorous denunciation of Camden was omitted from the *Life of Johnson*.

[1] Coke is, in fact, merely an old-fashioned spelling for Cook.

no doubt that they may attain to a perfect English pronunciation if they will. We find how far they attain to it; and there can be no doubt that a man who conquers nineteen parts of the Scottish accent may conquer the twentieth. But, Sir, when a man has got the better of nine tenths, he grows weary, he relaxes his diligence, he finds he has corrected his accent so far as not to be disagreeable, and he no longer desires his friends to tell him when he goes wrong; nor does he choose to be told. Sir, when people watch me narrowly, and I do not watch myself, they will find me out to be of a particular county. In the same manner Dunning may be found out to be a Devonshire man. So most Scotchmen may be found out. But, Sir, little defalcations do not hurt. I never catched Mallet in a Scotch accent; and yet Mallet, I suppose, was past five-and-twenty before he came to London."

BOSWELL. "It may be of use, Sir, to have a dictionary to ascertain the pronunciation." JOHNSON. "Why, Sir, my dictionary shows you the accents of words if you can but remember them." BOSWELL. "But, Sir, we want marks to ascertain the pronunciation of the vowels. Sheridan, I believe, has finished such a work." JOHNSON. "Why, Sir, will you consider how much easier it is to learn a language by the ear than by any marks. Sheridan's dictionary may do very well.[1] But you cannot always carry it about with you; and when you want the word, you have not the dictionary. It is like a man who has a sword that will not draw. It is an admirable sword, to be sure. But while your enemy is cutting your throat, you cannot draw this sword. Besides, Sir, what entitles Sheridan to fix the pronunciation of English? He has in the first place the disadvantage of being an Irishman; and if he says he will fix it after the example of the best company, why, they differ among themselves. I remember an instance. When I published the Plan for my dictionary, Lord Chesterfield told me the word *great* should be pronounced so as to rhyme to *state*, and Sir William Yonge sent me

[1] Thomas Sheridan (1719–1788), actor, manager of the Theatre Royal in Dublin, lecturer on elocution, and author, was the father of the dramatist Richard Brinsley Sheridan. His *General Dictionary of the English Language* was announced in 1762 and published in 1780. He had tutored Boswell in pronunciation. Johnson had a low opinion of him and was in the habit of alluding to him as "Sherry" and then as "Sherry derry".

word that it should be pronounced so as to rhyme to *seat* and that none but an Irishman would pronounce it *grait*. Now here were two men of the highest rank, the one the best speaker in the House of Lords, the other the best speaker in the House of Commons, differing so widely."

We talked of kelp. I have often observed that Mr. Johnson is very fond of talking of manufactures, or giving any instruction as to matters of utility. He advised Sir Alexander to refine his kelp to such a degree, before putting it on board a ship, that it might be put up in hogsheads and so be much safer from damage and cost much less freight.

I went home with Sir Alexander to dinner. He observed that a man should never interrupt another in conversation; because the man who is interrupted will only wait with eagerness to get in again, and while the other is talking will be thinking of what he himself is to say, and consequently the interrupter will be talking to no purpose. This is a just and good practical remark. There was nobody at dinner but my Lady and he and I. After dinner he and I took a walk in the fields, and met a Colonel Donald[1] Campbell returned from the East Indies, where he had been twenty years, and had received twenty wounds.[2]

We called together at Dempster's, who was gone abroad and had left his dining-room in perfect Scotch confusion. Colonel Campbell had some drollery, and I made him dictate; and partly from his dictating, partly from my own observation, I wrote down the following inventary of a Scotch Member of Parliament's dining-room furniture: Upon one table a stone basin with dirty water; a china *goglet*, as Campbell called it, or water-bottle with water in it; a case of razors; a shaving-brush, shaving-box and soap-ball, a strap, and a tin jug for warming water in. Upon one chair a pair of ruffles, dirty. Upon another chair a pair of white stockings and a pair of black ditto, a stock, a clothes-brush, a towel, and a shaving-cloth, dirty. Upon the arms of two chairs placed close together a flannel waistcoat without

[1] The fourth newly recovered portion of the Journal ends with this word. See above, p. 42 *n.* 2.

[2] Colonel Campbell was of Glensaddell. Fourteen sword wounds and a musket ball in the body, all received by him at the siege of Madura, 1763, are duly recorded by Major Sir Duncan Campbell of Barcaldine, *Records of Clan Campbell in the Military Service of the Honourable East India Company 1600–1858*, pp. 88–92.

sleeves. Upon another chair a dirty shirt. Upon another ditto a black waistcoat and a grey frock with black buttons. Upon another ditto four combs, a pair of scissors, and a stick of pomatum. Upon the carpet a large piece of blue and white check spread out, a tea-chest, two shoes at a considerable distance from each other, a flannel powdering-gown, a pair of slippers. Upon the chimney-piece innumerable packets of letters and covers to be franked, a book, a pamphlet, some newspapers, and a snuff-box. Hanging upon brass nails two hats, a sword and belt, a belt without a sword. Standing in a corner a very long cane with a gold head. Dempster's eldest black[1] could not well understand what we were about. We drank tea at Sir Alexander's. I then went to Mr. Johnson's. He was not come home half an hour past nine. I walked on to Mr. Dilly's, sat with him half an hour or so, and eat a crust of bread and drank a glass of wine.

I returned to Mr. Johnson about eleven. He was in excellent good humour and I ventured to lead him upon the subject of a future state, as to which Lady Colville and I have talked together of, having much curiosity to know his ideas. He said, "Why, Sir, the happiness of an unembodied spirit will consist in a consciousness of the favour of God, in the contemplation of truth, and in the possession of felicitating ideas." BOSWELL. "But, Sir, there is no harm in our forming to ourselves conjectures as to the nature and particulars of our happiness, though the Scripture has said but very little of it. 'We know not what we shall be.' " JOHNSON. "Sir, there is no harm. So far as philosophy suggests, it is probable. So far as Scripture tells us, it is certain. Dr. Henry More has carried it as far as philosophy can. You may buy both his theological and philosophical works in two volumes in folio for about eight shillings." BOSWELL. "One of the most pleasing thoughts is that we shall see our friends again." JOHNSON. "Yes, Sir; but you must consider that when we are become purely rational, many of our friendships will be cut off. Many friendships are formed by a community of sensual pleasures. All these will be cut off. We form many friendships with bad men because they have agreeable qualities and they can be useful to us; but after death they can no longer be of use to us. We form many friendships by mistake, imagining people to be

[1] Here eight more pages, removed for the *Life of Johnson*, are now restored.

different from what they really are. After death we shall see every one in a just light. Then, Sir, they talk of our meeting our relations. But then all relationship is dissolved; and we shall have no regard for one person more than another, but for their real value."—I was struck with the novelty of the thought; it was at least new to me; and if one could separate the adventitious ideas of this transitory state from those which must endure for ever, the thought would appear to be just.—"Sir," said he, "we shall either have the satisfaction of meeting our friends or be satisfied without meeting them." BOSWELL. "Yet, Sir, we see in Scripture that Dives still retained an anxious concern about his brethren."[1] JOHNSON. "Why, Sir, we must either suppose that passage to be metaphorical or hold with many divines and all the Purgatorians that souls do not all at once arrive at great perfection." BOSWELL. "I think, Sir, that is a very rational supposition." JOHNSON. "Why, yes, Sir; but we are not told it is a true one. There is no harm in believing it. But you must not compel others to make it an article of faith, because it is not revealed." BOSWELL. "Do you think, Sir, there would be any harm in a man's praying for the souls of his deceased friends if he holds the doctrine of purgatory?" JOHNSON. "Why, no, Sir." BOSWELL. "I have been told that in the liturgy of the Episcopal Church of Scotland there was a form of prayer for the dead." JOHNSON. "Sir, it is not in the liturgy which Laud framed for the Episcopal Church of Scotland. If there is a liturgy older than that, I should be glad to see it." BOSWELL. "As to our employment in a future state, revelation indeed says little. The Revelation indeed of St. John gives us many ideas, and particularly mentions music." JOHNSON. "Why, Sir, ideas must be given you by means of something which you know; and as to music, there are some philosophers and divines who have maintained that we shall not be spiritualised to such a degree but what something material—though of matter very much refined—will remain. In that case we may have music."

BOSWELL. "I don't know if there are any well-attested stories of the appearance of ghosts. You know there is a famous story of the appearance of Mrs. Veal prefixed to Drelincourt on Death." JOHNSON. "I believe, Sir, that is given up. I believe the woman declared upon

[1] Luke xvi, 19–28 ("Dives" is the Vulgate Latin for "rich man").

her death-bed that it was a lie."[1] BOSWELL. "This objection is made against the truth of ghosts appearing: that if they are in a state of happiness, it would be punishing them to bring them to this world; and if they are in a state of misery, it would be giving them a respite." JOHNSON. "Why, Sir, as the happiness or misery of an unembodied spirit does not depend upon place but is intellectual, we cannot say that they are less happy or less miserable by appearing upon earth."

We went down between twelve and one to Mrs. Williams's room and drank tea. I mentioned that we were to have the remains of Mr. Gray in prose and verse, published by Mr. Mason. JOHNSON. "I think we have had enough of him. I see they have published a splendid edition of Akenside's works. One bad ode may be suffered; but a number of 'em together makes one sick." BOSWELL. "Akenside's distinguished poem is his *Pleasures of the Imagination*.[2] But for my part I never could admire it so much as most people do." JOHNSON. "Sir, I could not read it through." BOSWELL. "I have read it through, but I did not find any great power or warmth in it."

I mentioned Mr. Elwall, whose trial Sir John Pringle gave me. JOHNSON. "Sir, Mr. Elwall was, I think, an ironmonger at Wolverhampton, and he had a mind to make himself famous by being the founder of a new sect which he wished much should be called Elwallians. He held that everything in the Old Testament that was not typical[3] was to be of perpetual observance; and so he wore a ribband in the plaits of his coat, and he also wore a beard. I remember I had the honour of dining in company with Mr. Elwall. There was one Barter, a

[1] Defoe's *True Relation of the Apparition of Mrs. Veal to Mrs. Bargrave* (apparently a journalistic rendering of a ghost story which was circulating in London in 1705) was prefixed to the fifth edition, 1707, of the English translation of Charles Drelincourt's treatise, *The Christian's Defence against the Fears of Death*. The two were published together during the rest of the century.

[2] Mark Akenside (1721–1770) became physician to Christ's Hospital in 1759 and to the Queen in 1761. The best of his minor poems, *Hymn to the Naiads*, was published in Dodsley's *Collection of Poems*, 1758. His blank-verse *The Pleasures of Imagination*, 1744–1757, pursues themes of neo-Platonic, pictorial, and associationist æsthetics made current earlier in the century by Shaftesbury, Addison, and Hutcheson.

[3] Symbolic.

miller, who wrote against him; and so you had 'the controversy between Mr. Elwall and Mr. Barter'. To try to make himself distinguished, he wrote a letter to King George the Second, challenging him to dispute with him, in which he said, 'George, if you be afraid to come by yourself to dispute with a poor old man, you may bring a thousand of your *blackguards* with you; and if you should still be afraid, you may bring a thousand of your *red* guards.' The letter had something of the impudence of Junius to this King.[1] But the men of Wolverhampton were not so inflammable as the Common Council of London, so Mr. Elwall[2] failed in his scheme of making himself a man of consequence."

I regretted that sitting up late hurt my health; otherwise I would have continued much longer listening to Mr. Johnson, whose conversation is truly admirable both for instruction and entertainment. I got home about two in the morning. I got the watch to light me along the streets till I met with a hackney-coach. Saturday night is the worst for meeting bad company on the streets of London.

SUNDAY 29 MARCH. Having received a kind invitation to breakfast with the Honourable Mrs. Stuart, an old and intimate friend of my wife's,[3] I accepted it with pleasure. She lived in Queen's Street, Mayfair. Before she appeared, I looked out at the window and saw almost opposite the late Lord Eglinton's house in this street, where he lived when I came first to London, where I lived with him, and where I

[1] "Junius" was the pseudonym of a political writer who contributed to *The Public Advertiser* from 21 January 1769 to 21 January 1772 a series of letters which aimed to discredit the ministry of the Duke of Grafton and to secure the return to power of the Earl of Chatham. In an artificial but vigorous style he poured vitriolic abuse on Grafton, the Duke of Bedford, Lord Chief Justice Mansfield, and King George III himself. The author's own collected edition of the letters had just appeared. It seems highly probable that Junius was Sir Philip Francis (1740–1818).

[2] The fifth of the newly recovered fragments of the Journal ends with this word. See p. 42 *n.* 2.

[3] A niece of Boswell's friends the tenth and eleventh Earls of Eglinton, she was married to James Archibald Stuart, younger brother of Boswell's friend Lord Mountstuart. For reasons now unknown, Boswell had frowned upon his fiancée's intimacy with her. In later years he himself came to have a high sentimental regard for her.

first learnt the knowledge of life in this metropolis. The many happy days which I have passed there and the recollection of his unhappy death affected me much as I mused by myself.[1] Mr. Stuart was in the country. Mrs. Stuart was in bad health but had a pleasing look, revived agreeable ideas of her as Peggie Cunynghame, and was very entertaining. She had two fine little girls for her children, who were brought into the room, I really believe more from real affection for them than to avoid any scandal by sitting alone with a gentleman. I don't remember how we introduced the subject of matrimonial infidelity. She candidly declared that from what she had seen of life in this great town she would not be uneasy at an occasional infidelity in her husband, as she did not think it at all connected with affection. That if he kept a particular woman, it would be a sure sign that he had no affection for his wife; or if his infidelities were very frequent, it would also be a sign. But that a transient fancy for a girl, or being led by one's companions after drinking to an improper place, was not to be considered as inconsistent with true affection. I wish this doctrine may not have been only consolatory and adapted to facts. I told her I was very happy; that I had never known I was married, having taken for my wife my cousin and intimate friend and companion; so that I had nothing at all like restraint.

Mrs. Stuart has a great deal of lively humour. She gave me a most characteristical anecdote of an English pedant, Dr. Smith, the present Head Master of Westminster School. Lady Percy[2] and she were going to see the procession of the Princess of Wales's funeral, and were to have places in Dr. Blair's, one of the prebendaries of Westminster, from whose windows they could see it well. There was so great a crowd that they could not get their carriage forward to Dr. Blair's. So they stopped at Dr. Smith's door, sent up their names, and begged

[1] See above, p. 1. Though Boswell did not live in Eglinton's house during his second visit to London, he visited it many times. See *Boswell's London Journal, 1762–1763*. Eglinton was shot and killed by a poacher in October 1769. The incident was described for Boswell in a letter from his fiancée (*Boswell in Search of a Wife, 1766–1769*, 24 October 1769).

[2] Her sister-in-law, Lady Anne Stuart, third daughter of the Earl of Bute, married (1764) Hugh Percy, later second Duke of Northumberland, but was divorced by him in 1779.

leave only to walk through his house to Dr. Blair's. They heard him answer the servant, "It cannot be. I will not let them go through; I'll do nothing to oblige the Dean and Chapter." It would seem that there had been some quarrel between him and the Dean and Chapter. But his thinking of that, and conducting himself sternly with a view to it while two pretty, young, agreeable ladies were waiting with impatience for the favour only of being allowed to pass through his house and could not reasonably be supposed to have any connexion with the Dean and Chapter, was truly ludicrous. They persisted in their request till at last Dr. Smith himself came downstairs and opened his back door, saying, "Well, you may go through. But remember, 'tis not to oblige the Dean and Chapter."

My old friend[1] Archie Stewart, Sir Michael Stewart's youngest son, came in; but was in a very bad state of health, having a rheumatism of a very violent kind. It had made one of his legs longer than the other, so that he was quite lame; and he was even bowed down to a great degree. He told me he had now got a fortune in Tobago[2] of about £20,000. I understood too that he had been successful at play this winter. He showed us £800 which he had picked up the night before. I dined with DOUGLAS. Castle Semple,[3] Laird Heron[4] and several more Scotch were there. We were elegantly entertained. I told him it made all a part of the general system with me who looked back on the Cause. He should look back too. It would do him good.[5]

[1] The friendship dated back to 1763, when Stewart, who was then settled in Rotterdam as a merchant, had been very kind to Boswell while Boswell was suffering an attack of intense melancholy.

[2] He was killed there in 1779 while repulsing some American privateers.

[3] William McDowall.

[4] Patrick Heron of Kirroughtrie had two months earlier (23 January) divorced Jean Home, daughter of Lord Kames. Heron was a chief promoter of the Douglas, Heron, and Company Bank, the collapse of which during 1772 and 1773 ruined so many shareholders, including Andrew Crosbie. See below, p. 232, for Heron's second courtship in the summer of 1774.

[5] Douglas disliked all reference to the Cause which had called his filiation in question, and finally broke with Boswell when Boswell, in *The Journal of a Tour to the Hebrides*, published Johnson's sceptical comment on the matter.

I went to Lord Mansfield's in the evening. Lord Mountstuart had told me that Lord Mansfield was so angry at me for having in some degree spoken well of Wilkes at his levée in spring 1768, the last time I saw his Lordship, though Lord Oxford only was present, that he had declared he would never let me into his house again. This was not well in Lord Mansfield, if true; for I doubt Lord Mountstuart has been mistaken.[1] As it is of some consequence to counsel who are to appear at the bar of the House of Lords to be well with his Lordship, I resolved to try how he would receive me. He took me by the hand, and seemed as courteous as I could wish. LORD MANSFIELD. "How does your father do?" BOSWELL. "I thank your Lordship." LORD MANSFIELD. "How long have you been in town?" BOSWELL. "About a fortnight, my Lord. I should have been sooner to pay my respects to your Lordship, but was afraid of intruding upon you." LORD MANSFIELD. "Glad to see you, Sir, at all times." I think this was enough.[2]

Dr. Mounsey, our Scotch Russian,[3] and some other gentleman were in the room. By degrees there was a succession of people, mostly Scotch: the Duke of Queensberry, Lord Adam Gordon, General Scott,[4] Sir William Hamilton, Ambassador to Naples,[5] Mr. Stewart

[1] See *Boswell in Search of a Wife, 1766–1769*, 22 May 1768.

[2] He later decided, however, that Mansfield really was angry. A copy of a letter to Mansfield among the Boswell papers at Yale, 14 February 1783, begins, "I reckon myself unlucky in having had less of your Lordship's attention than others not better entitled to it. I have been informed that I gave you offence several years ago by speaking too favourably in your presence of the gay and classical John Wilkes. *Nihil est ab omni parte beatum* [no situation in life is in all respects happy—Horace, *Odes*, II, xvi, 27–28]. I regret never having been invited to Kenwood, or to share any of the social hours of Pope's Murray, which few could have relished more than myself."

[3] James Mounsey of Rammerscales had been physician to the Empress Elizabeth of Russia.

[4] Major-General John Scott of Balcomie, M.P. 1754–1775, at this time for Fife. He was a noted gambler.

[5] Husband (1791) of Romney's famous friend and model and Nelson's mistress, Emma. On his visit to England this year, Hamilton sold his collection of Greek and Roman antiquities to the British Museum for a Parliamentary grant of £8,400.

Moncrieffe, Sir James Steuart,[1] Solicitor Dundas,[2] etc. There were also some English. I could not but smile within myself when my Lord Oxford came in.[3] Lord Barrington was there. It was curious to see him and Lord Mansfield together, whom I have seen so much abused in the newspapers. A report of several people having been killed in a sort of mob in the north of Ireland was mentioned. Lord Mansfield, smiling and addressing himself to Lord Barrington, said, "This beats St. George's Fields all to nothing." What would Junius, what would the Patriots, as they call themselves, have said had they been present! The massacre of St. George's Fields[4] has been a bloody and terrible charge against Lord Barrington in particular, and much, too, against Lord Mansfield. Many of the English would suppose that the great culprits would grow pale at hearing the very name of St. George's Fields; and yet here were they making it a point, a jest, in conversation. Satire is like a nettle. If you touch it gently and timidly, it will sting you. But if you come boldly up and seize it firmly, it is crushed and becomes quite harmless.

After Mr. Moncrieffe went out, we talked of his sumptuous entertainments. "I hope," said Sir James Steuart, "he will never again ask me to dine with him. He asked me twice and both times I took the gout, though I did not go to his entertainments." "Sir James," said I,

[1] Better known as Denham, the name which he assumed in 1773. A Jacobite who had received his formal pardon and had been received at Court in the preceding December; author of the first considerable work in English on economics, 1767.

[2] Boswell's college-mate at Edinburgh, brother of the Lord President of the Court of Session and son of a former Lord President, had been appointed Solicitor-General for Scotland at the age of twenty-four. See below, p. 246. *n.*

[3] Possibly because Oxford had spread the story that Mansfield would never admit Boswell again.

[4] This occurred on 10 May 1768, when troops fired into a mob in St. George's Fields who had gathered on a rumour that Wilkes was to be released from prison in order to be present at the opening of Parliament. Barrington was Secretary at War and publicly supported the action of the troops. Mansfield, Chief Justice of the Court of King's Bench, was very unpopular because he usually upheld the royal prerogative, and was much jostled by the crowd on his way to Westminster Hall on 8 June to decide the question of Wilkes's outlawry. His verdict in favour of a reversal was widely attributed to fear.

WILLIAM MURRAY,
first Earl of Mansfield (1705–1793), from an oil painting by John Singleton Copley, 1783, in the National Portrait Gallery, London

"you put me in mind of the man who had an antipathy at a cat and felt a horror as he passed under the sign of one, though he did not see it." The style of Lord Mansfield's levée was rather constrained. He himself sat with his tie-wig, his coat buttoned, his legs pushed much before him, and his heels off the ground and knocking frequently but not hard against each other, and he talked neatly and with vivacity. But the circle of company who sat around spoke little and low and I thought too obsequiously. Sir James Steuart alone spoke with freedom. I went and sat awhile with Lord Mountstuart.

MONDAY 30 MARCH. I called on Mr. Foote at his house in Suffolk Street, just as he got up. He was just the same man. He asked me to dine with him at North End on Thursday. He said Lord Mansfield's voice was a false one; that is to say, a voice which he has made to himself. He said Garrick's was the same (taking him off), and that his brother George and his very servants all imitated it. "My master, Sir, is not at home" (taking them off). Foote showed his usual inclination to attack Garrick. He took off his *aw-aw-aw* hesitating way of speaking, which is indeed strange, and added, "Sir, a man born never to finish a sentence." He said he lately made an extempore epigram upon him, as being perpetually playing a part:

> Garrick's the greatest actor of the age;
> For Garrick acts both on and off the stage.

I breakfasted with Archie Stewart. I had an immense satisfaction in comparing myself now with the wretched being that I was when he entertained me most kindly and humanely at his house in Rotterdam. I was then so low-spirited, melancholy, hypochrondriac, or whatever other name the affliction may have, that I was at times quite gone, and even when easy despaired of ever being well.[1] Now I am firm and cheerful and contented in general, and very rarely does a cloud darken my mind. Stewart carried me in his chariot to the House of Lords to hear the appeal, Willock, etc., against Ouchterlony. He left me there and I heard it out; and then had the pleasure of hearing Lord Mansfield speak, which I had never had before. He reversed the decree of the

[1] See *Boswell in Holland, 1763–1764,* 1 August–8 September 1763.

Lords of Session with an ease that gave me somewhat a disagreeable feeling of his supreme power over the property of Scotland. I was, however, charmed with the precision of his ideas, the clearness of his arrangement, the elegant choice and fluency of his language, and the distinct, forcible, and melodious expression of his voice. I recollected the excellent reversal of DOUGLAS, to comfort us under the idea of his supreme power; and, as an ancient Scotsman, it pleased me to see a younger son of the family of Stormont in so exalted a situation. The Chancellor did not speak.

I dined at St. Clement's Coffee-house with my good friend Mr. William Wilson and Mr. George Urquhart, the solicitor. Mr. Urquhart spoke to me strongly to come to the English bar. I argued against it. But was pleased to hear him, because I really do often wish to do it. Mr. Johnson is not against it; and says my having any Scotch accent would be but for a little while. My only objection is that I have a kind of idea of Scottish patriotism that makes me think it a duty to spend my money in my own country. Auchinleck indeed is my great object; and I have a notion I might be as much there if I were at the English bar as I can be while I practise in the Court of Session. Business is become necessary for me; and I had better follow it where I can make a great fortune by it than where I can make but little. But then I should be leaving a certainty of tolerable business for an incertainty, the consequence of which might either be success or disappointment. In this manner do I meditate on the subject, without its having any real influence upon my conduct. I am, however, resolved to go through the form of being called to the English bar. I went home and wrote my Journal all the evening.

TUESDAY 31 MARCH. I called on Mr. Garrick at his house in the Adelphi. I found him like a little minister of state, standing in the middle of a room, hurried and surrounded with several people, and among them old Cleland, in his youth the author of the *Woman of Pleasure*,[1] that most licentious and inflaming book, and now the grave and prolix *Parliamentarian* in the newspapers. He is the son of Major Cleland, the Will Honeycomb of the *Spectator*. He is a fine sly malcontent. Garrick was talking vainly of his being appointed the

[1] Better known as *Fanny Hill*.

executor of a clergyman by "that great man, Lord Camden." "Not a very great man," grumbled Cleland. I saw Mr. Garrick was not at leisure, so I went and breakfasted at the Mount Coffee-house.

I called on General Oglethorpe[1] and left a card telling him that Mr. Samuel Johnson and I were to dine at General Paoli's, where he would please send and let us know if he would be at home in the evening, as we would in that case drink tea with him. I went and called on Mr. Johnson, and he and I came to General Paoli's in a hackney-coach. As we came along he said that the wonderful expedition with which houses were built was one of the things that struck him most on his coming to London. We were very happy at General Paoli's. There was nobody else there but Count Gentili, who is of his household. It was no small disadvantage that the General did not well understand Mr. Johnson and could not well answer him. However, by my aid as an interpreter, things did pretty well.

We disputed if marriage was natural. The General maintained it was. "My dear Sir," said Mr. Johnson, "it is so far[2] from being easy and natural for a man and woman to live in a state of marriage that we find all the restraints and motives in civilised society are hardly sufficient to keep them together." The General said that in a state of nature a man and woman first uniting together would form a strong and constant affection by the mutual pleasure which each then received; and that they had not the causes of difference which occur between husband and wife in civilised life. "Sir," said Mr. Johnson, "they would have differences, though of another kind. One would choose to go a hunting in this wood; the other in that; one would choose to go a fishing in this lake, the other in that; or perhaps one would choose to go a hunting when the other would choose to go a fishing; and so they would part. Besides, a savage man and a savage woman meet by chance; and when the man sees another woman that pleases him better, he would leave the first."

This led into a disquisition on the dispute whether there is any beauty independent of utility. The General maintained there was not.

[1] General James Edward Oglethorpe (1696–1785), founder of the colony of Georgia, 1732, had introduced himself to Boswell in the spring of 1768.

[2] Here six pages, removed by Boswell for the *Life of Johnson*, are now restored.

Mr. Johnson maintained that there was; and he instanced a coffee-cup which he held in his hand, the painting of which was of no real use, as the cup would hold the coffee equally well if plain; yet the painting was beautiful. The General spoke English much better than I imagined he could do. "Sir," said Mr. Johnson, "you must speak it before your friends, with whom you need not care though you spoil a thought."

We talked of the practice of swearing. The General said that all barbarous nations swore from a kind of violence of temper that could not be confined to earth but was always reaching at the powers above. He said too that there was greater variety of swearing in proportion as there were among a people greater variety of religious ceremonies.

Mr. Johnson went home with me and drank tea, as no message had come from General Oglethorpe. He said he thought General Paoli had lost somewhat of that grandeur in his air and manner which he had when he came first to England. The observation is just, and the fact is easily accounted for. When he came first here, he was just arrived from being at the head of a nation. Wherever he had passed, and even here, he was addressed in that high character. But after having been near three years just in the style of a private gentleman, much of the majesty of his deportment must insensibly be lost.

Mr. Johnson said Goldsmith's *Life of Parnell*[1] was poor; not that it was poorly written but that he had poor materials; for nobody could furnish the life of a man but those who had eat and drank and lived in social intercourse with him.

I have a constant plan to write the life of Mr. Johnson. I have not told him of it yet, nor do I know if I should tell him. I said that if it was not troublesome and presuming too much, I would beg of him to tell me all the little circumstances of his life, what schools he attended, when he came to Oxford, when he came to London, etc., etc. He did

[1] Thomas Parnell (1679–1718), poet and friend of Swift and Pope, best remembered for his octosyllabic *Night Piece on Death*. Goldsmith's *Life of Parnell* appeared in 1770. Johnson, later writing a *Life of Parnell* for the edition of the English poets, confessed it was a task which he would "very willingly decline". "What such an author [as Goldsmith] has told, who would tell again? I have made an abstract from his larger narrative."

not disapprove of my curiosity as to these particulars, but said, "They'll come out by degrees."

He censured Ruffhead's *Life of Pope*. "Sir," said he, "he knew nothing of Pope and nothing of poetry." He praised Mr. Joseph Warton's *Essay on Pope*, but said he would publish no more of it, as he had not been able to persuade the world to think of Pope as he did.[1] "Sir," said I, "there is no matter. He is an ingenious counsel who has made the most of his cause; he is not obliged to win it." "But, Sir," said he, "there is a difference when the cause is of a man's own making."

I expressed how happy I was at having lived to make my father amends for what he suffered from my former folly and bad conduct. "Sir," said he, "I am glad to hear you talk so."

We spoke of the use to be made of riches. Said he, "If I was a man of a great estate, I would drive all the rascals whom I did not like out of the county at an election."

I consulted him whether a man should lay himself out to show great hospitality. This was an important subject for me who would naturally go to an excess of hospitality, both from inclination and from a notion that it makes a man of great consequence. "Sir," said Mr. Johnson, "you are to consider that ancient hospitality of which we hear so much was in an uncommercial country, when men, being idle, were glad to be entertained at rich men's tables. But in a commercial country, a busy country, time becomes precious and therefore hospitality is not so much valued. No doubt there is still room for a certain degree of it; and a man has a satisfaction in seeing his friends eating and drinking around him. But promiscuous hospitality is not the way to make one's self of real influence. You must help some people at table, before[2] others. You must ask some people how they like their wine oftener than others. You therefore offend as many as you please. You are like ———,[3] who said when he granted a favour, 'J'ai fait dix

[1] The first volume of the *Essay* had been published in 1756, but the promised second volume did not appear until 1782.

[2] The sixth of the newly recovered portions of the Journal ends here. See above, p. 42 *n.* 2.

[3] Louis XIV. In the *Life* Boswell filled the blank by "the French statesman".

mécontents et un ingrat.'[1] Besides, Sir, being entertained ever so well at a man's table impresses no lasting regard or esteem. No, Sir" (speaking with a low and earnest voice), "you will make sure of power and influence by lending privately sums of money to your neighbours, perhaps at a small interest, perhaps at no interest, and always having their bonds in your possession." This is an excellent thought. I am resolved to practise it to a certain extent if it shall ever be in my power; and the scheme of securing influence in the country is so admirably adapted to my high feudal notions that I shall never forget this afternoon when it was suggested to me by the great Mr. Samuel Johnson. I am persuaded that in this late age it will supply the place of the old attachment.

I told him that my father had never kept a hospitable house, that is to say, a house where people drank as much as they pleased and found themselves as at an inn. But by his knowledge and good sense and prudence he had given so many people good advice, and was still ready to do so, that he had much more influence in the country than those who were the immediate and temporary delight of visitors.[2]

I said I would employ part of my riches in educating young men of merit. "Yes, Sir," said he, "provided they fall in your way; but if you once have it understood that[3] you patronise young men of merit, you will be harassed with solicitations. You will have multitudes forced upon you; some will force them upon you from mistaken partiality and some from downright interest without scruple, and you will be disgraced.

"I would propagate all kinds of trees that will grow in the open air. A greenhouse is childish. I would introduce foreign animals into the country; for instance, the reindeer."

He said Bayes was a mighty silly character. If it was intended to be like a particular man, it could only be diverting while that man was remembered. But he questioned if it was like Dryden, as has been

[1] "I have made ten malcontents and one ingrate." *Dix* is the reading of the *Life*; Boswell left a blank in the Journal. Voltaire, in his *Siècle de Louis XIV*, and Johnson, in quoting the remark again in his *Life of Swift*, give *cent* (a hundred).

[2] This allusion to Lord Auchinleck was omitted from the *Life*.

[3] Here ten pages, removed for the *Life of Johnson*, are now restored.

said, as we know some of the passages said to be ridiculed were written since *The Rehearsal*; at least a circumstance mentioned in the Preface.[1] I maintained that it had merit as a general satire on the conceit of dramatic authors. But he held it very cheap.

While we were sitting, there came a card from General Oglethorpe that he would be glad to see us, he being just then come home; but we sent back that we were just going to the Pantheon. In a little, however, the polite old gentleman arrived himself in a chair. It was most agreeable to find him as lively, as full of knowledge, and as full of spirits as ever. When I was last in London he and Mr. Johnson wished to meet, and I was to bring them together. But, General Oglethorpe having gone to the country, I was disappointed of that pleasure. Goldsmith had brought them acquainted in my absence. "Who," said General Oglethorpe to Mr. Johnson, "would have thought that you would go to worship the heathen gods?" (Alluding to our going to the Pantheon.) After sitting a few minutes with the General, Mr. Johnson and I walked to the Pantheon. The *coup d'œil*, as the French say, on first view of it did not strike us so much as Ranelagh. The truth is Ranelagh is of a more beautiful form; more of it, or rather indeed the whole rotunda, appears at once. It is better lighted. However, as Mr. Johnson observed, we saw the Pantheon in time of mourning,[2] when there was a dull uniformity, whereas we saw Ranelagh when the view was charmed with a gay profusion and variety of colours of the different dresses.[3] Mrs. Bosville came up to us and had some con-

[1] In his *Life of Dryden*, which was written some years after the date of this conversation, Johnson states the view now generally accepted: that by Bayes ("the laureate") Dryden [who became laureate in 1668] was principally intended, but that the character was in early drafts of the play aimed at Sir William D'Avenant and Sir Robert Howard. "The design was probably to ridicule the reigning poet, whoever he might be." Malone, in later editions of the *Life*, pointed out that additions were made to *The Rehearsal* after it was first printed in 1672. The play is anonymous, but is believed to have been written by the Duke of Buckingham, with help from Samuel Butler, author of *Hudibras*, and Martin Clifford, Master of the Charterhouse.

[2] For the King's mother. See above, p. 63.

[3] Ranelagh Gardens, Chelsea, was a place of public amusement which boasted a rotunda 150 feet in diameter, with an orchestra in the centre and boxes around it.

versation with us. Mr. Johnson said she was a mighty intelligent lady. My old mistress Miss Blair was here, to my great surprise; for I did not know she was in London. I felt a kind of consciousness that I had not behaved altogether well to her. No man should trifle with young ladies who are candidates for matrimony. She however behaved at least as ill. So there's no harm done.[1] I had great satisfaction in watchfully and respectfully attending my revered friend through the mazes of this magnificent place of entertainment. The grandeur of the pillars in imitation of marble and the elegance of the finishing in every respect were well worth seeing.[2]

I said there was not half a guinea's worth of pleasure in seeing it. But Mr. Johnson observed that there was half a guinea's worth of inferiority to other people (or some such phrase) in not having seen it. I said I doubted if there were many happy people there. "Yes, Sir," said he, "there are many happy here. There are many people here who are watching hundreds and who think hundreds are watching them."

Sir Adam Fergusson[3] joined us. I presented him to Mr. Johnson. Sir Alexander Gilmour, Mr. Fordyce, and one or two more Scottish emigrants formed a circle round us. Sir Adam expressed some apprehension that the Pantheon would encourage luxury. Mr. Johnson said he was a great friend to public amusements, for they kept people from vice. "You now (addressing himself to me) would have

---

The Pantheon in Oxford Street, which was intended to be a "winter Ranelagh", had opened in the preceding January. As Boswell's remarks indicate, the chief feature of both buildings was a great rotunda in which people promenaded.

[1] The tale of Boswell's backings and fillings in the pursuit of Catherine Blair, heiress of Adamton, fills many of the pages of *Boswell in Search of a Wife, 1766–1769*. His own summary here seems candid. At one point she told him she wished she liked him as much as she did Auchinleck. See above, p. 3.

[2] "It amazed me. . . . Imagine Baalbek in all its glory! The pillars are of artificial *giallo antico*. The ceilings, even of the passages, are of the most beautiful stuccos in the best taste of grotesque. The ceilings of the ballrooms and the panels painted like Raphael's *loggias* in the Vatican. A dome like the Pantheon [in Rome], glazed. It is to cost fifty thousand pounds" (Horace Walpole to Sir Horace Mann, 26 April 1771).

[3] See below, pp. 211–12.

been with a wench had you not been here.—Oh, I forgot you were married."

Sir Adam threw out an idea that luxury corrupts a people and destroys the spirit of liberty, so that they become enslaved. "Sir," said Mr. Johnson, "that is all visionary. I would not give half a guinea whether I should live under one form of government or another. It is of no moment to the happiness of each individual. Why there now, the question about general warrants made a prodigious noise, and yet had you gone through England you could not have collected a farthing a head from the people to ensure them that they should never suffer from general warrants.[1] Sir, the danger of the abuse of power is nothing to each individual. What Frenchman is prevented from passing his life just as he pleases?" SIR ADAM. "But, Sir, in the British Constitution it is surely of importance to keep up a proper spirit in the people, so as to preserve a proper balance against the Crown." JOHNSON. "Sir, I perceive you are a vile Whig. Why all this childish jealousy of the power of the Crown? The Crown has not power enough. When I say that all governments are alike, I consider that in no government power can be abused long. Mankind will not bear it. If a sovereign oppresses his people to a great degree, they will rise and cut off his head. There is a remedy in human nature against tyranny that will keep us safe under every form of government. Had not the people of France thought themselves honoured as sharing in the brilliant actions of the reign of Louis XIV, they would not have borne him; and we [may] say [the same] of the present King of Prussia's people." Sir Adam brought in the ancient Romans and Greeks. "Sir," said Mr. Johnson, "the mass of both of them were barbarians. The mass of every people must be barbarous where there is no printing and consequently knowledge is not generally diffused. Knowledge is diffused among our people by the newspapers." Sir Adam mentioned the orators, poets, and artists of Greece. "Sir," said Johnson, "I am talking

[1] The question had arisen when in 1763 John Wilkes, author of the attack on Lord Bute in *The North Briton*, No. 45, was arrested on a warrant which did not name him specifically or describe him with any precision. Chief Justice Pratt (Lord Camden) declared such a warrant to be "unconstitutional, illegal, and absolutely void". See above, p. 71 *n*.

of the mass of the people. We see even the Athenians, what strange work they made of it." Demosthenes's orations were mentioned. "Sir," said Mr. Johnson, "the little effect those orations had upon them shows they were barbarians." He was very loud and violent.

Sir Adam was unlucky in his topics; for he suggested a doubt of the propriety of bishops being peers. "How so, Sir?" said Mr. Johnson. "Who is more proper for having the dignity of a peer than a bishop, providing a bishop be what he ought to be; and if improper bishops be made, that is not the fault of the bishops but of those who make them." He was disgusted by Sir Adam and called him to me a narrow Whig with just the commonplace arguments. I, however, told him afterwards that Sir Adam was a man who distinguished himself by his regard for religion, though his politics were bad. "O Sir," said Mr. Johnson, "politics go but a little way with me in comparison of religion. I forgive him his politics for his religion."

Mr. Johnson and I drank some tea together. He then met with a Mrs. Horneck and a very pretty girl, a Miss Horneck.[1] They engaged to take care of him. I saw him fairly into their coach, and then I came home.

WEDNESDAY 1 APRIL. I breakfasted at Lord Elibank's. He said Paterculus had well observed that Cicero and Virgil had spoiled or rather stopped oratory and poetry at Rome. So Shakespeare had put a stop to all great tragic poetry in England. The reason is when men of real genius see a thing carried to[2] the highest pitch of perfection, they think it is not worth their while to do anything, because fame is pre-occupied. They cannot hope for distinguished excellence, so they leave the field to inferior geniuses who have not such high ambition. Mr. Johnson had said, "Sir, I never am with Lord Elibank but I learn something from him." I told my Lord this, and he was much pleased. I dined at Sir John Pringle's, just he and I and Duncan Forbes,[3] easy and

[1] Goldsmith's friends, and already old friends of Johnson's. Gibbon, writing to his friend Holroyd in 1774, speaks of their seeing Mrs. Horneck at the Pantheon.

[2] The seventh newly recovered fragment of the Journal ends here. See above, p. 42 *n.* 2.

[3] Surgeon to the Second Troop of Horse Guards. It was he who directed the clearing of Boswell's constitution before his marriage.

comfortable. I drank tea at Mrs. Strange's,[1] and came quietly home.

THURSDAY 2 APRIL. Mr. Archibald Macdonald breakfasted with me. Lord Eglinton and Major Hunter and Crosbie came and chatted a little while. After they went, Sir Alexander Macdonald came, and he and I walked out together. Crosbie and Wight introduced me to Mr. Mayne, banker in Jermyn Street, who carried us in his coach to Mr. Foote's villa at North End, where we were invited to dine. Mr. Mayne was a genteel man. He told us that he rode in Hyde Park with Mr. Fitzherbert the day before he shot himself; and it being fine weather he observed to Mr. Fitzherbert that he had seen no accounts in the newspapers of anybody having hanged or drowned themselves. "Very true," said Fitzherbert, "I have not observed any."[2]

I walked a good deal at Mr. Foote's. He gave us a very elegant dinner, all served upon plate; and he did not say, "Gentlemen, there's Madeira and port and claret." But, "Gentlemen, there's *all* sorts of wine. You'll call for what you choose." He gave us noble old hock, of which he said he had purchased ninety dozen—"the stock of an ambassador lately deceased," as I said. It was indeed bought from an ambassador. He gave us sparkling champagne, Constantia, and Tokay. When the latter was served round, he said, "Now you're going to drink the best wine in England"; and it was indeed exquisite. His claret flowed of course. There was nobody else here but Nabob Gray, who had been my schoolfellow at Mr. James Mundell's.[3] Foote entertained

[1] Isabella Strange, besides being an extremely distant cousin of Boswell's, was sister to his friend Andrew Lumisden, who was Secretary to the Old Pretender and had shown Boswell many kindnesses when he was at Rome. Her husband, the distinguished engraver Robert Strange (later knighted), had also been out in the '45. When soldiers searched for him in her home after Culloden (they were then affianced), she is said to have saved him by hiding him under her hoop-skirt.

[2] William Fitzherbert, M.P., of an ancient Derbyshire family, witnessed the execution of some convicts on the morning of 2 January 1772, and that afternoon went to his stable and hanged himself. As he was a man of wide acquaintance and esteemed as a wit, his suicide was much discussed. For Johnson's character of him, see the *Life of Johnson*, 15 September 1777. Robert Mayne, who told Boswell this anecdote about Fitzherbert, committed suicide himself in 1782.

[3] George Gray, born in India c. 1738, the son of a surgeon, was sent back to Scotland to be educated, and in 1744 entered James Mundell's school in the West

us with taking off George Faulkner, who he said sorted his companies in the oddest way, and always characterised each guest on the ceremony of introduction. As thus: "This is the ingenious Samuel Foote, Esquire, reckoned one of the best table-companions in Ireland; this is Mr. such-a-one, who has more wit than any judge now upon the Bench; and this is Mrs. such-a-one, who has imported more of Dr. James's Powders into this country than anybody."

He said Mr. Johnson had once a great inclination to become a Methodist. But changed his mind upon occasion of one of their preachers, whom the people drove out of Long Acre, saying he was persecuted by the Jacobites. He said Johnson told him as follows: " 'This fellow was preaching in Long Acre. The people in the neighbourhood, wanting to get rid of him, attacked him with tongs, with spits, with frying-pans, and other culinary instruments, and drove him away. The rascal said it was the Jacobites. Now, for my part, I cannot see the connexion between a frying-pan and a Jacobite.' 'Ay, Sir,' said I, 'but there's a connexion between a *warming-pan* and a Jacobite.' "[1] This story made us laugh heartily; but Mr. Johnson has

Bow, Edinburgh. Since Boswell entered the school in 1746 and left it in 1748 or 1749, his association with Gray had occurred when they were both children. Gray attended the University of Edinburgh, but by 1756 (when he was presumably not more than eighteen) he was back in Bengal making his fortune. He was elevated to the Bengal Council, but engaged in questionable practices, and was sent home by Clive in 1766. In his India speech before the House of Commons three days before this dinner at Foote's, Clive had remarked that there had not been found among the "nabobs" a single one "sufficiently flagitious for Mr. Foote to exhibit on the theatre in the Haymarket". He spoke just in time, for Foote exhibited a satirical play, *The Nabob*, on 29 June 1772. Sir Matthew Mite, the hero of this piece, is a generic study, but besides embodying traits from Clive and General Richard Smith, he may also glance at Boswell's old schoolfellow. When Boswell once found fault with Foote for "indulging his talent of ridicule at the expense of his visitors", Johnson replied: "Why, Sir, when you go to see Foote, you do not go to see a saint: you go to see a man who will be entertained at your house and then bring you on a public stage; who will entertain you at his house for the very purpose of bringing you on a public stage" (26 October 1769).

[1] It was maintained at the time of the birth of Prince James Francis Edward (the Old Pretender) in 1688 that he was a supposititious child, introduced into the Queen's bed in a warming-pan.

since told me that it was not true, and that Foote had just made it to introduce his own saying. It was curious to see Foote showing his pedigree, the very thing for which he makes Cadwallader[1] so ridiculous.

I came home in Nabob Gray's chaise and remained quietly at home. Corresponding with my dear wife is a great happiness to me. I need not write down that I retain a constant regard and even love for her; or that my mind, while I am thus absent, is sometimes clouded with anxiety and sometimes cheered and illuminated with the warmest and brightest beams of gladness.

FRIDAY 3 APRIL. I breakfasted at home. Then was awhile at the House of Peers, hearing the appeal, Bruce Kinross[2] against Miss Bruce. I am now quite at home in the House, and take the Usher of the Black Rod's chair very regularly.[3] I went up by water to Paul's Wharf and then walked on to my friend Mr. Dilly's, with whom I had engaged to pass all this day and take a bed in his house at night. He and I and his brother dined comfortably. Then he and I went to the ———[4] Jews' synagogue, and heard Leoni, a fine singer; ———, a good strong one; and ———, a most admirable bass. It was curious to see the Jews talking and laughing together, and no kind of solemnity in their countenances. It was just a plain religion. They executed so much, like a task, and like boys at a task looked off and intermixed other things. Mr. Farquhar Kinloch, my travelling companion to London in autumn 1769, was here. He went with me to Mr. Dilly's, drank some coffee, and left us.

In the evening came a company of *literati* invited for me: Dr. Jeffries, Dr. Gilbert Stuart, a Mr. Leeson, and Kenrick, now Dr. Kenrick, who once wrote an 18d. pamphlet against me, but principally against Mr. Johnson, though it was entitled *A Letter to James Boswell, Esq*. Kenrick was quite a different man from what I expected to see.

[1] In his farce *The Author*.

[2] James Bruce-Carstairs of Kinross.

[3] The chief usher of the Lord Chamberlain's department and usher to the House of Lords. He carries an ebony wand surmounted by a golden lion. Boswell could have sat on a bench within Black Rod's box but not in his official chair.

[4] Ashkenazic, or Dutch; the "Great Synagogue" in Duke's Place, Aldgate.

His *Epistles, Philosophical and Moral* promised seriousness or rather profound gravity; and many of his other writings promised acrimony to a high degree.[1] But I found him a bluff, hearty little man, full of spirits and cheerfulness. He said devotion was not natural; that is to say, the devotion of the heart; that fear made people use ceremonies but did not inspire true devotion. He said he had a pronouncing dictionary almost ready, by which he hoped to fix a standard, as the varieties of pronunciation among people in genteel life were very few. He said he taught a man from Aberdeen to speak good English in six weeks. He said his great difficulty was to get him to speak at all. He told him, "Sir, you don't speak at all. You sing." We talked of my schoolmaster. "Sir," said he, "you have no chance; for, consider, the greatest part of the schoolmasters about London are Scotch. 'Now,' say we, 'if he beats the children of his own countrymen so terribly, what will he do with ours?' You must call the boys blockheads, Sir; though then I fear some of our Lords may have a fellow feeling with them." I remember little of what passed, though the evening went very well on. Joseph had brought me up a shirt, a nightcap, and slippers; so I was quite at home.

SATURDAY 4 APRIL. Mr. Charles Dilly and I went to the ——— Jews' and the ——— Jews' (where I was last night—the Dutch Jews') Synagogues.[2] I could not help feeling a kind of regret to see the certain descendants of venerable Abraham in an outcast state and sneered at and abused by every fool, at least to a certain degree. We came back to breakfast. I then walked with Mr. John Donaldson the bookseller and a Captain McCulloch out to Mr. Elphinston's, who keeps the academy at Chelsea. Mr. Hugh Buchan, the City Chamberlain of Edinburgh, and Mr. James Chalmers, Writer to the Signet, were there. I had just Scotch ideas. Mr. Elphinston is a worthy, hospitable man, but has an affectation, a pedantry, and an anxiety to please that make him in some measure disagreeable. He had a foolish laugh too, a

[1] He was no doubt the greatest scoundrel among the writers of the age. He had made gratuitous attacks on Johnson, Goldsmith, and Colman, and was in the following July to publish the vilest of the lot—his libel on Garrick called *Love in the Suds*.

[2] The blanks should be filled by "Sephardic" and "Ashkenazic" respectively.

made giggle. He took us and got us a sight of Kensington Palace. Some of the rooms are pretty good. But it is sadly stripped of its pictures.[1] We then drank tea with him, and Mr. Chalmers walked to town with me and my two companions out.

SUNDAY 5 APRIL. I called at Mr. George Lewis Scott's, for whom I had called several times but never found him till today. He and I went and called for Sir James Steuart, with whom we sat awhile. At neither of these places did I breakfast. I went to Mr. Johnson's and found him and his old attendant Mr. Levett drinking tea. I took none, but just got some biscuit at a pastry shop. I went to St. Paul's and heard the latter part of an excellent sermon by Mr. Sturges, one of the prebendaries. Then assisted at some prayers, stayed the communion, and received the Holy Sacrament in that grand edifice. I was elevated and bettered. I came back to Mr. Johnson.

He said Elphinston had a great deal of good about him, but was also very faulty in some respects. "His inner part," said he, "is very good. But his outer part is very faulty. You in Scotland do not arrive at that nice critical skill in languages which we get in our schools in England. I would not put a boy to Elphinston whom I intended for a man of learning. But for the sons of citizens, who are to learn a little, get good morals, and then go to trade, he may do very well." I mentioned my cause before the General Assembly where a preacher was opposed in his settlement because he had been guilty, or was accused of having been guilty, of fornication five years ago.[2] "Why, Sir," said

[1] George III had moved them to St. James's, Windsor, and Buckingham House.

[2] The case was Elders &c. of Portpatrick v. McMaster. William McMaster was presented to be minister of Portpatrick by Captain John Blair of Dunskey. The presbytery of Stranraer ruled that it could take no steps towards his settlement until his character had been cleared, and this action was affirmed by the synod of Galloway. The General Assembly (30 May 1771) reversed these sentences, but reserved the right of McMaster's opponents to give him "a libel in proper form", i.e. to attempt to prove their charges. Boswell received fees totalling four guineas in the case. His opponent was Henry Erskine. A year later (30 May 1772) it was reported to the General Assembly that the presbytery had found McMaster guilty of "uncleanness, falsehood, subornation of falsehood, and dissimulation", and had deprived him of his licence. The Assembly ruled that the sentence was final and dismissed McMaster's petition.

Mr. Johnson, "if he has repented of it, it should not be an objection. A man who is good enough to go to heaven is good enough to be a clergyman." I told him that by the rules[1] of the Church of Scotland, if a scandal, as it is called, is not insisted in for five years, it cannot more be insisted in unless it be of a heinous nature or again become flagrant. So there was a great dispute whether fornication was a sin of a heinous nature. I maintained it was not, as it was not atrocious, was not one of those sins which argued very great depravity of heart; in short, was not in the general acceptation of mankind a heinous sin. "No, Sir," said he, "it is not a heinous sin. A heinous sin is that for which a man is punished with death or banishment." BOSWELL. "But, Sir, while we argued that it was not a heinous sin, an old clergyman rose up and repeating the text, 'Neither whoremongers, &c., shall enter into the kingdom of God,' asked if it would not now be called a heinous sin." JOHNSON. "Why, Sir, observe the word *whoremonger*. Every sin persisted in will be heinous. Whoremonger is a dealer in whores, as ironmonger is a dealer in iron. But as you don't call a man an ironmonger for buying and selling his knife, so you don't call a man a whoremonger for getting one wench with child." BOSWELL. "Sir, his getting the woman to tell a lie and say another man was the father of the child was worse than the fornication." JOHNSON. "Why, yes, Sir. But you must say that argued his shame."

I came upon the subject of the inequality of the livings of the clergy in England and the mere trifles which some of the curates have. JOHNSON. "Why, yes, Sir. But it cannot be helped. You must[2] consider that the revenues of the clergy are not at the disposal of the State, like the pay of the Army. But different men have founded different churches, and some are better, some worse. The State cannot interfere and divide them equally. Now when a man has but a small living, or even two small livings, he can afford but little to a curate." He said he went more frequently to prayers than to sermon, as the people required more example to go to prayers than to sermon; hearing sermon being easier to them than to fix their minds on prayer.

[1] Two pages, removed by Boswell for the *Life of Johnson*, are here restored.

[2] Here the eighth of the newly recovered fragments of the Journal ends. See above, p. 42 *n.* 2.

I dined at Lady Margaret Macdonald's. Nobody but her son Archie was with us. All was in the most perfect neatness, I may say elegance. I was in admirable spirits, quite in the same humour as when the late Lord Eglinton was alive.[1] Archie went away. Lady Margaret and I had a great deal of common conversation. Sir John[2] and Lady Anstruther came in. I supped at Sir Alexander Macdonald's, where was Mr. Mitchelson. It was strange to dine with the mother and sup with the son, and they not in speaking terms.

MONDAY 6 APRIL. I breakfasted with Mr. Duncan Forbes, who keeps an admirable breakfast, bread and butter and marmalade. Then Crosbie and I went and saw Cox's Museum. The mechanism and rich appearance of the jewels were both very wonderful and very pleasing. We then went down to the House of Lords and heard Bruce against Miss Bruce. Mr. David Rae's English was terrible. I said that as people had a vanity in founding new sects, Mr. Rae had a mind to found a new language.[3]

I dined at Sir Alexander Macdonald's, where were Mr. Johnson and the Hon. Captain Thomas Erskine, Lord Buchan's youngest brother, a very pretty lad.[4] Mr. Johnson was very courteous to Lady

[1] Lord Eglinton was Lady Margaret Macdonald's brother. See above p. 55 *n.* 1.

[2] M.P. for Anstruther Easter Burghs.

[3] This leading Scots advocate, who in 1782 succeeded Lord Auchinleck in the Court of Session as Lord Eskgrove, had a notoriously thick and artificial pronunciation. "Whenever a name could be pronounced in more ways than one, he gave them all; and always put an accent on the last syllable. For example, syllable he called syllabill. And when a word ended with the letter G, this letter was pronounced, and strongly. And he was very fond of meaningless successions of adjectives. A good man would be described as one excellent, and worthy, and amiabill, and agreeabill, and very good man. The article A was generally made into *one*, and he generally cut a word of three syllables into two separate words, the first of two syllables, and the last of one, and even divided a word of two syllables into two words. Thus, 'I met a young friend as I was walking in the Canongate,' was converted by him into, 'I met one youngg friend as I was walk-ing in the Canongate.' " (Henry Cockburn, *Memorials of His Time*, New York, 1856, p. 119 *n.*)

[4] He was twenty-two years old, had been midshipman and lieutenant in the Navy, and was now ensign in the Army. In 1775 he sold his commission to study law, matriculated at Cambridge and took an M.A. degree, was called to the bar in 1778, and stepped immediately into a large practice. He was especially famous as

Macdonald. He said, "I will go to Skye with this lady. I'll go anywhere under this lady's protection." (By the by, he has told me that the language of conversation is somewhat different from the language of the pulpit. As, for instance, "I'll" for "I will", "receiv'd" for "received,"[1] are used in conversation.) Lady Macdonald said *Rasselas* was the finest novel she had ever read. Fielding was mentioned. "He's a blockhead," says Mr. Johnson. BOSWELL. "My dear Sir!" JOHNSON. "What I mean by his being a blockhead is that he was a barren rascal." BOSWELL. "But, Sir, will you not allow that he draws very natural pictures of human life?" JOHNSON. "Why, Sir, it is of very low life. Richardson used to say that had he not known who Fielding was, he should have believed he was an ostler. Sir, there is more knowledge of the heart in one letter of Richardson's than in all *Tom Jones*. I indeed never read *Joseph Andrews*." Captain Erskine objected that Richardson was tedious. JOHNSON. "Why, Sir, if you were to read Richardson for the story, your impatience would be so much fretted that you'd hang yourself. But you must read him for the sentiment and consider the story as only serving to give occasion to the sentiment."

A book of travels lately published under[2] the title of *Coryate Junior*, and written by Mr. Paterson, was mentioned. Johnson said this book was an imitation of Sterne and not of Coryate, whose name Paterson had chosen as a whimsical one. "Tom Coryate," said he, "was a humourist about the Court of James the First. He had a mixture of learning, of wit, and of buffoonery. He first travelled through Europe, and published his travels.[3] He afterwards travelled on foot

---

counsel for the defence in cases connected with the law of libel and treason; he defended Tom Paine, Horne Tooke, and Thelwall. In 1806 he received the Chancellorship, and was raised to the peerage. (In 1786 he would be "leading counsel" on Boswell's side in the latter's first case in the Court of King's Bench.)

[1] This seems to mean that clergymen in the pulpit still used an archaic or liturgical pronunciation: "re-cei-ved".

[2] At this point six pages, removed by Boswell for the *Life of Johnson*, have not been recovered. The text continues from the published *Life*.

[3] *Coryats Crudities Hastily Gobled up in Five Moneths Travells in France, Savoy, Italy*, London, 1611.

through Asia and had made many remarks; but he died at Mandoa[1] and his remarks were lost."

We talked of gaming, and animadverted on it with severity. JOHNSON. "Nay, gentlemen, let us not aggravate the matter. It is not roguery to play with a man who is ignorant of the game while you are master of it, and so win his money; for he thinks he can play better than you, as you think you can play better than he; and the superior skill carries it." ERSKINE. "He is a fool, but you are not a rogue." JOHNSON. "That's much about the truth, Sir."[2] BOSWELL. "So then, Sir, you do not think ill of a man who wins perhaps forty thousand pounds in a winter?" JOHNSON. "Sir, I do not call a gamester a dishonest man but I call him an unsocial man, an unprofitable man. Gaming is a mode of transferring property without producing any intermediate good. Trade gives employment to numbers, and so produces intermediate good."

Mr. Erskine told us that when he was in the island of Minorca he not only read prayers but preached two sermons to the regiment. He seemed to object to the passage in Scripture where we are told that the angel of the Lord smote in one night forty thousand Assyrians. "Sir," said Johnson, "you should recollect that there was a supernatural interposition; they were destroyed by pestilence. You are not to suppose that the angel of the Lord went about and stabbed each of them with a dagger or knocked them on the head, man by man."

After Mr. Erskine was gone, a discussion took place whether the present Earl of Buchan, when Lord Cardross, did right to refuse to go Secretary of the Embassy to Spain, when Sir James Gray, a man of inferior rank, went Ambassador. Dr. Johnson said that perhaps in point of interest he did wrong, but in point of dignity he did well. Sir Alexander insisted that he was wrong, and said that Mr. Pitt intended it as an advantageous thing for him. "Why, Sir," said Johnson, "Mr. Pitt might think it an advantageous thing for him to make him vintner

[1] He died at Surat, to which he is said to have walked, a distance of nearly 200 miles, from "Mandoa" (Mandú, ancient capital of the kingdom of Málwa).

[2] A short passage of the *Life* text here omitted was recorded as an afterthought by Boswell in his Journal, and hence appears farther on in the present text as the next to the last paragraph of this day's entry.

and get him all the Portugal trade; but he would have demeaned himself strangely had he accepted of such a situation. Sir, had he gone Secretary while his inferior was Ambassador, he would have been a traitor to his rank and family."

I talked of the little attachment which subsisted between near relations in London. "Sir," said Johnson, "in a country so commercial as ours, where every man can do for himself, there is not so much occasion for that attachment. No man is thought the worse of here whose brother was hanged. In uncommercial countries many of the branches of a family must depend on the stock; so, in order to make the head of the family take care of them, they are represented as connected with his reputation, that, self-love being interested, he may exert himself to promote their interest. You have first large circles, or clans; as commerce increases, the connexion is confined to families. By degrees, that too goes off, as having become unnecessary and there being few opportunities of intercourse. One brother is a merchant in the city and another is an officer in the Guards. How little intercourse can these two have!"

I argued warmly for the old feudal system. Sir Alexander opposed it, and talked of the pleasure of seeing all men free and independent. JOHNSON. "I agree with Mr. Boswell that there must be a high satisfaction in being a feudal lord; but we are to consider that we ought not to wish to have a number of men unhappy for the satisfaction of one."—I maintained that numbers, namely the vassals or followers, were not unhappy; for that there was a reciprocal satisfaction between the lord and them: he being kind in authority over them; they being respectful and faithful to him. . . . and[1] my superiors; or rather indeed have felt them when abroad; for in this country ideas of reverence are much weakened.

I should have remarked, when mentioning gamesters, that Mr. Johnson put his argument thus: "A man who only does what every one of the society to which he belongs would do, is not a dishonest man. In the Republic of Sparta it was agreed that stealing was not dis-

[1] Here the text is resumed in the manuscript Journal. The first part of this sentence, which may be all that is missing, probably ran somewhat as follows: "I have often experienced such feelings of satisfaction between myself . . ."

honourable but only the being discovered. I do not commend a society where there is an agreement that what would not otherwise be fair shall be fair. But I maintain that an individual of that society who practises what is allowed is not a dishonest man."

Mr. Johnson was pleased with this day's entertainment. Sir Alexander sent his coach for him before dinner, and he set down Mrs. Williams near the Middlesex Hospital; and in the evening Lady Macdonald and he went in it and took up Mrs. Williams, my Lady was set down at a rout, and Mr. Johnson and Mrs. Williams took the coach home. So much attention was very pleasing to Mr. Johnson. There was a fine contrast between his robust and rather dreadful figure and that of the beautiful Lady. Sir Alexander went home with me, eat some oysters, and drank a little port. I really like the Knight.

TUESDAY 7 APRIL. I breakfasted with Lord Eglinton, who keeps the best breakfast of any man in London, a complete Union of the good things of Scotland and England: bread and butter and honey and marmalade of oranges and currant jelly and muffins, well buttered and comfortably toasted. The Earl is pleasant, but his conversation does not furnish my Journal as his brother's used to do. I went to the House of Lords and heard out the appeal, Bruce-Carstairs against Miss Bruce. Lord Mansfield had been shaken in his opinion during the hearing; and therefore, though he affirmed, he gave his reasons, and indeed spoke in a most masterly manner. I dined at Mr. Bosville's. There was nobody there but Miss Wentworth. We were plain and comfortable.

In the evening I met at the Queen's Arms in St. Paul's Churchyard with the rest of the partners of *The London Magazine*.[1] It was truly satisfactory to me to find myself the only Scotsman among a company of English, and at the same time the distinction quite forgotten from our union of interest and from my perfect art of melting myself into the general mass. Most individuals when they find themselves with people of a different country cannot get free of their own particular national distinction. The individual, instead of being melted down, as I have remarked of myself, remains as hard as a piece of iron in a

[1] See above, p. 17. The other partners included Edward Dilly, John Rivington, Richard Baldwin, and Thomas Becket.

crucible filled with lead or silver. I should not wish to be melted so as not to be again separated from the mass. But when the heat is over, I gather myself up as firm as ever, with perhaps only a small plate or thin leaf of the other metal upon me sufficient to make me glitter, and even that I can rub off if I choose it. Our consultations this evening for the good of our magazine, with every monthly publication lying on the table before us, was quite in the style of London editors. I delighted in looking through our record, seeing the succession of proprietors and conductors, the rises and falls of our magazine in peace and in war, in short the whole circumstances of an undertaking which for so many years has entertained the public. I had more enjoyment in thinking of my share of the profits of this than if I had been to draw ten times the sum out of an estate. We had an admirable supper. Our first toast was "*The London Magazine*" in a bumper, and every partner present had a crown given him for his attendance by our Treasurer and Secretary. I had not been at a meeting for two years and a half, having been close in Scotland. I was a man of considerable consequence. The place of our meeting, St. Paul's Churchyard, the sound of St. Paul's clock striking the hours, the busy and bustling countenances of the partners around me, all contributed to give me a complete sensation of the kind. I hugged myself in it. I thought how different this was from the usual objects of a Scots laird. I had a joy in indulging my own humour. I drank more than I had done since I had come last to London, though not to excess. I was, however, heated a little; and Tom Becket the bookseller would fain have had me along with him, I suppose to stop by the way at another tavern, for Tom is too much given to his cups. However, my good friend Mr. Dilly insisted on my going home with him, which I did.

WEDNESDAY 8 APRIL. I got up early and was at Crosbie's lodgings in Suffolk Street, to breakfast and get him to assist me in drawing the case for Hastie the schoolmaster. He attended to it a little but was so miserably dissipated that I could not get him to fix to it for any time. I went a little to the House of Lords and heard the Earl of Home's appeal[1] against Mr. William Wilson.

[1] The case concerned a debt inherited by the ninth Earl of Home from the third Earl.

I dined at General Paoli's. He took notice of that speech in Shakespeare:

> If any spark of life should yet remain,
> Down, down, to hell, and say I sent thee thither.[1]

He admired the force of it. Count Gentili plagued us by disputing against it. Poor man! he is very troublesome to the General, who is very good to him. The General says the Count knows little but has great vanity, and will dispute upon all subjects. He is an odd mixed character. He is Corsican born, and his family, from being rich and distinguished, fell low; and he has been long in the German service. As a German, he is the openest kind-hearted fellow imaginable. But sometimes he becomes the discontented Corsican and his moroseness is visible. He has little true politeness, that is to say, little compliance or softness of manners, by which he offends the English. He is dogmatical in his little opinions too. He will tell you that there are no good soldiers in England because he sees that their hats are not cocked in the German fashion; and he will maintain that there is not a general in England fit to command because he sees no rodomontade, no roughness of manner. One day he will deny the being of a God. The next he will argue for implicit faith in the Pope. With all this, he has a good natural disposition (*un bon naturel*), so that he is worth being indulged. Such is the character which the General draws of Count Gentili. He has got £200 a year pension from the British Court. I went home, and wrote all the evening.

THURSDAY 9 APRIL. I breakfasted with my old friend Mr. Claxton of Lincoln's Inn.[2] I liked to see him just as formerly in his chambers. He was sensible and unaffected as usual, and asked me to dine at his house in Great Ormond Street next Monday; for although

[1] *3 Henry VI*, V, vi, 66–67 (slightly misquoted).

[2] Lawyer, Fellow of the Society of Antiquaries, later owner of an estate at Shirley, near Croydon; originally a Cambridge friend of Temple, who introduced him to Boswell in London in 1763. He named Temple and Boswell his executors in 1773, and in 1776 Temple gave his fourth son the names John James after Claxton and Boswell.

he lives in chambers, yet he has a house where his sister resides. I then called on Mr. Charles Fergusson[1] and had a full conversation with him about my brother David, whom I am anxious to have settled in London. Mr. Fergusson was very friendly, promised to look out for an opening, and I believe said with great justice that any young man who comes to London with a knowledge of business, diligence, and a pretty good tock may do very well. I went to the House of Lords and heard out the Earl of Home's appeal.

I should have dined at the Mitre with Sir John Pringle's club, but was too late; so I went to Mr. Johnson, but he would not go out and dine anywhere. He asked me to drink some tea. I insisted then to have some bread to it. So we went down to Mrs. Williams's room and had our tea, and something like what are called Yorkshire cakes. Mr. Johnson was gloomy today.

I introduced the subject of prayer, and the different notions of it in the writings of Abernethy and Ogden.[2] He had not read the last. The different notions of it are that the greatest number of the orthodox divines, or rather indeed all of them who reason philosophically, consider the effect of prayer to be merely as it improves the mind of him who prays, whereas others consider it as actually influencing the Supreme Being. "Sir," said Mr. Johnson, "to reason too philosophically about prayer does no good. To be sure, you cannot think that it makes GOD alter his purposes. But by producing good effects on the mind of him who prays, it disposes the mind in such a manner that the thing prayed for is insensibly attained." To this purpose did he reason, and showed me how the greatest powers may be enfeebled and cramped when confined by a system of orthodoxy. Undoubtedly, while the universal prescience of GOD even as to the operation of the human mind is supposed, prayer is to be held as in reality of no avail. It is only a link in the chain of things.

We talked of ghosts. Mrs. Williams said it was not true that Mrs. Bargrave[3] had declared upon death-bed that the story of the apparition

[1] Charles Fergusson, a wine merchant, was the younger brother of Sir Adam Fergusson. His son James succeeded to the baronetcy of Kilkerran in 1813.

[2] Boswell was to carry Ogden's *Sermons on Prayer* to the Hebrides.

[3] Here, and below, this name has been supplied by the editors.

prefixed to Drelincourt upon Death was not true; for she had indeed said nothing of it then; but Mrs. Williams knew Mrs. Bargrave's daughter, who said it was true. Mr. Johnson said he knew one man who was an honest man, and a sensible man, who told him he had seen a ghost. This was old Mr. Edward Cave, the printer at St. John's Gate. Mr. Johnson said that Mr. Cave did not like to talk of it, but seemed to be in great horror when it was mentioned. BOSWELL. "Pray, Sir, what did he say it appeared to be?" JOHNSON. "Why, Sir, something of a shadowy being."

I mentioned witches and asked what they properly meant. JOHNSON. "Why, Sir, they properly mean those who make use of the aid of evil spirits." I said I believed their having existed, as there was a general report and belief of it. JOHNSON. "Why, Sir, you have not only the general report and belief, but you have the confessions of many of them." BOSWELL. "Yet, Sir, it is said that, so soon as an Act of Parliament against prosecuting them was made, they ceased."[1] JOHNSON. "Sir, they ceased before that."

I went to my club at the London Coffee-house. Dr. Priestley read us *Corsica*, a poem by Miss Aikin[2] of Warrington. We were very well.

FRIDAY 10 APRIL. I breakfasted with Dempster. He had carried his election as one of the East India Directors;[3] so was surrounded with people congratulating him, and among others he had at his levée Count Lauraguais,[4] whom I could not bear, he seemed to be so very a Frenchman, and that too of the priggish style, speaking French as an Englishman who what we in Scotland call *knaps* (speaks) English. The *a* which ought to be broad he pronounced as the English do in *mammá*.[5] I could get no good of Dempster.

[1] The Act of 1603 against witches was repealed in 1736.

[2] Name supplied by the editors. Anna Laetitia Aikin is better known as Mrs. Barbauld, author of *Hymns in Prose for Children*. *Corsica* contains a very flattering passage about Boswell himself.

[3] Dempster had been an East India Director in 1769 but had not been re-elected in 1770 or 1771.

[4] After distinguishing himself in the Seven Years' War, he helped to introduce English gardens and horse-races to France. He was the first to show Parisians a race on the *plaine des Sablons* with English horses and jockeys.

[5] Boswell presumably means that Lauraguais substituted the vowel of *mal* [a]

I should have mentioned that I called on Mr. Murphy yesterday morning. He owned to me that writing in verse was very much a matter of habit. That his *Grecian Daughter*[1] had been written some years ago. That he had not written *any* verses for some years; and that when Mrs. Yates last winter prevailed with him to write an epilogue for her, he found he went about it very awkwardly. Murphy has admirable chambers in Lincoln's Inn. He has a very good collection of books, and they are all elegantly bound and gilt, an expense which I really think is well bestowed, as it makes a man read with more pleasure and consequently with a mind better disposed to receive benefit.

I this day heard the appeal between the magistrates of Edinburgh and the feuars[2] in the New Town. Lord Mansfield spoke as well as I could conceive any man to do. It was really a feast to hear him.

I dined at General Oglethorpe's, at his house in Lower Grosvenor Street. His lady, whose fortune is his support while our court shamefully neglects him, was a good civil old lady, with some affectation of wit, with which, however, she troubled us but little. Mr. Johnson and Dr. Goldsmith and nobody else were the company. I felt a completion of happiness. I just sat and hugged myself in my own mind. Here I am in London, at the house of General Oglethorpe, who introduced himself to me just because I had distinguished myself; and here is Mr. Johnson, whose character is so vast; here is Dr. Goldsmith, so distinguished in literature. Words cannot describe our feelings. The finer parts are lost, as the down upon a plum; the radiance of light cannot be painted.

We talked of armorial bearings. Mr. Johnson told us a circumstance which I doubt has not been observed by any herald: viz., that armorial bearings were as ancient as the siege of Thebes. This he

---

for that of *pas* [ɑ]. [a], which cannot be unambiguously illustrated by any English word, is "Harvard a", or the vowel used by fashionable English speakers when they pronounce *flower* as *flah*.

[1] First acted 26 February 1772.

[2] Persons who had subscribed for tracts of land in the extension of Edinburgh across the North Loch proposed by the magistrates and council of Edinburgh and were now protesting against certain unwelcome changes in the plans.

proved by Euripides, who in his tragedy ——— mentions ———.[1]

I started the question if duelling was lawful. The brave old General at once fired at this and said that undoubtedly a man had a right to defend his honour. Goldsmith said, "I ask you first, what you would do if you was affronted?" I answered, "No doubt I would fight." "Why, then," said Goldsmith, "that solves the question." "Nay, Sir," said Mr. Johnson, "it does not follow that what a man would do is therefore right." I said I wanted to know if duelling was consistent with Christianity. Mr. Johnson took up the question and indeed[2] treated it in a masterly manner; and so far as I have been able to recollect,[3] his thoughts were these: "Sir, as men become in a high degree refined, various causes of offence arise which are considered to be of such importance that life must be staked to atone for them, though in reality they are not so. A body that has received a very fine polish may be easily hurt. Before men arrive at this artificial refinement, if one tells his neighbour he lies, his neighbour tells him he lies; if one gives his neighbour a blow, his neighbour gives him a blow; but in a state of highly polished society, an affront is held to be a serious injury. It must, therefore, be resented, or rather a duel must be fought upon it; as men have agreed to banish from their society one who puts up with an affront without fighting a duel. Now, Sir, it is never unlawful to fight in self-defence. He, then, who fights a duel does not fight from passion against his antagonist but out of self-defence; to avert the stigma of the world and to prevent himself from being driven out of society. I could wish there was not that super-

[1] Boswell neglected to fill these blanks, and in the *Life* saved himself labour by altering the sentence to read, "proved by a passage in one of the tragedies of Euripides." James Boswell the younger in the fourth edition (1804) conjectured that Johnson's reference was to *The Phœnician Maidens*, l. 1120 (ll. 1106–1140 of a modern text). This may be right, but Aeschylus had already given a much longer and more striking version of the same material in *The Seven against Thebes*, ll. 375–652. In any case it is strange that Johnson should have maintained that a play of the fifth century proved anything about the siege of Thebes.

[2] Here four pages were removed by Boswell for the *Life of Johnson*, and have not been recovered. The text is continued from the printed *Life*.

[3] A notice that his record in the Journal was brief and that he is expanding it from memory at a distance of fifteen years or more.

fluity of refinement; but while such notions prevail, no doubt a man may lawfully fight a duel."[1]

Let it be remembered that this justification is applicable only to the person who *receives* an affront. All mankind must condemn the aggressor.

The General told us that when he was a very young man (I think only fifteen) serving under Prince Eugene of Savoy, he was sitting in a company at table with a Prince of Württemburg. The Prince took up a glass of wine, and, by a fillip, made some of it fly in Oglethorpe's face. Here was a nice dilemma. To have challenged him instantly might have fixed a quarrelsome character upon the young soldier; to have taken no notice of it might have been considered as cowardice. Oglethorpe, therefore, keeping his eye upon the Prince and smiling all the time, as if he took what his Highness had done in jest, said, "*Mon Prince*,"—I forget the French words he used; the purport however was, "That's a good joke; but we do it much better in England"; and threw a whole glass of wine in the Prince's face. An old general who sat by said, "*Il a bien fait, mon Prince; vous l'avez commencé*":[2] and thus all ended in good humour.

Dr. Johnson said, "Pray, General, give us an account of the siege of Belgrade." Upon which the General, pouring a little wine upon the table, described everything with a wet finger: "Here we were, here were the Turks," etc., etc. Johnson listened with the closest attention.

A question was started how far people who disagree in any capital point can live in friendship together. Johnson said they might. Goldsmith said they could not, as they had not the *idem velle atque idem nolle*[3]—the same likings and the same aversions. JOHNSON. "Why, Sir, you must shun the subject as to which you disagree. For instance, I can live very well with Burke: I love his knowledge, his genius, his diffusion and affluence of conversation; but I would not talk to him of the Rockingham party." GOLDSMITH. "But, Sir, when people live

[1] When Boswell's eldest son, Alexander, was killed in a duel with James Stuart in 1822, Francis Jeffrey, Stuart's counsel, read to the jury this passage and others in the *Life of Johnson* in which duelling is defended. Stuart was acquitted.

[2] "Good for him, your Highness; you started it."

[3] Sallust, *Catilina*, xx, 4.

together who have something as to which they disagree and which they want to shun, they will be in the situation mentioned in the story of Bluebeard: 'You may look into all the chambers but one.' But we should have the greatest inclination to look into that chamber, to talk of that subject." JOHNSON (with a loud voice). "Sir, I am not saying that *you* could live in friendship with a man from whom you differ as to some point: I am only saying that *I* could do it."[1]

Goldsmith told us that he was now busy in writing a Natural History, and, that he might have full leisure for it, he had taken lodgings at a farmer's house near to the six-mile stone on the Edgware Road, and had carried down his books in[2] two post-chaises (I suppose two return ones, as the cheapest mode of conveyance), and he was admirably situated for study. I promised to go and visit him.

We talked of ghosts. General Oglethorpe said he neither believed nor disbelieved apparitions. I boldly avowed my belief. Then Mr. Johnson mentioned his having heard a man of sense and veracity [say] he had seen one (viz., the story he told me of Mr. Edward Cave). Dr. Goldsmith said he also was told by his brother, the Reverend Mr. Goldsmith, that he had seen one. (I forgot to mention that when Dr. Goldsmith declared he could not live in friendship with a man from whom he differed in some considerable point, Mr. Johnson said, "You put me in mind of Sappho in Ovid.")[3]

We talked of my schoolmaster's cause. Dr. Goldsmith said that its consequences spread wide, and was for him, upon my state of the affair. We sat till past eight, only sipping a little wine; that is to say, the General and Goldsmith and I; for Mr. Johnson never tastes wine now but drinks only lemonade. I had a full relish of life today. It was somehow like being in London in the last age. I felt myself of some real personal consequence while I made one of such a company; and

[1] A sentence which comes in the *Life* at this point (see p. 109 *n.* 2) is here omitted because it occurs below in the Journal.

[2] Here the text is resumed in the manuscript Journal.

[3] Boswell left a blank for the quotation but never filled it. Sappho in Ovid's epistle *Sappho to Phaon* affords a sort of negative analogy to Goldsmith. She pleads that a dusky maiden can seem bright to the eyes of a lover. "Turtles and doves of different hues unite, And glossy jet is paired with shining white" (Pope's version, ll. 43–44).

nothing was wanting but my dearest wife to go home to, and a better fortune in the meantime to make her live as she deserves.

I supped at Mr. Spottiswoode the solicitor's. His wife was a good-looking woman. He had a kind of company of Jews and Portuguese. There was a Portuguese gentleman with an English wife and a Portuguese lady with an English husband. We had singing and laughing. Whether I was the unlucky cause of it, as being thought a wit, I know not; or whether [Spottiswoode] is usually in that style when he is gay, I know not; but I was surprised and plagued with a kind of punning and playing upon words with which he persisted to entertain us all the the evening, instead of being the sensible man of business that I had been accustomed to see him.

SATURDAY 11 APRIL. Sir Alexander Dick[1] had given me a letter of recommendation to Dr. Lowth,[2] the Bishop of Oxford. I had called for him and left it, and he had called for me when I was abroad. I called again this morning and found him at home in his house in Duke Street, Westminster. He seemed to be a neat, judicious little man in his conversation with me. His abilities as a writer are well known. I went with Mr. Spottiswoode to young Strahan's printing-house upon Snow Hill, where Hastie's case was printing. I made several additions, having carried up Mr. Johnson's *Corpus Juris* with me. Spottiswoode said it was the best case that had been drawn this winter, and he was confident that we would win our cause and get £100 costs. Strahan made us take beefsteaks and porter and a bottle of port with him. I said he should be called the *hospitable printer*, which was a much better title than the *patriotic* one.[3]

[1] One of Boswell's closest friends of the older generation, Sir Alexander was a physician, who, upon inheriting a baronetcy and a competency, had retired to his elegant mansion of Prestonfield near Edinburgh, and there indulged his tastes for the classics, agriculture, and a hospitable table.

[2] Professor of Poetry at Oxford 1741–1750, author of *Lectures on the Sacred Poetry of the Hebrews*, originally published in Latin in 1753—of which Johnson said all Scotland could not muster learning enough for them.

[3] It was his father, William Strahan, Benjamin Franklin's friend, who was the "patriotic" printer. Spottiswoode's son John married the elder Strahan's daughter Margaret; their sons Andrew and Robert carried on the elder Strahan's printing business.

Spottiswoode went home; but as Mr. Johnson had promised me his assistance and said he would be at leisure this evening, I was anxious to get our case as soon done as possible, as I could not get a copy of the case for the other side till we exchanged ours with theirs; and Mr. Johnson had told me that he could not make his remarks till he had seen their case. I waited patiently till past ten o'clock at night, when I got our case. I then hasted away, took a coach at Fleet Ditch, called at Mr. Johnson in passing and told him I should soon be back with the appellants' case,[1] drove to Spottiswoode's and got it, and then returned and got it fairly tabled before the great man. I got him to read the *Reasons*, and then said I hoped he would write down his thoughts upon the subject. Said he: "There's no occasion for my writing. I'll talk to you." I then proposed he should dictate and I would write. To this he agreed. I therefore sat with most assiduous care and eagerness, and he dictated to me a noble defence, which I preserve.[2] This lasted till after one in the morning. It was the only time that I ever did anything in a cause upon Sunday, except a criminal cause. This indeed might be considered as one, as the schoolmaster was standing trial for his all and for his character. Besides, writing down Mr. Johnson's observations was not properly *working* at my business. I could perceive that what he threw out upon the subject in conversation was stronger and had more fire than what he dictated.

I forgot to put down that last Sunday, when I was with him, the barber came in to shave him, when he said, "Come away, barber; you know I seldom give you this trouble on a Sunday." I said I had no scruple to be shaved on a Sunday. "Why, no, Sir," said he, "if you shave yourself or your servant does it. But if you employ a barber, and every one else employs him, the barber will have as much work to do on Sunday as on any other day." He said he approved of the custom some people had of having baked meat, a pie, on Sunday, as it could be baked on Saturday and might be eat cold or needed only to be warmed on Sunday, so that a servant was not kept from church.

[1] A number of copies of both the appellant's and respondent's cases, printed and bound at the expense of the appellant, had to be lodged in the office of the House of Lords. See Appendix B.

[2] See the *Life of Johnson* under this date.

This night we went to tea with Mrs. Williams between one and two. Mr. Johnson observed that Goldsmith had spoken at General Oglethorpe's without thought, as he often does, to keep you in mind of him, for fear you should forget he is there. BOSWELL. "Yes, he stands forward." JOHNSON. "True, Sir, but if a man is to stand forward he would choose to do it not in an awkward posture, not in rags." BOSWELL. "I like very well to hear honest Goldsmith talk away carelessly." JOHNSON. "Why, yes, Sir; but he should not like to hear himself." It was near three in the morning when I got home.

I should have mentioned that I this morning (Saturday) breakfasted with Mr. Campbell in Northumberland Street, one of the contractors for paving the streets of London. He is brother to Glenure,[1] and his nephew, Mr. Alexander Campbell, my brother advocate, introduced me to him. I had heard he had been a scholar of my client Hastie's and that he spoke well of him. But I was misinformed, for [he] had never been at his school.

SUNDAY 12 APRIL. Sir Alexander Macdonald called upon me and carried me to breakfast with him, after which we went together to Westminster Abbey. The solemnity of the grand old building, the painted glass windows, the noble music, the excellent service of the Church and a very good sermon, all contributed to do me much good. We surveyed some of the monuments. I particularly observed the tomb of Dr. Busby, the famous Master of Westminster School, whose severity was great, as well as his merit. I felt some enthusiasm for supporting my schoolmaster's cause, and the image of Busby served to inspire me with more. Wherever I can find a good opportunity for superstition of enthusiasm, I always indulge it. The warmth of my soul delights to expand itself. I should have been born in old times; or rather the expression should be "in early times". Or I should have been born in Spain.

I went and paid a visit to Dr. Campbell in Queen's Square. He has perhaps written as much as any man, and to very good purpose. He received me with the same cordiality as formerly. He has a manliness and a courteousness about him that I seldom observe. I take it the last age had more of it than this has. I ventured to ask him when his great

[1] Duncan Campbell.

work, *Britannia Elucidata*, would be published, as there have been great complaints of his delay. He assured me he was within a few sheets of being done; and he observed that it had ruined his health. Indeed, the close confinement and intense labour necessary for it must have been very prejudicial to him.[1] He said to me, "I have none of that fondness for literary fame which you profess."[2] He spoke strongly of the degeneracy of the age in point of reverence for government. I mentioned to him my schoolmaster's cause. "You'll lose it," said he. "The House of Lords have not force enough to venture to support any authority."

When I came home, honest Mr. William Wilson called upon me and sat awhile. I have seen him at all the appeals in the House of Lords, and have sometimes called on him at Mr. Murray's, bookseller in Fleet Street, where he lodged. I dined at Lord Advocate's. Crosbie was rather too late. When he appeared, I cried, "There comes Serjeant Crosbie." "I'm sure," said Miss Barbara Montgomery,[3] "he's not an *orderly* sergeant." This was quite an Edinburgh dinner, a number of Scots advocates assembled; so the conversation, though it served to fill up time and help digestion, made no impression on my memory.

Lord Advocate was to have carried Crosbie and me this evening to the Lord Chancellor's. But the Chancellor was so ill he did not see company. So Crosbie, Wight, Sandy Fergusson[4] and I took a hackney-coach and drove to Lord Mansfield's. We talked of their victory in their appeal over the Corporation of Edinburgh. By the by, I have not given myself credit yet for some good pleasant remarks on that occasion. I said to Sandy Hart, who, it was believed, was sent up by the town to attend the appeal, "Lord Mansfield will reverse, Sir."

[1] It was published in 1774 under the title *A Political Survey of Britain*, and is said to have had a rather disappointing reception, many of the original subscribers having died during the course of its composition.

[2] "For my part, I should be proud to be known as an author; and I have an ardent ambition for literary fame; for of all possessions I should imagine literary fame to be the most valuable" (Preface to *An Account of Corsica*, 1768).

[3] The Lord Advocate's daughter.

[4] Laird of Craigdarroch, noted for his convivial habits, winner in the contest celebrated by Burns in the song of *The Whistle*.

"Will he?" said he. "How will he do it?" Said I: "By sleight-of-hand, like Jonas or Breslau.[1] He won't tell you how he does it. But he'll let you see him do it." Hart stared and did not know what to think of this. After Lord Mansfield had made his fine speech for reversing, I said, "He has not only done it. But he has shown how he did it. The cause was like a great piece of veal or other meat. The Court of Session could not find the joint. It was handed about through the fifteen and they tried at it; but it would not do. Lord Mansfield found the joint at once and cut it with the greatest ease, cleanly and cleverly." I said that he put me in mind of Raphael's cartoon of Paul preaching at Athens.[2] Here was Hugh Buchan, the Town's Chamberlain, like one astonished and confounded philosopher. Here was Sandy Hart grinning like another. Here was the Solicitor appearing to be converted. Here was Mr. David Rae stupefied and become silly. We advocates were diverted at a coachful of us going to Lord Mansfield's. The rout was in the same style as usual. My Lord spoke more to Crosbie and Wight, who sat near him, than to anybody. He said flattering things of the Scots lawyers, observing that many of them wrote very well. He was clearly currying favour with our fraternity.

Douglas had called on me this morning, when I was abroad, and begged I would sup with him. I did so. Lady Lucy did not come in till about eleven; so we supped very late. Mr. Graham of Balgowan[3] was there.

MONDAY 13 APRIL. I dined at Claxton's. His sister was a plain, easy, cheerful girl. She will be of use to my wife when I bring her to London. I am resolved to bring my wife with me next year, and I am constantly considering and looking out in that view. A Mr. Haistwell dined with us and Mrs. Browne, the widow of Isaac Hawkins Browne, best known by his imitations of different poets in

[1] Jonas and Breslau were professional jugglers and magicians. Boswell saw Breslau perform twice at Edinburgh in October 1774.

[2] Among the pictures moved from Hampton Court to Buckingham House in 1764. See above, p. 97.

[3] Thomas Graham, later Baron Lynedoch of Balgowan. His distinguished military career did not begin until after the death of his wife, about 1791. He was one of the few men actually present at the death of Sir John Moore at Corunna.

his *Pipe of Tobacco* in Dodsley's *Collection*.[1] She seemed to be a genteel well-bred woman; but I could perceive no impregnation of genius, and I was not well enough acquainted with her to ask her as to minute particulars concerning her husband, which I wished to do. I have really a genius for particular history, for biography.

At seven I went to Crosbie's and consulted as to our plan of pleading Hastie's cause, which was to come on next day. I could not help being under considerable anxiety, partly for fear of my client, whom I had saved in the Court of Session, partly on account of myself, as I considered my first appearance at the bar of the House of Lords to be an important era in my life, on which my reputation as a speaker in this part of the island might depend. I called a little at Sir John Pringle's, with whom I had left a copy of our case, and talked a little on the subject with him. As it was a general question of police[2] and expediency, I thought everybody might assist me somewhat. I went home and studied my speech, introducing into it the great thoughts and masterly expressions which Mr. Johnson had given me. I did not take all that he gave me, but interwove a good deal as I wrote out my oration.

TUESDAY 14 APRIL. General Oglethorpe, with the activity of a young soldier and the zeal of a warm friend, was with me this morning by eight o'clock. I had sent him the cases the day before. He said the time was so short he could furnish me nothing. But bid me in general insist on the dangerous consequences of lessening the authority of a schoolmaster, and that the Court of Session had pronounced a most equitable judgment, not indulging the evil passions of deluded men. I had yesterday sent a copy of our case with a respectful card to Dr. Smith, the Head Master of Westminster School, who has been mentioned rather as an odd character in this my Journal, page 79. I thought that the master of so celebrated a school might very properly be consulted on such a question. Joseph had called in the evening for

[1] Browne's *Pipe of Tobacco* was first published as a pamphlet in 1736 and then in the second volume of Dodsley's *Collection of Poems*, 1748. The poets imitated are Colley Cibber, Ambrose Philips, James Thomson, Edward Young, Pope, and Swift.

[2] An equivalent, now obsolete, of "policy".

an answer; and the Doctor returned the case with only a verbal message that they did not correct in England as my client had done, and that he was no judge as to other points how far the sentence was just or not. Sending no written answer looked as if the Doctor was really as rough as Mrs. Stuart supposed him. But this morning I received a very polite card from the Doctor, in which he indeed gave an opinion against my client, but offered to answer any questions upon the subject that I might have to put to him. It was now too late; but I was pleased with his civility, and resolved to wait upon him.

Sir Alexander Macdonald sent to me that he would carry me to the House of Lords in his coach. He accordingly came. This mark of regard from the Chieftain pleased me much, and I thought I should always remember it and speak of it. We stopped at Mr. Crosbie's, where I put on my gown and (for the first time) a band.[1] Crosbie assured me that I had nothing to fear, and that we should prevail. But I was anxious and uneasy, and took an advice which Sir John Pringle gave me last night, which was to drink some wine. I drank a couple of large bumpers of white wine. It did me no good. It confused me without inspiriting me. When we got to Westminster Hall, I grew better. I amused my mind, sometimes with the idea of my being an English counsellor, sometimes with the idea of my being a Scots lawyer come up to plead one of the appeals from the court of his country, which was the truth. Before we were called in, Lord Advocate said to me he believed the House of Lords might let my schoolmaster stay where he was.

EDITORIAL NOTE: The reader will better understand what follows if he pauses to read Appendix B, or at least as much of it as relates to Scots appeals to the House of Lords. No eighteenth-century print

[1] Professor Ronald Ireland writes to the editors, "Until about fifteen years ago a Scotch advocate appearing in the House of Lords was required to dress as an English barrister. An advocate of Boswell's time did not wear bands but a stock (now a white necktie). A relic of the now obsolete rule is the practice of some members of the Scotch bar who have appeared before the House of Lords of wearing the English designatory or vestigial hat—sometimes wrongly thought to be a pocket for fees—on the shoulder of the gown."

THE HOUSE OF LORDS IN 1742,
from an engraving (1749) by John Pine. See p. ix. From an original in the Yale University Art Gallery

showing the Lords sitting as a court of appeal appears ever to have been issued, but the engraving reproduced facing page 118 will furnish a trustworthy basis for an imaginative construction. Imagine most of the figures in the engraving eliminated. The throne is empty, the dais cleared. The woolsack (a sort of ottoman upholstered in crimson) stands at floor-level in front of the throne. Three clerks sit at the clerks' table. Scattered along the side benches are perhaps a dozen or fifteen peers and a bishop or two. They all wear ordinary morning dress. Most, if not all, of the cross-benches have been removed. At eleven o'clock Lord Chief Justice Mansfield in his flowing scarlet robe and full-bottomed wig enters the chamber, preceded by the Serjeant-at-Arms bearing the mace on his shoulder. Lord Mansfield (who is deputising for the Lord Chancellor) takes his seat on the woolsack, and the mace is laid on a table behind him to show that the House is sitting. One of the bishops reads prayers, and the business of the day begins. The clerk reports that an answer in another appeal has been brought in, and then reads the title of the case we are concerned with: "Campbell et al. against Hastie." "Call in the parties," says Lord Mansfield to the Yeoman Usher, and the doors are thrown open. The lawyers and visitors assemble at the bar. After putting the formal questions from the woolsack, Lord Mansfield comes forward to a chair nearer the bar, and presides over the hearing from there.[1]

TUESDAY 14 APRIL [continued]. When the counsel were called in, I had a satisfaction in the solemnity and form of making three bows: one when we entered the door, one after advancing some steps, and one when we came up to the bar, we being all in a line, too, while making those bows, and nobody but peers being allowed to be in the House till we had reached the bar. The respondents are entitled to the right hand of the chair. Lord Advocate and our Solicitor-General, as being King's Counsel, had taken it, and took Sir John Dalrymple with them. Lord Mansfield corrected this error, saying, "Gentlemen, you have mistaken your sides." This piece of pleasantry helped my spirits. The Duke of Argyll was there, and more Lords than usual. Lord

[1] This note combines information from the *Journals of the House of Lords*; Michael Macdonagh, *The Book of Parliament*, 1897; and letters from Mr. C. S. A. Dobson, Librarian of the House of Lords.

Lyttelton attended at my request, and so did my friend my Lord Mountstuart. Without the bar there was an audience uncommonly numerous.[1] General Oglethorpe was there, and so was Mr. Garrick, and with him a *conseiller du Parlement de Paris*.

I was in a flutter till it was my turn to speak. When Lord Mansfield called out, "*Mr. Boswell*," and I mounted the little elevation on which the counsel who speaks is placed,[2] I felt much palpitation. But I knew I was master of my cause, and had my speech in writing. I had seen that Lord Mansfield was against us, which was discouraging. My client was now no longer at stake. I had only my own reputation to mind. I begun with a very low voice and rose gradually; but restrained myself from appearing anyhow bold or even easy. I spoke slowly and distinctly, and, as I was told afterwards, very well. I indulged only one sally of wit, or whatever such a sally as follows may be called. "My Lords," said I, "I speak with warmth for this schoolmaster who is accused of too much severity. I speak from gratitude, for [I] am sensible that if I had not been very severely beat by my master, I should not have been able to make even the weak defence which I now make for this schoolmaster."[3] Lord Mansfield smiled. Lord Gower

[1] The *Journals of the House of Lords* show that two bishops and twenty-three temporal peers (including Lord Mansfield) were in attendance on 14 April 1772, but a good part of this number no doubt came in after the Hastie appeal had been disposed of. The roll: the Bishop of Worcester, the Bishop of Lichfield and Coventry; Earls Gower, Denbigh, Westmorland, Sandwich, Doncaster, Abercorn, Marchmont, Rosebery, Oxford, Ilchester, and Northington; Viscounts Montagu and Weymouth; Barons Le Despencer, Paget, Sandys, Bruce, Walpole, Mansfield, Lyttelton, Scarsdale, Boston, and Sundridge. The Earls of Abercorn, Marchmont, and Rosebery were Representative Scots Peers. "Lord Sundridge" is the Duke of Argyll; he was not a Representative Peer and his Scots dukedom did not entitle him to a seat in the House of Lords, but his barony in the peerage of Great Britain did. Similarly "the Earl of Doncaster" is the Duke of Buccleuch. Lord Mountstuart's name does not appear in the roll because he was a commoner. As M.P. for Bossiney he may have been sitting in a section of benches not properly within the bar.

[2] Presumably the octagonal platform on which our illustration shows the Speaker of the House of Commons standing.

[3] If it were not for this statement and a similar one made earlier by Boswell in connexion with his client Hastie (above, p. 61), one might have concluded that he

and some other Lords called out, "Bravo!" Lord Mansfield was so much against my client that in the course of his questions during Mr. Crosbie's pleading he interpreted the evidence as if Mr. Hastie had given his scholars the play (or a holiday, as they say in England) every Friday. I had a satisfaction in obviating this, saying, "With the greatest submission, I cannot understand this holiday given on Friday as a general practice; for the evidence says, '*That* Friday was given,' etc., which points out a particular single Friday." His Lordship made a very fine speech for reversing, of which I and Longlands the solicitor together are to make out a copy. When he came to the Friday, he smoothed it over and said there was an *ambiguity* in the evidence. I should have mentioned that Dr. Smith, the Head Master of Westminster School, attended. So did my friend Archie Stewart, Mr. Dilly, Messrs. Strahan printers, elder and younger, and indeed a number of people who would hardly attend a Scotch appeal.

I was set down at home by Sir Alexander Macdonald, changed my wig, and then got a hackney-coach and drove to the celebrated Mrs. Montagu's. I had seen her in Scotland at Dr. Gregory's,[1] but did not think this entitled me to visit her in London. The Doctor had promised me a letter to her, but had forgot it. General Paoli had informed her that I was in town; so she sent me a card to meet him with her this day at dinner. There was he, Lord Lyttelton,[2] the Archbishop of York

---

entirely escaped the drubbings which were the general lot of eighteenth-century schoolboys. In the Sketch of his life that he wrote for Rousseau he says that as a small child he was considered too delicate for corporal punishment, and he records only one instance of parental chastisement: his father beat him heartily at an early age for telling a lie. But there is no reason to suppose that James Mundell's private school, which he attended from the age of five to the age of eight, though "advanced" in some respects, was any more sparing of the rod than other schools. Indeed, Boswell's intense dislike for the school which the Sketch records may have been due in large part to the punishments he now professes to approve of. Mr. Dun and Mr. Fergusson, who had entire charge of his education from the age of eight to the age of thirteen, would pretty certainly have had the power of the rod, but one gets no feeling from Boswell's many references to them that they ever availed themselves of it.

[1] See below, p. 171 *n.* 3.

[2] Lyttelton, who had been the friend of Pope and Thomson and enjoyed a con-

and his two eldest sons, and Mr. Anson of Staffordshire.[1] Whether Mr. Montagu was in town or not, I know not. We heard nothing of him. The house was grand and as elegantly finished and furnished as I can imagine. We had a fine dinner and dessert, Burgundy, champagne, sweet, and in short a rich variety of wines. Seven or eight servants attended us. I was introduced to the Archbishop and to Mr. Anson. The latter said little. The former was one of the pleasantest men I ever saw. Lord Lyttelton told me Lord Mansfield had said to him I spoke very well, adding, "Mr. Boswell is too good a counsel; for in order to assist his client he would give us a bad impression of his own character, when he tells us that when he was at school he would have done his master a mischief if he could." Lord Lyttelton said of me to the company, "He has been pleading for tyranny, a thing he never did before, nor never will do again." Mrs. Montagu got a great packet about her husband's coal-work, which is a considerable part of their riches. Lord Lyttelton joked, calling her "you cinder-wench". She found fault with some kind of husbandry where they sow wheat and barley, as I think, together. "Because," said she, "they are not ripe at the same time." Said the Archbishop, "We see many such kind of marriages." The truth is, Mrs. Montagu's own marriage was of that kind. Her husband is much older than she. They have not been ripe at the same time. The Archbishop spoke Italian with a fluency and a perfection of accent that was wonderful, though he had been but fifteen months in Italy and that a great many years ago. His Grace told me he was very happy to be acquainted with me, and asked me dine with him on the Saturday sennight. I was quite easy and happy today, and felt how excellent a place London is when one is in real good

---

siderable reputation himself as poet and statesman, had given Boswell praise and encouragement on the publication of *An Account of Corsica*. Mrs. Elizabeth Montagu, "the Queen of the Blues", was pre-eminent as hostess for the intellectual society of London. She had long been a close friend of Lyttelton's, and had contributed three dialogues to his *Dialogues of the Dead* (1760).

[1] The Archbishop was Robert Hay Drummond; his sons, Robert Auriol, who in 1787 succeeded his uncle as tenth Earl of Kinnoull, and Peter Auriol, who died in 1773. Thomas Anson of Shugborough was elder brother to the great Admiral.

company. General Paoli was so good as to accompany me in his coach all the way to Great Russell Street to my friend Mr. Bosville's, where I was engaged to sup. There was nobody there but Sir Alexander and Lady Macdonald and a Mr. ———. Sir Alexander sounded my praises. We had a good social evening.

WEDNESDAY 15 APRIL. I breakfasted by appointment with Mr. Garrick. He had there Mrs. ———, a fat sensible woman, and Mr. Pingo, the medal and bust maker. He and Mrs. Garrick were as agreeable as ever. By and by came in Mr. Smith, a ———, and Mr. O'Brien, formerly the player, who since his marriage with Lady Susan Strangways is quite *the fine man about town*.[1] I thought him agreeable. His foppishness appeared to be only vivacity and neatness. He told us that Fitzherbert was at Mr. Thrale's in Southwark, where Mr. Johnson lives so much, and being shown the brewery, particularly the great *tub*, he asked, "But where's *Diogenes*?" (Meaning Mr. Johnson.) Mr. Garrick complained of a passage in Mr. Johnson's preface to his Shakespeare, in which he insinuates that Mr. Garrick (for *he chiefly* has the old editions of Shakespeare) was not very ready to communicate them. "Now," said he, "not only did his black get any old plays that he sent for, but the key of them was left with the maid, with orders to have a fire and every convenience for Mr. Johnson." I was sorry to find any coldness between Mr. Johnson and Mr. Garrick. They had misunderstood one another. Mr. Garrick had imagined that showing his old plays was a favour. I have since learnt from Mr. Johnson that his idea was that Garrick wanted to be courted for them, and that on the contrary he ought rather to have courted him and sent him the plays of his own accord. He denied that his black ever got any of them. Mr. Johnson may perhaps be insensibly fretted a little that *Davy Garrick*, who was his pupil and who came up to London at the same time with him to try the chance of life, should be so very general a favourite and should have fourscore thousand pounds, an immense sum, when *he* has so little. He accordingly will allow no great merit

[1] The marriage, which had been contracted in 1764 without the consent or knowledge of Lady Susan's father, the Earl of Ilchester, had caused a great deal of talk. O'Brien had retired from the stage, and had held various appointments in America.

in acting. Garrick cannot but be hurt at this, and so unhappily there is not the harmony that one would wish.

I entertained them with an anecdote which I have omitted to put down in its proper place. Some evenings ago when I was at Mr. Johnson's, I took up *The London Chronicle*,[1] in which was an extract from a new book called *Theatrical Biography*. I read some of Mr. Garrick's Life aloud. At last I came to a sentence where the author says that so much having appeared about Mr. Garrick already he could say nothing new, but would only give some *original retouches*. I stopped at this strange expression, and asked, "Pray, Sir, what does he mean by *original retouches?*" Mr. Johnson, who was heartily weary of my reading aloud what he did not care for, answered, "What does he mean? Why, Sir, how can you ask what such a fellow means? Sir, if you were to ask himself, he can't tell what he means." The phrase was a true bull; and Mr. Garrick told me the book was said to be written by one Cooke,[2] an Irishman.

I pressed Mr. Garrick to come to Scotland, and said we had a right to a visit from him; that he had favoured Ireland with his presence, and why not Scotland? "Sir," said he, "when I went to Ireland, I went to get money. It was harvest time then with me. But when the barn's full" (stretching himself in his chair) "one grows lazy." "Well, Sir," said I, "but you have not yet had the harvest of *oats*. You must come and get that." He had lately had a correspondence both in prose and verse with Lord Chatham. I was astonished at the beauty of Lord Chatham's verses which Mr. Garrick read to us;[3] and in one of his

[1] 7–9 April 1772, p. 337.

[2] Perhaps William Cooke, later known as "Conversation Cooke", after a poem, *Conversation*, published in 1790. He was the anonymous author of the *Life of Johnson* published by Kearsley in 1785.

[3] Garrick and the celebrated statesman had during the winter and the spring of this year exchanged various compliments and flowery verses, which had been the subject in turn of further, anonymous, verses in *The London Chronicle*, copied in *The Gentleman's Magazine*. "More inquiries," wrote Garrick to Chatham on 26 February, have been "made after the verses addressed to me than after *Lear* or *Macbeth*." The following lines from Chatham's effort of 3 April, "To Mr. Garrick, in Answer to His Verses from Mount Edgecumb," are perhaps a fair sample:

Leave, Garrick, the rich landscape, proudly gay,

Lordship's prose letters there was a sentence to this purpose: "I think we are indebted to you not only for entertainment but for instruction; and I should have been very sorry not to contribute my mite towards discharging this favourite branch of the national debt." I thought this an excellent compliment from an old minister. Mr. Johnson, to whom I afterwards mentioned it, said it was pedantry, as it is pedantry in any man to introduce allusions to his own employment. There was a card which Lord Chatham had written to Mr. Berenger about Mr. Garrick, in which were words to this purpose: "Illustrious Shakespeare! but more illustrious Garrick! for the first sometimes goes out of Nature. The other never does." Garrick had written on the back of this card: "Rich and exquisite flattery!" It is fine when one enjoys flattery knowing it to be so. The card having been worn,[1] a piece of paper had been pasted on the back of it; so that it had just the appearance of a pass such as an old soldier or a man taken by the Turks carries about with him. I said it was Mr. Garrick's pass to fame. That he went about saying, "Lord bless your Honours; here is my pass." Mr. Garrick said I had done very well in the House of Lords, only might have been a little more animated. "But," said he, "you considered that they would be expecting to see the bold Boswell, and so you restrained yourself." This was really the case.

I went to the House of Lords and heard so much of the appeal, Innes against Gibson and Balfour; but I was too late to hear Dunning,[2] which I regretted much. I dined with Mr. Ross, the royal patentee of

---

Docks, forts, and navies, brightening all the bay:
To my plain roof repair, primeval seat! . . .
Come then, Immortal Spirit of the Stage,
Great Nature's proxy, glass of every age,
Come, taste the simple life of patriarchs old,
Who, rich in rural peace, ne'er thought of pomp or gold.

[1] Boswell clearly wrote *word*, and it is perhaps not quite certain what he meant. *Wore* as past participle of *wear* was in good usage in the eighteenth century, but *wored* seems not to occur after the fifteenth century.

[2] John Dunning, first Baron Ashburton (1731–1783), became in 1768 Solicitor-General in the Grafton administration but resigned the office in 1770. He was one of the most powerful orators of the day. Boswell did not hear him speak until 16 April 1776.

the Edinburgh Theatre, whom I must do the justice to say that he never forgets his obligations to me, in writing for him the Prologue which he spoke at the opening of our theatre and befriending him as far as I could. The party was just he and I, Mrs. Ross, and Walter Ross the Writer to the Signet, a forward creature and one of whom I have no favourable opinion.[1] I did not like his being there. It was curious to see the celebrated Fanny Murray[2] as decent a lady at her own table as anybody.

In the evening I called at Mr. Johnson's. Mrs. Williams told me that Mr. Langton was in town and that Mr. Johnson was to sup with him at the Crown and Anchor, with his brother-in-law, Lord Binning.[3] I went to the Crown and Anchor and found Langton, whom I had not seen since his marriage and having a son to keep up the ancient family which his is, and which is a thing that becomes very rare amongst either English or Scots gentlemen.[4] He had with him Lord Binning, who was just setting out for Utrecht with his tutor, Mr. Oliphant; Mr. ———, a young gentleman of Eton, and Mr. Johnston of Lincoln's Inn, son to Mr. Johnston of Carnsalloch.

In a little came Mr. Johnson. They were all afraid to venture forth. I as usual risked boldly in order to get him to speak. I observed that although he had been confident of my schoolmaster's success and done him all the service he could and still thought he should not have been turned out, he would nevertheless have a joke against him. It was in-

[1] Ross is now remembered as an enthusiastic antiquary who gathered and preserved many stone carvings removed from old Edinburgh buildings demolished in his lifetime; he also wrote *Lectures on the Practice of the Law of Scotland* (published posthumously in 1792), which became a classic textbook, and is still recommended to students. If Boswell had any special cause for disliking him, he has not recorded it.

[2] Celebrated, before her marriage to Ross, as a courtesan; probably the fashionable and frail beauty to whom the indecent burlesque *An Essay on Woman,* by Potter and Wilkes, had been addressed.

[3] Charles Hamilton (1753–1828), styled Lord Binning, was son and heir of the seventh Earl of Haddington and half-brother of Langton's wife.

[4] Boswell and Johnson had supped at the Crown and Anchor with this learned gentleman and original Club member on 7 June 1768. On 24 May 1770 Langton had married the widow of the ninth Earl of Rothes.

deed pretty clear that the schoolmaster did not open his school so many hours as he ought to have done. So when I again talked this night of his severity, "Why, Sir," said Mr. Johnson, "he had time for nothing more." Dr. Nowell was mentioned; and I spoke of him with applause for preaching his high Tory sermon on the 30th of January last. But I tried to say something against his expulsion of the six students from Oxford some years ago because they were Methodists, and would not desist from praying and exhorting.[1] JOHNSON. "Sir, that expulsion was extremely just and proper. What had people to do in an university who were not willing to be taught, but who would insist to teach? Where is religion to be learned but in an university? Sir, they were examined and found to be mighty ignorant fellows." BOSWELL. "But, Sir, was it not hard to expel them, for I believe they were good beings?" JOHNSON. "Yes, Sir, I believe they might be good beings. But they were not fit to be in the University of Oxford. A cow is a very good animal in the field. But we turn her out of a garden."

I would needs defend drinking, although Mr. Johnson looked very awful and cloudy upon me for doing so. "Sir," said I, "you know the maxim *in vino veritas*: a man who is warmed with wine will speak truth." JOHNSON. "Why, Sir, that may be an argument for drinking if you suppose men liars; but, Sir, I would not keep company with a fellow who lies as long as he is sober and whom you must fill drunk before you can get a word of truth out of him." BOSWELL. "But, Sir, you know all mankind have agreed in esteeming wine as a thing that can cheer the heart, can drive away care; in short, the common phrases used with regard to it prove it to be a good thing. Would not you, Sir, now, allow a man oppressed with care to drink and make himself merry?" JOHNSON. "Yes; if he sat next you." This was one of his great broadsides.[2] Langton, who is a timorous man, said, "I saw that you would bring something upon yourself."[3] I never was dis-

[1] See above, p. 49 *n.* 3. Nowell did not expel the Methodists himself, but he wrote a pamphlet defending their expulsion by the Vice-Chancellor and as a result was the target of several published replies.

[2] In the *Life of Johnson*, the broadside is removed from its context and put with undated material of 1772, where Boswell becomes simply "a gentleman".

[3] See below, p. 196.

turbed. I know Mr. Johnson so well and delight in his grand explosions, even when directed against myself, so much that I am not at all hurt.

Langton said he was just establishing a school upon his estate; but he expressed doubts which had been suggested to him that it might have a tendency to make the people less industrious. "No, Sir," said Mr. Johnson. "While learning to read and write is a distinction, the few who have that distinction may be the less inclined to work. But when everybody learns to read and write, it is no longer a distinction. A man who has a laced waistcoat is too fine a man to work. But if everybody had laced waistcoats, we should have people work in laced waistcoats. There are no people more industrious, none who work more, than our manufacturers. Yet they have all learnt to read and write." He said before this, "Sir, you must not omit doing a thing immediately good for fear of remote consequences of evil, for fear of its being abused. A man who has candles may sit up too late, which he would not do had he not candles; but nobody will deny that the art of making candles, by which light is continued to us beyond the time that that sun gives us light, is a valuable art and ought to be preserved." BOSWELL. "But, Sir, would it not be better to follow Nature and go to bed and rise just as Nature gives us light or not?" JOHNSON. "No, Sir; for then we should have no kind of equality in the partition of our time between sleeping and waking. It would be very different in different seasons, and in different places. In some of the northern parts of Scotland how little light is there in some parts of the winter!"

We talked of Tacitus. I ventured to say that I did not think him a good historian; that he had admirable sense and elegant sentences, but was too compact, had not sufficient fulness. This was risking pretty far. But to my great joy Mr. Johnson gave me his countenance. Said he: "Tacitus rather appears to have put down notes for writing a history than to have written a history." Although it was twelve o'clock at night when we parted, I went home with Mr. Johnson, and Mrs. Williams made tea for us. I told him what had been said of my appearance in the House of Lords. "Well," said he, "that was worth coming to London for."

THURSDAY 16 APRIL. Mr. Mickle, the author of that beautiful

moral poem *The Concubine*, breakfasted with me. He was very anxious about a tragedy he had written and which I had recommended warmly to Mr. Garrick. I told him that Mr. Garrick had said to me yesterday that he was engaged to as many plays as would fill up two years, but that if Mr. Mickle's play was altered so as to do for the stage, it should have its place. "At the same time," said he, "let Mr. Mickle try if Mr. Colman will take it. I know he is not full. If Colman takes it, good and well. If not, his refusing it would be no objection to me. My refusing a play would be an objection to him. I mean now my having had the first offer. But that, I say, is no objection to me; and were it one, I would get over it for a friend of yours." Mickle is but a silent man. It was rather a burthen to me to be obliged to entertain him, for I have not that perennial flow of spirits which Garrick has.[1]

I shall here put down some scraps of Garrick which I have omitted in my account of yesterday. He was strong against my schoolmaster and said he should have been whipped out of the town of Campbeltown. He told me he was now reconciled to Dr. Armstrong; but justly complained of Armstrong for insidiously giving him his tragedy to read as the production of a young man, and under that disguise getting Mr. Garrick's free opinion against it and then abusing him.[2] "Ah," said

[1] William Julius Mickle (1735–1788) is probably best known today for his ballad *Cumnor Hall*. As a young man in Edinburgh he had, like Boswell, contributed to Donaldson's *Collection of Poems*. After operating unsuccessfully a brewery inherited from his father, he became in 1765 corrector to the Clarendon Press. His Spenserian imitation *The Concubine* appeared in 1767, and in 1771 he published the first book of his *magnum opus*, a translation of *The Lusiad* of Camoens. Boswell, who had a sincere admiration for his talents, solicited subscriptions in Scotland for *The Lusiad*, and pushed the tragedy *Chateaubriant* (afterwards called *The Siege of Marseilles*) with Garrick. Mickle was touchy and resentful, interpreted as a personal affront Garrick's final rejection of the play (which happened later in this year), and saw sinister motives in a *contretemps* involving Garrick's subscriptions to *The Lusiad*. In spite of Boswell's tactful and patient counsel, Mickle wrote violent letters about Garrick and reflected on him in an angry note in *The Lusiad*. Boswell, caught in the middle, managed to keep on friendly terms with the furious poet and the contemptuous manager.

[2] John Armstrong's tragedy *The Forced Marriage* was written in 1754 and published in his *Miscellanies* in 1770, whereupon David Hume wrote to William Strahan: "It is certainly one of the worst pieces I ever saw. . . . He keeps an

Garrick, "these geniuses are no better than other men. They are *pulvis et umbra*."[1] He praised Beattie highly and said he would ride to Edinburgh to serve him. He said Dr. Robertson's persecuting Beattie for having attacked Hume had hurt the Doctor's character a good deal in England. "What?" said he, "here is a writer who is throwing loose those moral ties by which men are restrained from cutting one another's throats or picking one another's pockets" (acting it admirably all the time). "There comes another writer who attacks him. And shall a reverend clergyman persecute that writer who stands boldly forth on the side of religion?" It was really pretty to hear Mr. Garrick talk thus.

I called a little on Sir John Pringle, who told me he heard I had done well in the House of Lords, reminded me of his encouraging me to be a lawyer by saying I should come to London every spring for appeals, and was much pleased. I dined at General Paoli's; only Count Gentili there. The General said that Cato was a Tory and Caesar a Whig. The former was anxious to support the fixed government of his country. The other was for overturning it. I spoke of historians, and particularly praised Lord Lyttelton because he gives us what is said on both sides, balances, and draws a conclusion the justice of which he submits to his readers. I said no historian who relates transactions or draws characters which existed in times which he never saw has a right to give us a flowing confident narration, without telling us why he has such ideas of men and things. Most of them do so. But Lord Lyttelton is like a judge who sums up the evidence on both sides. The weather was wet and gloomy. I sat the evening at home.

FRIDAY 17 APRIL. This being Good Friday, I was in solemn frame. Absolute fasting would have hurt me. By way of penance, and upon honour seriously so, I went and breakfasted with Mrs. Christian Macdowal.[2] I then called on Lord Lyttelton. I told him my com-

---

anger against Garrick for above twenty years for refusing to bring it upon the stage; and he never since would allow him to be so much as a tolerable actor" (13 March 1770).

[1] "Dust and a shade": Horace, *Odes*, IV, vii, 16.

[2] Mrs. Macdowal is mentioned three times in Boswell's Condensed Journals, but without any indication why calling on her could be counted an act of penance.

pliment to him as an historian, which pleased him. He talked very prettily on gardening. He said he had a wild imagination. I answered, "Your Lordship has taken a good *bit* to curb it with, by applying to history." I was hurt at two things. He talked of Mr. Mickle as of one whom he had never seen, when I am sure Mickle is acquainted with him and has had a good deal of literary intercourse with him. And notwithstanding his high letter to Miss Marshall on her comedy, he talked of it very lightly.[1]

I called on Mr. Johnson, whom I found with a large folio Greek New Testament (at least so it was to the best of my remembrance) lying open on his table; and sometimes he would read a little with a solemn hum, and sometimes talk to himself, either as meditating or as praying. I would not disturb him on this day. I went in search of a church, to hear prayers, or say prayers rather. It was now past three in the afternoon, and I could find no church in the City but where prayers were over. So I had only silent devotion. I had passed St. Paul's from a desire to satisfy my curiosity by attending worship in some other church, and so I missed every place of prayer.

I drank tea at Mr. Dilly's; then drank tea a second time at Mr. Henry Baldwin's, our printer of *The London Magazine*. His wife was a pretty little genteel woman and his house in very good order. I then called for Mr. William Wilson. He carried me into his landlord Mr. Murray's, where was a company sitting after dinner, Sir John Dalrymple[2] and others. I took a glass or two of wine, and then went home. As I had promised something for *The London Magazine* next day and had fallen behind in my Journal, I resolved to sit up all night and write. I accordingly did so. The time was when I have sitten up four nights in one week in London. But I found this night very hard upon me.

I should have mentioned that I called this day on Langton, who

[1] Jane Marshall published her comedy, *Sir Harry Gaylove*, by subscription this year. Boswell himself had got a subscription for her on 26 February. In June 1769 he had read the play, and on 10 September 1769, *en route* back to London from the Stratford Shakespeare Jubilee, he had tried unsuccessfully to promote it with Colman.

[2] See below, p. 166.

joined me in complaining that Mr. Johnson was deficient in active benevolence; for instance, we could not mention anyone whom he had introduced to another. Mr. Langton told me that Mr. Topham Beauclerk,[1] another of Mr. Johnson's great friends, had also complained of him and said that he thought he could not perceive any difference in his taking leave of one when going to the East Indies or when going to ever so small a distance. I should have mentioned too that I met at Mr. Dilly's my old acquaintance Dr. Gibbons,[2] dissenting clergyman in London. We talked of George Lewis Scott, who published the continuation of Chambers's *Dictionary*, and of his separation from his wife (Mrs. Montagu's sister), who writes novels.[3] Said I: "*She* writes novels, and she married a dictionary-maker. It seems she can do without a dictionary."

SATURDAY 18 APRIL. Captain Hoggan breakfasted with me, and then he and I went and called at Sir Alexander Macdonald's. I was cold, and had a headache from my last night's sitting up. I strolled about in the forenoon, and dined at Clifton's Chop-house in Butcher Row, the place where my friend Temple and I used to dine when I lived in the Temple. I drank tea at Mr. Henry Baldwin's and delivered him the *copy*[4] which I had promised, and was quite a laborious author.

[1] See below, p. 172.

[2] Thomas Gibbons (1720–1785), minister of the Independent Church at Haberdasher's Hall and a tutor of the Dissenting Academy at Mile End, was made D.D. by the University of Aberdeen in 1764. Boswell heard him preach in Edinburgh 23 July 1769, and had him to dinner about the same time.

[3] Ephraim Chambers (c. 1680–1740) published in 1728 in two folio volumes the first edition of his *Cyclopædia, or an Universal Dictionary of Arts and Sciences*. Materials which he left for a supplement were committed to the mathematician George Lewis Scott (1708–1780), and two more volumes appeared in 1753. Scott's estranged wife, Sarah Robinson, a sister of the bluestocking Mrs. Elizabeth Montagu, was an industrious but dull writer of books of history and romance, all published pseudonymously or anonymously.

[4] "A Sketch of the Constitution of the Church of Scotland . . . with Specimens of the Oratory of Some of the Most Distinguished Members of that Church," in *The London Magazine* for April and May of this year. The "specimens of oratory" were an extended report of the debate in a case on patronage in the General Assembly of 1771 (see above, p. 14) in which he himself had been employed as counsel.

I called on Mr. Johnson, and found him in solemn mood, with the great New Testament open again. I have had a fondness for Sir Francis Osborne's[1] works, and was thinking to publish an edition of him with his life. I asked Mr. Johnson what he thought of Osborne. He answered, "A conceited fellow. Were a man to write so now, the boys would throw stones at him." I consulted him as to my applying for the Sheriffship of Ayrshire, and securing it by undertaking the office just now and engaging to let Mr. Duff have the salary for life. He said, "I would take it if I could get it when the old man dies. But not now on the terms you mention. That would be confining yourself the best years of your life for nothing. Your vacation of three months at a time is a good thing. You can come here; you can go to France; you can go to Italy." I have omitted to mention that one day since I came last to London, I spoke to Mr. Johnson of the good that following the law had done me by filling up my time and preventing me from being listless and unhappy. But that I thought a country gentleman might contrive to pass his life very agreeably. "Why, Sir," said he, "you cannot give me an instance of any man who is left to lay out his own time contriving not to have tedious hours."

I supped tonight at Sir Alexander Macdonald's, where were Mr. and Mrs. Bosville and Miss Bosville and Tommy. The Knight thought fit before supper to read aloud from some of the books of peerage a great deal of the history of the Wentworth family.[2] I was drowsy and could hardly keep up my eyes, and the *lecture* did not help to keep me awake.

SUNDAY 19 APRIL. It being Easter day, I was in an unusually good frame. I breakfasted on chocolate and sweet biscuits at General Paoli's. He then carried me in his coach to the Sardinian Minister's Chapel in Lincoln's Inn Fields.[3] He left me there, as he went to the Polish Minister's Chapel to hear a private mass.[4] There was a great

[1] Not "Sir", though Boswell here and elsewhere styled him so. See below, p. 147.

[2] Mrs. Bosville was a Wentworth.

[3] The Gordon riots of 1780 commenced with the demolition of this chapel. It was rebuilt, and here Fanny Burney was married to General D'Arblay, 1 August 1793.

[4] The Polish Envoy Extraordinary, Count Burzynski, was a friend of Paoli's and had come with him on the visit to Scotland in August 1771. See above, p. 22.

crowd. But I was happy enough to be conducted by a person in the Ambassador's livery to a seat just before the organ and fronting the altar. The solemnity of high mass, the music, the wax lights, and the odour of the frankincense made a delightful impression upon me. I was divinely happy. General Paoli was ready to receive me when mass was done. We drove to Mr. Johnson's. He was not come home from church. I asked Mrs. Williams to come upstairs to us, as she was very desirous to be in the General's company. She accordingly sat with us awhile, and was charmed with the General's attention and affability. She left us when Mr. Johnson came in.

We talked of the blind being able to distinguish colours by the touch. Mr. Johnson said that the great Saunderson mentions his having attempted to do it; but that he found he was aiming at an impossibility.[1] That, to be sure, a difference in the surface makes the difference of colours. "But that difference," observed Mr. Johnson, "is so fine that it is not sensible to the touch." The General mentioned gamesters and jugglers who could know cards by the touch. Mr. Johnson said that those cards must not have been so well polished as ours are.

We talked of sounds. The General said no simple sound was pretty, but only a harmony of sounds. I ventured to differ from this and mentioned the sound of a fine woman's voice. "No, Sir," said Mr. Johnson, "if a serpent or a toad uttered it, you would think it ugly." BOSWELL. "So you would think, Sir, were a fine tune to be uttered by one of those animals." JOHNSON. "No, Sir, you'd say 'twas well. We've seen fine fiddlers whom we liked as ill as toads, ha! ha! ha!"

He said difference of taste, with respect to its being a good or bad taste, was just difference of skill. "But," said I, "for instance, we find people differ much what is the best style of the English language. Some tell you Swift's is the best; others that a fuller and grander way of writing is the best." JOHNSON. "Sir, you must first define what you mean by style before you can judge who has a good taste in style and who has a bad. Those of the two tastes whom you have mentioned

[1] Nicholas Saunderson, blinded by smallpox at the age of twelve months, became in 1711 fourth Lucasian Professor of Mathematics at Cambridge. His *Elements of Algebra*, 1740, contains the disclaimer to which Johnson refers.

don't differ as to good and bad. They both agree that Swift has a good neat style. But one loves a neat style; another loves a style of more splendour. One loves a plain coat; another loves a laced coat; but neither will deny that each coat is good of its kind." The General pressed Mr. Johnson to come often to see him, without waiting for an invitation. Mr. Johnson said, "I will come with my friend Boswell, and so I'll get a habit of coming."

The General was good enough to drive me about till dinner-time, down Snow Hill, all the length of Holborn and Oxford Street, down Park Lane and along Piccadilly. He said of the Roman Historians, "*Livio un dio, Tacito un uomo di buon senso, Sallustio filosofo*."[1] I dined at Sir John Pringle's. Colonel Pringle and his lady, Willy Hall, and Mr. John Pringle, Lord Alemoor's brother, were there.[2] The latter controverted the common principle, which sticks much with me; viz., that it is a great loss to the country that the people of estates carry their money to the Capital. He said it naturally returned again to the country; and that there was no benefit to the country in having more money than what was sufficient to pay labourers, so that the people should never want work, which he observed was the case even now when such complaints are made of people carrying their money out of the country. I am no profound calculator or politician. But I cannot help thinking that the country must be in a much happier state when people of fortune live at home and make their rents circulate in the neighbourhood. At any rate, I am clear that the men of fortune who do so are happier.

We talked of the change to the worse on[3] the manners of Edinburgh; that now the gentlemen drink so constantly that the ladies are neglected, and you do not find gentlemen in the drawing-room and at

[1] "Livy is a god, Tacitus a man of good sense, Sallust a philosopher."

[2] Colonel James Pringle (later Sir James Pringle of Stichell) and William Hall were nephews of Sir John. They were also connected with the "Merse" Road Bill which Boswell mentions on 24 March: Colonel Pringle (M.P. for Berwickshire) being spokesman of the Committee which brought in the Bill, and Hall, as heritor of the county, a petitioner for certain changes in it. John Pringle of Haining, some kind of remote cousin of Sir John's, was M.P. for Selkirkshire.

[3] Quite clear in the manuscript, although apparently it cannot be explained as a Scotticism.

the tea-table, which was formerly the mode. For my part I am determined to try to revive it. In the evening I went and sat awhile with Lord Mountstuart. Our conversation was rational and calm.

MONDAY 20 APRIL. Captain Hoggan breakfasted with me. I then had General Paoli's coach and drove to the City, as my most attentive and indefatigable friend Mr. Dilly had procured me a ticket to my Lord Mayor's dinner and ball at the Mansion House. I called for Mr. William Wilson and wished him a good journey. I called at Mr. Waugh's in Sion Garden, Aldermanbury; but he was not at home.[1] I found Mrs. Waugh and sat a little with her, and then Mr. Dilly and I went to the Mansion House in General Paoli's coach, the General's coachman and Swiss footman in silver-laced liveries, and Joseph my servant also, mounted behind for the sake of grandeur. I should have mentioned that I saw from Mr. Dilly's windows the procession of the children belonging to the hospitals in their way to St. Bride's Church, and the procession of the Lord Mayor, Aldermen, and Sheriffs in their coaches.[2] We went to the Mansion House about three o'clock, according to invitation, but we had a long time to wait. There being such a crowd of carriages, it took a long time for the company to get in. The ladies were all in one room and the gentlemen in other two rooms before dinner. The Lord Mayor drank our healths in a glass of white wine, which was formally proclaimed by ———, who began, "My Lord Bishop of Peterborough," and so naming down the other people of distinction, and then I remember this: "My worthy masters, the Aldermen, Knights, Squires, and Gentlemen all, the Lord Mayor drinks your health." Mr. Dilly was acquainted with the Lord Mayor (Nash) and introduced me to him. He was a big comely man, without any pride of office. As I was acquainted with Mr. Wharton, whom his Lordship's interest had promoted to be a Commissioner of Excise in Scotland, I had some conversation with the Lord Mayor. Before dinner, Mr. Dilly and I went in to the Egyptian Hall and viewed the tables, which were indeed grand. We then waited at the door and saw

[1] John Waugh is listed in the directory as "merchant"; the reason for Boswell's interest in him is not known.

[2] To hear the famous Easter Monday charity sermon, known as the Spital Sermon. The preacher this year was John Hinchcliffe, Bishop of Peterborough.

dinner carried in. The review of dishes was prodigious. Everybody was kept out of the hall till dinner was set, the door being guarded by men with great staves, I suppose City officers. Then the Lord Mayor and Aldermen and ladies and their attendants or partners went in, and then the door was left free. As there were a good many more tickets given out than there were places in the hall, there was a terrible struggle who should get in first among us who had to shift for ourselves. I was sadly squeezed and not a little concerned lest I should lose Dilly, he being a very little man. However he and I got in soon enough to get good places. It was truly a superb entertainment, and made the metropolis of Great Britain appear in a respectable light. There was a great number of foreigners of distinction there. We had everything in the way of meat and drink that could be found, fruits, confections, ices in perfection. Burgundy and champagne were called for as we pleased. I had before me a bottle of each. During our entertainment a band of music played, and from time to time the crier announced a toast. There were three tables with about a hundred people at each. The Lord Mayor sat at the table in the middle. The company retired just as they chose, without any order.

The Lord Mayor and Aldermen and a select party adjourned to another room, where were a couple of long tables, with a range of bottles. I had not met with John Wilkes since I left him at Paris in spring 1766. I thought this a good opportunity to do it accidentally.[1] So when Dilly and I came into this room, I said with an audible voice, "This is excellent; this is like ourselves, quite Scotland." Wilkes turned about, and seeing me, we instantly shook hands. "Well," said I, "only think of me, comparing the grandeur of the Lord Mayor and Aldermen to Scotland." As we were sitting down, Wilkes said, "Don't sit by me or it will be in the *The Public Advertiser* tomorrow." However,

[1] Since 1766 Boswell's dealings with Wilkes had been unattractively correct. He had associated freely with the fascinating demagogue in Italy and France, though Wilkes was then under sentence of outlawry for declining to give himself up on a conviction for obscene and seditious libel. But in the London jaunts of 1768 and 1769, though Wilkes was then in London—the second time in gaol, serving his sentence—Boswell had deliberately avoided him. Wilkes had been elected M.P. and expelled the House; he had also been elected Alderman of London, and was now Sheriff.

the Recorder[1] very genteelly made way, and down I sat with Mr. Alderman Trecothick on my one hand and Mr. Wilkes on the other. "Well," said Wilkes, "Boswell, you was a pleasant fellow when I knew you. But now you're grown the gravest of grave mortals. You should have come and seen a friend in gaol." Said I: "I do assure you I am glad to meet with you, but I cannot come to see you. I am a Scotch laird and a Scotch lawyer and a Scotch married man. It would not be decent."[2] "Do you remember," said he, "how melancholy you was at Paris, when the news came of the Old Pretender's death? I kept your secret."[3] "Upon my word," said I, "you had a grand entertainment here today." Said he, "You did not see the sheep's-head. You did not see the haggis."[4] I said to . . .

EDITORIAL NOTE: The full Journal breaks off here at the foot of a page with a blank reverse, indicating that it was never carried further. The remainder of the London record for this year consists of rough notes. Later, when Boswell was writing the *Life of Johnson*, he seems not to have found the notes until after he had written the corresponding portion of the *Life*, and then to have used them with unusual carelessness. They show, for instance, that he was mistaken in the passage of the *Life* where he says that he first met Edmund Burke on the night of his own admission to the Literary Club in 1773; he was present with Burke, Goldsmith, and Beauclerk at a dinner given by Sir Joshua Reynolds on 6 May 1772, was struck with Burke's amiable conversation, and recorded two of his puns.

On 8 May Boswell had a specially fine conversation with another

[1] (Sir) James Eyre.

[2] He did not, in fact, resume easy relations with Wilkes until 1775, by which time Wilkes was Lord Mayor of London and had been allowed by the Government to take the seat in Parliament from which he had been repeatedly expelled.

[3] Boswell learned of the death of the Old Pretender 24 January 1766. ("Was dull a little.") Two days afterwards, at Wilkes's, he saw in *The St. James's Chronicle* a notice of the death of his mother. Wilkes made a very kindly attempt to console him for his loss.

[4] Sheep's or calf's heart, lungs and liver, minced, mixed with oatmeal, seasoned and boiled in the maw of the animal. This and the sheep's-head were considered especially Scotch.

Club member. "Garrick called on me ere dressed. He had called before and left [his name as] 'Rantum Scantum.'[1] Entered again: 'Here's Rantum Scantum.' Took me out to walk in St. James's Park. Fifteen guineas to Gentleman.[2] Took off Johnson: 'Davy is futile.' Then on Thames, when we talked of language, repeated, 'Hast thou a medicine for a mind diseased,' from *Macbeth*, ending, 'Throw physic,' etc.[3] Great." Almost a year later, in a letter written to Garrick shortly before the next London jaunt, Boswell waxed reminiscent. "I must beg and entreat that you will play *Macbeth* while I am in London. You may remember what an impression you made upon me by repeating only a few lines of it while we walked one morning last spring on the banks of the Thames near the Adelphi."

On 9 May Boswell had an audience with Lord North, apparently his only meeting with that unpopular statesman. "Breakfast Mr. Dilly's. Then coach and away to Lord North's. Waited. . . . Called in. Spoke well. Father's joke as to juries on rebels."

During this jaunt Boswell, who had left home on 14 March, sent letters to his wife on six days in March; on twenty-one days in April and on eight days in May before setting out for home on the twelfth. At the end of April he was "uneasy at valuable friend's complaints. Gloomy fate, or doubts as to it, clouded me." He was "hypped black." But on the next day: "Home evening. Good letter revived [me]." And two days later: "Drank hard. . . . These two nights went with bad women a *little*." At Mrs. Stuart's he had a "fine conversation on gallantry and love . . . and no second marriage." She had said to him on an earlier visit: "If all husbands here [were] like you, wives [would] not wish to go to heaven." On the day before he left London, he called on Mrs. Thrale and received her "kind invitation" to bring his "wife . . . next year." At Johnson's house late on the night before departure, they talked of their friends and the writing of

[1] A traditional phrase indicating nonsense or disorder ("harum-scarum").

[2] See above, p. 17, and below, pp. 175, 244, 247.

[3] *Macbeth*, V, iii, 40ff., quoted somewhat inaccurately. Garrick had first acted *Macbeth* in 1744, reviving the authentic text. Arthur Murphy in his *Life of David Garrick*, 1801, cites this passage to illustrate how much Garrick had done for the play by his restorations.

biographies. "I hope you'll write all their lives," said Johnson. "Farewell. God bless [you]."

TUESDAY 12 MAY. After about two hours sleep Hoggan arrived —obliged to get up before five. Mr. Dilly had chocolade. I had everything (almost) well settled. But still, as at death, some things remained. Took leave of Joseph.[1] Poor man! Tears and kissed hand. Leave of both Messrs. Dilly. Was a *little* in flutter. Out by Islington. Away—by St. Albans. . . .[2]

[1] Joseph was presumably to return by water, as he had come down (above, p. 40), and was not too confident of reaching his destination.

[2] He returned by the west road (Leicester, Loughborough, Derby, Manchester, Kendal, Shap, Carlisle, Langholm, Hawick), a route which he had perhaps not travelled since 1760.

1772–1773

Boswell's Life from the End of his London Jaunt in the Spring of 1772 to the Beginning of his Jaunt in the Spring of 1773. Boswell did most things eagerly. Eager to set out on his London jaunt in March 1772, he was, as the time approached, eager, if not to return home, at least to accomplish the journey with a maximum of satisfaction. It was always important to his happiness to have company. On Saturday 9 May, three days before his departure, he was writing to Johnston of Grange that Hoggan would be his companion on the west road by Carlisle and Langholm, would give him "a convoy as far as Hawick. I hope my wife will meet me there. You must be kind enough to be at Langholm on Friday forenoon, and meet us there, and go with us to Hawick. It will be an admirable friendly meeting." Despite several appeals from Temple, Boswell had no plans for seeing him. The trip from London to Mamhead was long and expensive. Boswell had made it in 1769. Perhaps we can forgive him if consciously or unconsciously he decided this year that the "conversation of the first geniuses" was more important than that of his old friend. Already Boswell had formed an "intention of coming to London every spring." "The House of Lords," wrote Temple, "will be a fine theatre for your talents. As you say, it will also afford you an opportunity of keeping up your acquaintance with those *great folks* who may be of use to you in your hopes of preferment." Another hope, that of coming to the English bar (years later so fruitlessly to be realised), had begun to form as early as the summer of 1769 or perhaps even during his London visit in the spring of 1768. But these practical aspects of the London plans could only somewhat extenuate the aspect of extravagance and guilt in them. In the letter to Grange he wrote: "I only regret that my valuable spouse and I have been separated, which has given considerable anxiety and uneasiness to both of us, and which therefore I am resolved shall never again happen for so long a time while we are in this world."

"Worthy" Grange in a letter written three weeks before Boswell's reply had described both his own state of nervous weakness (following his escape from some kind of amorous connexion) and the improved health of Mrs. Boswell.

"I have seen Mrs. Boswell frequently. She is pretty well, and by the time you return I hope you'll find her perfectly recovered. I was blaming her for being so much alone; indeed she has not many people here at present that she can be quite easy with, and those you know are the only company that are agreeable to a person recovering from any illness. I saw her last night. She was anxious anent your appearance in the House of Lords."

Grange was a good friend, but for some reason—because he was back in the country and did not receive the letter in time or because of his neurosis ("still . . . very uneasy, and incapable of fixing my attention on any particular subject")—he failed to keep the rendezvous at Langholm, as Boswell had "flattered" himself he might. "I went to the post-house there; but could get no intelligence about you." We have no evidence either that Mrs. Boswell went so far as Hawick in order to support the latter stages of the journey. Boswell at any rate got home and plunged into business. By the third of June he had "just got free from the Church Court" and had by it "cleared" his "house-rent, and five guineas into the bargain." Nevertheless, he planned to ask Grange for a loan of £250 on his personal bond. The London jaunt had scarcely put money in his pocket.

A notable event of the summer was a visit to Edinburgh by Sir John Pringle. Boswell offered him an apartment in his own house.

"I am much obliged to you for the kind offer . . . which perhaps I should have accepted of had I been to come single to Edinburgh; but as I carry a lady with me (*sub rosa sit*) and thereby make a sort of family, you see I can give no private house the trouble of my accommodation.[1]

[1] This should probably be set down as one of Sir John's jokes, for the circum-

But I will still avail myself of your friendship, and beg of you to send one of your servants to bespeak a lodging for me . . . consisting of two bedchambers and a dining-room, and a room for a manservant. Let the lodging be as handsome as shall become a friend of yours and as airy as you can get it."

Pringle stayed perhaps through a good part of the summer; he engaged in a grandfatherly flirtation with Mrs. Boswell's little niece Jeanie Campbell of Treesbank (who was on a kind of extended loan to the Boswell household); and although he must have left at about the moment when Boswell decided to attempt to remedy a certain long-standing cause of dissatisfaction in his relations with his father, he continued to furnish sober counsel.

"I was sorry to find you had made an unsuccessful attempt about recovering that deed you mention; but I must blame you for refusing your father's invitation to Auchinleck, which certainly you ought to have accepted, as I know he would have taken it well; and I even conjecture that if you had gone and shown no resentment at the refusal, he might of himself afterwards [have] done what you required of him. As things now stand, he sees that you have taken pet, a circumstance that ought never, and I dare say in this case never will, gain favour. I therefore take the liberty to advise you speedily to correct this *faux*

---

stances are against the obvious interpretation. He was writing from Stichell, the house of his brother, Sir Robert Pringle, and though Sir Robert was a widower, it does not seem as though Sir John would have "carried" a kept mistress to the ancestral seat. Boswell devotes many pages of his Journal to Sir John, but never refers to a mistress, and he was not likely to overlook such frailty on the part of a man who was always lecturing him for irregularities. In memoirs of Sir John which he wrote for Dr. Andrew Kippis he says, "What David Hume boasts in the panegyric on himself which he calls his life—that his company was very acceptable to modest women—was true of Sir John." Furthermore, as we know from the Edinburgh *Directory* for 1773–1774, Pringle took lodgings in James's Court, so that he could not really have meant that he wanted his arrangements kept *sub rosa*. Boswell's records tell us nothing whatever about Sir John's household in London, but as a physician he would probably have needed a housekeeper, and he may have been so dependent on her that he took her with him when he made extended visits. He had been briefly and unhappily married, but had been a widower for almost twenty years.

pas, by going to your father's house, either without any annunciation, or, which I should like better, by writing a letter apologising in some manner for what you had done and desiring leave to come to him if convenient for him. There I would have you stay till he went to Edinburgh, or as long as you found it agreeable to him, cheerful in his presence, attending him in his walks, and at other times applying yourself to those studies in which, you may remember, he told me he believed you to be deficient. If you will comply with this hint from me at this time and any other which I shall find necessary for preparing matters for my interfering, be assured that I will exert myself to the utmost in this affair. The world will do your father the justice to think that when he exacted that deed from you, he did wisely and equitably for his family; but at what time the same deed is to be given up, and you restored to what you call your birthright, may be a disputable point. You were several years in sowing your wild oats, and therefore, though there is all the appearance of your having exhausted that unprofitable grain, yet the same world will want to be sure, and perhaps demand a trial of you for as many years in the good husbandry as were employed in the bad. . . .

"Remember me . . . to my little rustic favourite, whom at my return to Edinburgh I shall expect to have made great progress in English manners. Let your next letter be dated from Auchinleck."—Pringle, 19 September.

And a few days later, Boswell received similar admonishment from Temple:

"Why not agree to such a settlement as your father desires? Your attachment to the family of Auchinleck is laudable, but you ought in the first place to consider yourself and Mrs. Boswell. It seems indeed the enthusiasm, or rather bigotry, of this passion, to sacrifice your own happiness and that of her you ought and profess to love more than yourself to a distant posterity who it is possible may have neither virtue or merit. Comply with your father's request, and I dare say he will make a settlement on Mrs. Boswell and do everything else to make you easy.

"I am sorry you did not go to Auchinleck. I would never appear to doubt of its being mine. The very apprehension in you may tempt to the reality in him. . . . Why imagine that lady ill-disposed towards you? Only both of you show her the respect and attention that is really due to her, and I dare say she will give you no reason for dissatisfaction. How could John be such a goose as to differ with her?"[1]

Subsequent letters from Pringle trace the continuation of Boswell's trouble.

"I should believe, dear Boswell, that you had quarrelled with me, considering the date of my last letter to you, an age ago, and to which you have never given an answer. The subject was finding you in the wrong and exhortation to act otherwise than you proposed to do at the time. On that condition, you know what I undertook to do for you. . . .

"I add my compliments to your little charge."—1 December.

"I have not forgotten my engagement. . . . I mean I have written about that affair to your father and have received a favourable answer. . . . I cannot, however, approve of your taking pet last autumn. . . . Remember in all cases of opposition, I shall be of the ministerial side; I mean on that of your father's, my oldest and best friend. You may inherit after him (if I should survive him) my first affections, but they cannot be alienated during his life. . . .

"Love to little Campbell."—4 March 1773.

About the time when Boswell "took pet" with his father, or early in August 1772, he began once more to keep a brief Journal. One early page, now partially destroyed by damp, seems to preserve a fragment of an entry (11 August) concerning that disagreeable incident. "⟨He offered to take⟩ me west. I told him that in the way I was in, I could not think of it. Parted having the advantage of him."

The Journal runs nearly to the end of January in the next year,

[1] Boswell's "strange" brother, Lieutenant John, had recently had a rift with Lady Auchinleck and had returned to his former retreat with Dr. Wilson at Newcastle.

giving us crowded hints of conviviality and business during an autumn recess and a winter session. Early in the autumn Thomas Pennant the traveller, topographer, and antiquary passed through Edinburgh, and Boswell had tea with this "neat little man". Somewhat later, Bennet Langton, the Lincolnshire squire and friend of Johnson's with whom Boswell had renewed his acquaintance in London the previous April, arrived with his wife, Lady Rothes, and they stayed in town until mid-December. On twenty-one days Boswell's Journal refers to engagements with Langton. He visited Auchinleck. Two other visitors to Edinburgh, during the first half of November, were Boswell's London acquaintances the South Sea explorers and naturalists Banks and Solander. When these empiricists came into contact with the learned and philosophic farmer and jurist Lord Monboddo, a notorious theorist about human kinship with the orang-outang, conversational results were worth a longer entry than usual. "Went with Dr. Solander and breakfasted with Monboddo, who listened with avidity to the Doctor's description of the New Hollanders, almost brutes—but added with eagerness, 'Have they tails, Dr. Solander?' 'No, my Lord, they have not tails.' "[1]

Business was good. Boswell was now one of the examinators of the Faculty of Advocates. (On 27 November he examined the historian of Edinburgh, Hugo Arnot.) He records a week (Saturday 12 December) in which he drew twenty-three guineas in fees—two guineas more than in any week since he came to the bar. He had been a Mason since his nineteenth year, had in fact served as Junior Warden and Depute Master of Canongate Kilwinning Lodge, and he now for the first time begins to mention Masonic activities in his notes. At the same time the record is streaked with some darker themes. He was drinking more heavily, and he began to yield to a periodic appetite for nocturnal gaming. Ten entries during November, December, and

[1] Monboddo "inquired for these long-tailed men of Banks and was not well pleased that they had not been found in all his peregrination" (Samuel Johnson to Mrs. Thrale, 25 August 1773). Monboddo had first announced his pre-Darwinian ideas in his preface to *An Account of a Savage Girl*, 1768, translated under his supervision from the French of La Condamine. He returned to the theme in the first volume of *The Origin and Progress of Language*, published early in 1773.

January refer to whist. On 6 January he had a card table for "the first time" in his own house.

He seems to have had during the autumn a first momentary relapse in the direction of his pre-marital promiscuity. Mrs. Boswell, after a slow recovery from her miscarriage of the previous winter, was pregnant once more. In a series of guarded phrases and cryptic symbols, Boswell confesses his malaise under the restraints now necessary (19–20 September), his resort, after "too much wine," apparently to a woman of the town (27 October), and later his "dire uneasiness," his "dreary fears" of the consequences. His "valuable Π" knew all and made him send for the doctor. "She is my best friend, and the most generous heart."

A minor document of the period, Boswell's notes on his reading of a book by the seventeenth-century gentleman-philosopher Francis Osborne, his *Advice to a Son* (1656), consists of page numbers and topical headings in Boswell's own words (more revealing than the actual text) for passages which impressed him. Among others: "Buy a house rather than build," "Marriage and polygamy," "Want of children no evil."

The return to London had perhaps done something—if something were needed—to revive his passion for authorship. His "Sketch" of the poet Gray, with Temple's "character" of Gray, in *The London Magazine* for March 1772, had been followed in the April and May issues by "A Sketch of the Constitution of the Church of Scotland . . . with Specimens of the Oratory of Some of the Most Distinguished Members of that Church," the first instalment of which we have seen him writing on 17 April while in London. His first act upon arriving in Edinburgh on 18 May was to post back to Dilly "two sheets" for *The London Magazine*, no doubt his second instalment. In June he followed these with an anonymous self-critique or "Sceptical Observations" upon a passage of his first instalment. He had promised Dilly a series of monthly essays for *The London Magazine* to be entitled "The Hypochondriack." But this effort was apparently too much for the present inspiration. During the autumn he made some abortive attempts to produce a first number, then postponed the scheme.

Immediately after the rising of the Court of Session, he was almost daily in the Laigh Parliament House reading the old records of the Privy Council of Scotland and copying "curious passages" with a view towards publishing a volume of extracts. This pleasant labour was to continue during several years, but nothing would come of it. It gave Boswell a bad conscience ("Records. Uneasy to think that this was the only thing that I really minded at present"). His friend Temple, however, wrote to him approvingly of the project and drew a contrast which reminds us of one sort of conflict which authorship might entail for the gentleman of that day:

"I am glad to find you have thoughts of publishing again. Such a work as you propose cannot but be curious. . . . Age makes every event and every character venerable. . . . You know neither Mrs. Boswell nor I ever liked your engaging in the magazine. Anything you write there will never be read by anybody but shopkeepers and farmers. Is it not surprising that the Baron of Auchinleck, the friend of Paoli, the author of the *Account of Corsica*, should be flattered with the admiration of hucksters and pedlars!"

The country was suffering from a widespread financial depression,[1] said to have been the worst since South Sea days. There is no reason to believe that Boswell had any special knowledge of finance, but in November he felt moved to write and publish anonymously the first of the series of "characteristical pamphlets" in which from time to time he was to proffer advice to the nation. This was entitled *Reflections on the Late Alarming Bankruptcies in Scotland*. The deplorable state of public affairs seemed to him to be somehow due to those features of contemporary Scottish life which generally annoyed and depressed him (and which occasioned perhaps some of his own most troublesome temptations). "For some years past there has been in Scotland an abominable spirit of levelling. . . . Ever since the seat of government has been removed from among us, we have been increasing in riches and barbarity. . . . Interest or amusement draw the greatest number of our people of fashion up to London. . . . There is no distinction of tables, as there is no distinction of ranks; all must have an equal number of dishes, all must have wines equally costly, as all

[1] See above, p. 80 *n*. 4.

think themselves equally *gentlemen*. . . . One great source of extravagance . . . is the practice of extensive and indiscriminate entertaining. . . . There is . . . more hard drinking in Scotland than in any other country in Europe. . . . Every drawing-room is like a nunnery, and the ladies hardly see the gentlemen. . . . We are shamefully deficient in dress, which is the least hurtful mode of expense." Boswell concludes with the hope that the late bankruptcies may have at least the effect of "restoring just notions of subordination" and "frugality". He was himself very likely the author of the favourable review in *The Edinburgh Advertiser* for 20 November. Otherwise the pamphlet seems to have attracted no attention whatever.

A letter written to Boswell by the actor-manager James Love from London on 19 November recommended a young visiting player to Boswell's "protection" and made apologies for intruding. "The hurry of business and necessary attention to matters of higher moment no doubt sufficiently tend to obliterate the traces of your former less important connexion. . . . If you have not entirely sunk all theatrical matters in more elevated pursuits. . . . " But the apprehension was by now perhaps ill-founded.

Boswell's relations with London seem scarcely interrupted during the year between his visit of 1772 and that which all along he must have been planning for the very next spring. Letters from Percy and Johnson[1] at the end of August gave him the inspiration for one to Garrick—a composition at once facetious and informative which deserves to be inserted here in its entirety.

[Boswell to David Garrick]

Edinburgh, 10 September 1772

DEAR SIR,—Let me in the first place thank you for the obliging care which you took before I left London to have my head externally improved by the addition of a handsome wig made by your own operator. Mr. *Gast* acquitted himself to admiration. The wig which you bespoke for me arrived in good time and, if I may play on words, has made me look the reverse of a*ghast*, giving me indeed an air much

[1] "Poor Hastie, I think, had but his deserts."

superior to what any other wig did, even those which I had from the celebrated *Courtier*.[1] I have not failed to do justice to Mr. Gast and at the same time have vaunted my being equipped by Mr. Garrick's wig-maker. This having given occasion to some pleasantry in divining for what character my wig was fashioned, my friend Captain Erskine observed, "To be sure, for *Benedict the married man*." My wife, however, cannot be reconciled to my wearing a wig, let it be ever so well made. I know not why it is, but women in general do not like wigs. Did every man's *strength* lie in his hair as Samson's did, the motive would be obvious and natural.

I have delayed writing to you till I should have it in my power to comply with your desire of having a copy of the catalogue of Mr. Samuel Johnson's writings drawn up by Dr. Percy. As the catalogue was communicated to me by Percy as a favour, I could not give a copy of it without his permission. This I asked by a letter to him before I left London; but I did not get his answer till the other day. He, however, freely consents to my letting you have a copy of the catalogue. He even says that as I contributed to its formation, I have all the right of an author over it. I therefore now send you a copy, and I beg that you may be good enough to give me any additions that you know. I can mention two: the epigram on Cibber's Birthday Odes, "Great George's praise let tuneful Cibber sing," and the original epitaph on Claudy Phillips which gave occasion to Mr. Johnson's fine one which I heard you repeat at the Archbishop of York's, and which I find is published in Mrs. Williams's *Miscellanies*. I wish to have the original one as a foil and to show how poor a hint was the occasion of a very bright sally which was in a manner extempore as Mr. Johnson and you sat at breakfast: "Davy, I can make a better."

I know you will give me your kind assistance in collecting everything that may be had with regard to your old preceptor, of whom you always entertain a high idea, notwithstanding the *hiatus valde deflendus*[2] in the *Preface* to his *Shakespeare*, for which I have often sincerely felt. If I survive Mr. Johnson, I shall publish a *Life* of him, for which I have a store of materials. I can with pleasure record many of his expressions

[1] This allusion remains obscure.

[2] "Omission greatly to be regretted."

to your honour; and I think I can explain with truth, and at the same time with delicacy, the coldness with which he has treated your public merit.[1] I had a letter from him a few days ago, informing me that he cannot come to Scotland this autumn; but he says, "I refer my hopes to another year; for I am very sincere in my design to pay the visit and take the ramble."

I send you a catalogue of books on sale here just now. Whatever other catalogues come out shall be sent to you; and I shall be happy to execute any commissions which you may have.

I had a letter the other day from Mr. Mickle. His tragedy in its improved state is I understand now with you. I heartily wish that it may be accepted.[2]

I offer my best compliments to Mrs. Garrick, and I ever am with sincere regard, dear Sir, your obliged friend and humble servant.

[JAMES BOSWELL.]

A letter from Boswell to the moral philosopher and poet James Beattie written at the end of October encourages Beattie to continue his Spenserian narrative poem *The Minstrel*, transmits some words of praise which Johnson had sent concerning Beattie's *Essay on Truth*, and concludes with a long essay paragraph arguing against the Horatian thesis that middling poetry ought not to be tolerated (*mediocribus esse poetis*). Garrick replied to Boswell about the list of Johnson's writings in November, and on Christmas Day Boswell celebrated by

[1] Boswell and others thought that Garrick's signal services in reviving Shakespeare on the stage and in bringing Shakespeare's own texts back into acting use deserved some mention in an historical introduction to Shakespeare such as Johnson's *Preface*. Johnson's defence (*Life*, 19 October 1769) had been couched in somewhat splenetic language: that Garrick was admirable only as an actor, " 'a poor player, who frets and struts his hour upon the stage' . . . a shadow." Later, in the Hebrides (23 September 1773), Johnson was to assert that Garrick had "been liberally paid for mouthing Shakespeare"; that he had "not made Shakespeare better known." The reader will remember that during the previous spring in London (above, 15 April 1772) Boswell had discussed with both Garrick and Johnson the even more delicate subject of Johnson's covert rebuke of Garrick for not being more forward in lending him his old editions of Shakespeare for collation.

[2] It never was. See above, p. 129*n.* 1.

writing letters to both of the London celebrities. To Johnson: "I communicated to Beattie what you said of his book." Beattie had been delighted and would find "a perpetual source of pleasure" in recollecting Johnson's "paternal attentions." To Garrick: Your kind "attention to me from the first hour of our acquaintance has been remarkable. I am much flattered by it and always retain a warm gratitude." Johnson's "noble" Drury Lane Prologue had been omitted from the list sent to Garrick simply by a mistake in transcription. "It is a *chef d'œuvre* and does great honour to our illustrious friend. When we meet, I shall without ceremony trouble you to give me all of him that I want."

A notable event in the life of Edinburgh during January 1773 was a masquerade given by Boswell's "cousin", the beautiful Lady Macdonald. In the Edinburgh and London newspaper accounts, which seem to have their source with Boswell, the affair is celebrated as the first of its kind ever given in Scotland. It seems to have been quite insipid. Boswell himself attended as a dumb conjuror. "It was regretted that this facetious gentleman's talents were locked up in dumb show."

FRIDAY 15 JANUARY. Digges obligingly called to settle with me about going to Lady Macdonald's masquerade. I was so ill I had great reluctance to go, but was afraid of offending her Ladyship. I went to the theatre at six. Digges and Yates assisted me to dress. Digges and I went together. It did pretty well. I came off early.

Samuel Johnson, who apparently read about the masquerade in *The Gentleman's Magazine*, made it the occasion of a pleasantly cool and philosophic reprimand in his next letter.

"I have heard of your masquerade. What says your synod to such innovations? I am not studiously scrupulous, nor do I think a masquerade either evil in itself or very likely to be the occasion of evil; yet as the world thinks it a very licentious relaxation of manners, I would not have been one of the *first* masquers in a country where no masquerade had ever been before."

Certain events of this winter curiously illustrate how Boswell's professional, and sometimes more than professional, interest in criminal trials could alternate rapidly with other kinds of excitement. In January occurred the notable trial of Alexander Murdison, a farmer of Peeblesshire, and John Miller his shepherd, for stealing sheep and reselling them with new markings. This gruelling trial continued steadily from eight in the morning of Friday 8 January throughout that day and night and all day Saturday until eleven at night. The jury sat until five on Sunday morning and returned its verdict of guilty on Monday. Boswell himself was not involved as counsel, but some of his close friends were—Alexander Lockhart, for instance, being so exhausted on Saturday evening that he was unable to speak for Murdison. Boswell's brief Journal for Friday seems to insert between references to the trial a confession of some kind of adventure—apparently one more lapse of the kind we have already alluded to for the previous October.

FRIDAY 8 JANUARY. . . . Dined. It was a jolly meeting of friends; but I drank too much and was greatly heated. We played a rubber at whist. . . . I had been in the morning for a little at the trial of Murdison and Miller for sheep-stealing. I went out to go again to it for a little. In my way—complete—for the first and I fancy last time. Trial a few minutes. Home. . . .

SATURDAY 9 JANUARY. Went to trial at ten o'clock. Jury, counsel etc. [li]ke ghosts—like Priam's judges.[1] Dined home. Evening heard Crosbie charge jury with manly ability for Murdison, Rae with fluency for Miller, but he was worn out.

Eight days later Boswell sent for his surgeon, Mr. Wood, and after another six days was "still much indisposed." "My wife's kind attention about me wonderful."

About the middle of March, in three of the busiest and most distracted days of his life, Boswell appeared as counsel for the defence in two of the trials resulting from the alarming "meal riots" that had broken out in Perth and Dundee in the previous December and January.

The cost of oat and barley meal (the staple of life for all but the well-to-do in Scotland) was at this time being artificially sustained by

[1] The reading is uncertain and the meaning doubtful.

export bounties and the control of imports. As a result, the numerous and growing class of artisans, who had no stake in agriculture and no influence in politics, rose in mobs to punish and intimidate exporters and either to destroy stores accumulated to be sent out of the country or to force sale on a free market. The local authorities were overwhelmed, the military was called out, and country gentlemen had to organise their tenants and labourers in self-defence. Public feeling among the agricultural interest was violent against the rioters.

The first of the trials in which Boswell appeared was that of Richard Robertson, a sailor from Dundee, who was indicted, along with five others who had absconded, for joining mobs that carried off grain from a warehouse and a vessel and pillaged the houses of merchants in West Muir of Fintry and at Mylnefield. This trial was set for eight in the morning of Monday 15 March. Some time in the previous evening Mrs. Boswell's labour pains began and her doctor was sent for. The pains continued all night, but in the morning the birth did not seem imminent. Boswell went to court probably after little or no sleep. As very little direct evidence could be adduced, the prosecution dropped all the charges against Robertson except that of his having joined in the riot at Mylnefield. Boswell got through addressing the jury and hurried home about four: "No hopes yet." He had to go at once to a consultation on the next trial, that of two men also from Dundee, Malcolm Cameron and Peter Tosh, which was set for next morning. "Between six and seven met Joseph—safe. Home; fine little thing, etc." In such terse and indirect fashion did he record the event he had so long yearned for: the beginning of a family of his own. Robertson's jury found unanimously that it was proven that he had engaged in the riot at Mylnefield, but that it was not proven that he had had any hand in destroying house or furniture.

On the next day, in the defence of Cameron and Tosh, Boswell enjoyed a complete victory. These two men were accused of having been in a mob that broke into, pillaged, and generally demolished the house of a grain-exporter at Elcho. The prosecution admitted, however, that there was no proof that the accused had joined in any of the acts of violence committed by the mob. Boswell and his colleague Alexander Lockhart spoke at the conclusion of the evidence. The jury next morning brought in a unanimous verdict of not guilty.

But on the same day, Wednesday, Boswell remained in court to plead the "import" of the equivocal verdict delivered Monday against Robertson. The prosecution having granted that a capital sentence was impossible but having asked the judges to impose "the next highest punishment which their Lordships could inflict," Boswell demanded a dismissal on the ground that since the jury had not found the accused engaged in the riot in a criminal manner, and had not specified the extent of his being engaged, "the fair and natural presumption" was that he had joined it actually in order to be of service to the merchant at Mylnefield whose house had been attacked—for instance, by giving him "timely notice of their approach" or by directing them in such a way as to prevent michief. "The counsel enforced his argument by ingeniously observing that their Lordships had, the day before, two instances before them of persons being [thus] laudably engaged in mobs." The Lords, after an adjournment to think things over, came back, expressed their horror of "the licentious practice of mobbing" and unanimously sentenced Robertson to transportation for life, the first seven years of his service to go to the contractor for transporting felons.

"Upon sentence being passed, the panel made a short speech informing the Court that he had a wife and children whose subsistence depended entirely on him, that though he did not acknowledge himself guilty of any crime, yet he was willing to undergo whatever punishment the Court should inflict upon him, however severe, if they would allow him to remain at home with his family; and concluded by saying that if they did not change his sentence from perpetual banishment, he would much rather be hanged than submit to it."[1]

Though Boswell's plea concerning the reason for Robertson's presence in the mob was probably more ingenious than plausible, the case was clearly one of hardship. Everybody knew that scores of people had been engaged in the riots, that the ringleaders had evaded arrest or had escaped from custody, and that only a handful of wretched people on the fringes had been swept up and put to the bar. Most of

[1] *Scots Magazine*, xxxv (June 1773), 330.

the witnesses against Robertson showed great reluctance to testify, and one of them was on the following day committed to the Tolbooth "for one month for having been guilty of prevarication upon oath and refusing to answer necessary interrogatories put him by the Court." The trial was fully reported in *The Caledonian Mercury* for 17 March, probably by Boswell himself. That evening at six his new-born daughter was baptised, receiving the name of her great-great-grandmother, Veronica van Aerssen van Sommelsdyck, Countess of Kincardine.

Murdison and Miller, the sheep-stealers, had appealed against their sentence to the House of Lords, but a Committee of the Lords had ruled that the House of Lords was not competent to receive appeals from the Court of Justiciary. On Saturday 20 March, Boswell went to the prison and "heard Murdison pray". On 24 March, Murdison, Miller, and a housebreaker named John Watson were hanged in the Grassmarket. Boswell's note reads, "The execution of three criminals. Effect diminished as each went."

Boswell's friendly advisers were voluble on the subject of his parenthood.

"I did not much mind the sex at this time, the great point being the mother's going out her full reckoning and bringing into the world a healthful infant: *c'est ne que le premier pas qu'y coûte.*[1] Providence, it seems, wants to deal out its blessings to you little by little, finding it not convenient for you to make you too happy at once. . . . You have reason to believe that, considering how well Mrs. Boswell has performed her part this time, you will have sons in plenty, and possibly anxiety enough about disposing of them. I should flatter myself that this circumstance of your becoming a father yourself will incline you more and more to give such attentions to the person who gave you being as perfectly to reconcile him to you, if anything then be yet wanting. I should imagine that upon an event (which must come, but which you piously wish may happen late) you'll find nothing to revolt you, but on the contrary everything consistent with the character of an indulgent as well as a prudent parent. . . .

[1] "The first step is the hardest."

"Remember me . . . affectionately to Jeanie and tell her that I am much flattered with her constancy and the preference she gives me to such a person as the Baron."[1]–PRINGLE, 25 March.

"Veronica, we trust, is but an earnest of many more of each sex, and that the race of Boswell is now to diffuse itself in wide and various branches. The event must be highly pleasing both to my Lord and Lady and will naturally be the means of removing all reserves and coldnesses. It was very well judged to baptise her according to the rites of the Church of Scotland.

"I am already dead; I am buried alive."—TEMPLE, 30 March.

On the first of March Boswell, had written to Percy in London: "My wife is to lie in this month. If it shall please GOD to grant her a good recovery, I intend being in London by the first of April, when I shall have the pleasure of meeting you." The most exciting business of the season in London waiting Boswell's arrival was Goldsmith's play *She Stoops to Conquer*. In his February letter containing the rebuke on the masquerade, Johnson had also written this pregnant proto-criticism of the play: "Dr. Goldsmith has a new comedy, which is expected in the spring. No name is yet given it. The chief diversion arises from a stratagem by which a lover is made to mistake his future father-in-law's house for an inn. This, you see, borders upon farce. The dialogue is quick and gay, and the incidents are so prepared as not to seem improbable."

On the day before his departure for London Boswell wrote no fewer than eleven letters, his general purpose being to announce the birth of his daughter. Two of the letters combine the announcement with a reference to *She Stoops to Conquer*, an obvious association because the play had opened on the same evening as that on which Veronica was born. To Garrick he wrote: "Your prologue to *She Stoops to*

[1] Possibly a jocular reference to Boswell himself (see above, p. 148). If the title is meant literally, the person is probably Robert Ord, Chief Baron of the Exchequer, whom Boswell, in *The Journal of a Tour to the Hebrides,* praises for splendid hospitality.

Conquer is admirable. . . . I hope to be with you for some time this spring." Boswell was not in the least uncertain as to when he was going to be in London; he had booked a place in the Newcastle fly for three o'clock the next morning and would arrive on the heels of his letter. But if he said so, Garrick would not write an answer, and an opportunity for securing a fine item for the archives at Auchinleck would be wasted. His letter to Goldsmith employs the same innocently unscrupulous tactics, and is in other respects one of the most successfully artificial that he ever wrote. He warms Goldsmith up by giving him back a flattering reflection of his own ideas and style. More than a decade earlier Goldsmith had declared war on the prevailing sentimental mode in English comedy, attacking it in *The Present State of Polite Learning* (1759) and in the preface of his first comedy, *The Good Natured Man* (1768). Up to 15 March 1773 the battle had gone against him. *The Good Natured Man*, produced by Colman, had been dubiously successful, while Hugh Kelly's *False Delicacy*, a sentimental comedy produced simultaneously by Garrick, had been a smash hit. Colman had been most reluctant to proceed with *She Stoops to Conquer*, and Johnson had had to use "a kind of force" to get him to put it into production. While the manager was vacillating, Goldsmith published in *The Westminster Magazine* (December 1772) *An Essay on the Theatre, or a Comparison between Laughing and Sentimental Comedy*. "Humour," he said, "at present seems to be departing from the stage, and it will soon happen that our comic players will have nothing left for it but a fine coat and a song. It depends upon the audience whether they will actually drive those poor merry creatures from the stage, or sit at a play as gloomy as at [Whitefield's] Tabernacle." Boswell plays variations on the theme.

[Boswell to Oliver Goldsmith]

Edinburgh, 29 March 1773

DEAR SIR,—I sincerely wish you joy on the great success of your new comedy, *She Stoops to Conquer, or The Mistakes of a Night*. The English nation was just falling into a lethargy. Their blood was thickened and their minds *creamed and mantled like a standing pool*;[1] and

[1] Shakespeare's *Merchant of Venice*, I, i, 89.

no wonder—when their comedies which should enliven them, like sparkling champagne, were become mere syrup of poppies, gentle soporific draughts. Had there been no interruption to this, our audiences must have gone to the theatres with their nightcaps. In the opera houses abroad, the boxes are fitted up for tea-drinking. Those at Drury Lane and Covent Garden must have been furnished with settees and commodiously adjusted for repose. I am happy to hear that you have waked the spirit of mirth which has so long lain dormant, and revived natural humour and hearty laughter.[1] It gives me pleasure that our friend Garrick has written the prologue for you. It is at least lending you a postilion, since you have not his coach; and I think it is a very good one, admirably adapted both to the subject and to the author of the comedy.

You must know my wife was safely delivered of a daughter, the very evening that *She Stoops to Conquer* first appeared. I am fond of the coincidence. My little daughter is a fine, healthy, lively child and, I flatter myself, shall be blessed with the cheerfulness of your comic muse. She has nothing of that wretched whining and crying which we see children so often have; nothing of the *comédie larmoyante*. I hope she shall live to be an agreeable companion and to diffuse gaiety over the days of her father, which are sometimes a little cloudy.

I intend being in London this spring and promise myself great satisfaction in sharing your social hours. In the meantime, I beg the favour of hearing from you. I am sure you have not a warmer friend or a steadier admirer. While you are in the full glow of theatrical splendour, while all the great and the gay in the British metropolis are literally hanging upon *your smiles*, let me see that you can *stoop to write* to me. I ever am with great regard, dear Sir, your affectionate humble servant,

JAMES BOSWELL.

[Written on wrapper] Pray write directly. Write as if in repartee. My address is James's Court, Edinburgh.

[1] This anticipates Johnson's famous remark on the play (29 April 1773): "I know of no comedy for many years that has so much exhilarated an audience, that has answered so much the great end of comedy, making an audience merry."

The stratagem failed with Garrick but succeeded with Goldsmith, perhaps even beyond Boswell's expectations. Goldsmith, a man who grudged any writing that he was not paid for, did write "directly . . . as if in repartee", producing one of the best of the few letters that survive from his pen. This was the first document which Colonel Isham acquired from Boswell's great-great-grandson Lord Talbot de Malahide in 1926, thus initiating the recovery of the "archives". One wonders whether Goldsmith would have been amused or vexed if he could have known that a century and a half later a letter of his would fetch a sum about equal to his total stage earnings from *She Stoops to Conquer*. Presumably the letter went to Edinburgh and was sent back to London, where Boswell received it a week after he and Goldsmith had met.

[Received 14 April, Goldsmith to Boswell]

London, Temple, 4 April 1773

My dear Sir,—I thank you for your kind remembrance of me, for your most agreeable letter, and for your congratulation. I believe I always told you that success upon the stage was great cry and little wool. It has kept me in hot water these three months, and in about five weeks hence I suppose I shall get my three benefits. I promise you, my dear Sir, that the stage earning is the dirtiest money that ever a poor poet put in his pocket, and if my mind does not very much alter, I have done with the stage.

It gives me pleasure to hear that you have increased your family, and I make no doubt the little stranger will one day or other, as you hint, become a Conqueror. When I see you in town, and I shall take care to let Johnson, Garrick, and Reynolds know of the expected happiness, I will then tell you long stories about my struggles and escapes, for as all of you are safely retired from the shock of criticism to enjoy much better comforts in a domestic life, I am still left the only *poet militant* here, and in truth I am very likely to be *militant* till I die, nor have I even the prospect of an hospital to retire to.

I have been three days ago most horridly abused in a newspaper, so like a fool as I was I went and thrashed the editor.[1] I could not help it. He is going to take the law of me. However, the press is now so scandalously abusive that I believe he will scarcely get damages. I don't care how it is, come up to town, and we shall laugh it off whether it goes for or against me. I am, dear Sir, your most affectionate humble servant,

OLIVER GOLDSMITH.

P.S. Present my most humble respects to Mrs. Boswell.

On the morning of 30 March, Boswell set out on his six-weeks' jaunt to London. Once more he marked his departure by the commencement of a fully written Journal.

[1] An author signing himself "Tom Tickle", generally thought to be Kenrick (see above, pp. 95–6), had written in *The London Packet* a grossly insulting letter comparing Goldsmith to an orang-outang and sneering at his affection for Mary Horneck, "the Jessamy bride", the "very pretty girl" whom Boswell had met at the Pantheon the previous year (above, p. 92). See also p. 165 *n.* 2 below.

JOURNAL IN LONDON

1773

TUESDAY 30 MARCH. Being to set out very early for London in the Newcastle fly, my clerk, Mr. Lawrie,[1] had sat up all night in the dining-room to be ready to call me at three in the morning, which he did, and made tea for me. He is a sober, diligent, attentive lad, very serviceable to me and I believe very sensible of my kindness to him. He goes to church regularly, which is rare in this loose age amongst young men of his profession. I had felt a kind of dreary reluctance the night before when I looked forward to the fatigues of my journey, especially the little sleep which one is allowed when travelling by the fly. But the agreeable prospect of being in London, which includes so many interesting and favourite objects, prevailed over the mists of apprehension; though I had still the awful thought that I might never return to Scotland and meet my dearest wife. Either of us might die during our separation. This thought, when it presses strongly upon the mind, is terrible. It is enough to make one never separate from a valuable spouse. Yet how weak would it be to be so influenced. I cannot explain how the mind takes different degrees of firmness and vigour at different times. I walked down the High Street of Edinburgh, which has a grand appearance in the silence and dusky light of three in the morning, and felt myself like an officer in a campaign. When the fly had rumbled me a mile or two, rational and manly sensations took the place of tender and timid feebleness. I considered that I had left my wife and little daughter well. That I was going to London, whither so many Members of Parliament, lawyers, merchants, and others go and return in safety to their families. I saw nothing dangerous, nothing melancholy. I had taken leave of my wife last night, which had affected my spirits a good deal. She is of an anxious temper at all

[1] See below, p. 285.

times; but being not yet fully recovered from child-birth, she was more anxious than usual. Luckily she did not wake when I set out this morning, so that we had not a second farewell interview.

The company with me in the coach were my brother John, who was going to Newcastle, an English buck who I suppose was a rider,[1] and a Scotchwoman who I suppose was a servant-maid. The buck said, "I have to go on horseback to *Duns*; and I am a *Dunce* for my pains"; upon which the Scotchwoman observed, "*The Lads o' Duns* is a bonny spring."[2] He and she went no farther than Kelso. John and I dined at Wooler. We had the coach to ourselves till we had passed that stage a good way, and then were joined by Mr. ———, steward to Lord Tankerville. At Newcastle we had Dr. Wilson[3] to sup with us; and after supper Mr. ———, who was to go on so far in the London fly next day, drank a glass with us. John and I had not exchanged many words. He is of a most unlucky frame.

WEDNESDAY 31 MARCH. I left John sound asleep in another bed in the room where I lay. He had not so much as bid me farewell. He has bad health, which, I take it, produces that sullen pride and unsocial obstinacy which he has. I find it in vain to try to have the comfort of a brother or a companion from him. I shall study to make him easy, but will not submit to take the load of him upon myself. It is difficult to describe how very heavy his disagreeable behaviour is to those with whom he lives. He is incapable of being pleased by them. Never was there a greater difference between human beings than between him and my brother David and me. Mr. ——— talked to me of the advantage of large farms: how easy it was for a steward to receive rents from men always able to pay; how they could make land produce much more than tenants could do who had but small stocks; and how tenants with small stocks were always unhappy, and were much better as servants to great farmers. He left me at Darlington. From thence I travelled alone to Wetherby, where the fly put up that night.

[1] A commercial traveller.

[2] A "spring" is a lively dance-tune. The rider's pun was better than most: a dunce was originally a *Duns man*, a follower of John Duns Scotus, who took his name from the place of his birth.

[3] In whose care John was to stay.

THURSDAY 1 APRIL. I travelled alone all this day, except for about half a stage when I had for my companion the chambermaid of the inn at Tuxford, who was returning home from a visit to her relations, and about the third of a stage when I had a good gentlewoman who was going to Newark. I remember the time when my mind was in such a state of fermentation that whenever the lid put upon it by the restraint of company was removed, it was like to boil over, or rather, to use a better metaphor, when not stirred by company but left to stagnate in solitude, it soon turned upon the fret. But now it has wrought itself into such a sound state that it will *keep* for a long time. The satisfaction which I feel from the comparison of my present with my former self is immense; though I must own that during my fermentation there were grand ebullitions and bright sparkles which I can no longer perceive. I came at night to Grantham. One Anderson, a Scotch tailor, had just married the widow of H. Crabtree, who kept the Angel Inn and who left her all he had. It seems she was a Scotchwoman, and had been first of all married to a tailor; so, when on a visit to her relations at Edinburgh, she had resumed in one sense her first love.

FRIDAY 2 APRIL. There came into the fly this morning Mr. ———, who had been a strolling player, and Master ———, a young gentleman at Grantham School, who was going to London to see his father and mother during the holidays. The former soon opened, told me he had been bred a coach-painter in Long Acre, London. But having always a violent inclination for the stage, he went upon it, as he said, with design to be cured of his fondness for it. He had now given it up, and was to settle in business as a grocer. He lived near Biggleswade, and told me that he had many Roman coins found in that neighbourhood. He promised to send me some to Donaldson's shop in London. He went out at Biggleswade. The young scholar was very silent. It was disagreeable going from Barnet to London at that time of the evening when robberies are committed. However, we got safe to our inn in Holborn; and I do maintain that for a man in good health who just wants to be conveyed from Edinburgh to London, the fly is an excellent method; better than going with a companion in a post-chaise such as chance supplies.

I got a hackney-coach and drove to Mr. Dilly's, where I always land in London and take up my residence till I have looked out for lodgings to my mind. I found here Herries the orator[1] and his wife, and Dr. Wharton, rector of Bridgetown, Barbados, and his lady: a kind of a bishop of the island. I supped comfortably, and went to bed, quite at home.

SATURDAY 3 APRIL. Luckily my servant Joseph, who had gone from Leith by sea, arrived this very morning. After breakfast I took him along with me till I should fix on lodgings. I went immediately to General Paoli's, who now lived in Jermyn Street, St. James's. He received me with open arms as usual, and asked me to dine with him this day and every other day when I was not otherwise engaged. I tried to get lodgings in the same street with him; but I make it a rule never to give more than a guinea a week, and could find no good ones there at that price. I went to the next nearest street to him, Piccadilly, and got a very pleasant apartment at the milliner's opposite Melbourne House. I dined at Paoli's after having sauntered about all forenoon, I know not how. I am writing this Journal on the 20 April from memory; so it must be very imperfect.

I shall make a transition to Mr. Samuel Johnson's, where I went between ten and eleven at night. He was not come home. I found Frank, his black, my old acquaintance, who showed me into Mrs. Williams's room. I am a favourite with Mrs. Williams. I read to her from *The London Chronicle* Dr. Goldsmith's apology for beating Evans the publisher.[2] I thought when I saw the story in the newspapers that it had been an invention, like Pope's stories of Curll, but on my coming to town I found it to be very true; and I was diverted to find my friend Dilly so keen on the side of the publisher, not only maintaining that

[1] Rev. John Herries, M.A. (d. 1781), author of *The Elements of Speech*, 1773.

[2] A military friend of Goldsmith's having stirred him up to "resent" the libellous letter in *The London Packet* (above, p. 160), Goldsmith went to the shop of the publisher of the paper, Thomas Evans, and struck him with his cane. A scuffle ensued, and the combatants were separated by Kenrick, the editor and probably the author of the libel. The newspapers, after their wont, shrieked at Goldsmith for infringement of the freedom of the press. His "apology" was a dignified and manly reply to this criticism. He finally compromised Evans's action for assault by paying £50 to a Welsh charity.

Goldsmith had been guilty of a great outrage and ought to be punished by criminal justice, but believing that Evans had beat him black and blue. Goldsmith's apology was written so much in Mr. Johnson's manner that both Mrs. Williams and I supposed it to be his. When Mr. Johnson came home he embraced me with sincere cordiality, saying, "I'm glad you're come." He said to Mrs. Williams, "Dr. Goldsmith's manifesto has got into your paper," meaning *The London Chronicle*. I asked him if Goldsmith writ it, with an air that made him see I suspected he had done it. "Sir," said he, "Dr. Goldsmith would no more have asked me to write such a thing as that for him than he'd have asked me to feed him with a spoon, or to do anything else that argued his imbecility. I as much believe that he wrote that as if I had seen him do it. Sir, had he shown it to any one friend, he would not have been allowed to publish it. He has indeed done it well; but 'tis a foolish thing well done. I suppose he has been so much elated with the success of his new comedy that he has thought everything that concerned him of importance to the public." I said, "I suppose, Sir, this is the first time that he has been engaged in such an adventure." JOHNSON. "Why, Sir, I believe it is the first time he has beat. He may have been beaten before. No, Sir, 'tis a new plume to him."

I mentioned Sir John Dalrymple's *Memoirs* and his discoveries against Russell and Sidney.[1] JOHNSON. "Why, Sir, everybody who had just notions of government thought them rascals before. It is well that all see them to be so." BOSWELL. "But I can imagine all that is said of them to be true without their being rascals." JOHNSON. "Sir, will you consider, would any of them [have] had it known that they intrigued with France? Depend upon it, Sir, he who does what he is afraid should be known has something rotten about him. This Dalrymple seems to be an honest fellow, for he tells equally what makes against both sides. But nothing can be poorer than his writing; 'tis the mere bouncing of a schoolboy: 'Great he, but greater

[1] See above, p. 119. Dalrymple's *Memoirs of Great Britain and Ireland* drew on unpublished documents in the Dépôt des Affaires Etrangères at Versailles to argue that Algernon Sidney and Lord Russell, champions of the popular party against Charles II and both executed after the Rye House Plot of 1683, had been acting under French influence.

she,' and such stuff."[1] We drank tea and sat till near one in the morning.

SUNDAY 4 APRIL. I drank chocolate at General Paoli's; then found Sir John Pringle, whom I had missed yesterday; by the by, I found Dempster yesterday, quite in spirits. I found Sir Walter Montgomerie-Cuninghame.[2] Time passed till it was too late for church. I dined at my worthy kinsman's, Mr. Bosville's. Sandy MacLeod, who was out in the year 1745 but has been allowed to come home, was there. I had never been in company with him before. I met Captain Bosville, whom I had not seen for several years, as he had been travelling. He still had no aptitude to speak. When I came home I found a kind card from the Hon. Mrs. Stuart, regretting that she had not seen me when I called in the morning and begging I might come as soon as I could. As she is my wife's most intimate friend, I went directly and drank tea with her and her husband. They now lived in Hanover Square. I came home at ten and went to bed early. I should have been at my Lord Mansfield's rout. But unluckily my servant had forgot to put up the breeches of my full-dress suit; so when I was going to dress, I found a deficiency that could not be supplied. When I told the story to Spottiswoode the solicitor, he laughed and said that I might have gone to wait on the Scotch Lord Chief Justice without breeches.

MONDAY 5 APRIL. I know not how it is, but I am less anxious in being absent from my valuable spouse this year than I was last.[3] Perhaps her having a little daughter to amuse her makes the scene more lively to my imagination; but then ought I not to feel a double anxiety this year, when I am absent both from a wife and a child? In whatever

[1] "He great in this last act of his life, but she greater" (Dalrymple's description of the parting of Lord and Lady Russell). Johnson returned to the burlesque of Dalrymple's style on a later occasion (*Hebrides,* 20 November 1773).

[2] The oldest of the Lainshaw children, Mrs. Boswell's nephew. He had succeeded his grandfather in 1770 in the baronetcy of Corsehill.

[3] During this jaunt Boswell sent letters to his wife on 30 and 31 March and thirteen times in April up to the twenty-second. On 24 April he entered in his Register of Letters: "and during the rest of the month many to my wife." He received four letters from her up to 17 April and on 28 April entered the note: "and during the rest of the month many from my wife."

way it is to be explained, I have mentioned the fact. Yet I am certain that I am as fond of my wife as I was last year; nor do I know that my mind is become more rational so as to throw off any vain fears that may arise, as sparks[1] of water are thrown from a grindstone. I wish I may continue as I am while absent from my family.

I breakfasted with Mr. Spottiswoode. The appeal concerning the estate of Linplum[2] was to come on before the House of Lords today; but as Dempster had told me that there was to be a grand debate in the House of Commons upon East India affairs and that Lord Clive was to pronounce an oration in defence of all his conduct, I chose to be there rather than in the House of Lords. I called on Mr. David Kennedy, and found him the same joker as formerly and nothing more. It struck me a little to think that the gentlemen of Ayrshire should be represented in Parliament by a good, honest, merry fellow indeed, but one so totally incapable of the business of legislation, and so devoid of the talents which distinguish a man in public life.[3] I threw myself into the humorous rattling style and plagued him with a new-invented dialogue between his brother, Lord Cassillis, and him when setting out for London. "My Lord, provisions are grown dearer, you must allow me a little more." "Davy, you have very well already." "But, my Lord, I have learnt to drink porter in London." "Well, Davy, you shall have another £100." Kennedy took me into the House of Commons. Captain Robert Preston[4] came in. He and I and a Captain Thomson in the India service sat together. Lord Clive did not open.[5] We had not the great boar, but we had exceeding good hare-hunting. I heard Dowdeswell, Jenkinson, Stanley, Dyson, Thurlow, Pulteney,

[1] "A spirt, jet; a small spot of dirt or liquid mud; a small quantity of liquid" (*English Dialect Dictionary*: a Scotticism).

[2] This cause, like some of those heard by Boswell during his London visit of 1772, concerned a Scottish inheritance.

[3] See above, p. 39 and below, p. 211.

[4] Boswell's cousin; third son then living of Sir George Preston of Valleyfield. He commanded the *Asia* in the East India Company's service.

[5] His speech, which Chatham thought one of the finest he had ever heard, was made on 3 May. On that day Boswell went to the House of Lords to hear a poor lieutenant in the Army, John Maclellan, establish his claim to the Kircudbright peerage.

Governor[1] Johnstone, and my friend Dempster speak. But I was also fortunate enough to hear Mr. Edmund Burke speak twice. It was a great feast to me who had never heard him before. It was astonishing how all kinds of figures of speech crowded upon him. He was like a man in an orchard where boughs loaded with fruit hung around him, and he pulled apples as fast as he pleased and pelted the Ministry. It seemed to me, however, that his oratory rather tended to distinguish himself than to assist his cause. There was amusement instead of persuasion. It was like the exhibition of a favourite actor. But I would have been exceedingly happy to be him. Lord North spoke a considerable time with calmness, perspicuity, and sufficient elegance. Speaking in Parliament appeared to me to be not very difficult. If a man knows pretty well the subject of debate and has good animal spirits, he may make a very good appearance. Preston and Thomson and I went and dined together, or supped rather (as it was between eight and nine) at the Piazza Coffee-house.

TUESDAY 6 APRIL. I breakfasted at Harry Davidson's, and after leaving cards at several doors, I went to the House of Lords and heard Forrester speak in the Linplum cause. I never heard him before. I liked his manly manner, with something of that air of business as a lawyer which I have figured in my imagination, seldom see, and cannot describe. Lord Advocate also spoke, very tediously. I had heard Counsellor Bearcroft speak in a question about a bill of divorce before they began.[2] I am now a kind of enthusiast in my profession and have great pleasure in observing different specimens of it. Lord Mansfield, though he affirmed the decree, made a speech on the cause, as it was a singular one, where it was argued that the meaning was different from the words. He observed that where there was any principle in a settlement, either that of justice or that of family, there was room to conjecture a man's meaning from circumstances; but in a settlement made from whim only, how could meaning be conjectured? and

[1] Of West Florida, 1765.

[2] Philip Cade was suing for divorce from his wife, Catharine Whitworth Cade, for adultery with Lord Aylmer, who had already had judgement passed against him for criminal conversation with Mrs. Cade. The divorce was granted, and Lord Aylmer married the lady. Their daughter was Landor's Rose Aylmer.

therefore he must take the words simply. I relished highly hearing him again; that full, easy, and choice expression of which he is possessed is truly admirable. I met here my cousin Claud, who was now in London for the first time. He preserved the manners of Scotland pure, and his engagements lay in a different channel from mine.[1] Sir Walter and I dined at the Hon. James Stuart's. We were hospitably treated with a family dinner, and I was glad to find Mr. Stuart become sedate and informing himself as to Scotland.

This was the monthly meeting of the partners of *The London Magazine*, at the Queen's Arms in St. Paul's Churchyard. Whoever is there before a quarter after eight by St. Paul's clock receives a crown. I was too late at one of the meetings last year. So I was resolved to be up in time tonight. I said I had run for the plate and won it. Indeed it cost me very hard running from Mr. Stuart's. But I would rather have had that crown than a guinea. I have a happy talent at making myself interested and pleased with small things. The partners were all glad to see me. We have always a good supper, and, besides Madeira, our landlord Betts's excellent old port at half a crown a bottle. He is a jolly fellow, and it is said is worth £20,000. As he had been much obliged to the Stationers' Company, he always attends himself upon the partners of *The London Magazine*. He told me he had eight hundred dozen of that port. Our editor[2] supped with us. This is a new custom, which I do not much like; it is a kind of restraint upon us. I went home with Mr. Dilly at twelve, as I always do upon these occasions. John Rivington rises the moment that twelve strikes, and Dilly and I follow his example.

I neglected to mention that this forenoon I waited on Lord

[1] Though Claud Boswell was two years younger than James Boswell, his father and Boswell's grandfather were brothers. In 1799 he succeeded Lord Monboddo in the Court of Session, with the title Lord Balmuto. On the jaunt to Ireland, 29 April 1769, Boswell told Margaret Montgomerie that Claud Boswell had narrow views. "He had thick high stone walls . . . except when I surprised him by sometimes taking a hammer and beating a hole in his walls so as to give him a peep of the fields of fancy, which made him caper."

[2] Unidentified. On 4 April 1775 Boswell gives the editors as Henry Mayo and Captain Edward Thompson, but speaks as though they had been appointed since he had last been in London.

Lyttelton. He had known Lord Chesterfield long.[1] He said that Lord Chesterfield had admirable parts so far as they went. That he was not fit to be Prime Minister, but he was very fit to be a Secretary of State. That his judgment in planning was not great, but that he was exceedingly capable in execution. That he could not determine whether it was proper to make a peace. But that no man could make it so well. That he was a believer in God and a future state, though in no fixed mode. In the younger part of his life he indulged himself, as was the fashion of wits, in sallies against revelation, but as he grew older he treated it with more reverence, though he never was properly a Christian. That after he was forty he went through the Roman classics under Lord Lyttelton's direction, having neglected them when young. That he at first submitted to the trouble of consulting a dictionary, till by degrees Latin became easy to him. That he was quite master of French and Italian, particularly of French, which he spoke in perfection. Count Guerchy paid him a very handsome compliment upon it. After they had conversed some time in French, he stopped him on a sudden: "Pardonnez-moi, Milord. Parlez-vous anglais?" That he was constantly saying witty things even to the last. Speaking of his old friend, Lord Tyrawley, he said, "Tyrawley and I have been dead this twelve-month, though we have chosen to keep it a secret."[2] Tall Sir Thomas Robinson was very ill, and somebody told Lord Chesterfield he was dying by inches. "So am I," said he. "But as Sir Thomas has a great many more inches in highth than I have, he will take longer time to die." I observed that Lord Chesterfield had been happily placed in situations just suited to his abilities. I thought the first *bon mot* true wit; the last only a conceit. Lord Lyttelton and I joined in lamenting the death of Dr. Gregory.[3] I observed that few men are missed when they die. They are like trees cut down in a thick forest. We do not perceive the blank. But that Gregory was a distinguished tree, as the apple tree among the trees of the wood.

[1] Chesterfield had died only a few days before: 24 March 1773.

[2] Tyrawley died 14 July 1773.

[3] John Gregory (1724–1773), M.D., Professor of Medicine at Edinburgh University, had practised for some years in London, where he had been an acquaintance of Lyttelton's.

"Ay," said Lord Lyttelton, "and a tree whose shade had no noxious effect, but was benign to all around it."[1]

I have omitted to mention that on Sunday forenoon I called on General Oglethorpe, and found him in his usual spirits. He had a Bible lying upon the table before him. Whenever[2] I appeared, "My dear Boswell," cried the fine old gentleman, and pressed me in his arms. I value his acquaintance very highly and it is the more pleasing to me that I owe it entirely to my own merit; for he came and introduced himself to me at my lodgings in Half Moon Street, Piccadilly, the spring when my *Account of Corsica* came first out.

WEDNESDAY 7 APRIL. After breakfasting at Mr. Dilly's I walked down to the Adelphi and called on Mr. Garrick. His coach was at the door to carry him into the country; so I just had time to shake hands with him and make a bow to Mrs. Garrick, who was seated in the coach. Mr. Garrick, however, had time to tell me that he now admired Mr. Johnson's conversation more than ever; expressing himself in a strong picturesque manner the particular phrases of which have escaped my memory. I then called on the Hon. Topham Beauclerk, who has also a house on the terrace of the Adelphi. I was shown into a very elegant parlour. I liked his large gilded lion, a cast from the antique, supporting his sideboard. He received me politely but not with so much ardour as I wish to find. However, the truth is, I never was in company with Beauclerk but twice—once dining at Sir Joshua Reynolds's, and once supping at Garrick's when I was last in town.[3] He then invited me to see him when I should return; and Langton told me that my open downright manners had pleased him, and he had said, "I do love Boswell monstrously." Beauclerk's high-bred behaviour may have been construed by me as distant coldness. His great veneration for Mr. Johnson and Johnson's love for him are enough to make me value him; and from what I have seen of him he appears to be a man of wit, literature, and fashion in a distinguished degree.

[1] Lyttelton himself died only four months later, 22 August 1773.

[2] As soon as.

[3] This dinner, on Wednesday 6 May 1772, was the one at which Boswell met Burke also for the first time. See above, p. 138. The supper at Garrick's occurred three days later.

He said Mr. Johnson was grown much better-natured of late and would bear a great deal more than he used to do. That Goldsmith was talking of there being a playhouse for the representation of new plays solely, as a scheme to relieve authors from the tyranny of managers. That Mr. Johnson opposed the scheme. Upon which Goldsmith said, "Ay, it may do very well for you to talk so, who have sheltered yourself behind the corner of a pension"; and that Mr. Johnson bore this and said nothing severe to Goldsmith that evening. Beauclerk said he always expected it would come; for that Mr. Johnson could delay his vengeance for a considerable interval. As an instance of which, Mr. Johnson dined with him one day when there was a Captain Brodie in the company who had married a relation of Beauclerk's.[1] That after dinner Mr. Johnson rose and walked to the end of the room in a fit of meditation and threw himself into some of those attitudes which he does when deep in thought. Brodie, who knew nothing of his character but was just a jolly sea-officer, a blunt tar who wished to put the bottle about and did not like to see a man who did not drink as the rest of the company did, turned to Mr. Johnson and said, "Sir, if you be for dancing a minuet, had not you better go to the ladies?" Brodie had no bad intention. But it may be well conceived what a shocking speech this was to the majestic Rambler. A dreadful explosion was to be expected. Mr. Johnson took no notice whatever of the speech for a good while. At last he came and sat down, and all at once, turning to Mr. Beauclerk, said, "Don't you think this Brodie a very coarse fellow?"[2]

I said Mr. Johnson's accepting a pension from a prince whom he had called an usurper was a circumstance which it was difficult to justify with perfect clearness; and that if I had been rich enough, I would rather have paid it myself than that he should have accepted of it; "though indeed," said I, "he may look upon it as a tribute due to him from the nation and only conveyed to him by the hands which have the

1 Captain David Brodie, R.N., had lost his right arm. He was a Scotsman and a relative of Lady MacLeod. His wife was the Mary ("Molly") Aston whom Johnson thought the loveliest creature he ever saw; she was first cousin to Beauclerk's mother.

2 Brodie's encounter with Johnson was omitted from the *Life of Johnson*.

custody of the nation's money." "Yes," said Beauclerk, "the King has so much money allowed him for pensions to men of genius and literature; and accepting of such a pension has nothing to do with the right of the King. He accepts it as a literary man. An ingenious Roman Catholic may accept a pension in that way without any injury to his principles." "Why," said I, "though Mr. Johnson has been represented as a violent Jacobite, I have heard him say that if holding up his hand would have made Prince Charles's army prevail, he would not have done it. Nothing can be more moderate than that; but indeed it was after he had his pension that I heard him say so. I was not acquainted with him sooner." "But," said Beauclerk, "I heard him say so before he had his pension."

Just as I came out of Mr. Beauclerk's I met Dr. Percy. He had Sir John Hawkins[1] with him, to whom he introduced me. He carried us to his study at Northumberland House to show us a picture of Cleveland the poet, his relation, which he had bought at Mr. West's sale.[2] I drank a dish of chocolade here, and resting myself after much hard walking I listened with pleasure to Percy's active schemes of curious and amusing literature.

I had called on Dr. Goldsmith at his chambers in Brick Court in the Temple as I passed along in the morning. He was not up, and I was shown into his dining-room and library. When he heard that it was I, he roared from his bed, "Boswell!" I ran to him. We had a cordial embrace. I sat upon the side of his bed and we talked of the success of his new comedy, which he saw that I sincerely enjoyed, and of his beating Evans the publisher. He said there was no other method left; and he was determined to follow it. He showed me in some newspaper two paragraphs of scandal about Mr. Johnson and Mrs. Thrale. How an eminent brewer was very jealous of a certain author in folio, and perceived a strong resemblance to him in his eldest son. "Now," said he, "is not this horrid?" "Why," said I, "no doubt though to us

[1] Later to be Boswell's chief rival as biographer of Johnson.

[2] Percy was great-grandson of William Cleveland, younger brother of John Cleveland, the poet. He had acquired the portrait (which was by Isaac Fuller) very recently. The sale of the pictures of James West, the great antiquary, had begun on 31 March 1773.

who know the characters it is the most ludicrous nonsense, yet it may gain credit with those who do not. The assertions of a newspaper are taken up insensibly. I long believed Burke to be a Jesuit." I went into the dining-room. He rose and came to breakfast, and I sat by him. He is the most generous-hearted man that exists; and now that he has had a large supply of gold by his comedy, all the needy draw upon him. I found on his table a letter full of gratitude to him from his countryman, poor Francis Gentleman, with a promissory note for fifteen pounds.[1]

I dined at Sir John Pringle's. He was indisposed; and though he sat with the company in very good humour, he was not able to act as master of the house, but deputed me. Mr. Pennant, author of the *Tour to Scotland*, was there. I had just seen him at Edinburgh and was glad to see more of him. Mr. Johnson told me he had read his *Tour* all through and was well entertained with it. He is a neat, lively man. Mr. John Pringle and some other Scotch gentlemen were there. We were very social, though I remember little of what passed. I only remember a remark of my own on Sir William Chambers's *Oriental Gardening*, which the *Heroic Epistle*[2] to him had made an universal topic of conversation. He talks most seriously of introducing terrible objects into a garden. I said this put me in mind of a paragraph in Faulkner's *Dublin Journal* which in describing some fine place in Ireland mentioned the prodigious rocks impending over one's head, so as that the *delighted* spectator imagines every moment that they are to fall down and crush him to pieces.[3]

Between seven and eight, I set out for Mr. Thrale's in Southwark, where Mr. Johnson now was. I intended waiting upon that family in the morning, but was prevented by the several interruptions which I have marked above. I am much obliged to them. I went to Hungerford

[1] See above, p. 139, and below, pp. 244, 247.

[2] An anonymous satire by the poet of *The English Garden*, William Mason.

[3] Compare Richard Payne Knight, *Principles of Taste*, 1805, and Thomas Love Peacock, *Headlong Hall* (1816), Chapter VI: "Here is the same rock, cut into the shape of a giant. In one hand he holds a horn, through which that little fountain is thrown to a prodigious elevation. In the other is a ponderous stone, so exactly balanced as to be apparently ready to fall on the head of any person who may happen to be beneath; and there is Lord Littlebrain walking under it."

Stairs and got a boat to take me over the river. None of the watermen would go farther.[1] It was a fine moonlight, and it was very agreeable to be on the Thames. After being landed, I walked along the shore till I came to Mr. Thrale's. I found Mrs. Thrale and Mr. Johnson and another gentleman at tea. The gentleman soon went away, and then we were quite well.

I repeated the stories of Lord Chesterfield which Lord Lyttelton had told me. Mr. Johnson said most of Lord Chesterfield's witty sayings were puns. He however allowed his saying of himself and Lord Tyrawley to be good wit. Everybody has heard that Mr. Johnson had a difference with Lord Chesterfield, that he broke off all communication with him, and wrote a most severe letter to him on the occasion. It is curious to find how a story that has no foundation may be confidently told for years, gain credit without hesitation, and even appear to be well vouched. As an instance of this, it has always been said that the occasion of the difference between Mr. Johnson and the Earl was that Mr. Johnson was one day kept waiting two hours in his ante-chamber and then Colley Cibber came out from the Earl; and that this provoked Mr. Johnson so much—that he should be kept waiting for a player—that he went off in a great passion. Lord Lyttelton, a great friend of Lord Chesterfield's, spoke of this as of a thing well known. Nay, in justifying Lord Chesterfield, he even explained the particulars. "I suppose," said he, "Lord Chesterfield was very busy when Mr. Johnson called. And you are not to imagine that Cibber had been all the time with my Lord. He was his old acquaintance, and had been introduced by a back stair, perhaps only ten minutes before, and Mr. Johnson was too hasty." Now Mr. Johnson told me this evening that he never was kept waiting while Cibber came out; so that the story has not the least basis.

I gave an account of Burke's speaking on Monday last, and naturally used some action. Mr. Johnson fell into his usual paradoxical argument that action can have no effect upon reasonable minds. "Action," said he, "may enforce noise but never can enforce argument.

[1] From Hungerford Stairs to the landing in Southwark nearest the Thrales' was over a mile by water. The watermen probably did not wish to go so far at night, with the risk of not picking up a return fare.

If you speak to a dog, you use action; you hold up your hand thus, because he is a brute; and in proportion as men are removed from brutes, are reasonable beings, action will have the less influence over them." Said Mrs. Thrale, "What then becomes of Demosthenes's saying, 'Action, action, action'?" JOHNSON. "Why, Demosthenes spoke to an assembly of brutes, to a barbarous people." I saw Mrs. Thrale did not agree with him any more than I did. It is truly amazing that this great master of human nature should deny the power of action over reasonable beings, when it is certain and proved by innumerable facts that its influence has been very great. Reasonable beings are not solely reasonable. They have fancies which must be amused, tastes which must be pleased, passions which must be roused. May I venture to think that Mr. Johnson's opinion as to action proceeds from some defect in the finer parts of capacity—in the powers of delicate perception?

He talked of Percy's intended edition of *The Spectator*, with notes, of which Percy has done a part himself, and committed the care of the rest to one whom he superintends.[1] Mr. Johnson observed that all works which describe manners require notes in sixty or seventy years or less. He said he had told Percy what he knew, and others had told him what they knew. He spoke of Addison's Sir Andrew Freeport, a true Whig who argued against giving charity to beggars, and such topics; but that Addison thought better, and made amends by making him found an hospital for decayed farmers.[2] He made me take down the volume in which that is told, and he read it to us. To hear him read is fine.

Since I have mentioned Percy, I may here remark that in my last year's Journal I have given a bad edition of Mr. Johnson's lines in ridicule of *The Hermit of Warkworth*.[3] I had them so from Garrick. But when I repeated them as from him this year, Mr. Johnson said, "Then he has no ear"; and he gave me them right, as thus:

[1] Dr. John Calder, secretary to the Duke of Northumberland.

[2] *Spectator* No. 549, by Addison. Sir Andrew's argument against giving charity to beggars is in *Spectator* No. 232, which, however, is not by Addison.

[3] In his Notes for 9 May 1772.

I put my hat upon my head
And walked into the Strand,
And there I met another man
Whose hat was in his hand.

I mentioned Burke's using Scripture phrases; such as, in describing that the same sentiment will have quite a different effect when it comes from the Treasury bench from what it has when it comes from the side of Opposition, he said when I heard him, "It is sown in weakness here; it is raised in power there."[1] Mr. Johnson said, "I'm afraid Burke sacrifices everything to his wit. 'Tis wrong to introduce Scripture thus ludicrously." I have a difficulty upon this head. I am not clear that Scripture is hurt by being introduced in the manner that Burke did it here. It is like using a highly classical phrase. It has its effect at once; and very good Christians have not scrupled to use Scripture phrases so. It is not throwing ridicule upon them. I own it should be done with reserve; and it is hard to make a proper distinction. When a wit, who is said to have been Dr. Pitcairne, remarked, on a poor mason's falling from a high house and part of what he was building falling after him. "Blessed are the dead which die in the Lord; they rest from their labours, and their works do follow them,"[2] there was both inhumanity and impiety. Mr. Thrale came home. I sat here till one in the morning, got a hackney-coach, and drove home.

THURSDAY 8 APRIL. I breakfasted with Mr. Crosbie. I dined at General Paoli's. Situation has a great share in the production of every character. While I was with the General at the head of his nation in Corsica, I could collect many memorabilia. Now I cannot recollect anything that passed this day. (Indeed I am now writing in the night between the 30th April and 1st May.) I drank tea at my old acquaintance Love's, of Drury Lane Theatre. I then went to Mr. Johnson's and sat with him a good while, though he hardly spoke at all.

I observed Burnet's *History of His Own Times* in Mr. Johnson's

[1] 1 Corinthians, xv, 43.

[2] See Revelation, xiv, 13. Archibald Pitcairne (1652–1713) was a Scots Jacobite physician with a considerable reputation for Latin verse. He was grandfather to Boswell's friends Lady Colville and the Hon. Andrew Erskine.

library. I was curious to hear his opinion of it. He said it was very entertaining; that the style was mere chit-chat (I think); that he did not believe Burnet intentionally lied, but that he was so prejudiced that he did not try to find out the truth. He was like a man who resolves to regulate his time by a certain watch, but will not inquire whether the watch is right or not.[1] I can remember no more of this night, but only that when I said, " 'Tis twelve o'clock," he said, "What's that to you and me?" and bid Frank tell Mrs. Williams that we were coming to drink tea with her, which we did. I was very desirous of seeing Mr. Johnson at church and could not get a better opportunity than the Holy Week; so I told him I would come and go to church with him tomorrow. He allowed me.

FRIDAY 9 APRIL. This morning being Good Friday, I went in good frame to Mr. Johnson's. Frank said there was nobody with him but *Dr.* Levett.[2] I never knew till now that Levett had that title, or rather took it. We had good tea and good cakes, I think cross-buns. I then accompanied Mr. Johnson to St. Clement's Church in the Strand. He was solemn and devout. I went home with him after. We did not dine on this venerable fast. He read to himself the Greek New Testament. I looked at several books, particularly Laud's Life by ———. I observed a saying of King Charles II which I may introduce into my essay on the profession of a lawyer, viz., that he could not be one because ———.[3] Mr. Johnson said it was false reasoning, because every cause has a bad side; and a man is not overcome though the cause which he has pleaded is decided against him.

[1] Gilbert Burnet (1643–1715) was a Scot who became Bishop of Salisbury and a favourite adviser to King William. His *History of My Own Times* was published posthumously, 1724–1734. Johnson's objections to it relate to the fact that Burnet was a Broad Churchman in both politics and religious doctrine.

[2] "Dr." Robert Levett was a self-taught practitioner of humble origin who lived with Johnson and sometimes prescribed for the members of his household.

[3] Boswell filled the blank in the *Life*: "I cannot defend a bad, nor yield in a good cause." The saying (which was uttered not by Charles II, but by Charles I, before he came to the throne) is quoted from Laud's diary for 1 February 1623/4. Boswell was probably reading Henry Wharton's *History of the Troubles and Tryal of the Most Reverend Father in God and Blessed Martyr, William Laud,* to which Laud's Diary is prefixed. The essay on the profession of a lawyer was never written.

He spoke of a gentleman who has an estate being called in duty to reside so much upon it, and do good there. He observed strikingly to me that whoever comes and settles in London in any capacity will have his children English and quite strangers to his estate, as much as Frenchmen, and that one of the great disadvantages of plunging into the ocean of life (or dissipation) here is that almost every man runs out his fortune. He said if he were Langton, he would go resolutely to France and live on £100 a year rather than sell a mass of land which his family could never get back.

I told him how Goldsmith said to me the other morning, "As I take my shoes from the shoemaker, and my coat from the tailor, so I take my religion from the priest," and I was regretting this loose way of talking. "Sir," said Mr. Johnson, "he knows nothing. He has made up his mind about nothing."

To my astonishment Mr. Johnson asked me to dine with him on Sunday. I never supposed he had a dinner at home. "Sir," said he, "I generally have a pie on Sunday." I most readily accepted the invitation. We went back to St. Clement's in the afternoon. There was sermon both forenoon and afternoon, by different clergymen; but what they were I cannot say. They must indeed have been remarkable discourses that the very shadow of the great mind of Johnson would not have obscured; that the very idea of his power would not have annihilated. I may be on stilts, but my mind has sprung up and lights upon anything she first meets. I saw him to his door after sermons. I then went and drank tea at Mr. Dilly's. Mr. Mayo, the dissenting minister,[1] was there. I called at Woodfall's, who directed me to the Chapter Coffee-house to find books of *The Public Advertiser*. I found there my old essays.[2]

[1] Johnson's antagonist in the long argument about toleration at Dilly's on 7 May of this year.

[2] Three essays published by Boswell in *The Public Advertiser* before this date are known through their inclusion in *The Hypochondriack* (Nos. XLVII, XLIX, LXVIII). Another series, as yet uncollected, was published there over the pseudonym "Rampager". The earliest reference to these yet noted occurs in a letter of Temple to Boswell dated 5 July 1770. See also Boswell's remark in the Journal, below, 24 August 1774. Henry Sampson Woodfall was the publisher of *The Public Advertiser*.

SATURDAY 10 APRIL. I breakfasted ———. I dined at Mr. Bosville's. More I cannot recollect.

SUNDAY 11 APRIL. This being Easter Day, I found myself in such a frame as I could wish. I breakfasted at the Chapter Coffee-house, which I had last night[1] found to be an excellent place, and a little after ten went to St. Paul's. I made myself be shown into a seat just by Mr. John Rivington. He invited me to his family dinner, a fillet of veal and a pudding, but I told him I was engaged with Mr. Johnson; but I promised to drink tea with him, and go with him to hear music and see the children sup at Christ's Hospital.[2] Mr. Wilson, a residentiary, preached to us on this text: "But we trusted that it was he who should have redeemed Israel."[3] He gave us a neat and clear deduction of the evidence of Christianity. I was struck and elevated as usual by the service, and though I did not feel that firm conviction which I have done at different periods of my life, owing I believe to an indolence of mind making me not recollect or feel the importance of settling the truth one way or other, yet my heart and affections were pious, and I received the Holy Sacrament with considerable satisfaction. I was above three hours in church today.

When I came to Mr. Johnson's, he was not yet come home. By and by he arrived. I had gratified my curiosity much in dining with Rousseau, and I thought it as curious to dine with Mr. Johnson. I supposed we should hardly see knives and forks, and only have the pie which he mentioned. But to my surprise I found everything in very good order. He and I and Mrs. Williams and a Miss ———[4] were the company. We had a very good soup, a boiled leg of lamb and spinach, a veal pie, an excellent rice pudding, pickled walnuts and onions, porter and port wine. I dined as well as ever I wish to do. The lamb made him tell me a joke. He said Mr. Thrale's sister, Lady Lade, when

[1] Either this should read "Friday night" or the last sentence of the entry for Friday (a crowded interlinear addition) should have been entered under Saturday.

[2] Rivington was a governor of Christ's Hospital.

[3] Luke xxiv, 21.

[4] Mrs. Piozzi says that this was "Poll" Carmichael, but she was probably only guessing.

she saw Sir George Colebrooke in a white waistcoat and green coat, said he was like a leg of lamb and spinach.[1]

We spoke of Dr. Campbell, author of *The Lives of the Admirals*. He said he was a very inquisitive and a very able man, and a man of good principles, though he has been deficient in practice. "Campbell," said he, "has not been within a church for many years; but he never passes by one but he pulls off his hat. This shows the man to be radically right, and we may hope it will some time or other produce a right practice."

He owned Hawkesworth was his imitator, but did not think that Goldsmith was. BOSWELL. "Sir, everybody thinks so." JOHNSON. "Sir, he has great merit." BOSWELL. "Yes. But he owes his getting so far up much to you." JOHNSON. "Perhaps he has got sooner to it by that."

Mr. Johnson observed that the books printed in Scotland before the Union were very few; that he had seen a collection of all of them at the Hon. Archibald Campbell's, a relation of the Duke of Argyll's, and they were very few. He asked me what books of religion our clergy recommended to the common people. I was at some loss to tell him, but mentioned Henry *On Prayer*—Guthrie's *Trial of a Saving Interest in Christ*—*The Life of God in the Soul of Man*.[2] I spoke of my scheme of writing Ruddiman's Life.[3] He said he'd be glad in helping me to do honour to him, but that his farewell letter to the Faculty of Advocates might have been written in Latin.

He told me he had twelve or fourteen times attempted to keep a Journal, but never could persevere. "The great thing," said he, "is the state of your own mind; and you ought to write down everything that you can, for you cannot judge at first what is good or bad; and write immediately while the impression is fresh, for it will not be the same a week after." I told him how uneasy I was at having lost eight hundred

[1] The MS reads "Lady———". Sir George was at the moment involved in spectacular bankruptcy.

[2] By Henry Scougal.

[3] Boswell, first and last, entertained some forty similar "schemes" which came to nothing.—Thomas Ruddiman (d. 1757) was a distinguished Scottish philologist, Librarian of the Advocates' Library.

pages[1] of my Journal, which were sent from Utrecht, where I had left them, and that I was chiefly uneasy for fear that somebody had them, as they really contained a full state of my mind when in a deep melancholy. He comforted me by saying that probably they had fallen into the hands of somebody who could not understand them, and would be destroyed as waste-paper. I am, however, much vexed at this loss, and at the apprehension that they may be lying concealed.

I asked him if he could tell when he was born, when he came to London and such things. Said he, "You shall have them" (or "I'll give you them") "all for twopence. I hope you shall know a great deal more of me before you write my Life." He said Dame Oliver's giving him gingerbread (for which see my last year's Journal)[2] was as high a proof of merit as he could conceive. That she read the black letter and asked him to borrow her from his father a Bible in that character. That he next went to an English master, Tom Brown, who wrote an English spelling-book and dedicated it to the Universe; but that he feared no copy of it could now be had. That his father knew Latin pretty well, but no Greek; that he did not read so much as he might have done, and was rather a wrong-headed man. That the sale of books at Lichfield was not sufficient to procure a livelihood, and that he used to have shops or places for sale in different towns whither he went to the fairs, and would even carry books in his saddle-bags to these places, or take them home to those who commissioned them; and had a great deal of bodily activity. I talked of going to see the Reverend Mr. Adams at Shrewsbury, who was Mr. Johnson's tutor at Oxford.[3] "Sir," said he, " 'tis not worth while. You know more of me than he does."

I drank tea at Mr. John Rivington's. I had the full impression of an eminent London bookseller—a governor of Christ's Hospital—being in the very middle of St. Paul's Churchyard on a Sunday. I was pleased

[1] Boswell probably exaggerates unconsciously. The first page surviving beyond the hiatus in his Holland Journal of 1763–1764 is numbered 537.

[2] His Notes for 24 April 1772.

[3] Dr. William Adams, who became Master of Pembroke College in 1775, would have been Johnson's tutor had Johnson returned after December 1729. In 1776 Adams told Boswell: "I was his nominal tutor; but he was above my mark." "That," said Johnson, "was liberal and noble."

to see him so comfortable with his wife and family. We went to Christ's Hospital. There was a great crowd of company there. It was truly agreeable to hear prayers read by one of the boys; to see them all take their wholesome frugal supper, bread and butter and beer, and then walk in procession and bow to the governors, each division with a nurse who takes care of them. I was particularly pleased to see the Steward, a *steady* man as advertisements say, who had been a boy in the Hospital himself, and now had authority over them all.[1] We had lastly an anthem sung, the organ accompanying it. Copies of the anthem were put into the hands of the company, written by the boys, with the name of the writer at each. They were generally taken back. I kept my copy. It was very well transcribed. I shall endeavour to learn what becomes of the writer.[2] The celebrated Richardson was brought up here. Mr. Rivington showed me the different wards. It is indeed a noble charity.

I ran home, dressed, and went to Lord Mansfield's. Jenkinson was with him, but went away just as I came. My Lord and I were then left tête-à-tête. His cold reserve and sharpness, too, were still too much for me. It was like being cut with a very, very cold instrument. I have not for a long time experienced that weakness of mind which I had formerly in a woeful degree in the company of the great or the clever. But Lord Mansfield has uncommon power. He chills the most generous blood.

I spoke of the coal cause, Alexander against Montgomery, where a rare event happened that the House of Lords divided.[3] Lord Mansfield

[1] John Perry, steward 1761–1785. He is the "old and good steward", so much beloved of the boys, whose death is recorded in Charles Lamb's "Recollections of Christ's Hospital". In "Christ's Hospital Five-and-Thirty Years Ago" (which deliberately presents the other side of the picture) Perry's administration is charged with some laxity.

[2] Boswell's copy survives. The transcriber's name was Joseph Allen. The name of the poet does not appear. The music was by Robert Hudson, music master at the Hospital and at St. Paul's Cathedral.

[3] All members of the House of Lords had the right to vote when the House was sitting as a court of appeal, but as a general thing decisions were left to the Law Lords. Lord Mansfield alone had reversed Hastie's case in the previous year (above, p. 121).

took care to mention that he was not there, to keep me in mind that if he had, the division would not have happened. I mentioned to him that when it was first determined in Scotland, my father and Lord Kames could form no opinion. At the second determination they did form an opinion, and the President and two Lords altered their opinions, one the one way, one the other; and then I said, "It was a cause which any man might have determined." Here was a piece of *étourderie* which laid me fairly open; and Lord M., who had observed that it would be very dangerous if a division should often happen, did not miss me. "What!" said he, "was a cause in which your father and Lord Kames could at first form no opinion, and as to which the President and other judges altered their opinions, one that any man might determine?" I, however, recovered: "I mean, my Lord, a cause of fact in which there was no law; where the question was merely whether there was a bargain between man and man—a cause to be determined by a jury." MANSFIELD. "Yes, a jury if directed." BOSWELL. "Do juries always take direction, my Lord?" "Yes, except in political causes, where they do not at all keep themselves to right and wrong." I obliged him to laugh by telling him that from our custom in Scotland of trying to account for decisions by extraneous circumstances, we had observed that the peers who were for fixing the coal contract were all the coal-masters: the Lords Abercorn, Cathcart, and Rosebery; whereas Lord Marchmont,[1] who had only a large peat-moss, was for setting the parties free.[2] Lord Mansfield laughed pretty heartily, crying, "Did ye?"

[1] All four were Representative Peers of Scotland in the House of Lords.

[2] Robert Alexander had discovered coal on his estate of Blackhouse, near Ayr, but before sinking capital in the development had tried to enter into an agreement with a neighbouring colliery at Newton for the sale of a fixed annual quantity of his coal at a stipulated price. On Alexander's refusal to restrict his output to the quantity which the colliery agreed to buy and thus to protect them from competition in the local market, the agreement fell through. Alexander, alleging that on the faith of an exchange of letters he had taken measures to work the coal, then brought suit for implement of the agreement. On 26 June 1771 the Lord Ordinary pronounced an interlocutor in favour of the colliery; the Inner House reversed this on 21 November 1771; but on a second reclaiming petition the court reversed its own ruling on 6 March 1772. Alexander then appealed to the House of Lords, and

I then resolved to satisfy my curiosity whether Andrew Stuart's letters had made any impression on him.[1] So I added, "This is as good reasoning as Andrew Stuart's *Letters*. They are very well written. I got your sister Mrs. Murray to promise to read them. I told her she'd be very angry, but that they were worth reading" (or words to that purpose). I looked steadily at him during all this, and he was not a bit affected. He said nothing. I said, " 'Tis a cruel thing on poor Douglas, now that he's settled and the question over so long ago." MANSFIELD. " 'Twill do him no harm. 'Twill not take the estate from him." I also made him laugh by telling him that I had met the new schoolmaster at Campbeltown, who told me that the boys were beginning to be rebellious and to talk of the reversal of the decree in Hastie's case, but that I told him *meo periculo*, "Don't spare them. Lord Mansfield allows you to whip them with a *rod* or *taws* (the loose leather, you know, my Lord) as much as you please; but don't take improper modes of correction." MANSFIELD. "Nor correct in passion. You said right" (laughing).

I had plucked up enough of resolution by this time, and perhaps had probed his Lordship more than was proper. He is all artificial. He affected to know little of Scotch appeals when over. I catched him, though! I spoke of the one, Parkhill against Chalmers, in a way that showed him I did not think the judgment a good one. Said he, "Were there not particular circumstances there?" I bowed without answering and let him take his own way; upon which he went on,

---

the Lords dismissed the appeal. Boswell's remark that "any man might have determined" the cause was not so silly as might appear. The determination whether an exchange of letters constitutes a contract is not so much a matter of law as of common-sense construction of the meaning of the English language. The account of this case in Thomas S. Paton's *Reports of Cases Decided in the House of Lords upon Appeal from Scotland from 1757 to 1784* ends with this note: "The judges in House of Lords seem to have been as much divided in this case as the judges in the Court of Session. After the debate the votes of the Lords were equal—four for reversing and four for affirming, whereupon it was determined that the interlocutor should not be reversed. It would seem from this that the lay lords joined in the voting."

[1] Stuart had been agent for the Duke of Hamilton in the Douglas Cause. In his *Letters to the Right Honourable Lord Mansfield*, privately printed in January of this year, he had attacked Mansfield for partiality in the Cause.

"Ay, there were so and so"—and showed that he well remembered what he affected not to remember.[1] It is unpleasant to see so high an administrator of justice such a man. I mentioned Mr. Johnson. He said he was a man of great learning and abilities. I told him I had a mind to try the law of vicious intromission[2] by agreement between the parties. He said if collusion was suspected, the House would not hear a cause, because it would not be fairly pleaded and the country might have bad law established. I told him of my debates in the Justiciary Court on the Mob Act being only in cases of sedition or rebellion, and that carrying off furniture by a mob was not robbery.[3] He agreed with the Court of Justiciary's interlocutors on both questions. I then called at Sir John Pringle's, where I found Captain Constantine Phipps[4] and some more company.

MONDAY 12 APRIL. The celebrated female historian, Mrs. Catharine Macaulay,[5] her brother the Rev. Mr. Sawbridge, and another gentleman had £10,000 lent on the estate of the Laird of MacLeod,[6] and for two years had received no interest. My good friend Dilly had directed them to me for advice; so their attorney, Mr.

[1] The House of Lords had upheld the decision of the Court of Session on 12 February of this year.

[2] An old principle of Scots law that "whoever intermeddled with the effects of a person deceased, without the interposition of legal authority to guard against embezzlement, should be subjected to pay all the debts of the deceased." The Court of Session, continues Boswell in the *Life of Johnson*, "had gradually relaxed the strictness of this principle, where the interference proved had been inconsiderable. In a case which came before that Court the preceding winter, I had laboured to persuade the Judges to return to the ancient law." Before leaving London in May 1772 Boswell had succeeded in getting Johnson to dictate a long argument on this characteristically Boswellian legal theme.

[3] The "debates" must have occurred in the trials of the "meal rioters" just before Boswell came to London. See above, pp. 153–6.

[4] Phipps, later second Baron Mulgrave (1744–1792), was M.P. for Lincoln in 1773. He was a Fellow of the Royal Society and of the Society of Antiquaries; he owned the best nautical library in England.

[5] Her *History of England* appeared in eight volumes, 1763–1783.

[6] Norman MacLeod, Chief of the clan, the "old Laird of MacLeod" of Boswell's *Journal of a Tour to the Hebrides*, had died in the previous year, much in debt, and had been succeeded by an eighteen-year-old grandson. See above, p. 65.

Heaton of Lincoln's Inn, was to retain me. In the meantime I engaged to breakfast with Mrs. Macaulay this morning and look at her securities. I first drank a dish of tea with Dempster, who I regretted was so busy that I could see little of him. Mrs. Macaulay and I had a very cordial, polite meeting, and she gave me a good breakfast, like any other woman. I looked at her securities and found them good. I dined at Mr. Bosville's. At night I went to Covent Garden and saw *She Stoops to Conquer*, the author's second night. I laughed most heartily, and was highly pleased at once with the excellent comedy and with the fame and profit which my friend Goldsmith was receiving. It was really a rich evening to me. I would not stay to see the farce.[1] I would not put the taste of Goldsmith's fruit out of my mouth. Sir Walter, who was to set out for his regiment at Minorca next day, and his brother Sandy, who was at an Academy at Kensington,[2] eat some cold beef at my lodgings and drank a parting glass. I could not forget their father, the honest Captain Montgomerie-Cuninghame.

TUESDAY 13 APRIL. Longlands the solicitor breakfasted with me, and we revised Lord Mansfield's speech in the appeal, Campbell against Hastie.[3] Mr. Johnson and Dr. Goldsmith called on me and we went to General Oglethorpe's, where we were engaged to dine. Last year we had a noble day there. I was anxious a little lest this should fall far short, but it did not. There was nobody there but ourselves, a Miss Lockwood, a[4] very well-behaved woman,[5] and a fine girl, a Miss

[1] The play had opened on 15 March and played for the twelfth time on 31 May, the closing night of the season. This was Boswell's first opportunity to see it. Goldsmith's profit for the evening was £171. 17. 0. The afterpiece which Boswell would not stay to see was *The Apprentice*, by another acquaintance of his, Arthur Murphy.

[2] Perhaps Elphinston's. See above, pp. 68, 96.

[3] That is, revised the report of the speech which both of them had taken down at the trial the year before. British courts did not yet make official stenographic reports of their proceedings.

[4] Boswell here removed five pages to use as copy for the *Life of Johnson*. They were not recovered till 1940, and are now printed for the first time as Boswell originally wrote them. See above, p. 42 *n.* 2.

[5] Miss Lockwood was present, along with Goldsmith, at Oglethorpe's again on Thursday 29 April. Apparently some sort of benevolent plot was on foot to bring the two together. See below, p. 216.

Scott, a natural daughter of the late Duke of Buccleuch as the world has it; but General Oglethorpe maintains that her mother was married to the Duke. The General produced before dinner a glass of what he called palm wine, the true canary; indeed truly rich. It seems the grape of that wine is the Rhenish vine transplanted into the Canaries. The General also called it sack; but Mr. Johnson told us it was not the sack which Falstaff drank, which was a sherry sweetened with sugar.

Goldsmith took up the common topic that the race of our people was degenerated and that this was owing to luxury. "Sir," says Mr. Johnson, "in the first place, I doubt the fact. I believe there are as many tall men in England now as ever there were. But, secondly, supposing them grown less, that is not owing to luxury; for, Sir, consider to how very small a proportion of our people luxury can reach. Our soldiery surely are not luxurious, who live on sixpence a day; and so you may take other classes. Luxury so far as it reaches the poor will do good to the race of people. It will increase them. Sir, no nation was ever hurt by luxury; for, as I said before, it can reach but to a very few. Sir, I admit that the great increase of commerce and manufactures hurts the military spirit of a people; because it gives them a competition for something else than martial honours, a competition for riches. It also hurts the bodies of the people; for you will observe there is no man who works at any particular trade but whom you may know from his appearance to do so. One part or other of his body by being more used than the rest deforms in some degree his body. But, Sir, that is not luxury. A tailor sits cross-legged, but that is not luxury." GOLDSMITH. "Come, you're just going to the same place by another road." JOHNSON. "Nay, Sir. I say that is not *luxury*. Let us take a walk from Charing Cross to Whitechapel, through I suppose the greatest series of shops in the world. What is there in any of these shops (if you except gin-shops) that can do any person any harm?" GOLDSMITH. "Well, I'll take you. The very next shop to Northumberland House is a pickle-shop." JOHNSON. "Well, Sir. Do we not know that a maid can in one afternoon make pickles sufficient to serve a whole family for a year? Nay, that five pickle-shops can serve all the kingdom? Besides, there is no harm done to anybody by the making of pickles or the eating of pickles."

We drank tea with the ladies, and Goldsmith sung Tony Lumpkin's song and a very pretty one to the tune of *Balamagairy* which he had designed for Miss Hardcastle; but as Mrs. Bulkley, who played the part, could not sing, it was left out.[1]

Mr. Johnson and Dr. Goldsmith walked home with me. I have forgotten much of this day's conversations. Goldsmith went away. Mr. Johnson drank some tea with me. I told him that Mrs. Macaulay said she wondered how he could reconcile his political principles with his moral, his notions of inequality and subordination with wishing well to the happiness of all mankind, who might live so agreeably had they all their portions of land, and none to domineer over another. "Why, Sir," said he, "I reconcile my principles very well, because mankind are happier in a state of subordination. Were they to be in this pretty state of equality, they'd soon degenerate into brutes, they'd become Monboddo's nation. Their tails would grow. Sir, all would be losers were all to work to all. They'd have no intellectual improvement. All intellectual improvement arises from leisure. All leisure arises from one working for another."

Talking of the family of Stuart, he said it would seem that this family had now established as good a right as the former family by the long consent of the people, and that to disturb this right might be considered as culpable. At the same time he owned that it was a very difficult question when considered with respect to the House of Stuart. That he thought to oblige people to take oaths as to the disputed right was wrong. That he knew not if he could take them. But he did not blame those who did. So conscientious, so delicate, and so mild is he upon this subject as to which so much noise has been made against him.

Talking of law cases, he said the English reports were very poor: the half of what has been said taken down, and of that half much mistaken. Whereas in Scotland, the arguments on each side were deliberately put in writing to be considered by the court; and he thought a collection of our cases upon subjects of importance, with the opinions of the judges upon them, would be valuable. Said he,

1 "Ah me! when shall I marry me?" See below, p. 218.

"You have not had time yet to have a volume. But you may be collecting."

WEDNESDAY 14 APRIL. I should have marked yesterday that Mr. ———, the ———[1] of Mr. Heaton, called on me and gave me a retainer for Mrs. Macaulay's . . .

EDITORIAL NOTE: The Journal ends at the bottom of a full page, with a catchword; as the reverse is blank, it was probably not carried further. But Boswell continues the story of his jaunt, in rough notes and separate papers, until the end.

The crowded days went whirling by. Small wonder if he did not find time to keep more than notes. " . . . Lord Mountstuart, supped." "Dined Paoli's." "Foote's puppets. Supped with him." "Called Percy." " . . . Mrs. Montagu's." "Mr. Johnson and Mrs. Williams . . . in Strahan's coach and took me." "Dined Mr. Thrale's." "Goldsmith at home." "Away to Drury Lane. . . . Garrick lively and fine."

TUESDAY 27 APRIL. Breakfast Garrick's. . . . Then Beauclerk's. Shown up to drawing-room. Very elegant. Lady Di comely and well behaved. . . . We talked of hanging. . . . As we walked up Johnson's Court, I said, "I have a veneration for this court." BEAUCLERK. "So have I." Found him alone. . . . Talking of Goldsmith, Johnson said, "He should not attempt as he does, for he has not [the] temper for it. He's so much hurt if he fails. Sir, a game of jokes is partly composed of skill, partly of chance. A man may be beat at times by one who has not the tenth part of his wit. . . . " We came away.

THURSDAY 29 APRIL. . . . Mr. Johnson was waiting for me. He and I went for General Oglethorpe's on foot. In Berkeley Square [we were] called to and taken up by Sir Joshua and Goldsmith. They told [us] they were at [a] loss where to go. "So," said I, "you took us as guides." JOHNSON. "I wondered, indeed, at their great civility."

A grand moment, towards which Boswell must have manœuvred

[1] This blank should probably be filled by some such word as "partner" or "clerk".

with some care—and some genius—came at the end of April in his admission to the Literary Club. ("Sir," said Johnson a few months later, "you got into our Club by doing what a man can do." "I suppose Dr. Johnson meant," adds Boswell, "that I assiduously and earnestly recommended myself to some of the members, as in a canvass for an election into Parliament.") On Friday 16 April, Boswell sent a note to Percy: "I hope you will remember me at the Club tonight. Sir Joshua, Mr. Johnson, and Dr. Goldsmith have obligingly engaged to be for me. They are all to dine at my lodgings on Saturday sennight, the 24th April. May I beg you will do me the favour to join us?" On Friday 23 April, Johnson wrote to Goldsmith, who was chairman at the Club that evening, "I beg that you will excuse my absence to the Club. I am going this evening to Oxford. I have another favour to beg. It is that I may be considered as proposing Mr. Boswell for a candidate of our Society, and that he may be considered as regularly nominated." In his diary entry for that day Percy recorded: "At the Club: Mr. Boswell proposed."

The following Friday produced Notes which Boswell later developed in a first draft of the *Life of Johnson*—thus:

[Manuscript of the *Life of Johnson*][1]

On Friday 30 April I dined with him at Mr. Beauclerk's, where were Lord Charlemont, Sir Joshua Reynolds, and some more company. . . .

The gentlemen went away to their Club, and as one black ball could exclude, I sat in such anxious suspense as even the charms of Lady Diana Beauclerk's conversation could hardly relieve. Mr. Beauclerk's coach returned for me in less than an hour with a note from him that I was chosen. . . . I hastened to the Turk's Head in Gerard Street, Soho, and was introduced to such a society as can seldom be found: Mr. Edmund Burke, Dr. Nugent, Mr. (now Sir William) Jones. There were also present, I remember, Mr. Garrick, Dr. Gold-

[1] The manuscript of the *Life of Johnson* now at Yale shows the book in all the stages of its composition. Boswell's first draft (with the single exception indicated in the next footnote) serves as the text for this and later passages.

smith, and the company with whom I had dined. [Upon my entrance, Johnson . . . placed himself behind a chair, on which he leant as on a desk or pulpit, and with humorous formality gave me a *charge*, pointing out the duties incumbent upon me as a good member of the Club.][1]

("They were afraid of you, Sir," said Boswell on the Hebrides tour, "as it was you who proposed me." "Sir," replied Johnson, "they knew that if they refused you, they'd probably never have got in another. I'd have kept them all out.")

FRIDAY 30 APRIL. . . . Fixed with Johnson [to] dine Mitre next day alone. Home in high spirits. Resolved [to] sit up and journalise. Did so. Not able as formerly, but wrote twenty-six pages.

SATURDAY 1 MAY. To Dempster's and breakfasted. Was ill. Conversation a fatigue; inclined to go to bed again, but resolved not. Dempster and I sallied out. Called Burke's, after having walked in Park; not in. Then he took me to walk on Thames—a kind of philosophical saunter. I had a strange thought on fate. . . . Went to Mr. Johnson's.

In the course of a relaxed and desultory conversation Boswell received what he must have prized as one of the highest compliments Johnson could pay him. "We dined by ourselves," he wrote in the *Life* manuscript, "at our old rendezvous the Mitre Tavern. He was placid but not much disposed to talk. He observed that the Irish mixed more with the English than the Scotch did; that their language was nearer to English, as a proof of which they did very well as players, which Scotchmen could not. 'Then, Sir, they have not that extreme nationality which we find in the Scotch. Sir, I will do you the justice to say that you are the most *unscottified* of your countrymen. You are almost the only instance of a Scotchman that I have known who did not at every other word bring in some other Scotchman.' "

On Friday 7 May, Boswell "settled all at lodgings. Was really calm. Left Joseph to set out. Took boat to Borough." At breakfast with the

[1] The passage in brackets was added in a revision of the first draft of the *Life*. The Notes of 1773 have the detail: "In flutter—prayed in coach."

Thrales occurred a conversation in which Boswell, retrospectively "seduced, perhaps, by the charms" of his hostess on the evening of his uneasy wait for the note from the Club, attempted now to vindicate her divorce by Act of Parliament from Viscount Bolingbroke and her present marriage to their friend Beauclerk. Johnson was "angry". "Go to Scotland! Go to Scotland! I never heard [you] talk so foolishly." For which Boswell in the *Life* manuscript has Johnson say: "My dear Sir, never accustom your mind to mingle virtue and vice. The woman's a whore, and there's an end on't."[1]

Temple had come to town, and Mrs. Temple. On first seeing his "old friend and spouse" together this afternoon Boswell was "hurt a little" at their "appearance". But a grand dinner-party was arranged at Dilly's in the Poultry. Temple and Claxton were there. Goldsmith and Langton, and two clergymen, the dissenting Dr. Mayo and the hymn-writer Mr. Toplady. "[The subject of] *toleration* was introduced by me, I know not how." The energetic argument which followed between Johnson and the liberal Dr. Mayo gradually squeezed out the less authoritative voice of Goldsmith, until there came one of those junctures for which Goldsmith was so unhappily noted.

[7 May, Manuscript of the *Life of Johnson*]

During this argument Goldsmith sat in great agitation from a wish to get in and shine. Finding himself excluded, he had taken his hat to go, but remained for some time with it in his hand, like a gamester who at the close of a long night waits for a little while to see if he can have a favourable opening. Once when he was beginning to speak he found himself overpowered by the loud voice of Johnson, who was at the opposite end of the table and did not perceive Goldsmith's attempt. Thus disappointed, Goldsmith in a passion threw down his

[1] Boswell in writing up his Notes for the *Life* often remembers details for which Notes have no equivalent. It seems very likely that Johnson made both these remarks on the morning of 7 May, or perhaps he delivered his crushing characterisation of Lady Di at some other time when the conversation was on the same topic. Boswell's Notes, by his own definition, are not so much minutes as hints for remembering, and he admits to occasional conflations.

hat, crying in a bitter tone, "*Take* it." When Toplady was going to speak, Johnson uttered some sound which Goldsmith supposed to be beginning again and taking the word from Toplady. Upon which he seized this opportunity of venting his own spleen under pretext of supporting another person. "Sir," said he to Johnson, "the gentleman has heard you patiently for an hour. Pray allow him to speak." JOHNSON (angrily). "Sir, I was not interrupting the gentleman. I was only giving him a signal of my attention. Sir, you are impertinent to me." Goldsmith made no reply but continued in the company for some time.

FRIDAY 7 MAY. . . . Langton, who was so quiet and so prudent, said, "Is there not a difference between opinions that lead to action and opinions merely speculative—for instance, [the] doctrine of [the] Trinity?" JOHNSON. "Sir, I'm surprised that a man of your piety [can introduce this subject here]." LANGTON (timorous like [a] ghost). "I only hinted [at the question from a desire to hear your opinion upon it]."[1] JOHNSON. "Well, then, Sir, I think that permitting to teach any opinion contrary to established doctrine of [the] Church is so far to permit the forces of that religion to be weakened." LANGTON. "[The] question may be whether [it is] most politic to tolerate or not." JOHNSON. "We have been talking of *right*. This [is] another question. I think [it is] not politic to tolerate."

[7 May, Manuscript of the *Life of Johnson*, continued]

He and Mr. Langton and I took a coach together to the Club, where we found Mr. Burke, Mr. Garrick, and some other members, and amongst them our friend Goldsmith, who sat silently brooding over Johnson's having called him impertinent. Johnson perceived this and said aside to some of us, "I'll make Goldsmith forgive me," and then called to him in a loud voice: "Dr. Goldsmith, something passed today where you and I dined. I ask your pardon." Goldsmith answered placidly: "It must be much from you that I take ill." And

[1] The extended passages in brackets are supplied (the second with some adaptation) from the *Life* manuscript.

so at once the difference was over, and they were on as easy terms as usual, and Goldsmith rattled away.

[FRIDAY 7 MAY, continued] . . . Johnson went out. Langton told of Goldsmith, and he of Langton. I said, "I'd [have] given five guineas rather than not [have] seen that exhibition. I so often tossed, and he laughing—to see his long legs in [the] air!"

In August Boswell would write to Langton: "I cannot help having a kind of joy in recollecting that you with all your timid caution got a drubbing at Dilly's. The truth is, it was observed when you was here that you assumed a kind of superiority over me, as if you was never touched by that awful rod which has been so often applied to my back. It is natural then for me to feel some satisfaction in thinking that you had your share."

At breakfast with Langton on 10 May Boswell learned something which displeased him much. Langton was on his way to his lawyer, Robert Chambers, to make a will devising his estate to his three sisters in preference to a remote male heir. This plan, so strongly antipathetic to Boswell's feudal inclinations, was the occasion of that grotesquely hilarious farewell hour with Johnson which found its way, only a little muted, though without Langton's name, into the *Life*. For it was at Chambers's house in the Temple that Johnson appointed Boswell to meet him that evening, and there Johnson, after recovering from an attack of "some violent internal complaint," launched with "noble enthusiasm" into a discourse on "keeping up the representation of respectable families. . . . He maintained the dignity and propriety of male succession in opposition to Langton." (Boswell had presumably let out the news.) He called Langton's sisters "three *dowdies*."

[10 May, Manuscript of the *Life of Johnson*]

He said with as stately a spirit as the boldest baron in the most perfect days of the feudal system, "An ancient estate should always go to males. It is mighty foolish to let a stranger have it who marries your daughter and takes your name. I would not let a rascal take my name. As for an estate newly got by trade, you may give it if you will to the dog *Towser* and let him keep his *own* name."

I have known him at times exceedingly diverted at what seemed to others a very small sport. He now laughed immoderately at Langton's making his will, called him Langton the *testator* and added, "I dare say he thinks he has done a thing, a mighty thing. He won't stay till he gets home to produce this wonderful deed. He'll call up the landlord of the first inn on the road, and after a suitable preface upon mortality and the uncertainty of life will tell him that he should not delay making his will. 'And here, Sir,' will he say, 'is my will, which I have just made with the assistance of one of the ablest lawyers in the kingdom.' And he will read it to him" (laughing all the time). "He believes he has made this will, but he did not make it. You made it for him. I hope you had more conscience than to make him say, 'being of sound understanding.' Ha, ha, ha! I hope he has left me a legacy. He should leave hatbands and gloves to all the Club. I'd have his will turned into verse like a ballad." In this manner did he run on, as full of drollery as a man could be, but surely such drollery as one should never expect from the author of *The Rambler*. Yet it must be very amusing and please us in a high degree to find that our mighty moralist and philologist could be so playful. Chambers did not by any means relish this jocularity upon a matter *quorum pars magna fuit* and seemed impatient till he got us out of his chambers. Johnson could not stop his merriment but continued laughing all the way till we got without the Temple Gate. I cherished it, calling out, "Langton the testator, Langton Longshanks." This tickled his fancy so much that he roared out, "I wonder to whom he'll leave his legs?" And then burst into such a fit of laughter that he seemed almost in a convulsion; then in order to support himself he laid hold of one of the posts which were then at the side of the pavement and bellowed forth such peals that in the dark silence of the night his voice resounded from Temple Bar to Fleet Ditch.

This most ludicrous scene of the awful and melancholy Johnson happened well to counteract the feelings of sadness which I used to experience when parting with him for a considerable time. I accompanied him to his door, where he gave me his blessing.[1]

In the Notes of 1773 Boswell wrote: "I got to Mr. Dilly's between one and two, raised him, and got all ready. Took leave, and James carried my portmanteau to the inn."

[1] After the phrase "rascal take my name", the Notes add: "(I'm not quite sure of this.)" The same version has: "Chambers accompanied us to the Temple Gate."

1773–1774

Boswell's Life from the End of his London Jaunt in the Spring of 1773 to the Beginning of the Summer Session in Edinburgh, June, 1774. Boswell's friend Temple, feeling no doubt that he had been neglected by Boswell at the end of the 1772 jaunt, had this year taken pains to prevent a similar occurrence. Even before Boswell set out for London, Temple had sent him advice where to lodge, with a suggestion that the Temples might join him to make up a friendly household and later travel north with him. Temple experienced a few days of panic at the thought that an impending visitation by his archdeacon might prevent his escape, and he had qualms about the expense of the trip proposed. But Temple and Mrs. Temple, as we have seen, did arrive in London, and they set out with Boswell on 11 May for the journey north, as far as Cornhill, a village just south of Berwick. At Morpeth the three dined with Temple's aunt Mrs. Collingwood. "Temple and I in the garden there as happy as ever; our college ideas quite lively." They had a good night at Wooler Haugh Head. "A fine trout and negus. Just we three, calm and fine." The disagreeable occurrence which might have been feared from Boswell's earlier opinion of Mrs. Temple took place next day during the breakfast stop at Cornhill. Boswell's Notes for the day and a periphrastic retrospect by Temple written at Gainslaw in June suggest that the three became involved in a more and more animated discussion about principles of government, feudalism, aristocratic privilege, and "subordination". Boswell apparently undertook to defend his usual allegiances in a style which he imagined Samuel Johnson might have used with the egalitarian Mrs. Macaulay in London. "I was rough to Mrs. Temple about her children being clerks, stewards to noblemen, etc. I was wrong." Temple replied: "You certainly were indelicate. . . . You should not . . . have been so severe and rough with your friend. The tears she shed were bitter ones. She says she forgives you, but I fear I cannot persuade her to pay you a visit." Boswell arrived home from his trip late at night on 15 May—"very ill with a cold. Could not speak to be rightly heard." During his absence his wife had sublet Hume's apartment where they had been living and had moved downstairs into a "large new house"—"very handsome and spacious rooms"—in the same building. (This was level with the ground on the side fronting the Lawnmarket, but four flats up on the steep north side.) Boswell wrote soon to Temple, two letters before he was answered—offering his apologies for the "tears at Cornhill."

Temple came on to Edinburgh—alone—and stayed eight days. ("Friday 9 [July]. Tea at D. Hume's with Mr. Temple.") Other visitors during the summer were Edward Dilly (in town about six weeks), Pringle (at least a month), Percy, and the Jacobite partisan Andrew Lumisden, who had been so kind to Boswell in Rome—now pardoned and back in Scotland after an exile of more than twenty-five years. In *The London Magazine* during this spring and summer Boswell was demonstrating his powers as a reporter in a series of "Debates in the General Assembly of the Church of Scotland." On St. John Baptist's Day (24 June) he was elected Master of Canongate Kilwinning Lodge. The honour was to be conferred on him again in 1774 and 1775. The summer was a busy one, with many cases before the General Assembly and the Court of Session. In July, before the Court of Session, he won his highly important cause concerning literary property, his friend and client Alexander Donaldson's pioneer fight against the London booksellers for the right to publish freely books not protected by the express terms of the Copyright Act, and hence in effect for the right to publish cheap reprints of the English classics.

During this summer Boswell was also engaged for the defence, concurrently, in two conspicuous criminal trials. In one of these his client was a pathetic victim of circumstance and apparently suffered a considerable injustice; in the other, a pair of clients got what they deserved. Thomas Gray, a poor Chelsea Pensioner who lived in the village of Fisherrow, had a quarrel one night in January of this year with his wife, and as a result was beset by a mob of young persons teasing and baiting him; these went so far as to climb on his roof, break a hole in it, and throw in sticks and stones. In a sudden frenzy he ran out and stabbed a man who was passing (his best friend, as it happened) and killed him. Gray was brought to trial on 26 July, and Boswell, opposing Solicitor-General Henry Dundas, argued at length and eloquently that his client was of "weak intellects", that he had been under the influence of liquor and had been emotionally upset to the point of not being able to judge between right and wrong, that the stabbing of his friend could hardly have been premeditated. The jury "with one voice" brought in a verdict of guilty. Boswell and Crosbie, on the tardy plea that Gray was now actually insane, had the minor consolation of getting the pronouncement of sentence delayed until the autumn. Search in the Register House has not yet revealed his fate, but has unearthed a grim memento: the actual knife which did the deed, tied up in the bundle of papers forming the process.

On 9 August, Boswell briefly records witnessing the conclusion of a trial in which he must have taken a specially keen technical interest. Callum McGregor, charged with having committed a murder in Abergairn twenty-six years earlier, was acquitted on a plea of "prescription"—that is, in virtue of the length of time elapsed between the crime alleged and the trial. Lord Auchinleck spoke in approval of the plea. The case seems to have set a precedent in Scots jurisprudence for more than a century—being cited, though without success, as late as 1934.

In the other trial where Boswell himself was engaged—it ended on 11 and 12 August in a session lasting through the night to four in the morning—Boswell and Crosbie and Henry Erskine, opposing the Lord Advocate and the Solicitor-General, defended two tinkers who, in company with three girls, had called one night at the lonely hut of a rag-gatherer on the Carnwath moorland to inquire their way, had found him defenceless with his wife and daughter, had knocked him down, inflicting an injury from which he died, and had plundered the place before leaving. John Brown and James Wilson were a pair of sturdy young ruffians: one night in June before the trial began they broke out of "cage" and stocks in the Tolbooth, cut through a floor, and reached the roof—on which they were then recaptured. Boswell and his colleagues can scarcely have conducted this trial with very high hopes. After a month on bread and water in the Tolbooth, Brown and Wilson were hanged on 15 September in the Grassmarket.

But by that time Boswell was many miles away, in the Isle of Skye, happy in the realisation of a long-cherished dream.

For about ten years, or ever since their early acquaintance in London during the spring and summer of 1763, Boswell had entertained and had been encouraged in a plan of getting Samuel Johnson to Scotland, and to the Hebrides. In London during the past spring he had industriously thickened the plot. Letters to the historian Robertson, to the moralist Beattie, to the elegant amateur of letters Lord Elibank, put them up to writing back in terms that could be read to Johnson as further encouragements to the adventure. "Express yourself . . . so . . . as to operate strongly upon him." "Write to me . . . that I may read it to the mighty sage." "Send me an epistle full of insensible attraction for Mr. Johnson." From Edinburgh at the end of May he wrote back to Johnson, urging him to "persevere in his resolution." "Let me know," replied Johnson, "the exact time when your courts intermit." "I am in high spirits at present," wrote Boswell to General Oglethorpe on 14 August. "Mr. Johnson is actually come as far north as Newcastle, and I expect him here this evening." "I am in very high spirits at present," he repeated to Langton in another letter written on the same day. "Mr. Johnson is actually come as far north as Newcastle; and I expect to have him under my roof this night."

Johnson got out of his post-chaise at Boyd's Inn in the Canongate on the evening of Saturday 14 August, three days after the rising of the Court of Session. ("Mr. Johnson sends his compliments to Mr. Boswell, being just arrived at Boyd's.") He stayed three days at Boswell's house in James's Court, receiving the homage of the "great, the learned, and the elegant" at breakfasts, dinners, teas, and suppers. (Mrs. Boswell "had tea ready for him" on his arrival and "insisted that, to show all respect to the sage, she would give up her own bedchamber to him and take a worse.")

On Wednesday 18 August, Boswell and Johnson, accompanied by Boswell's Bohemian servant, Joseph Ritter, set out. They travelled by post-chaise for twelve days, up the east coast of Scotland, by St. Andrews and Aberdeen, and then along the north coast to Inverness, and thence by horseback ("equitation") to Glenelg and by boat to the Isle of Skye. For seven weeks of September and October they moved about through the inner Hebrides—by horse, by "little" horse or island "sheltie", and by foot in the roughest places, by long-boat and oars, by small sail-boat, by a "vessel of twelve tons" and by another apparently somewhat larger. They stayed on Skye, on Raasay, on Coll, on Mull, Ulva, Inchkenneth, and Iona. On 22 October they reached the mainland once more at Oban in Argyllshire and were a few days later once more "in a country of bridles and saddles" and then of "post-chaises". Almost everywhere it rained (all but one and a half days of a solid month), and they were kept indoors, or at least prevented from travelling forward, during long periods when they had to impose on the patience of their island hosts. They had gone to the Hebrides in search of something primitive—in order to "contemplate a system of life almost totally different . . . to find simplicity and wildness, and all the circumstances of remote time or place." They had found some wildness, some rudeness and squalor, and they had been accordingly disgusted and depressed. At times they had yearned to be home. Boswell had often worried about the long separation from his wife. On the other hand, they had found moments, even extended spells, of "civilisation" and elegance, and almost always a warm-hearted, open-handed and touching feudal hospitality. They had talked and eaten their way through the country-side (Boswell had also danced, sung, and drunk), entertained and attended on all sides by lairds and their ladies, by their families, tenants, factors, and retainers, by innkeepers, by the clergy, by doctors and soldiers. On the mainland they were received by the military governors of two forts. Intervals of notable felicity were the four days spent early in the tour with John MacLeod and his family of ten lively daughters and three sons on the island of Raasay and the week spent at the castle of Dunvegan, the seat of MacLeod of MacLeod, in Skye. A notable instance of displeasure came with their first landing on Skye and their uncouth and parsimonious entertainment by Boswell's friend Sir Alexander Macdonald and his beautiful but "insipid" lady, Boswell's "cousin". (Boswell's record of this incident, even when severely pruned for publication in 1785, was so offensive that it came close to causing a duel.) A notable instance of humble and rough hospitality and of prolonged imprisonment by bad weather, endured with honour on both sides, was the nine days spent after being driven by a tempest to the outlying island of Coll. The most deliberate rendezvous with romance was the night spent in Skye at the farm of Kingsburgh, where the mistress was Flora Macdonald, the heroine who had sheltered Prince Charles after the '45. ("Each bed had tartan curtains, and Mr. Johnson's was the very bed in which the Prince lay.")

The moment of greatest solemnity—carefully worked up to, though at the end almost missed through loss of time and failure of nerve—came when after a forty-mile trip by long-boat along the shore of Mull and an overnight encampment in a barn on Iona, they stepped out at morning among the ruins of the cathedral and monastery, the sepulchre of many ancient Irish, Scottish, and Scandinavian kings. ("We were now treading that illustrious island which was once the luminary of the Caledonian regions, whence savage clans and roving barbarians derived the benefits of knowledge and the blessings of religion.")

On the mainland, the last important stop was for six days at Auchinleck, where Boswell's "honoured father" and his "respected friend" only momentarily forgot themselves and "came in collision", staging a contest of "intellectual gladiators" which Boswell, in his public account of the affair, decided would be unbecoming in him to "exhibit . . . for the entertainment of the public".[1]

At Inverness, on the way out, Boswell had written to Garrick. It was an elaborate literary letter, rich with allusions to *Macbeth*: to Forres (where they had passed a night), to the heath, the witches, the castle. At Inveraray, on the way back, tasting once more the luxuries of civilised life, he had found "one of the most elegant" of such luxuries in Garrick's reply, "a pineapple of the finest flavour". At the beginning of the adventure Boswell had taken advantage of the surge of good feeling generated by Johnson's presence in Edinburgh to renew

[1] He put some of the repartee into his copy for the printer, however, and did not strike it out till the stage of proofs. See the forthcoming edition of the *Hebrides* in this series.

friendly relations with Lord Hailes. At Auchinleck he now assumed the office of peacemaker in a letter to Langton, informing him that Mr. Johnson seemed to "imagine" that the rough work of last spring had been taken too seriously. "It seems you left London without calling for him."

The travellers arrived in Edinburgh on 9 November, having been absent for eighty-three days of the most "vigorous exertion". "For five weeks together, of the tempestuous season," nobody at home had received any word of them. Boswell almost immediately had to take up his work during the mornings before the Court of Session. But Johnson stayed on for ten days more of breakfasts, dinners, teas, and suppers, receiving the homage of the Edinburgh literati. "On the mornings when he breakfasted at my house, he had from ten o'clock till one or two a constant levée of various persons. . . . My wife was so good as to devote the greater part of the morning to the endless task of pouring out tea for my friend and his visitors."

During almost the entire journey Boswell had kept writing up his Journal, showing it in instalments to Johnson, who was highly pleased. Boswell now had two large notebooks and a smaller one and some sheets of loose paper all filled with the narrative. This was the record which after Johnson's death Boswell would with the help of Edmond Malone trim more or less discreetly as the first instalment of his biography of Johnson, *The Journal of a Tour to the Hebrides*, 1785.

On 20 and 21 November Boswell accompanied Johnson as far south as Blackshiels, fourteen miles on the road to London, and saw him into the fly for London on the next morning. "I came home last night," wrote back Johnson on 27 November, "without any incommodity, danger, or weariness. . . . I know Mrs. Boswell wished me well to go." "In this," wrote Boswell much later in a note to the *Life of Johnson*, "he showed a very acute penetration. My wife paid him the most assiduous and respectful attention while he was our guest; so that I wonder how he discovered her wishing for his departure. The truth is that his irregular hours and uncouth habits, such as turning the candles with their heads downwards when they did not burn bright enough, and letting the wax drop upon the carpet, could not but be disagreeable to a lady. . . . And what was very natural to a female mind, she thought he had too much influence over her husband."

Before their descent upon Auchinleck in October, Boswell had elicited from Johnson a promise to avoid talking with Lord Auchinleck on three topics: "Whiggism, Presbyterianism, and—Sir John Pringle." From the point of view of Boswell's domestic life, the best tail-piece to the Hebrides episode is perhaps a sportive letter of the following Christmas season from Sir John Pringle to his sweetheart in the Boswell household, Jeanie Campbell.

My DEAR JEANIE,—As there is some difference between your uncle and me in point of ceremony, whether he ought to write me first or I to him, till that be settled you will forgive me for giving you this trouble, to tell him that I congratulate his safe, though I cannot say speedy, return from his western expedition. Indeed he was so long away that I began to apprehend that instead of his having conducted his companion to the Isle of Skye, the Doctor had carried him to the island of Utopia or that other of Prince Rasselas—I have forgot the name of it, but you will help me out, as I dare to say you are now well acquainted with it and all Dr. Johnson's geography. . . .

I have been (you must know) very jealous of Dr. Johnson, lest he should have gained your affections and made you forget others who had a prior right. His genteel manner and polite conversation made me very anxious about the impression that might be made upon a heart so young and tender as yours, and especially in absence of one of so opposite a character. If so matters be as I suspect and that the Doctor is now the happy man, all I beg is that you would at least continue my friend and speak betimes a good word for me with Veronica. . . . Adieu, my good girl, and learn fast the London manners, whether to please Dr. Johnson or me.

[Unsigned]

In the following June, beginning once more a daily record of his life with the opening of the summer session at Edinburgh, Boswell looked back and recollected:

Review of My Life for Some Time Previous to This Period

After Mr. Samuel Johnson left me, which was on Monday the 22 of November, when we parted at Blackshiels, I was long in a state of languor. My mind had been kept upon its utmost stretch in his company. I had exhausted all my powers to entertain him. While he was with me, his noble exuberance of genius excited my spirits to a high degree, so that I did not feel at the time how much I was weakened. I was like a man who drinks hard and is kept in high glee by what is wasting his constitution, but perceives its enfeebling effects as soon as he lives without it. I was not, however, in a state of despondency. I waited patiently till my force should be restored. From the confusion of credit and scarcity of money, there was less business done in the Court of Session, Winter Session 1773–1774, than almost ever was known. I had not near so much practice as in former winters, which happened well for my indolent and listless state. I wrote few papers, and never was up any one morning before eight. Yet there was no great deficiency in the amount of my fees. I got one hundred and fifty guineas. I was engaged in several criminal trials: that of Cant and Muir for wilful fire-raising, in which a number of lawyers appeared, all gratis except Mr. Lockhart,[1] who spoke with as much spirit as ever upon the relevancy. I did not speak at all. Informations were ordered. But the matter was compromised, and they were banished. I charged the jury in three other trials: those of Margaret and Agnes Adams[2] for murder (I charged for Margaret); James Brown for . . .

There Boswell breaks off. Surely one of the causes operating to produce his slump of spirits during the winter of 1773–4 must have been the unusually crowded procession of his unhappy criminal clients. A comic poem by his witty fellow advocate Henry Erskine, *Patrick O'Connor's Advice to Henry McGraugh*, shows that by the summer of 1774 his reputation for quixotic and unprofitable defences was hardly less than Crosbie's. McGraugh was a destitute Irishman who had been

[1] See below, p. 229 *n.* 7.

[2] That is, Margaret Adam and Agnes Adam. Scots usage assigns plurals to proper names.

sentenced to public whipping because he had gone into taverns and ordered meals which he could not pay for. At the very time when Boswell was making his great effort for the sheep-stealer John Reid, he looked McGraugh up in the Tolbooth and wrote a bill of suspension that saved him from his ignominious sentence. "Patrick O'Connor's advice" to McGraugh was that he become a bailie.

> Then each day you may guzzle, at the city's expense,
> Without Crosbie or Boswell to plead your defence.[1]

The experiences which had established this reputation were, however, far from comic. On 24 January of this year Boswell appeared in court, against the Solicitor-General, Henry Dundas, in defence of two girls, Margaret Adam, aged twenty-two, and her sister Agnes, not yet sixteen. They were charged with the robbery and murder of a woman who kept a huckstery shop in Glasgow. If we may suppose a degree of truth in the last statement of Margaret, some sort of drunken party and brawl had occurred inside the shop when the girls retreated there from the attentions of "some worthless fellows of their acquaintance". The fellows made a noise at the door. Mrs. McIntyre "would have" the girls go away. "She threw a glass of spirits upon them. . . . Margaret . . . gave her a sudden thrust away from her. . . . In her fall her hind head struck against a stone wall, and she never stirred." Boswell spoke at length and eloquently, moving a separate trial for Agnes (so that her sister could appear as a witness in her defence), and he charged the jury for Margaret. Next day the girls were sentenced to be hanged in the Grassmarket and their bodies to be given to Dr. Alexander Monro, Professor of Anatomy in the University, for dissection. Agnes got a reprieve during the King's pleasure. Boswell's Journal for 2 March has the brief entry: "At M.A.'s execution."

Again, on 7 and 8 February, Boswell was in court addressing the jury for a Glasgow carter, James Brown, accused of horse-stealing. Despite a petition by the defence for a sentence only of banishment, "on account of several alleviating circumstances . . . such as his

[1] Erskine's poem is collected in James Maidment's *The Court of Session Garland*, 1839.

having an aged mother to support, with a wife and five children", the Solicitor-General won from the jury a unanimous verdict of guilty. They recommended mercy, however, and after being sentenced to be hanged in the Grassmarket, Brown received a pardon on condition of transporting himself.

And once more, on 14 March, Boswell was in the Justiciary Court, this time representing five clients, in two separate trials relating to two different forms of the crime of arson ("fire-raising"). John Andrews, William Wilson, and William Love were accused of breaking into, burgling, and attempting to set fire to a warehouse at Paisley. In a trial that lasted through the day until three o'clock the next morning, Boswell and Crosbie and two associates, by impugning the reliability of two key witnesses, won a perhaps hardly expected victory in a unanimous verdict of "not proven". On the very same day was concluded another trial in which Boswell had participated, though without speaking, during the past December. A pair of wrights, Thomas Muir and James Cant, were tried on an indictment at the instance of the Sun Fire Office of London for setting fire to their own property in Leith Walk. Boswell's "Review" of his life for these months, which we have already quoted, records the result: ". . . the matter was compromised, and they were banished."

Boswell's slump in spirits during the winter of 1773–1774—his first serious fit of depression since his marriage and a decidedly ominous experience—was not something which he tried to conceal from his friends. "Your writing law papers and pleading causes with such attention," wrote Temple, "does not seem very consistent with the languor and indolence of which you complain." "An interruption of business and some degree of disappointment has given a faint idea of that state of melancholy and despondency under which I almost continually suffer. . . . I suppose you'll plead your *little practice* as an excuse for not seeing Mamhead." (Temple's own troubles continued, of course, unabated. His special effort had recently been *An Essay Concerning the Clergy*, in eleven chapters. This inevitably had to be submitted to Mr. Hume. And Mr. Hume inevitably did not care much for it and sent back through Boswell his definition of a clergyman—echoed in Temple's letter to Boswell: "*A person appropriated to teach hypocrisy and inculcate vice.* How ungenerous, how unhandsome!")

Among the sources of uneasiness and despondency for Boswell that winter, the old domestic ones persisted strongly enough. Pringle wrote in February to admonish him:

"I was sorry to find that you should so obstinately continue Goth and Vandal with regard to your feudal system. I was in hopes that more reflection, your attachment to English manners, and parental affection would have by this time conquered those prejudices which none should preserve but a Parliament House agent.[1] How will it sound a hundred years hence in the annals of these times 'that J.B. of A. after making his tour through Europe, being the friend of Paoli and of Johnson and a member of the wits' club at the Turk's Head, should have left his estate to the son of a dancing-master of his own name, in preference to his own daughter, a dutiful child, married to a gentleman of character and the mother of a fine family of children, and of that number, three boys of the greatest hopes.' "[2]

And Boswell's other most faithful critic:

"Nothing but your own conduct can prevent your succession to the estate and influence of your family. But was ever anything so imprudent, so disrespectful, as to engage your interest without your father's approbation? . . . I am sorry Lord Auchinleck should talk with such contempt of Mr. Johnson. . . .

"Your unhappy brother John! O Boswell, how fatal those sort of reflections are to the veneration and love we owe the Parent of Nature! Disease, folly, melancholy entailed on families!"

[1] A Parliament House agent was what Boswell would have called a writer, and the English a solicitor: a lawyer not admitted to the bar who manages law cases and draws wills, deeds, entails, and the like (see above, p. 6 *n.*). Pringle seems to intimate that lawyers of that sort would be in favour of feudal prejudices because they make more complicated settlements and hence more work for lawyers. An *advocate* should be more liberal.

[2] See above, pp. 53 *n.* 2, 61 *n.* 4.

The single phrase of Temple's letter referring to Boswell's engaging his interest without his father's approbation is our only clue to an early stage in one of Boswell's most bitter experiences of this period. The right to vote for a Member of Parliament to represent a Scots county was in the eighteenth century severely restricted: a voter must hold land of the King and that land must further meet certain requirements (sometimes complicated and technical) as to assessed value. In the General Election of 1768, by pooling their "interest" (the votes of the friends, dependants, and acquaintances whom they could persuade or could control by patronage) two large landholders of the County of Ayr, the Earls of Loudoun and Cassillis, had secured the election as M.P. of Lord Cassillis's younger brother, that "joker" David Kennedy whom Boswell in the spring of 1773 had declared "totally incapable of the business of legislation".[1] In the General Election of 1774, the same coalition, now strengthened by the adherence of the Earl of Eglinton, proposed to re-elect Kennedy. But a group of landed gentlemen of the County, restive, as they said, at having the representation dictated by a coalition of peers and certainly restive against the coalition in power, banded together with the Earls of Glencairn and Dumfries in opposition and put up as their candidate that Sir Adam Fergusson of Kilkerran, whom we have seen Boswell introduce to Johnson in March 1772. ("Sir, I perceive you are a vile Whig.")[2] They also set themselves vigorously not merely to the reviving of dormant votes, but also to the creation of votes of a kind that Lord Auchinleck had taught Boswell to abhor as "nominal and fictitious."[3]

Though Boswell himself did not possess the qualifications of a voter in Ayrshire, he threw himself into this struggle with characteristic energy. As would have been expected, he put allegiance to feudal principle before candidate and came out on the side of the "old interest", the "noble association". He had previously expressed even extravagant admiration for Sir Adam Fergusson, but was now deeply offended with him because Fergusson thought himself not bound to

[1] Above, p. 168.

[2] Above, p. 91.

[3] See below, p. 269 *n*. 3.

pay a Corsican subscription for which Boswell and Crosbie had advanced the money. Boswell also held the "independent gentlemen" in disapprobation because of their aggressive policy of making votes. Lord Auchinleck had not engaged in politics for many years. Boswell probably assumed—most rashly—that his father would allow him to organise the Auchinleck "interest" and deliver it to the "noble association". And then came the grievous affront. Lord Auchinleck, surely not unhappy at a chance to slap down a young laird who was showing too great independence, yielded to the solicitations of the Lord President of the Court of Session, Robert Dundas, and not only promised his interest to Fergusson, but even made for him a number of the "faggot votes" which he had previously inveighed against. Thus, to use Boswell's passionate and deeply partisan language, the house of Auchinleck had joined in an odious combination by which the interest of "the old families in the County" was to be "defeated by an upstart," "the great-grandson of a messenger." (His gibe at Sir Adam's ancestry has never been substantiated. The Fergussons of Kilkerran, by all accounts, were an older family than his own.) But remarks uttered in the heat of politics are not made upon oath. He was deeply hurt both by this threat to the "old interest in elections" and by the frustration of his own hopes of playing a political role in the county. His father had thwarted, had "crossed" him, had rendered him insignificant in his "own county"—in short, had reduced Boswell to a "cipher". On 6 August of the coming summer he would firmly refuse an invitation to dine with the Lord President at Lord Auchinleck's house. This unhappy relation with his father was no doubt further aggravated during this winter by the fact that notions about a London career were now steadily enlarging in Boswell's mind. Thus Pringle:

"I still find you set upon fixing here. Possibly it may answer, but the hazard I should think would be too great for a man with a wife and a growing family of children. The person you quote for favouring the scheme has certainly wit,[1] but it is wisdom that is wanted in a coun-

[1] See above, p. 84, Boswell's encouragement from a solicitor named Urquhart and possibly from Johnson. Pringle, who thinks of the Club at the Turk's Head as "the wits' club" (see above, p. 210) may now be referring to Johnson.

sellor on this occasion. I shall keep your secret, and I would advise you to tell it to as few as possible, because if people get a notion that you are so unsettled, they will become shy of employing one whose head, they will imagine, is turned upon other subjects. But of all things obtain your father's consent, for possibly he may have reasons for going into the scheme, and if so, you will have the world on your side in going, and a good apology for you if you should go and fail."

In the background, then, appear Boswell's ultimate plans for attaining the metropolis. More immediately, the question whether he could persuade himself that he ought to indulge in his annual spring jaunt. Before Christmas he seems to have thought he might well make it. In February, Johnson concluded a letter: "Let me know . . . how fees come in and when we are to see you." But there were serious obstacles, among them the fact that Mrs. Boswell was once more in an advanced stage of pregnancy. On 5 March, Boswell tried to balance his reasons in a letter to Johnson. "I wrote to him," he says in the *Life*, "requesting his counsel whether I should this spring come to London. I stated to him on the one hand some pecuniary embarrassments which, together with my wife's situation at that time, made me hesitate; and on the other the pleasure and improvement which my annual visit to the metropolis always afforded me; and particularly mentioned a peculiar satisfaction which I experienced in celebrating the festival of Easter in St. Paul's Cathedral; that to my fancy it appeared like going up to Jerusalem at the feast of the Passover, and that the strong devotion which I felt on that occasion diffused its influence on my mind through the rest of the year."

The appeal was well enough calculated to elicit from Johnson some word of sanction that would incline the hesitating conscience in the desired direction. But Johnson's answer was the death-knell of the year's hopes.

"I think there is no great difficulty in resolving your doubts. The reasons for which you are inclined to visit London are, I think, not of sufficient strength to answer the objections. That you should delight to come once a year to the fountain of intelligence and pleasure is very natural; but both information and pleasure must be regulated by propriety. Pleasure which cannot be obtained but by unseasonable or unsuitable expense must always end in pain; and pleasure which must be enjoyed at the expense of another's pain can never be such as a worthy mind can fully delight in.

"What improvement you might gain by coming to London you may easily supply, or easily compensate, by enjoining yourself some particular study at home or opening some new avenue to information. Edinburgh is not yet exhausted; and I am sure you will find no pleasure here which can deserve either that you should anticipate any part of your future fortune, or that you should condemn yourself and your lady to penurious frugality for the rest of the year.

"I need not tell you what regard you owe to Mrs. Boswell's entreaties; or how much you ought to study the happiness of her who studies yours with so much diligence, and of whose kindness you enjoy such good effects. Life cannot subsist in society but by reciprocal concessions. She permitted you to ramble last year, you must permit her now to keep you at home.

"Your last reason is so serious that I am unwilling to oppose it. Yet you must remember that your image of worshipping once a year in a certain place in imitation of the Jews is but a comparison, and *simile non est idem*.[1] If the annual resort to Jerusalem was a duty to the Jews, it was a duty because it was commanded; and you have no such command, therefore no such duty."

Among Boswell's consolations this winter, a chief one was the decision in the House of Lords concerning the question of literary property. After his victory for Alexander Donaldson the previous July in the Court of Session, Boswell had shown Johnson his notes on the case—eliciting of course only a very limited appreciation from this sturdy champion of the London booksellers. Towards the end of December, however, Boswell began to get these notes in shape, and, about the end of January, Donaldson brought out in both Edinburgh and London *The Decision of the Court of Session upon the Question of Literary Property . . . Published by James Boswell, Esq., Advocate, One of*

[1] "Things may be like without being the same."

the Counsel in the Cause. In 1769 Donaldson had had judgment passed against him regarding literary property in the Court of King's Bench in London and was now appealing that decision to the House of Lords. It was important that Boswell's pamphlet, containing the opinions delivered by the Scots judges, should be out in time to be read before Donaldson's appeal came on (4 February). On 26 February Boswell learned the "great news" that Donaldson had won without a division and went at once to drink "tea with Lord Monboddo to triumph over him," Monboddo being the only member of the Court of Session who had voted against his client in the Edinburgh trial. Donaldson v. Becket[1] is still the basis of all English and American copyright acts.

The year was punctuated by letters to Boswell from island lairds and antiquaries (Maclean, Lochbuie, Macqueen, Kingsburgh) asking help or offering information. And Boswell carried on a brisk exchange of short notes with Johnson and the Thrales. He plied Johnson with information, reminders, and promptings; he sent him his "box" of collected curiosities. Even before reaching the Hebrides (on the mainland, sitting on a green bank in Glen Clunie), Johnson had begun to think that he might turn his memories (and perhaps his long letters to Mrs. Thrale) into *A Journey to the Western Islands of Scotland*. By January he was "seriously engaged" in exploiting this opportunity. "You must make haste and gather me all you can, and do it quickly, or I will and shall do without it." In May, Boswell found himself in the position of double "negotiator" between Johnson and Lord Hailes—on the one hand asking Hailes about the meaning of a Highland institution of cattle dowry, and on the other sending on for Johnson's criticism some specimens of Hailes's work in progress, *Annals of Scotland from the Accession of Malcolm III, Surnamed Canmore, to the Accession of Robert I.* On 21 June, Johnson had sent to the press the first sheets of the *Western Islands*, committing to print in the first paragraph a passage which it would give Boswell much pleasure to discover.[2]

On 9 April, Boswell received the shocking news that, five days before, Goldsmith had died. He had been carried off, in his early forties,

[1] One of Boswell's co-partners in *The London Magazine*: see above, p. 104. He was not the pursuer in the Edinburgh trial.

[2] See below, p. 226.

apparently by a kidney infection, his resistance, as Johnson believed, having been weakened by worries induced through his habitual improvidence. During the autumn of the previous year letters between Boswell and General Oglethorpe had lamented the failure of a kind of plot to get Goldsmith, "the Unfortunate Knight of Parnassus", to Cranham Hall at the right moment for bringing about a marital alliance with a certain wealthy "nymph"[1] and thus rescuing him from his financial distresses. The first effect on Boswell of learning about Goldsmith's death was a suddenly awakened sense of distance from other, still living, members of the Club, a feeling of opportunity neglected, of guilt in letting his correspondence go unattended to. On 10 April he wrote to Langton:

"The death of one friend endears to us still more those who survive. I got the news yesterday that we have lost Goldsmith. It has affected me much, and while I lament his departure and am warmly impressed with affection and regard to you who are one among the few whom I highly value, it gives me much pain to reflect that I have been so many months indebted to you for an excellent letter without acknowledging it. The same tenderness of disposition which makes me feel my being in the wrong to you with extraordinary sensibility makes me at the same time comfort myself with a kind sympathetic feeling that you will readily forgive me."

On the next day (11 April) Boswell thought of Garrick's letter which had reached him in the previous autumn at Inveraray, and now he answered that too: "That I have not thanked you for it long ere now is one of those strange facts for which it is so difficult to account that I shall not attempt it. . . . Dr. Goldsmith's death would affect all the Club much. I have not been so much affected with any event that has happened of a long time. I wish you would give me who am[2] at a distance and who cannot get to London this spring some particulars with regard to his last appearances." The most ambitious appreciation

[1] The Miss Lockwood mentioned above, p. 188.

[2] The original letter in the Hyde Collection and Lawrie's copy at Yale both read *are*.

of Goldsmith which Boswell received from any of his friends was written by Oglethorpe "immediately" after Goldsmith's death, though it was not posted until 15 June.

"Our Goldsmith is no more! I was with him Easter Sunday. He was then light-headed with a fever and died next day. When Johnson dined here with us, Mrs. Oglethorpe and the ladies joined Goldsmith in persuading Johnson to publish his delightful ramble to *Ultima Thule*. (Goldsmith was then in high health.) . . .

"I dined with Garrick and his Club about fourteen days before the catastrophe, when Goldsmith shined and by the command of the monarch of the stage pronounced excellent laughing epitaphs in rhyme on all of the Club. The members little thought then he should so soon want a serious one."

Garrick's now well-known account of the matter was that Goldsmith's epitaphs were written as a reply to one produced by himself extempore at an earlier gathering:

> Here lies Nolly Goldsmith, for shortness called Noll,
> Who wrote like an angel but talked like poor Poll.

For this Garrick had received at least as good as he gave.

> He threw off his friends like a huntsman his pack,
> For he knew when he would he could whistle them back.[1]

In *The London Magazine* for June, Boswell published a finely turned tribute to Goldsmith—a grace-note to public mourning—of a kind which he was uniquely well prepared both by his habits as collector and chronicler and by sympathetic temperament to execute.

[Boswell to the Editor of *The London Magazine*]

Sir,—I send you a small production of the late Dr. Goldsmith

[1] The epitaphs made up Goldsmith's unfinished anapaestic poem *Retaliation*. See below, p. 240.

which has never been published and which might perhaps have been totally lost had I not secured it. He intended it as a song in the character of Miss Hardcastle in his admirable comedy *She Stoops to Conquer*. But it was left out, as Mrs. Bulkley, who played the part, did not sing. He sung it himself in private companies very agreeably.[1] The tune is a pretty Irish air called *The Humours of Balamagairy*, to which, he told me, he found it very difficult to adapt words. But he has succeeded happily in these few lines. As I could sing the tune and was fond of them, he was so good as to give me them about a year ago just as I was leaving London and bidding him adieu for that season, little apprehending that it was a last farewell. I preserve this little relic in his own handwriting with an affectionate care. I am, Sir, your humble servant,

JAMES BOSWELL.

Song by Dr. Goldsmith

Ah me! when shall I marry me?
    Lovers are plenty but fail to relieve me.
He, fond youth, that could carry me,
    Offers to love but means to deceive me.

But I will rally and combat the ruiner;
    Not a look, not a smile shall my passion discover.
She that gives all to the false one pursuing her
    Makes but a penitent, loses a lover.

Boswell's second daughter, Euphemia, was born on 20 May. As the opening of the summer session on 14 June approached, he began but did not go far with the "Review of my Life for Some Time Previous to This Period" which we have already quoted. On the first day of the session he again resumed his fully written Journal.

[1] See above, p. 190.

453

Song by Dr Goldsmith
intended for Miss Hardcastle
in his Comedy She Stoops to conquer.
He gave me it in London Spring 1773.
It is in his own hand-writing.

Ah me when shall I marry me
Lovers are plenty but fail to relieve me
He fond youth that could carry me
Offers to love but means to deceive me

2

But I will rally and combat the ruiner
Not a look not a smile shall my passion discover
She that gives all to the false one pursuing her
Makes but a penitent loses a lover.

A SONG BY GOLDSMITH,
originally intended for inclusion in *She Stoops to Conquer;* with heading written by James Boswell. From the original in the Yale University Library

JOURNAL BEGINNING 14 JUNE

1774

TUESDAY 14 JUNE. I began to rise at seven. This day I got home another servant, James Dalrymple, a young man from Dumfriesshire who had been with Dr. Hunter at Moffat. He had a wife and two children in Edinburgh. Seemed to be clever and obliging. Between nine and ten called on my father, who had come from Auchinleck in one day and arrived late the night before. The Court of Session seemed to be crowded. I said, "There must be carrion in the wind when there's so many of us." The President was ill. Cosmo Gordon[1] affected much concern, and perhaps felt some. I neither felt nor affected any. "Cosmo," said I, "upon this subject you and I are Heraclitus and Democritus, the weeping and laughing philosophers." "And," said Maclaurin,[2] "I am the Stoic between you." I was in good sound hearty spirits, and found many of my brethren at the bar in the same humour. The Outer House is a scene of unbounded conversation and merriment. Everything is thrown out, and amongst such a quantity of stuff some good things cast up. I have marked some of this day in my *Boswelliana*.[3] I dined quietly at home. Nobody with us but Mrs. Montgomerie.[4] My father, Lady Auchinleck, and Dr. Young[5] drank tea. My father was pleased with Veronica, who applied to him for raisins which he had for her.

WEDNESDAY 15 JUNE. We dined at my father's. George

[1] Baron of Exchequer, 1777.

[2] He became a judge in the Court of Session as Lord Dreghorn in 1788. In 1776 he collaborated with Boswell and others in composing *The Justiciary Garland*, comic verses in "the Form of Trial before a Criminal Court."

[3] The discussion turned mainly on the absence of the President.

[4] Mrs. Boswell's widowed sister-in-law had arrived on 3 May.

[5] Professor of Midwifery at the University, Mrs. Boswell's obstetrician.

Frazer, George Webster, and Claud were there.[1] At five I was at the Solicitor's for my first consultation this session. I have at the beginning of several sessions felt a peculiar cast of ideas by which I could distinguish, in my own mind, one session from the rest. This came on quite simple. It was just the Summer Session 1774 without any other perceptible mark. I began to receive my fees this session, as I begin to eat my two eggs on any night, with a pure sameness. I called on Maclaurin as I returned and drank tea with him. I should have observed that as I was walking out to the Solicitor's with Taylor, Sandy Mackenzie's clerk—the consultation being on the cause, Ross of Auchnacloich against Mackenzie of Ardross—Taylor said we would not be the worse of the President's being present; that both he and Gardenstone were good friends to Ardross.[2] I said there was now very little to be expected on the Bench from private regard. It is true. For in the first place, the nation is more civilised and judges have better notions of justice. But, secondly, there is actually not such strong friendships or family attachments[3] as were long ago. I do not blame our judges of the last age so much as many people do, because at that time there were many of them plain country gentlemen, not lawyers at all, and because the warmth of their hearts gave them a considerable imperceptible bias to one side. And it must be owned that of the many causes that come before the Court of Session there is a good proportion such as the judges will differ upon merely in cool opinion. No wonder then that regard casts the balance without their knowing it. Maclaurin and I sat an hour very socially. I had a consultation on Earl Fife's politics[4] at eight, and the session opened well.

[1] George Frazer was an excise officer; George Webster (the son of Dr. Alexander Webster; see below, p. 223 *n.* 3) was a cousin of Boswell's.

[2] This case was a phase in a long series of suits concerning the reversion of some mortgaged lands of the Ross estate of Tollie. Boswell had been engaged in the case at least since the previous summer. Francis Garden, Lord Gardenstone, was a Lord of Session.

[3] Scots grammar in the present tense of the verb employs a form that looks like the third person singular for all three persons and both numbers unless the subject is a personal pronoun immediately preceding. Boswell rarely uses this construction; Mrs. Boswell, frequently.

[4] "Evening, consulted Lord Fife's politics. My getting into them was a great

THURSDAY 16 JUNE. After the House rose, I walked half round the Meadow with Lord Monboddo. He talked to me of the severe stroke of his son's death.[1] But I saw he bore it with philosophical composure. His conversation was manly; and, while he discussed his favourite subject of language, I felt my own inferiority to him in knowledge and precision of ideas. But we are so formed that almost every man is superior, or thinks himself superior, to any other man in something; and, fixing his view upon that, he is in good temper with himself. I was busy with session papers till near nine o'clock, when the Hon. Sandy Gordon[2] called on me to go and walk. I was sitting with my escritoire open. He saw the word *Milton*, which began a copy of verses, and his curiosity was attracted. I indulged his curiosity and my own vanity by reading a good deal to him both of my *Boswelliana* and my "Ten Lines".[3]

---

prize in the lottery of business. I was suggested by James Hay, my friend Charles's brother" (Journal Notes, 10 December 1772). James Duff, Earl Fife, was struggling with the Duke of Gordon for control of the counties of Banff and Elgin. Both sides were "making" as many votes as they could, while contesting those made by the other. Henry Dundas was among the lawyers of the opposition.

[1] Arthur Burnett, whom Johnson had examined in Latin at Monboddo, on the way to the Hebrides, died at Edinburgh on 27 April of this year at the age of eleven. He was Lord Monboddo's only son.

[2] He was a younger son of the Earl of Aberdeen and about three years older than Boswell; he became Sheriff-Depute of Kirkcudbrightshire in 1764, and a judge in the Court of Session as Lord Rockville in 1784.

[3] On 1 May 1774, Boswell, after an interval of nine years, had resumed his old exercise in self-discipline; he kept it up until 14 July. The lines on Milton were his task for 15 June. The lines for 30 May may be cited as a better specimen, both as verse and as biography:

Extremely wretched sure all men must think
A virtuous man who is inclined to drink;
Who feels an inward suction in his breast,
A raging vortex which is ne'er at rest.
Such is my woeful state; for I require
No jovial fellows to excite the fire.
It burns spontaneous in my vital parts,
And to my throat the keenest thirst imparts.
Mere love of liquor, and not social glee,
To drunken meetings leads unhappy me.

Nairne[1] called, and Gordon and he and I walked round the Meadow. We met Macqueen walking, which I said was an emblem of idleness, as grass growing at the Cross of Edinburgh was an emblem of desolation.[2] Gordon came home with me and took a little supper and some port negus.

FRIDAY 17 JUNE. Lady Preston and Miss Preston—Sir George[3] being somewhere else—dined with us; as did the Reverend Mr. William Macqueen, minister of Snizort in the Isle of Skye and brother to Mr. Donald Macqueen, who was so obliging to Mr. Johnson and me.[4] I was happy in being civil to him. In the evening I went to Mr. Stewart Moncrieffe's.[5] I played at sixpenny brag, and found I was as keen as ever. Luckily I lost only eight shillings. I was in excellent spirits for that kind of club.

SATURDAY 18 JUNE. I walked out to Prestonfield,[6] and was in the same social pleasant humour that I always am there. There was nobody there but the eldest Miss Keith[7] and Mr. Andrew Bennet, nephew to the minister. After dinner Sir Alexander and he and I and Mr. Sharp, the tutor, had a stout match at the bowls. Miss Keith and I had a dispute as to the preference of sons over daughters. She said, "I would not prefer sons as sons to daughters as daughters, as neither of

[1] William Nairne, John Maclaurin, and Andrew Crosbie were in the long run Boswell's closest associates in the Faculty of Advocates. At the start of the tour to the Hebrides, Nairne had accompanied Boswell and Johnson as far as St. Andrews. In 1786 he rose to the Bench as Lord Dunsinnan.

[2] Robert Macqueen, who next to Alexander Lockhart enjoyed the greatest practice at the Scots bar, rose to the Bench as Lord Braxfield in 1776; in 1780 he succeeded Lord Auchinleck as Lord Justiciary and in 1788 became Lord Justice-Clerk in place of Sir Thomas Miller. He served in some degree as model for Stevenson's Lord Hermiston in *Weir of Hermiston*.

[3] Baronet of Valleyfield. His wife was Boswell's mother's aunt. Sir George and Lady Preston supplied to a considerable extent the warmth of parental affection which Lord Auchinleck could not give.

[4] Clergyman and antiquarian, defender of Macpherson's Ossian, he accompanied Boswell and Johnson for eighteen days on their tour on Raasay and Skye.

[5] This elderly and not distinguished advocate lived in the Horse Wynd and had a fancy garden at his estate of Moredun. He was noted as "a maker of great feasts".

[6] See above, p. 112 *n.* 1.

[7] Daughter of the retired Ambassador, Robert Keith.

them make themselves." I answered, "We prefer a man to a dow (dove), and yet neither of them make themselves." I had very near said a man to some other animal, I forget which. But the remark would have been rude; whereas by choosing so delicate and pretty a creature as a dove no offence could be taken; and the comparison was very just. Said I, "We do not give an estate to a dove."

SUNDAY 19 JUNE. I was at the New Church[1] both forenoon and afternoon. Dr. Blair[2] and Mr. Walker preached. I dined at my father's between sermons. In the evening I read several of Ogden's sermons to Mrs. Montgomerie. She and I supped at Dr. Webster's.[3] Nobody there but Lieut. Wellwood. George rather merry. Had the usual ideas of prayers there—looking to Heriot's Hospital,[4] Mary Cochrane's picture and all the associations.[5] Drank wine and water and came home calm.

MONDAY 20 JUNE. It was wet. I was at home all day writing law papers, except being at a consultation from four to six at Mr. Rae's on Earl Fife's politics, where we had a tedious reading of papers, which is really an irksome operation. I observed Rae[6] pretty sound asleep at one time; and I myself was once or twice in that drowsy

[1] "We next went to the great church of St. Giles, which has lost its original magnificence in the inside by being divided into four places of Presbyterian worship. . . . We entered that division which was formerly called the New Church and of late the High Church, so well known by the eloquence of Dr. Hugh Blair" (*Hebrides*, 16 August 1773).

[2] Professor of Rhetoric and Belles Lettres in the University of Edinburgh, and one of the most admired preachers in the Church of Scotland. Johnson liked his sermons and recommended their publication to Strahan.

[3] Dr. Alexander Webster, Boswell's uncle by marriage, was one of the best-known figures in Edinburgh, a five-bottle consumer of claret ("Dr. *Bonum Magnum*") and a leader of the fundamentalist party of the Church of Scotland. See below, pp. 243, 271.

[4] The hospital or school for fatherless boys founded in 1623 by the royal jeweller George Heriot. The seventeenth-century structure, now a famous day school, could be seen from the windows of Webster's house, on the Castle Hill.

[5] A family party. Lady Mary Cochrane was great-grandmother to Boswell, George Webster, and Lieut. Robert Wellwood (Sir George Preston's daughter's son).

[6] See above, p. 99 *n*. 3.

nodding state which is very disagreeable. How much attention a lawyer ought to give to the causes in which he is employed is not easy to say. But it is certain that when there are many lawyers employed in the same cause not one of them gives as much attention as he would do were he single. In the evening I received a long letter from General Oglethorpe.[1] It stirred my mind, revived my idea of my own consequence in London, and made me impatient to be there and not lost in this provincial corner where I find nothing to engage me warmly.

TUESDAY 21 JUNE. Still wet. Mrs. Montgomerie and I went in a chaise to Bob Chalmers's country-house on the seaside, near Musselburgh, to eat a fish dinner. My wife would not venture out, the day was so bad and she was but a month and a day brought to bed. I know not how it has happened that we have had no intercourse since our marriage with Bob Chalmers's family; though, before that, both of us used to visit and be well entertained there.[2] We had refused several invitations from them and never asked them again. These cessations of acquaintance will happen unaccountably. Mrs. Montgomerie's being with us renewed the intercourse, and it was this day renewed as to me very effectually; for I eat of nine kinds of fish and drank various drams and a great deal of port, and was really much intoxicated. Mr. Baron Mure,[3] his lady, and Miss Annie were there. With them, too, I have had no intercourse, though invited, and though he is so much connected with Lord Mountstuart, my *carus Mæcenas*, and is a friendly, sensible, agreeable man. However, things are put to rights at once by some happy occasion. I engaged him, his lady, and daughter to dine with us on Friday, and at the same time Mr. and Mrs. Chalmers; and I engaged that we should dine at the Baron's the week after. I was talkative and vociferous from the liquor which I had drank.

I supped at Sir George Preston's with my wife and Mrs. Montgomerie. Dr. Webster was there with his son Jamie, now Colonel Webster, just arrived from Ireland. I was by this time outrageously intoxicated and *would* drink a great deal of strong port negus, which

[1] See above, p. 217.

[2] Chalmers was a "writer" (solicitor).

[3] William Mure of Caldwell, Baron of Exchequer.

made me worse. After I got home, I was very ill; not sick, but like to suffocate—a dangerous state—and my valuable spouse was much alarmed.

WEDNESDAY 22 JUNE. I had a miserable headache and in pleading a short cause before Lord Elliock I felt myself incapable of any distinctness. I was vexed at my conduct.

THURSDAY 23 JUNE. Young Cowhill[1] and McGeorge of Cocklick, two of my clients, and Grange and Adam Bell[2] dined with me. I was in a tolerable frame.

FRIDAY 24 JUNE. Baron Mure, his lady and daughter, and Bob Chalmers dined with us. Sandy Gordon, who was engaged also to come but had sent an apology, came to us after dinner. We were cheerful and easy. Mrs. Chalmers was not well, so could not come. We did not drink much. The Baron and Mr. Chalmers and I drank tea calmly. I then went to St. John's Lodge, it being St. John the Baptist's Day, on which the election of officers is made. I was chosen Master for the second year. Dr. Cairnie[3] was there for the first time for, I believe, some years. I was but moderately in Mason humour; though I have associated ideas of solemnity and spirit and foreign parts and my brother David with St. John's Lodge, which makes it always pleasing to me. Such agreeable associations are formed, we know not how, by a kind of chance, as the foam of the horse was by the dashing down the painter's brush on the canvas. I suppose the picture might be easily washed off. But it would be losing a satisfaction which perhaps we cannot equal by design.

SATURDAY 25 JUNE. Mr. Samuel Johnson has often recommended to me to keep a Journal, of which he is so sensible of the utility that he has several times tried it, but never could persist. I have at different periods of my life persisted a good time, and I am now hopeful that I may continue longer than ever. I shall only put down hints of what I have thought, seen, or heard every day, that I may not have too much labour; and I shall from these, at certain periods, make

[1] Charles Maxwell of Cowhill.

[2] Like Grange, a writer.

[3] Dr. John Cairnie had helped Boswell manage the affairs of his illegitimate infants Charles and Sally in 1762 and 1769.

up masses or larger views of my existence. Mr. Johnson said that the great thing was to register the state of my mind.[1]

I went out today to Lady Colville's, and had a most agreeable walk with her Ladyship and Lady Anne and Captain Andrew before dinner. My mind has of late years been so sound that I can assure myself of being suitably affected by certain objects. At Lady Colville's I am always soothed, comforted, and cheered.[2] The cares of life are taken off with a velvet brush. I observed to Captain Andrew that we never have a long continuation of agreeable life. It is frequently interrupted. A company who have been very happy together must have the pain of parting. After every enjoyment comes weariness or disgust. We never have a large lawn of agreeable life. It is cut to pieces with sunk fences, ha-has, even where it is smoothest. Captain Erskine always revives notions of family and antiquity and Toryism in my mind. There was nobody there today but one young lady who was quiet and inoffensive. So we were quite in our own style. I drank hardly any; so was undisturbed. After tea Captain Andrew walked into town with me.

I found a letter from Mr. Samuel Johnson, informing me that the first sheets of his *Journey to the Hebrides* were sent to the press. This gave me a lively joy; and I was much elated by his writing, "I have endeavoured to do you some justice in the first paragraph."[3] One must pause and think, to have a full feeling of the value of any praise from Mr. Johnson. His works and his majesty of mind must be kept in view. I had the same sensation tonight as on hearing from General

[1] See above, p. 182.

[2] The co-author of the facetious *Letters between the Honourable Andrew Erskine and James Boswell, Esq.*, 1763, had sobered with the years. But Boswell had affectionate memories of him and of his sisters ("The ladies of Kellie", above, pp. 48 *n.* 4, 54–5). Captain Andrew (a suicide by drowning in 1793 after losses at whist) and his twice-widowed sister, Elizabeth Lady Colville, lived together for many years at Drumsheugh House.

[3] "I . . . was in the autumn of the year 1773 induced to undertake the journey by finding in Mr. Boswell a companion whose acuteness would help my inquiry, and whose gaiety of conversation and civility of manners are sufficient to counteract the inconveniencies of travel in countries less hospitable than we have passed." Boswell received a copy of the book from Johnson in January.

Oglethorpe: that it was hard that I should not be in London. It is true Hume, Robertson, and other greater geniuses than I am prefer Scotland. But they have neither that peculiar and permanent love of London and all its circumstances which I have; nor are they so much in unison with the English as I am, which I have clearly perceived, and of which Mr. Johnson has assured me. I supped at Sir George Preston's with my wife and Mrs. Montgomerie.

SUNDAY 26 JUNE. Was all day at the New Church; Dr. Blair in the forenoon, ——— in the afternoon. At my father's between sermons. Dr. Webster, the Colonel, and George there, as also my wife and Mrs. Montgomerie. In the evening sauntered with my wife and Mrs. M., with intention to go to the Methodists' meeting or Lady Glenorchy's Chapel[1] to hear some remarkable evening sermon. They went to the latter; I went in only for a little, and heard a Mr. Davidson from England. Then went home by myself. It is amazing how all impressions of gloom upon a Sunday evening, which used formerly to hang so heavy on my mind, are quite effaced. We supped at Dr. Webster's, and were in an extraordinary flow of spirits.

MONDAY 27 JUNE. I went to see the foundation-stone of the Register Office[2] laid. I was very angry that there was no procession, no show or solemnity of any kind upon such an occasion. There was a fine sight both of well-dressed people and mob, so that there was spirit enough in the country to relish a show; and such things do good. It should have been laid either privately in the morning, or with some dignity. But cards were sent to all the judges as private men, and they accordingly dropped in, one by one, without their gowns and several of them with bob-wigs. The Lord Provost[3] too was there as a private man. To appear so at noon before a crowd of spectators was very poor.

[1] Very recently opened (8 May 1774); a large church built at the expense of a pious young noblewoman for the preaching of "pure evangelical doctrine" and to provide free seats for the poor. The Rev. Robert Walker (above, p. 223) preached the opening sermon.

[2] The Register House, designed by Robert Adam, was and remains one of the noblest monuments of the expansion of Edinburgh that followed rapidly on the opening of the North Bridge in 1772. At the time of its erection it stood isolated at the east end of Princes Street.

[3] Gilbert Laurie, Esq.

I was for satirising the Lord Register, who tripped about *delicately*. I would not just have hewn him like King Agag, but would have lashed him smartly—"Lord Freddie with a foolish face."[1]

We dined at Dr. Grant's[2] with a large company, amongst whom was Captain Schaw of the 66 regiment, and his lady, my old acquaintance Miss Thomson.[3] They had taken the house under us, and I had paid them a visit this forenoon, my wife and I having missed them last week and had our visit returned the same day. I had a consultation at four on Earl Fife's politics and returned to tea.

TUESDAY 28 JUNE. The President was in the chair. His animal spirits made the court seem more alive. It was like ringing the glasses at a drinking bout, or striking a shuttlecock with a sounding battledore. Balbarton[4] dined with us. I was a plain, good-humoured, hospitable kinsman to him. It is comfortable to be in that state. M. Dupont[5] drank tea with us, as did two sons of Dr. Wilson's at Newcastle.

WEDNESDAY 29 JUNE. We dined at Baron Mure's, where was a kind of second-rate grandeur but much cheerfulness. I sat by Miss Campbell of Carrick. Sandy Gordon was there, and Bob Adam[6] the

[1] The Lord Clerk Register was Lord Frederick Campbell, brother of the Duke of Argyll. He was accompanied in this ceremony by the Lord Advocate and the Lord Justice-Clerk. Agag, king of the Amalekites, came delicately before Samuel, who hewed him to pieces before the Lord (see 1 Samuel xv). Sir James Fergusson writes to the editors: "Lord Frederick Campbell receives less than justice from Boswell. It was largely owing to his persistent efforts that the building of the Register House was at last begun (nine years after the Royal Warrant for it had been granted), with the Adams as architects, and he rendered great public services in recovering missing records and encouraging the arrangement and cataloguing of the whole national archives. Incidentally, he was considered, both in youth and old age, one of the handsomest men of his time."

[2] Dr. Gregory Grant, celebrated for his "musical suppers", lived in James's Court on the fourth floor of the same entry as Boswell.

[3] In 1761–1762 Isabella Thomson had stood high on Boswell's list of matrimonial candidates. She had now been married to Captain Frederick Bridges Schaw for some twelve years.

[4] Another James Boswell, an elderly distant cousin.

[5] Rev. Pierre Loumeau Dupont, minister of the Huguenot congregation.

[6] Boswell rather surprisingly wrote "Adams", both here and in the entry for 1 July.

architect, who was lively enough, though vain, for which I forgave him. I drank rather too much. I drank tea there too. Then called for a little at Lady Mary Cunynghame's.[1] We all supped at Sir George Preston's.

THURSDAY 30 JUNE. Captain and Mrs. Schaw and their daughter, Dr. Grant, Colonel Webster, Miss Webster, Fairlie,[2] Matthew Dickie,[3] and Mr. George Haldane[4] dined with us. I was in as calm a frame as I ever remember; did not speak much and drank port and water, yet contrived that the company was very social and had five bottles of claret. I rose from table quite cool and several of us drank tea with the ladies. This was an inoffensive day.

FRIDAY 1 JULY. I dined at Lord Monboddo's, where we had Miss Fletcher, Baron Winn,[5] Crosbie, Maclaurin, Sandy Gordon, etc., and Bob Adam. We were sufficiently jovial. To go home to business seemed dull. However, after drinking tea (the only man except my Lord himself), I did go home and had a short consultation; and was pleased that Mr. Lawrie was out of the way, so that it was not my fault that I was idle. I supped at the Horse Wynd Tavern and drank my bottle of old hock, which did me no harm. There was but eight of us. Lord Monboddo was one.

SATURDAY 2 JULY. Dined at Craighouse,[6] and had a party at bowls both before and after dinner. It was wonderful to see Mr. Lockhart,[7] who has now stood fifty-two years at the bar, playing with all the keenness of a young man. Maclaurin and I led one another on to bet and I lost thirteen shillings. To play for a crown, as we did, is incongruous with the healthful field-sport of the bowls. It poisons it

[1] Sister to the Earl of Eglinton and mother to the Hon. Mrs. Margaret Stuart (see above, pp. 78–9).

[2] Alexander Fairlie of Fairlie, an Ayrshire neighbour.

[3] See below, p. 285.

[4] An advocate.

[5] George Winn, Baron of Exchequer.

[6] Alexander Lockhart's seat.

[7] Dean of the Faculty of Advocates and head of the bar in respect of practice. His elevation to the Bench having been long delayed because of his Tory (not to say Jacobite) politics, he was made a Lord of Session in 1775 as Lord Covington. He was then seventy-five years old.

with a certain degree of avaricious anxiety. I resolved never to play for more than a shilling.

SUNDAY 3 JULY. Was at New Church in the forenoon. The Reverend Dr. Ewing of Philadelphia[1] preached admirably on "My ways are not as your ways," etc. At my father's between sermons. Afternoon, Tolbooth Church; heard Dr. Webster, as well as ever. We all again took our Sunday's supper with him. We were comfortable and more quiet than last Sunday. I was for setting up a hogshead of wine as a Lord of Session in place of a drunken judge. Dr. Webster said it was a good thought; and let the parties or their agents take glass about, and he who happened to get the last glass win the cause. This he said would be cheaper than giving a salary to a judge and feeing lawyers. It is curious how a thought once started may be pursued. A reclaiming petition would come in against an interlocutor of Vintage 1754, Ordinary. Parties might agree before the hogshead was drank out.

MONDAY 4 JULY. Was busy all day. I had a consultation at seven in the morning—"Sub galli cantum consultor ubi ostia pulsat"[2]—to draw a bill of suspension, which was done by eleven. Dr. Wilson's sons dined with us. I finished a long memorial before night. Andrew Stewart, Junior, drank tea with us.

TUESDAY 5 JULY. Dined at Charles Hay's with Mr. Rose, Lord Fife's factor, and some others. We were social enough, without any rioting. Dr. Webster and Miss Webster came at night and supped with us.

WEDNESDAY 6 JULY. My wife, Mrs. Montgomerie, and I dined at Sandy Gordon's. Lord Monboddo, Crosbie, Stewart Moncrieffe, Cosmo Gordon, etc., etc., were there. Crosbie was obliged to go to the Commissary Court immediately after dinner to attend a process of divorce. I said it was a severe divorce to him to dissever him from us. It was a separation *a mensa*.[3] Monboddo was in excellent spirits and

[1] John Ewing, D.D., pastor of the First Presbyterian Church of Philadelphia and (later) first provost of the University of Pennsylvania. He had come to Britain to solicit funds for an academy in Delaware.

[2] "When at cock-crow a client knocks at the door"—Horace, *Satires*, I, i, 10.

[3] "From table," alluding to the legal phrase *divortium a mensa et thoro*, separation from bed and board.

did not seem inclined to rise. Cosmo Gordon and I sat to cherish his festivity, and we were really joyous. I repeated my ballad, *The Boston Bill.*[1] Lord Monboddo said it would do well in America. It was better than *Lilliburlero*, which brought about the Revolution; and Cosmo Gordon said it was equal to anything of Sir Charles Hanbury Williams. I had drank rather too much and was a good deal heated, and at the same time had several papers to write which hung heavy upon my mind. One representation was to be done this very night. I did it, however; though to be sure not very sufficiently. Social dinners and the practice of the law are really incompatible. I must restrain myself from them; and yet there is not company here to make them but in session time, and life must be enjoyed—

Think, O think it worth th' enjoying.[2]

I was this night firmly resolved to go to the English bar if ever I should be quite my own master; or at any rate to pass half my time in London, where my talents have their full value.

[1] On 16 December 1773 had occurred the Boston Tea Party. The Government in retaliation passed the Boston Port Bill, which closed Boston Harbour. Boswell from the first sympathised with the Americans. His "ballad" may be found in *The London Chronicle* for 21–23 July 1774. Three stanzas of eight (the third, fifth, and last) will be an ample specimen:

The blade of Burke and Dempster's dirk,
  From Irish bog and Scottish hill,
Were brandished bright, in the Court's sight,
  In vain against the Boston Bill. . . .

To the Upper House it went up souse,
  Of no effect was Chatham's will;
His quivering crutch could hardly touch
  The borders of the Boston Bill. . . .

Come let us sing long live our King,
  For we are sure *he* means no ill,
And hope the best for the oppressed
  By the unhappy Boston Bill.

[2] Dryden, *Alexander's Feast*, l. 104.

THURSDAY 7 JULY. Many of my brethren in the House asked to hear *The Boston Bill*, which I repeated with excellent applause. I lost two causes in the Inner House, I thought unjustly; and I spoke in both with a manly ease. Mr. MacLeod, brother to Raasay,[1] Mr. Bannatyne MacLeod,[2] the Reverend Mr. William Macqueen and his nephew (son to Mr. Donald), and Dr. Grant dined with me. I was quite in the Highland humour. We sang "Hatyin fome eri."[3] Adam Bell joined us, and then consulted me. I then was at a consultation at Mr. Ilay Campbell's;[4] then at St. John's Lodge, where were but six present. But my spirits made a choice meeting.[5]

FRIDAY 8 JULY. Lord and Lady Dundonald and Lady Betty Cochrane, Mr. Heron of Heron,[6] and Dr. and Mrs. Hunter dined with us. It was a substantial creditable dinner, without my being obliged to drink any. It was curious to see Lord Dundonald,[7] at the age of eighty-three, stout and fresh, with a flow of spirits. The tide, to be sure, appeared to be out. But there was a high sea. In the evening, after a

[1] Host to Boswell and Johnson, 8 to 12 September 1773.

[2] An Edinburgh advocate.

[3] Boswell's English phonetics for the Gaelic refrain of a Jacobite song which he had learned in the Hebrides: *Tha tighinn fodham éiridh* ("It comes upon me to arise").

[4] A leading counsel for Douglas in the Douglas Cause, he was later to be Solicitor-General, Lord Advocate, M.P. for the Glasgow burghs, and, in 1789, President of the Court of Session. In 1808 he was made a baronet.

[5] The minute of this meeting, still preserved, is entirely in Boswell's hand: "The Lodge having met, although there were very few brethren present, for which those who were absent should be reprimanded, the evening was passed in most social glee, every brother having sung (though not as a precedent), and the Lodge was adjourned to the first Thursday of August next." "These indications of social glee," says Dr. John Murray, who was generously allowed to examine the record, "are reinforced by a large splash of claret on one of the pages of the Minute Book."

[6] Patrick Heron was perhaps already courting Lady Betty, whom he married at the end of the next year. See above, p. 80 *n.* 4.

[7] Army captain in 1716, M.P. in 1722, Commissioner of Excise in 1730, the eighth Earl was brother of Euphemia Cochrane, Boswell's grandmother, father of Lady Betty and of Major Charles Cochrane (below, p. 236), brother-in-law of Sir George Preston (above p. 222 *n.* 3), and brother of Commissioner Basil Cochrane (below, pp. 237, 332).

long consultation on two causes of Colonel Rickson's widow, I felt myself in a pleasing indolence. I yielded to it and went early to bed.

SATURDAY 9 JULY. The state of my mind must be gathered from the little circumstances inserted in my Journal. The life of every man, take it day by day, is pretty much a series of uniformity; at least a series of repeated alternations. It is like a journal of the weather: rainy—fair—fair—rainy, etc. It is seldom that a great storm or an abundant harvest occurs in the life of man or in the progress of years. Of this week I can observe that my mind has been more lively than usual, more fertile in images, more agreeably sensible of enjoying existence.

An important part of my life should be my practice as a lawyer. I must record an anecdote. The Reverend Mr. William Macqueen had a legacy of two thousand merks Scots left to him by a testament subscribed in the Isle of Skye by one notary and two witnesses. He consulted me to know if it was good. I gave him my advice as a friend, and was of the opinion that it was not good, as the Act of Parliament, ———,[1] requires the subscriptions of two notaries and four witnesses to all deeds concerning heritage, and to all deeds of importance, i.e., which convey £100 Scots. At the same time, I said I had some faint idea that there was an exception as to a testament; and I should *think* of the subject. I talked with some of my brethren. *Sandy Murray*[2] said it would not do; and that there was no hardship upon people in remote countries where it was difficult to get two notaries, as clergymen were held as notaries in the case of testaments. *Crosbie* was clear it would not do. He said the Act was express; and how absurd would it be to allow one to make a settlement with less formality and fewer checks against imposition when he was ill than when in good health. I then told honest Mr. Macqueen that I was sorry to find that he would make nothing of his legacy, as some of my brethren agreed with me; but that

[1] Act of 1579, c. 18 (*Acts of Parliament of Scotland*, iii, 1814, p. 145).

[2] Alexander Murray became Solicitor-General next year and in 1783 was raised to the Bench as Lord Henderland. In the published *Journal of a Tour to the Hebrides* (1785) Boswell hinted that Murray's marriage to a niece of Lord Mansfield had not hurt his chances of promotion.

I should also ask his namesake, Mr. *Macqueen*. I did so; and Macqueen, with that excellent candour which he always has, told me that he really could not tell how the matter stood; that he thought it would not do. But like myself he said he had some kind of idea of a testament being privileged. I asked him if he actually did not know so plain a thing one way or other. He declared he did not. "Well," said I, "that flatters me very much, for I'm like to hang myself when I cannot answer a question, and here are *you* at a loss." He desired me to look into the law books, and had I at first *read*, instead of *thinking* and *asking*, I might at once have been made certain. Upon looking into Erskine,[1] I found it to be clear that testaments to any extent were good with one notary and two witnesses. This is a curious practical anecdote. I must observe that *Nairne* seemed to think it would do, and *Charles Hay* was certain it would do. A man picks up his firmest particles of knowledge occasionally. Charles told me that he knew this of the testament well, because he happened to call on Michael Nasmith when he was examining a notary, and heard that point mentioned. I made honest Mr. Macqueen very happy by telling him that his legacy was good.

This day I had fixed for paying a bet of five guineas to the Hon. Andrew Erskine, Grange, James Currie, Sandy Abercrombie and James Loch, writers, which I had lost six years ago. It was agreed at the time of the bet that it should be a supper at *Thom's*, in whose house I had paid two former bets.[2] But Thom having now given up his tavern, and the sum being handsome, we resolved to have a dinner at Fortune's. Dr. Webster was with us as chaplain; and we had an excellent dinner at No. 9 and abundance of drinking. While Webster sat, we had several good stories and songs. He left us between seven and eight, and then we grew very noisy and drunk, but very cordial as old friends. In short we had a complete riot, which lasted until near

[1] "Let the subject of a testament be ever so valuable, one notary signing for the testator, with two witnesses, is sufficient . . ." (John Erskine, *An Institute of the Law of Scotland*, Edinburgh, 1773, ii, 434).

[2] The nature of this bet is not recorded but is perhaps indicated by Boswell's account of one of the former suppers: "I gave a supper to two or three of my acquaintance, having before I left Scotland laid a guinea that I should not catch the venereal disorder for three years, which bet I had most certainly lost and now was paying. We drank a great deal . . ." (Boswell to Temple, 8 March 1767).

twelve at night. We had eleven Scotch pints[1] of claret, two bottles of old hock, and two of port, and drams of brandy and gin; and the bill was 6. 18. 5. So my five-guinea bet turned to a seven-guinea one; for I gave the waiter the balance of that sum over the bill. In our great warmth we signed an agreement to meet annually on the second Saturday of July, as we had "now met, after an interval of six years, in the same good humour and with the same cordial regard for each other that we then did, and considering that such things were rare and valuable in human life." I sat after the rest were gone and took a large bowl of admirable soup, which did me much good, for I was not sick; though after I was in bed my dear wife was apprehensive that I might die, I breathed so ill.

SUNDAY 10 JULY. Though I was neither sick nor had hardly any headache, I was, as it were, half boiled with last night's debauch, and I was vexed to think of having given my valuable spouse so much uneasiness; for she had scarcely slept any the whole night watching me. The reflection, too, of my having this summer so frequently been intoxicated, galled me. A circumstance occurred this morning which I hope will have a lasting impression upon me. There had come a letter to me from Mr. Samuel Johnson last night. My wife improved it well. She said she would not give me it, as I did not deserve it, since I had put myself into a state of incapacity to receive it when it came, and that it would not have been written to me had the writer of it known how I was to be. She would therefore send it back. She thus made me think how shocking it was that a letter from Mr. Samuel Johnson should find me drunk. She then delivered it, and it was a more than ordinary good one.[2] It put me in the best frame, and I determined vigorously to resist temptation for the future.

I was soberly at the New Church in the forenoon. Mr. Logan, minister at Leith, preached. I then walked down to Lord Dun-

[1] A Scotch pint equals about three Imperial pints; in U.S. measure, it is between three pints and two quarts.

[2] See *Life of Johnson*, 4 July 1774. Johnson announces his departure the next day on the tour to Wales, which was to take nearly three months, in company with Mr. and Mrs. Thrale. It did not, observes Boswell in the *Life*, "give occasion to such a discursive exercise of his mind as our tour to the Hebrides."

donald's and dined. He was in great spirits. Colonel Webster and Major Pitcairn, Charles Cochrane's father-in-law, were there. We three drank a bottle of claret each, which just cheered me. We drank tea there, and at night we all met at Dr. Webster's Sunday supper. The Major was a sensible, good-looking, well-bred man, and my second cousin through the family of Wishaw.[1] We were merry rather to excess.

MONDAY 11 JULY. My Saturday's debauch had relaxed me so as that business seemed irksome; and yet I had a number of papers which I was absolutely obliged to write in a short time, and some of the agents were complaining of delay. In the forenoon Captain Erskine called and gave me a special invitation from Lady Colville to dine with her. To accept of it seemed incompatible with my present state of business. Yet I could not resist. I considered that it would only throw me an hour or two more behind, and that I should be so refreshed with the agreeable interview with quality friends in the country air that I should be able to labour twice as well. I accordingly went. We had only the two Captains, Lady Dalrymple, and her grandchild, Lady Anne Lindsay.[2] I was gently happy and did not heat myself at all with wine. My wife came and drank tea. Captain Erskine walked with me as far as the New Town. I came home in admirable spirits and dictated papers with ease and alacrity.

TUESDAY 12 JULY. This was just a busy day. I drank tea with Nairne.

WEDNESDAY 13 JULY. The jovial party of Saturday, all but Dr. Webster, dined at Currie's. We were hearty and social; and he allowed every man to drink as he pleased. I resolved to keep myself sober. But I hobbed and nobbed so cordially that, although I was not

[1] Major John Pitcairn was sent to Boston later in this year; was in command of the British regulars at Lexington Common, 19 April 1775, when the first blood in the War of Independence was shed, and fell mortally wounded in the Battle of Bunker Hill, 17 June 1775. Pitcairn's grandmother, Mary Erskine, second wife of William Hamilton of Wishaw, was sister to Boswell's grandfather, Colonel John Erskine.

[2] "The two Captains" were Andrew Erskine and his brother Archibald, later Earl of Kellie. Lady Anne Lindsay, not yet twenty-four, was already the authoress of "Auld Robin Gray".

the worse of liquor and went home at six o'clock, I was restless and idle and did little or nothing. I supped at Sir George Preston's with my wife and Mrs. Montgomerie.

THURSDAY 14 JULY. My father and Lady Auchinleck, Commissioner Cochrane, the Laird of Fullarton and his mother, Mr. Nairne, Dr. Boswell,[1] and Messieurs Alexander Mackenzie and Andrew Stewart, Junior, dined with us. The company went away gradually till I was left with Fullarton, who drank nothing at all hardly, and the two writers,[2] who were both very social. In such circumstances my strong attraction from within requires little aid from any external impulse and easily makes me think that it is a kind of duty or necessity for me to drink. I took rather too much and was to a certain degree feverish with it. I must steadily keep in mind that no man is more easily hurt with wine than I am, and that there is no real advantage gained by being a good bottle-companion, and whenever I am set with company after dinner or after supper I must beware of thinking of Duncan Forbes,[3] whose hard drinking often misleads me. It was unpleasing today to see my father not at all frank or cordial with me or my wife. At seven Lady Dundonald came herself and consulted me about a lawsuit which she had with a weaver whom she had employed to make some rich table linen. I was vexed to find myself confused while her Ladyship talked with me. However, I was prudent and plausible. In the evening I wrote a very good representation in a cause concerning a bill, which consoled me so far. I had been much pressed to sup at Walter Campbell's with Maclaurin and Sandy Gordon. But I resisted and kept at home.

FRIDAY 15 JULY. This was a day of complete sobriety and diligence; and I extricated myself from a very difficult cause by persevering till I was master of it. I went in the afternoon

[1] Lord Auchinleck's younger brother, a physician. He resembled Boswell in temperament much more than he did Lord Auchinleck. See below, pp. 268. 335.

[2] Mackenzie and Stewart.

[3] Lord President of the Court of Session; died 1747. Lord Kames remembered that Forbes had the "singular faculty of being able after drinking to read his papers as well as in the forenoon".

to the prison and conferred with my old client John Reid.[1]

SATURDAY 16 JULY. Mrs. Montgomerie, my wife, and I dined at Mr. Mitchelson's[2] at Corstorphine. He sent his chaise, which carried us out. I was unusually delighted with the prospect of the country. Mr. Aytoun, Writer to the Signet, and Mr. Claud Boswell were there. We were perfectly sober. At six I had a hackney-coach which carried Mrs. Montgomerie, Claud, my wife, and me to the play. There was just forty people in the boxes and pit. The play was *The Man of Business*, and the farce, *Cross Purposes*.[3] It was wonderful to see with what spirit the players performed. In one view it was more agreeable tonight than being at a crowded play. One could attend fully to what passed on the stage, whereas in a great audience the attention is distracted and one has a great deal to do in behaving properly. The difference was the same as viewing a country when upon a calm horse at a slow walk or viewing it upon a fiery horse at a gallop, when you must attend to the reins and to your seat. But the laughable passages did not go off so well as in a crowd, for laughter is augmented by sympathetic power. Supped quietly at home.

SUNDAY 17 JULY. Was in a calm, reflecting frame. Considered how very little I read during the course of a week except mere matter of business. I thought of lying in bed all forenoon and indulging the humour in which I then was. I had a slight conflict between what I really thought would do me most good and the desire of being externally decent and going to church. I rose and breakfasted; but being too late for church, I read a part of my Bible and began the Life of Bishop Sanderson by Walton, which I have heard Mr. Samuel Johnson commend much and which I had borrowed from the Advocates' Library, being resolved to read all Walton's *Lives*, as Mr. Johnson had written to me of a design that Dr. Horne of Oxford had to reprint them,[4] but which he gave up upon Mr. Johnson's telling him

[1] John Reid, a butcher from Stirlingshire, had been Boswell's first criminal client in 1766, when Boswell and Crosbie obtained his acquittal in a trial for sheep-stealing. He had now been arrested on another charge of the same kind.

[2] Samuel, Senior, Writer to the Signet. See above, p. 63.

[3] By George Colman and William O'Brien, respectively.

[4] In the letter which Boswell had been given by his wife on 10 July.

that Lord Hailes had the same design. This, however, was a mistake. Lord Hailes only wished to have them reprinted, but was willing to give any aid that he could in the way of illustration. So that I was to write to Mr. Johnson that Dr. Horne should proceed. I wished to read what Mr. Johnson valued, and thought that perhaps I might be able to give some little aid to Dr. Horne. I read Sanderson's Life today, all but some leaves which were a-wanting in the copy which I had. I shall get the defect supplied.[1] The simplicity and pious spirit of Walton was, as it were, transfused into my soul. I resolved that amidst business and every other worldly pursuit I should still keep in mind religious duty. I had stripped and gone to bed again in my night-gown after breakfast, which favoured my tranquillity. A man who *knows himself* should use means to do him good which to others may seem trifling or ridiculous.

My wife and I dined at my father's, where were Sir George Preston and George Webster. There was the usual constraint joined with the usual small conversation. In the afternoon I was at the New Church and heard Dr. Blair preach. My wife and I drank tea at home by ourselves. We all supped at Dr. Webster's.

MONDAY 18 JULY. Mrs. Montgomerie, my wife, and I dined at Lady Colville's, where we had Sir George Preston, his lady, and daughter. Captain Andrew was not there. I was in a disagreeable humour, domineering and ill-bred, insisting to have Sir George's punch made stronger, and in short being really rude. A fit of impatience and coarse violence of temper had come upon me. I was angry at myself and yet so proud that when I saw it was observed with dissatisfaction, I persisted. We drank tea, and I grew calmer. Lady Anne walked in with my wife and me.

TUESDAY 19 JULY. Lord Alemoor[2] and his sister, Lord Mon-

[1] The volume, still in the Advocates' Library (National Library of Scotland), bears the following note in Boswell's hand on the fly-leaf: "Having borrowed this excellent life out of the Advocates' Library, I found that it wanted seven leaves. Having purchased the same edition at the Reverend Dr. Patrick Cumming's auction, with a head of the Bishop which has been taken away from this copy, I had the seven leaves supplied in manuscript by my clerk; and I now return it, hoping that it may edify many readers.—JAMES BOSWELL. 1780."

[2] Andrew Pringle, Lord of Session.

boddo, Mr. Walter Campbell and wife, and Miss Douglas Ker, Crosbie, and Charles Hay dined with us. It was a very creditable and agreeable meeting, for we were all in good humour. After the ladies went to the drawing-room, there was too much drinking. Lord Alemoor sat by till about seven and was very pleasant. I gave them my *Boston Bill* and read some of Goldsmith's *Retaliation*,[1] which dashed some finer genius in our jovial cup. Crosbie spoke more than usual. He had consultations both at six and seven. But he did not stir. He told me afterwards, "I could not tear myself away from you." Monboddo was excellent company. It pleased me to have my good professor, Charles Hay, in a party which satisfied him to the full. The future Shawfield was steadily merry.[2] I had a consultation at Mr. Rae's on Earl Fife's politics at seven. But I thought there were enough there without me—that I could read the papers by myself—and that I should come in long before their tedious conference was over. In the situation I then was, I could not get away. At eight my company insisted to break up. I went to Mr. Rae's and got as much of the consultation as was necessary. I was a good deal intoxicated, but had as much command of myself as to be decent.

WEDNESDAY 20 JULY. My hearty sociality of yesterday did not distress me much. The Journal of this day is marked above a week after its elapse; and it is the only day as to the history of which I could not swear. I am pretty certain that I passed it in the plain course of business without being in company.

THURSDAY 21 JULY. Mr. Alexander Donaldson and his son, Mr. Charles Hay, Mr. Michael Nasmith, and Grange supped with me. I told Mr. Alexander Donaldson that, as Alexander the Great sat down and wept that he had no more worlds to conquer, he might now, after his victory on Literary Property, sit down and weep that he had

[1] See above, p. 217 *n*. The poem was published a fortnight after Goldsmith's death. On 7 May Boswell, answering an inquiry from Lord Hailes, had not seen it and doubted if it was genuine.

[2] "The future Shawfield" is Walter Campbell; Charles Hay is called "my good professor" because he and Boswell had been studying law together during the recess. Hay (later Lord Newton), seven years younger than Boswell, had the reputation of being equally profound in law and in drink. He and Boswell were at this time close friends, but seem later to have quarrelled or drifted apart.

no more booksellers to conquer. We were jovial and merry. My wife and Mrs. Montgomerie were at the play, and sent to us not to wait supper for them. They came to us about eleven, and enlivened us. We sat till one in the morning.

FRIDAY 22 JULY. I dined at Lord Dundonald's with my wife and Mrs. Montgomerie. Old General Colville,[1] Captain Blair, Mr. Nairne, and George Webster were there. The Earl was in great spirits; but it was not quite agreeable to hear a man of eighty-three swearing and talking bawdy. One regretted that such admirable vivacity had taken such habits. He, however, showed a sense of piety; for he said he "never rose in the morning nor lay down at night without thanking God for his goodness" to him. I, in my way, rattled too much, and being grand-nephew to the Earl, who did not drink himself, I willingly thought it incumbent on me to be landlord, and pushed about the bottle pretty briskly. We drank tea. I felt myself somewhat flustered with wine; was at a consultation at the Solicitor's at seven. Then being unquiet after I got home, so that I could not work, went to Mr. Stewart Moncrieffe's, betted at the whist table, and lost a crown, which I grudged. We were ten at supper, Colonel Seton and Castle Stewart[2] for the first time. I indulged in old hock and became very drunk. Colonel Murray,[3] the Duke of Atholl's brother, joined me in supporting male succession. Seton and I were warm friends. Matthew Henderson[4] was very profane. Somebody said he would be

[1] Charles Colville (1691–1775), second son of Alexander (d. 1717), *de jure* fifth Lord Colville, entered the Army early, and saw much service, including Malplaquet in 1709 and Culloden in 1746. He became a lieutenant-general in 1770. He died unmarried.

[2] Colonel James Seton later became Governor of St. Vincent in the Windward Islands. William Stewart of Castle Stewart was M.P. for the Wigtown burghs 1770–1774 and for the stewartry of Kirkcudbright 1774–1780. He was forced to sell his estate c. 1783.

[3] ". . . of the old Highland regiment" (Journal, 4 May 1769). He was the Hon. James Murray, second son of Lord George Murray.

[4] Henderson, the antiquary, befriended Burns, who wrote a moving elegy on him in 1790. "He was," says the poet, "an intimate acquaintance of mine; and of all mankind I ever knew, he was one of the first for a nice sense of honour, a generous contempt of the adventitious distinctions of men, and sterling though sometimes *outré* wit" (*Letters of Robert Burns*, ed. J. DeL. Ferguson, ii, 33).

made answer for his sins. He said, "I wish I was impanelled in a future state. I would agree to take two hundred years of hell to be ensured of a future state." "Well," said I, "*there* is something spirited. A noble wish for the immortality of the soul. I tell you, Matthew, I shall meet you in a future state, and though, to be sure, you must do penance for some time, yet I am persuaded you will be forgiven." Drinking never fails to make me ill-bred. I insisted to know Moncrieffe's age. He parried me well. How I appeared this night to others, I know not. But I recollect having felt much warmth of heart, fertility of fancy, and joyous complacency mingled in a sort of delirium. Such a state is at least equal to a pleasing dream. I drank near three bottles of hock, and then staggered away. I got home about three in the morning. Mr. Nairne had supped at my house, expecting me home. Mrs. Montgomerie had sat up till two waiting to see me, as she was to set out next morning. I was incapable of knowing anything; and my wife was waiting all the time, drowsy and anxious. What a price does such an evening's, or rather night's, riot cost me!

SATURDAY 23 JULY. I had been sick without being sensible of it. But I was so ill at seven that I could not bid adieu to Mrs. Montgomerie. I however grew so well as to be able to get up and go to the Parliament House at nine. I was still quite giddy with liquor, and, squeamishness having gone off, I was in a good, vigorous, sparkling frame, and did what was necessary to be done in several causes, and was most entertaining amongst my brother lawyers. I described Castle Stewart as a castle impregnable by wine—that could not be *sapped*—that had a deep moat of wine around it. I dined at Crosbie's, where were the Lords Alemoor, Elliock, and Monboddo, a very good fifth of the Bench; as also Dr. Lind,[1] Wattie Campbell, and Cullen.[2] I was in prodigious spirits, dined with a great appetite, and drank beer copiously to allay the thirst of last night's drinking. We had a deal of merriment; and I drank old hock, which just cooled my fever and really sobered me. The judges sat well. I talked of the long time that

[1] Shelley's beloved friend, years afterwards, at Windsor; the old hermit in *Laon and Cythna* and Zonoras in *Prince Athanase*. He was at this time thirty-eight years old.

[2] See above, p. 51 *n*. 3.

the same Bench had sat. "As long as Duncan Forbes drove the same horses" (as I expressed his being at the head of the same Lords). "I am glad," said Lord Alemoor, "you give us so good an epithet as *horses*."[1] As the wine went freely about, he said, "You'll make a vacancy tonight." Said I: "Maclaurin has Lord Kennet dining with him today, to try what he can make of *him*. We are fighting the Bench in parties." I afterwards (not this day) observed that Kennet's insipidity and Maclaurin's peevishness would make poor work. It would be like skate and vinegar. It was pleasant to have the Bench and the bar so easy together as we were today, but in my opinion the ease was too much. The character of a judge should not only have dignity but reverence. Wattie Campbell and Cullen and I sat till between eleven and twelve, when Crosbie, who had drank very faithfully, seemed much overcome. He pressed us to sit, but none of us were drunk and we all came off. I walked home with great composure.

SUNDAY 24 JULY. I was very well, and was at the New Church all day and at my father's between sermons. Dr. Blair preached well in the forenoon on, "Who art thou that judgest another man's servant?" He recommended calmness in judging of others to man, who has so much need of indulgence from his Maker. The sermon was very applicable to me. I took it home and resolved to check violence of temper and make allowance even for the President. Sir George drank tea with us; and at night we took our Sunday's supper at Dr. Webster's, the sixth Sunday without interruption to me. I had just the usual ideas; and took, as I had done for these several Sundays, a short walk in the garden with George just before supper to point my appetite. We talked tonight of a future state very pleasingly. At supper, where was only young Grant, whom we had last Sunday, we were too vehement and vociferous. The sons bore down the father as much as they could. The father cried, "Have patience." Said George to him, "I would not like to take a month's tickets for patience from you"—thereby attacking the Doctor's own heat of temper. George has fancy. I was taking him short in an argument. He cried, "Don't cut me down yet. The crop's too green." I was more moderate than usual in talk, drank

[1] Sir James Fergusson suggests that this is a sly allusion to Lord Kames's favourite epithet for his colleagues: *bitches*.

little, and came home in good time, pretty much fatigued with the sociality of the two preceding days.

I omitted to mention that I called this evening on Sir William Forbes[1] and had a long comfortable tête-à-tête with him upon literary subjects and religious principles, and on the conduct of life. He told me that he kept an accurate account of his expenses, which he was resolved to do to the day of his death; that from his being so much used to figures, it was quite easy to him; that it served as a kind of Journal of his life; that perhaps once a quarter he classed his expenses under different articles, and so saw where to retrench, where to extend. I determined to have myself put in a way by him of doing the same. I value him highly and regret that we are not more together, for, as I told him tonight, I am always the better of being with him.

This day in church while I thought of Mr. Samuel Johnson's death happening some time hence, my mind was damped. I had then a very pretty lively thought that worthy Langton and others, who were touched by that noble loadstone and whose souls would point to heaven like needles to the pole, would remain to console me. It is very wrong that I do not write oftener to Langton. Sir W. Forbes showed me this evening two letters which he had from him.

MONDAY 25 JULY. Passed the day principally in writing law papers. I received a letter from Mr. Gentleman that he was in distress and begging the loan of five guineas.[2] My wife very genteelly was for my complying.

[1] Sixth Baronet of Monymusk, partner in the banking-house of Forbes, Hunter, and Co.; he was to become one of Boswell's most trusted friends and advisers. Boswell showed him portions of his unpublished Journal, appointed him guardian of his children and executor of his estate, and in addition made him one of his three literary executors.

[2] "A knowledge of and a thorough confidence in your character and feelings encourage me, though with much reluctance, to the following trespass upon your time and patience. Within the last eighteen months I have had a sad series of calamities in my family; the expensive sickness and irreparable loss of a valuable wife, the sickness and death of two children since her departure. . . . My infirm state rendered me incapable of joining Mr. Foote this summer . . ." (Francis Gentleman to Boswell [c. 20 July 1774]). See above, pp. 17, 139, 175.

TUESDAY 26, WEDNESDAY 27 JULY. [There are no entries for these days.]

THURSDAY 28 JULY. Mr. Wood the surgeon having called on us a little before three, we persuaded him to stay and dine. He very earnestly spoke to me to agree to make such a settlement of the estate of Auchinleck as my father chose, that my wife and children might have provisions secured to them in case of my death; and he said it was his opinion my father's chance of life was better than mine. This struck me much. But I felt a firmness in my old male feudal principles, though honest Wood could not see them but as wild romantic fancies. I have a strong conflict in my mind between my concern for my valuable wife, who in case of my death would be left in a miserable state of dependence, and those principles which are interwoven with my very heart, and which I hold myself bound in honour to maintain, as my great-great-grand-uncle gave the estate to his nephew, my grandfather,[1] in prejudice of his own four daughters; so that all who receive it as a male fief should faithfully transmit it as such. Mr. Johnson confirmed me in that principle and inculcated upon me that the chance of my wife and children being in a bad situation was nothing in the general calculation of things. I shall therefore be steady, conscious of my sincere affection for my wife and children, and trusting that I may have it in my power to make them all easy.

FRIDAY 29 JULY. Between one and two in the forenoon Mr. William Wilson and I went to a consultation at Mr. Lockhart's on a perplexed question between Fairholm's trustee—Johnston—and Mitchell and Buchanan of Mountvernon. It vexed me that I could not understand it upon reading the papers. It was astonishing to see Mr. Lockhart, who had only read them over as I had done, much master of the cause. He is certainly a prodigy in his profession. My wife and I dined at Lord Alemoor's. Lord Gardenstone, Macqueen, Crosbie, and Cullen were there. I was in very good spirits, but rather too much in the rough style of joking. As a specimen: Mr. Pringle, Lord Alemoor's brother who is in Parliament,[2] had a white rose; I had a red

[1] Actually his great-grandfather. See above, p. 53 *n.* 2; *Life of Johnson*, January 1776.

[2] See above, p. 135.

one. "Come," said I, "let us change." He did so readily. "You see," said I, "with what case a Member of Parliament changes sides. I wanted to try him; and he goes through his exercise like a dragoon horse when he hears a drum beat."

We had an elegant dinner, but I do not recollect much conversation that passed. Lord Alemoor observed that story-telling was the fashion of the last age, but that our wits now entertained with their own sayings. He asked me if I ever studied beforehand the good things which I said in company. I told him I did not. Crosbie agreed that it was so, but said I spoke enough about them *afterwards*; a very just remark. My wife and I stayed to tea. I was well warmed with wine here, and as Lord Gardenstone and Macqueen spoke jovially of supping at Moncrieffe's, this being the last night of meeting for the season and a neck of venison being promised, I determined to go. I did so, and flashed away. Castle Stewart talked of several voters who were against him having died. "If this goes on," said I, "you'll have a *dead* majority." I was really excellent company. I never saw any man more pleased with another than Seton seemed to be with me. There was very hard drinking. I however did not exceed a bottle and a half of old hock. But, with what I had taken at dinner, I was far gone.

SATURDAY 30 JULY. My head was inflamed and confused considerably. However, I went to the Parliament House a little after nine. I found the Solicitor, who had been with us last night and drank heartily, standing in the outer hall looking very ill. He told me he was not able to stay, so he went home. He had struggled to attend his business, but it would not do. Peter Murray told me he had seen him this morning come out of a dram-shop in the Back Stairs, in all his formalities of large wig and cravat. He had been trying to settle his stomach. In some countries such an officer of the Crown as Solicitor-General being seen in such a state would be thought shocking. Such are our manners in Scotland that it is nothing at all.[1] I kept up well all forenoon, and after the court rose attended a Faculty meeting, made

[1] Boswell's contemporary at college Henry Dundas became a few months later M.P. for Midlothian in 1775, Lord Advocate, and in 1782 Keeper of the Signet—the "uncrowned King of Scotland", holding the patronage of all official positions. He became Viscount Melville in 1802.

two motions, and presented some antiquities sent as a present to the Faculty by the Reverend Mr. Donald Macqueen in Skye.[1]

John Reid's trial was to come on next Monday. Michael Nasmith, who at my desire was agent for him, seemed anxious. I promised to him what I had resolved in my own mind: that I should taste no wine till the trial was over. In the afternoon I went with my wife and Veronica to Heriot's Gardens, which soothed and refreshed me. Veronica walked briskly, with a little help, pulled flowers, and I held her up till she pulled a cherry for the first time. I played a party at bowls with Adam Bell and so many more, drank tea at home calmly, as I had dined, and made up for yesterday's excess. In the evening when it was dusky I visited John Reid. I felt a sort of dreary tremor as he and I walked together in the dark in the iron room. He would own nothing to me. But I need not insert any account of him in my Journal, as I shall write concerning him separately.[2] I sent for a pot of lenitive electuary at night, that I might open and cool my body, and took a part of it. I had not taken physic before for two years. I wished to do a kindness to poor Gentleman, who had always paid me much attention, but my debts far exceeded my funds. I sent him an order on Messrs. Dilly for three guineas.[3]

SUNDAY 31 JULY. The physic had a benign effect. I took the rest of the pot this morning, and lay in bed all forenoon except when a *motion* made me rise. I read the Lives of Dr. Donne, Sir Henry

[1] "There is a sacrificial knife, an elf or Druidical spade, which was used in opening up the ground at one of the annual solemnities, a sling stone, so I am told, of which you are a better judge, if you have been in the Balearian Islands. But all these were indeed used here, where they knew nothing of metals. There is also another crusted stone, which I lately picked up at the foot of one of our mountains. If any of these or the whole of them may be thought a curiosity by the honourable faculty of which you are a member, I desire they may be laid up in their library as a small expression of my gratitude for the access I had to their books in Mr. Thomas Ruddiman's time. . . . Did I give you an elf arrow, or do you think it worth the sending?" (Donald Macqueen to Boswell, January 1774).

[2] He means in his Register of Criminal Trials. See the beginning of the entry for 1 August.

[3] "Believe me I regret that debts contracted in my days of folly still hang heavy upon me and make me unable to give you such assistance as I could wish to do" (Boswell to Gentleman, 30 July 1774).

Wotton, Mr. Hooker, and Mr. George Herbert, by Izaak Walton. I read them, all but a part of the last, in the forenoon, and was in the most placid and pious frame. I put in marks at all the places where I either observed errors of the press, or had any remarks to make, that I might give my aid, along with Lord Hailes, to Dr. Horne, Master of Magdalen College, Oxford, who was about to publish a new edition of these valuable Lives.

I was in a fine state of preparation for John Reid's trial, which was to come on next day. Michael Nasmith, who at my desire had agreed to be agent, called on me between one and two, when I got up and talked with him. Crosbie positively refused to appear for John Reid, as he had warned him after his last trial, but he was willing to give his aid privately. I went in a chair to his house at two, and consulted with him as to my plan of conducting the trial. He instructed me as to the subject of a charge of being habit and repute a thief. He asked me to dine with him, but as he had a company who I knew would drink, I declined his invitation, being resolved to keep myself perfectly cool. I went to the New Church in the afternoon and heard Dr. Blair preach. Sir George and Lady Preston and Miss Preston drank tea with us. In the evening I finished what remained of Walton from the morning. Looked into Sir George Mackenzie's *Criminals*,[1] meditated on the various circumstances of John Reid's trial, and examined separately two exculpatory witnesses as to his getting the sheep (with the theft of which he was charged) from one Gardner. One of them seemed so positive, notwithstanding my earnest request to tell me nothing but truth, that I began to give some credit to John's tale; but it afterwards appeared that great endeavours had been used to procure false evidence. Notwithstanding all my care to be cool, anxiety made me restless and hot after I went to bed.[2]

MONDAY 1 AUGUST. Having passed an uneasy night from anxiety as to the defence of John Reid, who was my first client in

[1] See below, p. 254 *n*. 2.

[2] "That the learned Bouricius who writes *De officio advocati* relates that he had passed many sleepless nights in preparing for capital trials, and that he must himself say that he had shut his eyes but for a very short space the preceding night" (deleted passage in a draft of Boswell's opening plea "for the panel").

THE TOLBOOTH, EDINBURGH,

engraved from a painting by Alexander Nasmyth. From an original in the Edinburgh Central Public Library

criminal business, I rose between six and seven and dictated to Mr. Lawrie my pleading on the indictment. My dear wife, who always takes good care of me, had a bowl of soup ready for my breakfast, which was an excellent morning cordial. The history of this day will be found in my Register of Criminal Trials.

EDITORIAL NOTE: Boswell's Register of Criminal Trials has not been found. He preserved, however, a considerable collection of separate papers relating to the Reid trial. An extended record of this trial is also to be found in the Justiciary Records, Books of Adjournal and Processes, in the Scottish Record Office.

At eight o'clock on the morning of 1 August, before the High Court of Justiciary, consisting for the moment of four judges: Thomas Miller of Barskimming (the Lord Justice-Clerk), Alexander Boswell Lord Auchinleck, Henry Home Lord Kames, and George Brown Lord Coalston, the trial of John Reid began with the reading of the Lord Advocate's indictment.

JOHN REID, flesher, lately residing at Hillend,[1] near to the west bridge of Avon, in the parish of Muiravonside and shire of Stirling, at present prisoner in the Tolbooth of Edinburgh, you are indicted and accused, at the instance of James Montgomery of Stanhope, Esquire, His Majesty's Advocate, for His Majesty's interest: THAT WHEREAS, by the laws of this and of every other well-governed realm, *theft*, especially *sheep-stealing*, and *reset of theft*, or the being art and part of both or either of said crimes, by stealing, receiving, or feloniously keeping, or having in one's possession a number of sheep, knowing them to have been stolen, for the purpose of selling, consuming or making gain of them, or by feloniously disposing of the carcasses or skins of part of such sheep, knowing them to have been stolen, are crimes of a heinous nature, and severely punishable, especially when committed by a person of bad fame, habit and repute to be a thief, or sheep-stealer: YET TRUE IT IS, that you, the said John Reid, are guilty actor, or art and part, of said crimes of theft, or sheep-stealing and

[1] A place about twenty miles west of Edinburgh, just north of the River Avon and a little downstream from the "west bridge".

reset of theft, or of one or other of said crimes, aggravated as aforesaid; IN SO FAR AS you did, upon the sixth day of October last, or upon one or other of the days or nights of the said month of October or of the month of September immediately preceding, or of November immediately following, steal, or feloniously away take from the farm of Medwenhead, in the county of Peebles, the property of William Lawson of Cairnmuir, and rented by Alexander Gray tenant in Lyne,[1] in the said county of Peebles, nineteen sheep, or some other number of sheep, the property of the said Alexander Gray; and, having stolen the same, you did by yourself, or with the assistance of others, your associates, drive said sheep to your said house at Hillend, near to the west bridge of Avon, in the parish of Muiravonside and county of Stirling; and having kept them there and in the neighbourhood thereof, did there kill a certain number of said sheep, and did sell or dispose of the same, or part of the carcasses and skins thereof, to different persons at Falkirk, and in the neighbourhood of your said house, or in the town of Linlithgow; and Robert Paterson, herd to the said Alexander Gray, suspecting that you had stolen said sheep, having gone from said farm of Medwenhead, after the said sheep had been a-missing from thence, to your said house of Hillend, upon the eleventh, or one or other of the days of the month of October aforesaid, he did there discover three of said sheep in a park near to your house, which had been put there by you to graze; and having thereafter gone into your flesh-house or booth, where you was in use to kill sheep, he there found two of said sheep, which had been killed, hanging up without the body-skin, but which, by the marks on their heads, which were not separated from their bodies, he knew to be part of said sheep which had been stolen from the farm of Medwenhead as aforesaid; and you, being conscious of guilt, did immediately, or soon after the arrival of said Robert Paterson at your said house, abscond and fly therefrom; and thereafter, the property of said three living sheep, and the heads of said killed sheep, having been proved to belong to said Alexander Gray, before the deceased Michael Ramsay of Mungall, Esq., one of the Justices of the Peace for the shire of Stirling, the same were, by his order, delivered to said Alexander Gray. From all which it is evident,

[1] See below, p. 253 *n*. 2.

that you the said John Reid are guilty actor, or art and part, of the said theft and reset of theft. AT LEAST, time and place aforesaid, a parcel of sheep, amounting to nineteen, or some other number, the property of said Alexander Gray, were stolen from said farm of Medwenhead; and you did feloniously receive part of said sheep, knowing them to have been stolen, or did feloniously keep the same in your possession, with a view to dispose thereof, and did actually dispose of part thereof, or of part of the carcasses or skins thereof, knowing said sheep to have been stolen; or was otherways guilty actor, or art and part, of said theft and reset of theft, or of one or other of said crimes; and you are a person of bad fame, habit and repute a sheep-stealer. AND you the said John Reid, having been brought before Archibald Cockburn of Cockpen, Esq., His Majesty's Sheriff-Depute of the county of Edinburgh, did, upon the twenty-third day of March last, emit a declaration, tending to show your guilt in the premises; which declaration, signed by you and said Archibald Cockburn, being to be used in evidence against you, will, in due time, be lodged with the clerk of the High Court of Justiciary, before which you are to be tried, that you may see the same. ALL WHICH, or part thereof, or that you the said John Reid are guilty actor, or art and part, of the said theft, and reset of theft, or of one or other of said crimes, aggravated as aforesaid, being found proven by the verdict of an assize before the Lord Justice General, Lord Justice-Clerk, and Lords Commissioners of Justiciary, you ought to be punished with the pains of law, to deter others from committing the like in time coming.

(signed) JAMES MONTGOMERY.[1]

On one side of the bar were arrayed four "procurators" for the prosecution: James Montgomery of Stanhope, Esquire, His Majesty's Advocate; Mr. Henry Dundas, His Majesty's Solicitor; and two other advocates, Mr. William Nairne and Mr. Robert Sinclair. Opposed to this formidable team stood: "Procurator in Defence, Mr. James Boswell, Advocate".

The first phase of the trial was a "pleading on the relevancy" of the "libel". "Boswell for the panel represented that":

[1] The Indictment has been taken from the printed copy in Boswell's collection of the trial papers.

[He] does in general deny the libel as laid. . . . If he has been so unlucky as to have sheep found in his possession which were stolen, he solemnly avers that he did not know them to be so, but although that had been the case, he humbly contends that this libel is irrelevant in so far as it concludes for the pains of law, the import of which he understands to be a capital punishment, upon the second alternative charged; for he is advised that reset of theft is not punishable with death. . . . As to the charge of his being a person of bad fame, habit and repute as sheep-stealer . . . he was tried for that very charge in December 1766, and a verdict of his country was returned finding it not proved, and nothing is better established than that a man cannot be again tried for the same charge of which he has been acquitted; and supposing this charge to be restricted to the time since his former trial, it is well known that when a man has had the misfortune to be tried for any crime, a prejudice is thereby created against his character which is seldom entirely removed from vulgar minds, though he obtains a verdict in his favour.[1]

Boswell concluded with a compliment to the candour and humanity of the Lord Advocate.

ADVOCATUS. I do not wish it should be understood that in this stage of the cause or any after stage I am to insist for any particular kind of punishment. I understand theft to be the subject of arbitrary punishment, and it is in your Lordships' breasts to determine. I am obliged to my learned friend for his compliment to my humanity. But I should not think it a proof of it were I to bring any of His Majesty's subjects to trial for a crime of which he was formerly acquitted. But the solid answer to the argument as to habit and repute is that it is only a circumstance. I should be sorry if the witnesses mix what is ancient. They will speak to his character, as to his complexion. It respects only the punishment, and your Lordships will not carry it farther than it ought to go. . . .

[1] Scottish Record Office, a minute, in Mr. Lawrie's hand, signed by Boswell, headed "Defences for John Reid". Other texts appear in the Books of Adjournal and among Boswell's own papers. Apparently the defence was required to present a signed outline of its arguments.

AUCHINLECK. As to habit and repute, it is not a crime in our law. It is a misfortunate thing when a man has it, but a man cannot be punished for having a bad character. It is pretty fair if we get them punished when there is both habit and repute and a proof of the crime. Then habit and repute [is] not only an aggravation but a strong circumstance of guilt.

Court all agreed.

I moved that the time should be restricted to since 1766. . . .

KAMES. If he is habit and repute when the theft was committed or now, that is enough; not that he was habit and repute forty years ago.[1]

The Court had sent summonses in the name of the Crown to forty-five Edinburgh tradesmen and craftsmen, and from these they now chose fifteen to serve as "assize" or jury: seven merchants, two engravers, two jewellers, two booksellers, one printer, one watchmaker.

The first witness called for the prosecution was Robert Paterson, aged fifty and upwards, herdsman. He deponed at great length and most circumstantially about the matters narrated in the indictment: namely his missing nineteen of his master's sheep and finding three of them feeding in a park near John Reid's house and three of them slaughtered in Reid's flesh-house, all three skinned but two with the heads still on, and his being absolutely sure, both from the natural marks and faces of the sheep and from certain "lug marks", burns, and tar marks, that these were his master's sheep (he "would have known them among a thousand"). And:

"That the distance from Medwenhead to the panel's house may be sixteen or eighteen computed miles,[2] and that it is easy to drive a parcel of sheep from said farm to the panel's house from sun-setting of one day to sun-rising of another in the month of October.

"That soon after he had challenged the three living sheep, William

[1] Boswell's trial papers, manuscript in Boswell's hand.

[2] See above, p. 250. Lyne is a small parish, near the centre of Peebles; it lies about twenty-four English miles (or perhaps a little more than twenty-one Scottish miles), at its most northerly point, from Hillend on the River Avon.

Black sent off the panel's daughter to go in quest of her father and bring him to see what he had to say; that the girl returned soon after without her father and spoke something to William Black by themselves which the deponent did not hear, and depones that he never saw the panel while he was about his house on the above search, except at the time . . . when he first came there and when he did not know him, but now knows the panel to be the same person whom he then saw and conversed with.''[1]

A second shepherd was called as witness (as he finished his testimony "Lords Pitfour and Kennet came into court"), and then a boy, the son of Paterson, the first witness.

Boswell for the panel objected that this witness is clearly inadmissible, he being not yet thirteen years of age, and having been but a little past twelve at the time when the facts charged are said to have happened. The law is expressly laid down by Sir George Mackenzie in his *Criminals*: Title: Probation by Witnesses, §5. And the same learned author, §12 of the same title, says that if a witness was not *habilis* at the time, he cannot be admitted though he be *habilis* and *major* at the time of his deposition.[2]

Sinclair for the prosecutor answered that it was proposed to examine the boy only in the way of declaration, and whatever may have been the opinion of Sir George Mackenzie upon abstract principles, nothing is now better established in practice than to receive declarations of this kind. . . . [3]

AUCHINLECK. I remember in the first trial I was on, which was for a murder, a little girl swore to having seen the panel mix a powder, which clenched the evidence of poison.

[1] Boswell's trial papers, manuscript in Boswell's hand. This version of the testimony is closely paralleled by that in the Books of Adjournal.

[2] Sir George Mackenzie of Rosehaugh, *The Laws and Customs of Scotland in Matters Criminal*, Edinburgh, 1678, Part II, Title XXVI ("Probation by Witnesses"), [§] 5 (p. 531), "How minors are to be admitted witnesses," [§] 12 (p. 536), "What time is considered in the hability of a witness."

[3] Books of Adjournal.

COALSTON. There is a great difference between civil and criminal questions. In the first, people have the choice of their witnesses. In the other, they have not.

He was called.

JUSTICE-CLERK. Boy, do you go to the Church?—to the Kirk?

BOY. No. I gang to the meeting-house.[1]

AUCHINLECK. You know that God made you?

BOY. (Stupid).

AUCHINLECK. Wha made you?

BOY (with shrill voice). God!

AUCHINLECK. You ken it's a sin to lie?

BOY. Ay.

PITFOUR. You know you are always in the presence of God, and that an over-ruling Providence superintends us all, and that you will be severely punished both in this world and the next if you say what is not true?

(*Pitfour Examinator*—Age[2] and childhood—strange work! Justice-Clerk and Lord Advocate tried him. But all in vain except as to some trifles. *Dismissed*. Afterwards, Justice-Clerk having said it was no evidence unless taken down, boy called back.)[3]

The testimony of the boy was followed by that of Alexander Gray, the tenant farmer who had owned the sheep; and then the prosecution adduced William Black of Hillend ("aged forty years and upwards, unmarried"). "Solemnly sworn, purged of malice and partial counsel, and interrogate," he deponed:

"That he is acquainted with the panel, who stays in his neighbourhood at Hillend and lives in a house belonging to the deponent and deals in killing of sheep and cattle sometimes, though not to any extent. . . . That the panel went from home upon a Wednesday or Thursday morning and returned with the sheep some time in the night

[1] The boy means that he belongs to a congregation of Seceders, not to the Church of Scotland.

[2] Pitfour was seventy-four years old.

[3] Boswell's trial papers, manuscript in Boswell's hand.

or next morning early; for the sheep were come before the deponent arose and were not there when he went to bed. That the deponent, said morning, saw part of the sheep going below the panel's house, and the panel was employed in killing some of them. That the deponent at the time had some suspicions that the panel had not come honestly by the sheep, though he had no conversation with him on the subject so far as he remembers, and the reasons of his suspicions were that he had brought home these sheep in the night-time and was in use to bring sheep in the night and did not commonly take the sheep to the markets to be sold but disposed of them privately in the town of Falkirk and the neighbouring towns and not in the public market-place, and that the panel is a person suspected of sheep-stealing by report of the country. . . . That the deponent said [to Robert Paterson] he ought to get a constable and to claim the sheep before some honest neighbours and consign them in some person's hand until he proved the property. The deponent accordingly got William Marshall, a constable, and James Inglis, and in their presence Robert Paterson claimed the sheep as belonging to his master, Mr. Gray, and showed his master's marks upon them. . . . That when Robert Paterson came in search of the sheep on said Monday the deponent went with him into the panel's house, but was told he was not at home, but at Bridgehill, which is not a quarter of a mile distant. That the deponent sent one of the panel's daughters to tell her father that a man had come to the town claiming the sheep and desired he might come and speak with him, that soon after the girl returned and was crying or *greeting*, said her father would not come back, but desired the deponent would put it up with the man the best way he could. Depones that after that he never saw the panel at his own house, though he was told he had been at it afterwards; but if it was, it must have been in a concealed manner, as the deponent never saw him. That in about two months thereafter the deponent was informed that the panel had been apprehended in his own house about twelve o'clock at night, but the deponent did not see him, as the party had carried him away before he got up.

"And being interrogated for the prisoner, depones that he purchased from the panel a leg of one of the sheep or a side, that is, of those which he brought home in October as aforesaid, but does not remember having purchased mutton from him at any other time. And being interrogated if when he bought the said leg or side he suspected that the sheep had been stolen, depones that there was a general suspicion against the panel, and the deponent was not in use to buy mutton from him, but as nothing had been proved against him and the deponent knew nothing as to that particular parcel, and that others were buying mutton from him at the time, he also bought as said is. That about three years ago or thereby, one William Gardner, who as the deponent believes is now in Stirling Gaol, purchased some cows or stots[1] at Falkirk Muir which the panel slaughtered, that the deponent heard that the panel and Gardner had afterwards some disputes together and left off dealing with each other, so far as he has heard, and the deponent never heard that said cattle had been improperly come by. And depones that as he was in bed when the panel came home in October last, he cannot say whether the panel drove home the sheep himself or if they were brought to the panel by some other person. And being interrogated if it does not consist with his knowledge that the panel was in bed in his own house all the night preceding the sheep's coming there in October last, depones that it does not consist with his knowledge whether the panel was in his bed or not that night; all he knows is that the panel went away in the morning, as already deponed to, and was not come home so far as the deponent knows when the deponent went to bed, but was at home next morning when he arose. And depones that there is not six yards between the panel's house and his, and that the panel has a wife and three children."[2]

The prosecution adduced also Robert Shaw of Bridgehill, aged fifty, married, who deponed:

"That he lives within half a mile of the panel's house, that he has known him for many years, that he has a bad character in the neighbourhood and has for several years past been suspected of sheep-

[1] Young oxen or steers.

[2] Boswell's trial papers, manuscript in Boswell's hand, closely paralleled in the Books of Adjournal.

stealing. That upon a Monday in the month of October last . . . the panel came over to the deponent's house in order to settle some accounts betwixt them, that when they were so employed the panel's daughter came and said, 'Father, come home as fast as you can,' or words to that purpose, upon which he rose, went to the door with his daughter, and did not again return to the deponent's house. That in a little time after, Jean Neilson came to the deponent's house and told him that the sheep which were in the panel's possession had been challenged as stolen sheep, upon which he went to the door and saw the panel upon the south side of the Water of Avon going westwards and away from his house, which is upon the north side of the Water of Avon; that he was sometimes running and sometimes walking hard, and that he observed him two different times look back. That at this time he saw some men driving three live sheep towards the bridge of Avon, which he afterwards understood were three of the stolen sheep that were challenged that day. Depones that the panel some time ago used to butcher both cattle and sheep, but for some time past only some sheep, and that he has sometimes bought mutton from him. And being interrogated for the panel, depones that the panel never wronged him in any dealings which the deponent had with him."[1]

Two other witnesses for the prosecution, interrogated by Lord Auchinleck, deponed that John Reid had the general reputation of a sheep-stealer. And then, without opposition from Boswell or the need of bringing witnesses, the prosecutor introduced, to be read before the court as promised in the indictment, Reid's "declaration":

At Edinburgh, the twenty-third day
of March, 1774 years

The which day in presence of Archibald Cockburn, Esquire, of Cockpen, advocate, Sheriff-Depute of the Sheriffdom of Edinburgh, compeared John Reid, flesher, lately residing at Hillend, near to the west bridge of Avon, in the parish of Muiravonside and shire of Stirling, presently prisoner in the Tolbooth of Edinburgh, who being

[1] Boswell's trial papers, manuscript in Boswell's hand, closely paralleled in the Books of Adjournal.

examined and interrogate declares that the week before last Michaelmas market at Crieff the declarant was the whole week at home at his own house at Hillend, where he slept every night that week, and that he possesses his house from one William Black, who is his next neighbour. Declares that he killed several sheep that week and sold some of them at Falkirk Market and likewise at home. Declares that he is acquainted with James Inglis, farmer at Haining Miln, and that Inglis was in the declarant's slaughter-house said week, when there were some dead sheep hanging there, but whether tups or ewes the declarant does not remember. And declares that at the same time the declarant had some sheep belonging to him going upon Black's pasture near the house, and being interrogate where he got or bought the sheep that he killed that week and sold either at home or Falkirk Market and also where he got or bought the sheep that were going on Black's pasture, declares that he got them all from one William Gardner in Parkhead of Hillend, who brought them to the declarant's house on the Thursday morning, on which day the declarant began to kill them. Declares that the number of sheep brought by Gardner to the declarant was nineteen, and that he told the declarant he got the said sheep from some horse-copers[1] about Carnwath with whom he had dealings. And being interrogate when he left his own house after Gardner had delivered the said sheep to him, declares that it is very likely he left it on the Monday after, but he will not say that he left it that day. And being interrogate what was his reason for leaving his own house so suddenly, declares that he will not answer that question or any more questions this day, having answered enough already. This he declares to be truth.[2]

Boswell and Reid had formally summoned (on 31 July) no fewer than thirty-three of Reid's neighbours and acquaintances as exculpatory witnesses (eight of these, including William Black, appearing also on the prosecution's list of thirty witnesses). On the same day, as we have seen, Boswell had examined two such witnesses with dis-

[1] Horse-dealers.

[2] Boswell's trial papers, manuscript in a clerk's hand, closely paralleled in the Books of Adjournal.

concerting results. He now attempted to adduce only a single witness.

I offered to prove by Andrew Auld what Gardner said as to a bargain between him and Reid as to these sheep.

SOLICITOR. Gardner himself was kept in the prison of Stirling, where he now lies, on purpose that the panel might bring him as an evidence if he thought proper.[1] Instead of doing which, we are to have a proof of a *hearsay* from him.

BOSWELL. I understood that a man convicted by the verdict of his country of house-breaking is infamous and intestable. Besides, though Gardner had been admitted, I should not have chosen to trust the panel's life to the testimony of one in his circumstances.

ADVOCATUS. I agree that the witness shall be examined as to what he has heard from Gardner.

KAMES. I am not for yielding to the King's Advocate to wound the law—to go out of rule to take a hearsay, instead of adducing Gardner.

ADVOCATUS. I am sure I want to do nothing to wound the law. I hold it to be clear law that if Gardner had been transported, what he said as to a bargain between him and the panel might have been proved, as that was the best evidence the nature of the thing would admit. But Gardner stands not transported, though convicted. Mr. Boswell says he thought him intestable and did not adduce him. *There* I put my concession.

KAMES. I never understand that the mistake of a lawyer was to make law. I submit, but I give my testimony against it.

JUSTICE-CLERK. If the prosecutor passes from an objection to a witness, it has been usual for the Court to admit. Had the opinion of the Court been called upon, we probably should all have been unanimous.

I stated that if Gardner had been called and the Lord Advocate had

[1] On the list of witnesses inscribed on Reid's indictment (Scottish Record Office) and signed, like the indictment, by James Montgomery, appears "William Gardner in Parkhead of Hillend, present prisoner in the Tolbooth of Stirling". Gardner had been tried before the spring Circuit Court at Stirling, convicted of stealing a piece of scarlet cloth from a shop in Falkirk, and sentenced to transportation. He was, like Reid, a tenant to Reid's neighbour William Black of Hillend.

admitted him, the same objection might have come from the Court: that the King's Counsel could not make, by their consent, illegal evidence be received:—so that in either case I should have been deprived of evidence.[1]

Andrew Auld, "indweller in Westcraig", was called. "Could only say that Gardner told him of a bargain between the panel and him above a year ago." "Depones nothing material and dismissed."

"No more witnesses called for the panel."

Boswell himself, however, introduced at this point a reminiscence:

BOSWELL for the panel represented that as there was here a charge against the panel of being habit and repute a common thief, notwithstanding of his being acquitted of that charge by a verdict of his country in the year 1766, it was of great importance to the panel to show cause for such bad report having prevailed, and he offered to prove by two of the jury upon his last trial that after a verdict of his country was returned acquitting him, the five judges present strongly expressed their disapprobation of the verdict and in such terms as to convey to the minds of a numerous audience that notwithstanding that verdict he was still a guilty man.

His Majesty's Advocate answered that in order to save the time of the Court he had no objection to admit the fact as above stated.[2]

The trial now concluded with speeches of summation by the Lord Advocate and Boswell.

Boswell seems to have been calculating that if he could to some extent discredit the aspersion of "habit and repute a thief", then Reid's own declaration concerning Gardner's role, along with the cross-examination of William Black and perhaps some further intimations from Auld, might persuade the jury that it was at least possible Reid had received the sheep from Gardner innocently. At the

[1] Boswell's trial papers, manuscript in Boswell's hand, closely paralleled in the Books of Adjournal.

[2] Books of Adjournal.

same time Boswell was careful not to adduce Gardner himself at the trial, fearing no doubt that his testimony would clearly convict Reid of the crime of "reset of theft" (that is, receiving stolen sheep knowing them to be stolen). We shall see that a few days after the trial Boswell made strenuous efforts to bring Gardner forward, when through Crown action it was no longer possible. Whether a verdict finding Reid guilty only of "reset" would have elicited from this Court the less severe sentence of transportation, we can scarcely now be sure, though Boswell may have had clear enough intimations to the contrary. The allusions to the alternative of reset, in the imperfectly reported speech by the Lord Advocate which follows, are apparently to be read, in the light of legal logic, as meaning that since this alternative has not been advanced by the defence, then the possibility of it should not be allowed to complicate the jury's judgment that Reid's possession of the sheep was guilty: that is, guilt of some kind is obvious, and only one kind is now admissible. Boswell's response will try, on the contrary, to suggest that at least one kind of guilt, the partial guilt of reset, has been abandoned by the prosecution, and that, given the simple alternatives of full guilt and innocence, it is more just to decide for the latter.

LORD ADVOCATE'S CHARGE. . . . As it is impossible for the Public Prosecutor, whoever he may be, to know whether a person accused may not, where there are only circumstances, prove that he bought them, reset is libelled. If there is evidence brought to satisfy the minds of a jury that he did not steal, then there is reset. Here there is no occasion for it; for if this man is not guilty of the actual theft, he is an innocent man. My learned friend has mentioned his former trial. Surely he cannot mean that the respectable judges (whom I have in my eye) having declared their opinions that it was a bad verdict will do him good. I therefore cannot imagine what use he is to make of it. . . .

Let us consider corroborating circumstances. What is the conduct of this panel? Does he appear like an honest man? . . . Black, his next neighbour, does not see him for two months, till the law, too cunning for him, overtakes him, and the officers catch him sleeping in his bed. These circumstances speak strongly to the mind. Had he been innocent, had he bought these sheep from Gardner, would he not have come and told the officers so and said, "This man must be a rascal"? . . . Now consider how improbable it is in calculation that on the same day the same number of sheep stolen were sold to the panel. It may perhaps be said Gardner stole the sheep, and therefore the number must be nineteen. But of this the panel has brought no evidence. He has not adduced Gardner. . . . My learned friend, who always does great justice to his clients, especially in this court, but is sometimes righteous overmuch (it is excusable when pleading for a panel), set out with a distinction between theft and reset. But he must have greater abilities than he really has (and he has great abilities) if he can persuade you that there was here not a theft but a reset. I do not think that in every case reset should be punished as theft. Here though proof had been brought that the panel had received the sheep from Gardner, the presumption would have been that it was reset. But it appears to me that the proof of actual theft is abundantly strong. Perhaps it may appear stronger to me as I am connected with a sheep country. You gentlemen will judge and will bring in your verdict accordingly.

My Charge. Gentlemen of the jury, you are now to deliberate concerning the life of [a] fellow citizen who stands at this bar charged with the crime of sheep-stealing. My Lord Advocate has summed up the evidence upon the part of the Crown with his usual ability, but with a warmth unusual for his Lordship on such occasions. He has indeed fairly explained the reason for this—his being connected with a sheep country. But you and I, gentlemen, who have no such connexions, will consider the matter calmly and coolly. You at least will, whose duty it is to form a judgment upon it. The indictment charges the panel with three several accusations: theft, reset of theft, and being a person of bad fame, habit and repute a thief. The reset of theft my Lord Advocate has given up, for he has admitted that unless the panel shall be found guilty of the theft in this case, he is to be held as an innocent man. I have therefore to speak only of two accusations, his being guilty of theft and his being habit and repute a thief. I shall begin with the last, and as I had occasion to state to the Court when pleading upon the relevancy of this indictment, I again state. . . .[1]

Mr. James Boswell "summed up the evidence . . . in a very masterly and pathetic manner, which did him great honour both as a lawyer and as one who wished for a free and impartial trial by jury" (*Edinburgh Advertiser*, 2 August 1774).

At about five o'clock that afternoon, the Court ordered the jury to be enclosed. They chose the bookseller William Gordon to be their chancellor and the printer John Robertson to be their clerk. They reached a verdict and signed it that evening before supper, and it was known about town, though not to be delivered until the next afternoon.

MONDAY 1 AUGUST [continued]. Michael Nasmith came home with me between five and six, when we dined, drank some porter and port and a bottle of claret. I was in a kind of agitation, which is not without something agreeable, in an odd way of feeling. Having heard that a verdict was found against John Reid, I went at eight to Walker's Tavern, where the jury were met (I having first visited my client and intimated his fate to him), and being elated with the admirable appearance which I had made in the court, I was in such a frame as to think myself an Edmund Burke—and a man who united pleasantry in conversation with abilities in business and powers as an orator. I enjoyed the applause which several individuals of the jury now gave me and the general attention with which I was treated. The Crown entertains the jury on an occasion of this kind, and the bill is authenticated by the initials of the chancellor. We drank a great deal, and by imposing a fine of a pint[2] of claret on any man who mentioned the trial, bets, etc., we had six pints of claret secured for a future meeting; and we appointed to dine together in the same place that day sennight. There was a strange mixture of characters. I was not much pleased at being fixed for another meeting. However, I considered it as un-

[1] Boswell's trial papers. The Lord Advocate's Charge is in Boswell's hand; the opening fragment of Boswell's Charge, all that is preserved, is in Lawrie's hand.

[2] See above, p. 235 *n.* 1.

avoidable, and as the buck in one of our farces says, 'twas *life*. We parted about twelve. I was much in liquor, and strolled in the streets a good while—a very bad habit which I have when intoxicated. I got home before one. My dear wife had been very anxious.

[Michael Nasmith to Boswell]

[Edinburgh] 1 August [1774], 7 o'clock

DEAR SIR,—This is truly miserable. The most unjudicious verdict that can be. But what is still more miserable, it is just: a verdict in general "finding the theft proved" against him. The gentleman who informs me is a stranger to judicial style, thinks these are the capital words. Capital enough! I wish it had been otherwise, for the sake of that respect which *belongs* to a jury and of the dignity that the panel's charge merits. Could we get an innocent panel! But what can be done for guilt? I am in low spirits notwithstanding the good cheer within me. Alwise, my dear Sir, yours most sincerely,

M. NASMITH.

TUESDAY 2 AUGUST. My bad rest during the night between Sunday and yesterday, the anxiety of the trial, and the debauch of last night made me in a woeful plight and very unwilling to rise. Worthy Sir John Hall called between seven and eight. I got up, and though hurt by the comparison between his decent sobriety and my riotous conduct, I was comforted to find myself entrusted by him, and the friendship of the family of Stichell continued to one of our family by his connexion.[1]

In the court in the forenoon I received great applause for my spirited behaviour yesterday; and I could also see Scottish envy showing itself. John Reid received his sentence at two o'clock, or rather a little before three.

EDITORIAL NOTE: When the jury had at two o'clock delivered its verdict—"all in one voice" finding "John Reid the panel guilty of the

[1] Sir John's mother was a daughter of Sir John Pringle, second Baronet of Stichell; he was therefore a nephew of Sir John Pringle the physician.

theft libelled"[1]—"Mr. Boswell moved the Court to delay pronouncing sentence for a few days, as he would endeavour to show that a capital punishment should not be inflicted."[2] We have Boswell's hastily scribbled record of the words that followed:

AUCHINLECK. I'll own I think theft by our law a capital crime, more especially as here, where 'tis a *grex*;[3] were it not so, farmers would be in [a] miserable situation. If nineteen not capital, a hundred not, and there would be an end of that useful business. I have therefore no sort of difficulty. If there was anything special, I should be for indulging [the] panel's counsel. But as we have often had this before us, [it] would be indecent.

KAMES. I have no doubt that theft of nineteen, nay of nine, [is] capital. If not, as my brother said, [it] would be dismal, as we could not repress it. And there would be no remedy. 'Tis done by low people. They cannot make reparation. I should like that better. At [the] same time, as we have no act making it capital, though we have had long practice, I'm for indulging [the] young man.

PITFOUR. I will confirm doctrine.[4]

COALSTON. If I thought there was any difficulty or any of your Lordships thought [there was any] difficulty, [I] would delay. But as 'tis clear, [it] would be wrong to delay. This case [is] not new to me. I had occasion to consider it not only by reading all on the subject but by searching [the] records. And so [I] formed [my] opinion. [I have] always followed [this procedure] since I had the honour to sit. I came to [a] clear conclusion. One act of theft [is] not always capital, as of a small thing, as one sheep. But [it is] also clear [that] one theft [can be] capital, as *abigeatus*.[5] And so far as I know, [there is] no instance where when sheep [were] stolen [it has] not [been] capital.

KENNET. I'm willing to grant all indulgence to [the] panel or panel's counsel. I applaud Mr. Boswell's zeal on this occasion and

[1] Verdict (Scottish Record Office).

[2] *Edinburgh Advertiser*, 2 August 1774.

[3] A flock.

[4] This sentence (an interlineation) may be the conclusion of Kames's remarks. The last word is uncertain and the "I will" could equally well be " 'Twill".

[5] Cattle-stealing.

which he has shown on many others. I think delay here improper, as much as if [in a case of] murther.

JUSTICE-CLERK. Your Lordships have a point of law fixed since the Monarchy, that theft [is] capital. It would then be improper and even indecent for the Court to delay upon the relevancy. All your Lordships agreed that theft [is] capital, and indeed [it] would hurt my mind to think that a *grex* should not be capital. So judgment [should be given].

AUCHINLECK. 'Tis a disagreeable part of our office to pass sentence of death on any man. But so are mankind made that it must be. This man [was] before us before, and all of us [were] called on in [the] course of our duty to declare that the verdict was contrary to evidence. Now we have from a most respectable jury a verdict finding [him] guilty of [the theft of a] *grex*. Were he to get off, [he] would go on. His former escape emboldened [him]. We have no choice. I propose that on Wednesday, etc.

JUSTICE-CLERK. John Reid, nothing remains to me now but to pronounce that judgment we the Court unanimously agreed should be pronounced. I am very sorry it is necessary. Your former trial should not have been mentioned, had it not been forced on [the] Court by your counsel, who has exerted all his talents and abilities in your defence. But the facts coming out in evidence put it out of his power to do you any service. I do not desire to revive the memory of what is past. God and your own conscience know [as to that.] But, Sir, you are now convicted[1] by verdict of your country of the theft of nineteen sheep. You could not commit that without other crimes. But it can do you no harm to join with my brothers in giving you . . .

[Sentence of Death Against John Reid]

The said Lords . . . decern and adjudge the said John Reid to be carried from the bar back to the Tolbooth of Edinburgh, therein to be detained until Wednesday the seventh day of September next, and upon that day to be taken forth of the said Tolbooth and carried to the common place of execution in the Grassmarket of Edinburgh, and then

[1] The ending of this word is not quite certain.

and there betwixt the hours of two and four o'clock in the afternoon of the said day to be hanged by the neck by the hands of the common executioner upon a gibbet until he be dead, and ordain all his moveable goods and gear to be escheat and inbrought to His Majesty's use, which is pronounced for doom.

THOMAS MILLER
ALEXANDER BOSWELL
HENRY HOME
JAMES FERGUSON
GEORGE BROWN
ROBERT BRUCE[1]

TUESDAY 2 AUGUST [continued]. My wife and I dined at Lord Alva's.[2] The only company were a Mrs. Bradshaw, wife to an officer of the 66 regiment lying in the Castle, and Mr. Cosmo Gordon. We were kindly, easily, and luxuriously entertained. My Lord's son *only* was at home.[3] At four I went to a consultation at Mr. Rae's on Earl Fife's politics. It lasted a very little while. I then returned and drank a few glasses of wine. I drank tea and was introduced to Mr. Robinson,[4] a young student, a nephew of Mrs. Montagu's. My wife and I supped at Sir George Preston's. Nobody there.

WEDNESDAY 3 AUGUST. Adam Bell, who consulted me, drank tea. My uncle the Doctor came and took a dish. He applied to me for the loan of £20. My heart was moved to think he needed it; and I promised to send him it next morning. I was at Macqueen's at seven, consulting with him and the Solicitor on Sir Allan Maclean's plea for recovering a part of the estate of his ancestors from the family of Argyll.[5] My blood stirred at this consultation.

[1] Books of Adjournal.

[2] James Erskine, Judge in the Court of Session and distant cousin of Boswell's.

[3] John Erskine of Aberdona, aged about sixteen years.

[4] Morris Robinson, aged seventeen, student at the University, later third Baron Rokeby.

[5] Boswell and Johnson had stayed with Maclean at Inchkenneth during the Hebrides tour, and he had conducted them to Iona. He had written on 17 June this year asking Boswell to find out if his agents were yet "prepared to take the field". "When that happens, I flatter myself you'll appear as one of my best friends."

THURSDAY 4 AUGUST. Sir John Dalrymple told me, either yesterday or today, that my behaviour in John Reid's trial would have made my fortune in England. This increased my desire to go; and, either yesterday or today while I walked in the Meadow with Maclaurin, he seemed to think I would do well to try. He said very handsomely, "*I decus, i, nostrum! melioribus utere fatis.*"[1] He and I had some conversation on the effect of tunes, and we agreed that there is a *ludicrous* in music independent of the association of ideas. He tried Pope's "Universal Prayer" to the tune of "Our Polly she's a sad slut" and it was quite ridiculous. This might arise from association. Yet "Down the burn, Davie" is in its subject by no means solemn; and I tried it and it suited the "Universal Prayer" very well. Balbarton dined. I was tonight at St. John's Lodge. Rather a dull meeting. I was then at Signora Marcoucci's[2] ball.

FRIDAY 5 AUGUST. [No entry for this day.]

SATURDAY 6 AUGUST. In the morning my father asked me to dine with him today, as he had the President with him. I told him I would do anything to oblige him, but that I really wished not to be with the President. He said it was on my account, to have me with people of respect. "Then," said I, "I'll be obliged to you if you will not ask me today." It gave me concern to have different views from my father. But as I cannot help having a bad opinion of the President—as he behaved in a most ungentlemanly manner to me, in privately persuading my father to make votes in Ayrshire against the nobility whose cause I had warmly espoused, and [had] done a most unfriendly thing to my father in leading him to do the very thing which he had for a course of years condemned[3]—I think it more honest and more

[1] *Æneid*, VI, 546: "Go, our glory, and enjoy a happier fate!"

[2] The mistress of a dancing school. A few years later Boswell would see his daughters dancing at her balls for young ladies. She lived in James's Court. In the spring of 1777 she was "on the same flat" with Boswell, they went tête-à-tête in a coach to a dinner at Prestonfield, and Boswell was "enlivened to Italian pitch".

[3] Only freeholders with a considerable property qualification could vote in Parliamentary elections, but some of the large landholders had hit upon the device of selling for nominal sums redeemable life-rents and "wadsets of superiority" devised for the sole purpose of splitting their qualifications, that is, of enabling them, through friends and dependants, to cast more than one vote. Lord Auchin-

spirited to show him that I will have no connexion with him; and notwithstanding his pride of office and the gross flattery which he receives, he must be sensible that he is not what he ought to be.

Sandy Gordon begged as a particular favour that I would dine with him as a friend and be present at the baptism of a son which was born to him last night.[1] I accepted. Dr. Webster was there. We drank cheerfully, but I had resolution not to take too much, being engaged to sup at Captain Schaw's with Lord Pembroke. I came home between seven and eight somewhat heated, but wrote a paper well enough. My wife was at the play with Mrs. Schaw. About eleven we assembled. Lord Pembroke, to whom I had been introduced some years ago in London, was very affable to me. We had a very genteel company, and the most brilliant table that ever I saw in a private house in Edinburgh: a row of crystal lustres down the middle of the table; fruits and flowers interspersed in gay profusion. There was as little good conversation as at any genteel supper.

SUNDAY 7 AUGUST. Was at New Church in the forenoon and heard Dr. Blair. Then called on Lord Pembroke and Colonel Stopford of the 66th regiment, who lodged in the same house with him (in Gosford's Close, a strange place).[2] My Lord was lively and easy. He told me that Mr. Johnson was lately at Eton, where the Doctors entertained him with all their curiosities and with a very good dinner, after which, in order to be as much in spirits and as good company as they could, they pushed about the bottle briskly. Johnson seemed to be displeased. Somebody asked him what was the matter. He answered,

---

leck had always maintained that such votes were fictitious. He had expressed his disapproval of them in his *Observations on the Election Law* dictated to Boswell at Auchinleck in the autumn of 1771. See above, p. 15. At the election on 13 October of the present year both candidates were liberally provided with "made" votes, but when it was demanded that the oath of *bona fide* possession be taken, five of Kennedy's voters discovered qualms of conscience while all of Sir Adam's (including one clergyman) swore through thick and thin, and he was elected. He held the seat for Ayrshire for the next ten years.

[1] Lt.-Col. Alexander Gordon, killed at Talavera, 28 July 1809.

[2] It was old-fashioned, but nonetheless a fashionable residential quarter.

"Why, Sir, this merriment of the parsons is very nauseous to me." I had given Lord Pembroke a letter of recommendation to Paoli when he went to Corsica. This made a connexion. I asked the honour of his company to dinner. He agreed to come any day I pleased. I fixed Thursday. I said, "We Corsicans should meet." Colonel Stopford also engaged to come.

My wife and I dined at my father's between sermons. Dr. Boswell, Sir George Preston, and Mr. Webster were there. Veronica always visits there at that time and gets raisins from her grandfather. In the afternoon I went and walked in St. Anne's Yards and the Abbey of Holyrood House. I was like Isaac meditating in the fields.[1] My wife and I drank tea at home by ourselves, then went with our children and walked pleasantly in Mr. Webster's[2] garden. We supped there. He himself sent that he was not to be home to supper. We were uneasy a little; but it turned out that he had gone to baptise a child, and I suppose had found good wine.

MONDAY 8 AUGUST. Breakfasted at Lady Colville's and engaged her and Lady Anne and Captain Erskine to dine on Thursday with Lord Pembroke. Walked in the garden and was much refreshed. Mrs. Gordon of Stair,[3] who was now in town, took a family dinner with us. I drank tea most comfortably with Grange. We talked seriously. I had this sally: our grave reflections on the vanity of life are part of the farce—like the grave ridiculous in comedy—for, after making them, we take a jovial bottle as if we never had thought. Lady Betty Cochrane, Lord Advocate, Sandy Gordon, Sandy Murray, Maclaurin, and Mr. Henderson (Sir Robert's son)[4] supped with us. This was a good genteel company. We spoke against drinking, but drank four pint bottles of claret. No conversation to be marked. The jury which should have dined together today put off the meeting.

TUESDAY 9 AUGUST. Mr. Bruce of Kinnaird, who was just

[1] Genesis xxiv, 63.

[2] Boswell had known him for years as "Mr.", before he became D.D. in 1760.

[3] Boswell had listed "Miss Gordon" (presumably her daughter) as a matrimonial possibility in 1761–1762.

[4] Aged twenty-two years, later M.P. for various constituencies, and baronet.

returned from his most curious travels, was in the Court of Session, a tall stout bluff man in green and gold.[1] I was very desirous to be with him. Monboddo set him dead, and Maclaurin snuffed him keen.[2] Bob Chalmers introduced me to him, saying, "I thought you two would be glad to see one another." I said I was extremely happy to have the honour of being known to Mr. Bruce, and wished much to see him, not merely to make a formal bow. He said he would be very glad to meet with me, or something to that purpose. All this was very well. Good, unmeaning, commonplace politeness from him. I was quite impatient to hear him talk. I consulted with Monboddo and Maclaurin, and set out to try what I could do to get an appointment made to dine or sup in a tavern. He had now gone out of the Court. I went home, changed my wig, and then went and called for him at his lodgings in Mrs. Reynolds's in Miln's Square. Luckily he was just come in, and I found him alone; and a most curious scene I had with him. I conjectured that he had come to London with high expectations from Government and had been disappointed. This had soured his temper, not very sweet originally; and he had come to Scotland, at which he had conceived a strong aversion when young from the bad usage of a stepmother who had obtained unjust settlements from his father—and come in bad humour with it and its inhabitants, just to try how much he could squeeze out of his estate to support him in England. In this frame, he seemed to be the very reverse of Banks—impatient, harsh, and uncommunicative. I at first felt myself feeble and awkward with him, owing in part to my consciousness how very ignorant I was of the very rudiments of the knowledge respecting the countries which he had been seeing. My curiosity and vanity united, were, however, sufficient to impel me, and as he grew more rough I grew more forward; so that I forced in a manner a good deal from him, while he looked big and stamped and took me short and held his head high and talked with a forcible loudness as if he had been trying whether the room had an echo. As this was a very remarkable scene

[1] He had, as he supposed, discovered the source of the Nile; actually of its largest tributary, the Blue Nile.

[2] They went after him like bird dogs. Compare Monboddo's interest in the travellers Banks and Solander, above p. 146.

with a very remarkable man, I shall as well as I can put it down in its very form as it passed.

BOSWELL. "Pray, Mr. Bruce, was it true that you was bit by a serpent as the newspapers told us?" BRUCE. "I, Sir, bit by a serpent? No, Sir." BOSWELL. "We were told so, and that your leg was hurt." BRUCE. "That was a worm, Sir." (Here, to be sure, he had me fairly as a man of inaccuracy.) BOSWELL. "Where?" BRUCE. "I was ill at Marseilles, but I believe I brought it with me from Nubia. It is a worm which fixes itself into the——" (here he gave the technical term). BOSWELL. "It is spiral like a screw." BRUCE. "Yes, and but small." (Then, letting down his stocking, he showed me the scar.) "The people in that country will have a number of them fixed in their bodies at a time, but they are expert at twisting them out; and then they suffer nothing. My servant broke the worm in my leg, which occasioned all the mischief. At [Jiddah on the Red Sea][1] I met with eleven English vessels from the East Indies. I was then dressed like a poor Turk. I had a mind to try the captains of these vessels. The first I called on was a Scotsman, a Captain *Boswell*. He bid me begone, though I told him I was an unfortunate countryman. He had seen too many such vagrants as me. I then went to an English gentleman, Captain Thornhill, who received me with politeness and humanity, saying, 'I am sorry to see a countryman in distress. You shall have a passage to the East Indies in my ship. You need not go abroad again.' Then called to his servant, 'Let this gentleman have an apartment in my house. Sir, I shall do all that is in my power to make you easy.' Several other English captains behaved well to me. I then said I was happy to find such behaviour to a countryman. I should always tell it to their honour. I would now show them what I was. Upon which I produced my credentials from the Ministry in England and other letters of consequence, and a credit for £2000. I dined with all the captains that day; and *how* they did roast Boswell, my *gude* countryman. When I sailed for Abyssinia, all the ships put out their colours and saluted me with their guns as I passed. Boswell had out his colours but did not fire a gun; only called out with his speaking trumpet, 'Mr. Boswell wishes Mr. Bruce a good voyage.' " I said I was sorry that a countryman

[1] Blank in MS, filled by the editors. Bruce's *Travels* were published in 1790.

and my namesake had behaved so ill. Mr. Bruce seemed to delight in the thought that this Boswell was a *Scotsman*.

I asked what kind of architecture they had in Abyssinia. BRUCE. "Architecture, Sir, in a barbarous, mountainous country!" BOSWELL. "What kind of houses have they?" BRUCE. "Huts." BOSWELL. "Of what are they made?" BRUCE. "Why, of branches of trees—of mud—and of mud and stone together." BOSWELL. "Have they any large towns? Do many of them live together?" BRUCE. "Why, 25,000 in one town." (Bob Chalmers came in and sat by us.) BOSWELL. "Has the King no better house than the rest?" BRUCE. "Yes. He has a large palace built by the Jesuits of stone, in which he might defend himself against all Asia, were it not that they have chosen a place where there is no well." BOB CHALMERS. "What may be the precise colour of the Abyssinians?" BRUCE. "Size and colour, Sir!" CHALMERS. "Precise colour, I said." BRUCE. "Why, tawny copper coloured; though they are fair enough under the line."

In this manner was information dug from him, as from a flinty rock with pickaxes. I shall throw together all that I gathered from him into an essay or sketch for *The London Magazine*.[1] I tried to make an appointment with him to dine or sup, but in vain. I asked in particular that he would meet Lord Monboddo. "No," said he. "I'll neither see Justiciary Lords nor Lords of Session. If I commit murder, I shall see the one; and if I have a civil action, I shall see the other." I made a most entertaining recital to some of my companions of this interview. I entertained Monboddo with it much. I afterwards found that Mr. Bruce was communicative enough if you let him alone, but could not bear to be questioned; at least I was told so, and it is very natural. He was like a ghost, which, it is said, will tell you a great deal of itself, but nothing if you question it. All extraordinary travellers are a kind of shows; a kind of wild beasts. Banks and Bruce however were animals very different one from another. Banks was an elephant, quite placid and gentle, allowing you to get upon his back or play with his proboscis; Bruce, a tiger that growled whenever you approached him. I made a good apology for him to Maclaurin, saying that my ignorant questions could not but fret him. "Suppose," said I, "an Englishman

[1] See below, pp. 283, 284.

should come with the utmost civility, and say, 'Mr. Maclaurin, I beg leave to apply to you as a man who can give me the best information. Pray, do your judges determine causes on foot or on horseback?' Some of my questions to Bruce," said I, "were almost as provoking." I dined quietly at home, and wrote law papers in the afternoon.

[Received 9 August, John Finlayson to Boswell]

Stirling, 8 August 1774

SIR,—Yours directed to my son, who died about three months ago, was yesterday brought to me, which I opened and read, and this day I spoke with the gaoler of the prison here, who is a very sensible and obliging man, and desired him to ask Gardner in ane overly and friendly manner if ever he had given or sold any sheep to Reid, and not let Gardner know that he was desired by any to ask the question at him. The gaoler answered that he had been several times alongst with the Sheriff-Substitute when he came to the prison and examined Gardner, and that Gardner alwise refused his giving or selling of sheep to Reid. However, he would try to ask that question at him this day, and which he said he did, and that Gardner returned him the answer he formerly had given. I also asked one of my clerks, who I sent alongst with the Sheriff-Substitute to Falkirk and Muiravonside to write the precognitions against Reid, and who also wrote these taken here, if ever he heard any of the persons examined, or Gardner, say that he, Gardner, had given or sold Reid any sheep, and he declares to me he never did. At least if ever there was any such thing emitted in the examinations, he does not remember it. I give you the trouble to make my best compliments to Mr. Maclaurin, whom it shall give me pleasure to serve at all times, as it will to you, though I have not the honour of being acquainted with [you]. I am, Sir, your most obedient and most humble servant,

JO. FINLAYSON.

WEDNESDAY 10 AUGUST. This forenoon I met in the Court of Session an old friend of Temple's and mine, the Reverend Mr. Nicholls, whom I had not seen for twelve years. His cousin Miss

Floyer, whom I had seen in England, was married to young Erskine of Mar, and Nicholls and Mrs. Erskine's brother and his lady were come down to visit Erskine and his lady. Captain James Erskine invited me to dine with them at Sir James Dunbar's house in Young's Street, Canongate, which he or they had taken for the race week.[1]

This last week of the session was not a very busy one to me. But I had several little petitions to draw today. I called on Mr. William Wilson about one of them in the afternoon. He was drinking a glass with Dr. Young and Mr. Speirs[2] of Glasgow. He insisted on my joining them; and, though I was not fond of being at all fevered with liquor in the end of a session when I might have sudden calls to write, yet, as Mr. Wilson gave me my first guinea and has always been my very good friend as a man of business, I complied and was solidly social. I really can adapt myself to any company wonderfully well.

In the forenoon I had visited John Reid, whom I found very composed. He persisted in averring that he got the sheep from Gardner. I really believed him after I had adjured him, as he should answer to God, to tell me the truth. I told him that I was of opinion that a petition to the King would have no effect, but that his wife had applied to me, and I should draw one which he should sign; but that he must not expect anything but death. He very calmly assured me he would expect nothing else. I wondered at my own firmness of mind while I talked with a man under sentence of death, without much emotion, but with solemnity and humanity. I desired John to write his life very fully, which he promised to do. I bid him say nothing as to the *facts* with which he was formerly charged. He had been acquitted by his country. That was enough. His acknowledging that he had been guilty might hurt some unhappy panel who was innocent by making a

[1] Norton Nicholls is best known as the disciple of the poet Gray in his last years. Nicholls's cousin Mrs. Erskine was a daughter of Charles Floyer, who had been Governor of Fort St. David, Madras, 1747–1750. Her brother, Charles, Jr., was a "nabob". Young John Francis Erskine succeeded to the restored Earldom of Mar in 1824. Captain James was his younger brother. The week's racing was held on Leith Sands and was sponsored annually by the Company of Hunters.

[2] Alexander Speirs was a founder of the Glasgow Arms Bank in 1750 and was a great importer of tobacco. In July 1779 Boswell describes him as a "low man".

jury condemn on imperfect circumstantial evidence. It will be a curious thing if he gives a narrative of his life.

In the evening I called in at Mr. Bell the bookseller's shop, where I found Mr. Paton of the Customs, who varied the ideal prospect of my mind by presenting to it his remarks and anecdotes concerning Scottish antiquities. He told me of a curious manuscript in the Advocates' Library, the diary of Birrel, a citizen of Edinburgh, in which all things that happened in that man's time (from 1532 to 1605)[1] are recorded. It will help me in my intended History of Edinburgh. A man's mind is like a ——— glass.[2] He must endeavour to find a variety of prints to look at; otherwise, let the glass be ever so good, he will tire of the sameness. At night I gave John Reid's wife a letter to Lord Erroll,[3] from whom she hoped for some assistance, her father having been his tenant these forty years.

[Boswell to the Earl of Erroll]

Edinburgh, 10 August 1774

MY LORD,—This will come to your Lordship's hands along with an application from Clarke, an old tenant of your Lordship's, in favour of John Reid, a client of mine who lies under sentence of death here for sheep-stealing. Reid it seems is son-in-law to Clarke. I may perhaps have been prejudiced, but I really did not think the evidence against Reid sufficient to convict him; and I am afraid his suspicious character determined the jury, which I take to be a dangerous principle. The stolen sheep were found in his possession; but he has uniformly averred that he had them from one Gardner, who has been since sentenced to transportation. He indeed could not *prove* this; but

[1] Boswell's manuscript reads "from 15—— to 16——." Robert Birrel's diary was first printed in 1798.

[2] Perhaps an "optical glass", also known as a "zograscope", and today sometimes, mistakenly, by antique dealers and others, as a "shaving mirror". It consisted of a stand holding a vertical lens and a mirror at an angle of forty-five degrees. A picture placed upside down under the mirror was seen magnified and with enhanced perspective.

[3] Boswell and Johnson stayed overnight with Lord Erroll at Slains Castle, 24 August 1773.

this story is by no means improbable. I am to draw a petition for him to the King in hopes of obtaining a transportation pardon, the evidence being defective and the crime of stealing nineteen sheep being at any rate too small for a capital punishment. If your Lordship will take the trouble to write to Lord Suffolk, it may have great influence, and as the unhappy man's petition will be much better read if a letter from Lord Erroll comes along with it, I shall delay transmitting it for some time till I know your Lordship's determination.

I beg leave to offer my most respectful compliments to Lady Erroll, and with a very grateful sense of your Lordship's civilities to me, I have the honour to be, my Lord, your Lordship's most obedient, humble servant,

[James Boswell].

THURSDAY 11 AUGUST. The confusion and hurry of the last day of the session were much the same as usual. I philosophised, thinking that in all probability all the members of Court would not be alive against another session, though indeed it is remarkable that the members of our College of Justice live long. Death makes as little impression upon the minds of those who are occupied in the profession of the law as it does in an army. The survivors are busy, and share the employment of the deceased. Archibald McHarg, writer, died this session, and though he had a great deal of business, he was never missed. His death was only occasionally mentioned as an apology for delay in giving in a paper. The succession in business is so quick that there is not time to perceive a blank.

Lord Pembroke had hurt his leg and been confined to the house for two days. I was afraid that he would not dine with me today. I called on him in the morning about ten. He was not up; but his servant said he was much better. I had good hopes of seeing him, but still was uncertain. I had a good company besides his Lordship invited; but he being the capital person, I should have been much disappointed if he did not come. My vanity made me very anxious; and I paid the tax of suffering a very disagreeable suspense till he arrived. The company was: Lord Pembroke (whom I contemplated as the *Herbert*, the master of *Wilton*, etc., and was happy that one of the family of Auchinleck entertained an English nobleman of such rank), Lady Colville, Lady Anne and Captain Erskine, General Lockhart of Carnwath, who had also been in Corsica, Colonel Stopford (Lieutenant-Colonel of the 66 regiment and brother to Lord Courtown, an Irish earl), and Colonel Webster. Everything went on with as much ease and as genteelly as I could wish. This was not my own idea only, for I was told so by Lady Colville and Lady Anne, who were attentive as friends. My wife was just as I should have been satisfied to see her in London. Lord Pembroke was lively and pleasant; General Lockhart was more affable than usual. Veronica was brought in after dinner, and Lord Pembroke shook hands with her. I was really the man of fashion. We drank only two bottles of wine after dinner, and then drank tea and coffee with the ladies. So agreeable a day I have not seen in Edinburgh. I went to the Assembly in the evening, not having been at one since I was married. I felt no awkwardness, but saw a very fine company with cheerful satisfaction. Lady Anne Erskine and my wife and Captain Erskine and I met there. I had a full crop from my entertainment of Lord Pembroke, it was so well known. Keith Stewart[1] came up: "Boswell, what have you done with your guest Pembroke?" LORD HADDINGTON.[2] "Mr. B-B-Boswell, what have you done with Lord P-embroke?" He and Colonel Stopford had gone to the play and came in to the Assembly after it. Douglas and I met tonight. His coldness to his best supporters makes him appear to great disadvantage. I told him I intended being at Douglas Castle this autumn. Bruce was here. I tried him again a little, but with very small success. Nicholls was introduced to him, and in my hearing put several questions to him, but received very dry answers. Two Spanish gentlemen were here: a grandee, a Count de Fernan-Nuñez,[3] and a Chevalier Comano. Nicholls introduced me to them. I had a good deal of conversation with the Chevalier, who was an inquisitive, clever little man. It hurt

[1] Naval officer, ultimately vice-admiral, son of the sixth Earl of Galloway.

[2] Father-in-law of Bennet Langton. See above, p. 126 *n.* 3.

[3] "Count ———" in the MS. The two Spaniards, on a tour through England and Scotland, appeared at the races as well as the Assembly and were noticed in the *The Scots Magazine.*

me to find myself much rusted both in Italian and French, while Nicholls spoke both very fluently.

FRIDAY 12 AUGUST. At seven went and saw my father set out for Auchinleck. I had engaged to breakfast at Lady Colville's and go in her coach with Lady Anne and her brothers to see the King's Purse run for on Leith Sands. I accordingly went; but, one of her little nieces having been seized with a fever, Lady Anne could not go. However, Captain Erskine[1] and I took the coach, and on our reaching Edinburgh we were joined by Captain Andrew and the Hon. Captain Elphinstone. It was the only good race this week, and there was a fine show of company. I dined according to invitation with Captain Erskine[2] and his party. Old Erskine the father,[3] his sister Mrs. Rachel, and Colonel Stopford were there. Mrs. Floyer was a Portuguese East Indian, a fine woman. We had an excellent dinner of two courses and a desert of fruits, ices, etc. We plied the wine well in the time of dinner but drank little after it. Nicholls had engaged to sup with me tonight. I asked the Erskines and Mr. Floyer. They were engaged; but Captain Erskine said they would all come to me on Sunday evening. I do not approve of having an entertainment on Sunday, chiefly because I think it should be a day of rest to servants. But I was taken suddenly here, so had not presence of mind to waive the offer. Besides, it was only to be a supper, which does not interfere with public worship. My wife and I afterwards called for the ladies and left a card of invitation for them. The company went to the concert.

I went home, and till Nicholls joins me, I shall take a short review of this summer session. I never was so busy, having written fifty law papers, nor made so much money, having got 120 guineas. I had been up almost every morning at seven, and sometimes earlier. I had been in the Court of Session almost every morning precisely at nine,

[1] Captain Archibald.

[2] Captain James.

[3] James, advocate and Knight-Marshal of Scotland. He was grandson and heir male of the tenth Earl of Mar, and his wife, Frances Erskine, was daughter and heir of line of the eleventh (forfeited) Earl. Their son, John Francis, was restored to the title in 1824. The Erskines of Kellie and the Erskines of Mar were rather remote cousins. Boswell himself, through his mother, was "descended in the line of Alva from the noble House of Mar".

Charles Hay and I having agreed that whichever of us was later of coming than the other, after the nine o'clock bell was rung out, should lose a shilling; and I think I was a few mornings a little late, and he a few, so that upon the whole we were equal. I had advanced in practice and kept clear of the President, I had distinguished myself nobly in a capital trial. I had been a good deal in company, and in the best company of the place, both in my own house and in their houses. I had therefore great reason to be satisfied, having enjoyed, withal, good health and spirits. BUT I had been much intoxicated—I may say *drunk*—six times,[1] and still oftener heated with liquor to feverishness. I had read hardly anything but mere law; I had paid very little attention to the duties of piety, though I had almost every day, morning and evening, addressed a short prayer to GOD. Old Izaak Walton had done me good; and frequently in the course of the day I had meditated on death and a future state. Let me endeavour every session and every year to improve.

Nicholls came to me in the evening. I had Grange also as a friend of Temple's; but there was little intercourse between his Honour and Nicholls, who was full of spirits, quite the fine gentleman, and talked of nothing but of his travels in Italy. It was agreeable to me to find Nicholls after twelve years very happy to meet me.

[Received 12 August, John Finlayson to Boswell]

Stirling, 9 August 1774

SIR,—I think it my duty to acquaint you that Gardner was this day transmitted to Glasgow in order to his being transported abroad. It shall give me great pleasure to serve you at all times in everything in my power, or any of Lord Auchinleck's family, of which I now understand you are, and for whom I have and entertain the greatest respect, having had the honour of his acquaintance for a great many years. I will beg the favour of you to make my best and humble compliments to his Lordship. Wishing all happiness to attend him and you, I am with much regard, Sir, your most obedient and most humble servant,

JO. FINLAYSON.

[1] On 21 June, 9, 19, 22, and 29 July, and 1 August.

SATURDAY 13 AUGUST. After breakfast I went to Belleville and waited on Lady Dundonald about a lawsuit which she had with a weaver whom she had employed to weave some fine table linen, but who had not done it well. She was to carry my wife to the race today, and she insisted that we should dine at Belleville. I agreed to stay on condition of being allowed to write letters, for which purpose I had set apart this day. Accordingly, after taking a dram of excellent brandy with the old Earl, I had the drawing-room to myself and, in all the good spirits that I ever enjoyed, I wrote to General Paoli and my brother David. There was nobody at dinner but Miss Roebuck. We drank tea. I supped at Mr. William Macdonald's, Writer to the Signet, where were Counsellor Archibald Macdonald, Longlands the solicitor-at-law, Sinclair the advocate, etc. There was a great deal of noisy mirth. I drank Madeira—not to excess.

SUNDAY 14 AUGUST. I lay too long and was not ready to go to church in the forenoon. I read in Dodsley's *Fugitive Pieces* "A Journey into England by Paul Hentzner, a German, in 1598", published by Horace Walpole, a curious account. My wife and I went to the New Church in the afternoon, and after I came home I read Burke's *Vindication of Natural Society* in the style of Lord Bolingbroke.[1] I was struck with the quantity of knowledge and abundance of imagery which it displays, and happy to think that it was an admirable antidote against irreligion, as the Preface well points out. Captain Erskine's company that I had engaged on Friday, Lady Betty Cochrane, Captain and Mrs. Schaw, and Colonel Stopford and Lieutenant Vowel of the same regiment, supped. I was in the same easy genteel style as on Lord Pembroke's day, and so was my dear wife. I never saw a supper go on more agreeably. We drank socially in the time of supper; and after it just one bottle of claret and a little out of a second. Ladies and gentlemen rose from table together. It was quite as I could wish.

MONDAY 15 AUGUST. The day that Lord Pembroke dined with me, I should have mentioned a dispute among the military gentlemen

[1] Hentzner's *Journey into England* was published by Walpole at Strawberry Hill in 1757. Burke's *Vindication of Natural Society* appeared in 1756. It is written not only in the style but "in the character of [Bolingbroke] a late noble author". Both pieces were reprinted by Robert Dodsley in his *Fugitive Pieces*, 1761.

whether experienced soldiers or young ones were best. Colonel Webster was for experienced ones, if they had not been wounded. Colonel Stopford and also General Lockhart for young ones, saying that there was an ardour in men advancing to action for the first time, under officers of whom they had a good opinion, which soldiers who had seen service had not. The question does not seem clear. I think it has been held that veterans are most effectual troops. Yet I observe in Hentzner's travels that on the tomb of Henry III in Westminster Abbey there was this motto: *War is delightful to the unexperienced*. Whether it is there still, I know not.[1]

This day I paid a visit to the worthy Lord Chief Baron,[2] whom I had not waited on for a long time, which was very wrong, as he had all along treated me with great kindness. I found him much better than I expected, as he had been ill a good while and was said to be much failed. He revived ideas of the dignity of the English law. His son was now with him, but was not in. I afterwards met him, and he and I went with Mr. David Hume to the philosopher's own house[3] and sat awhile, and from both of them I got many particulars of Mr. Bruce's travels, which I gathered with much attention, as I intended to draw out some account of them for *The London Magazine*. I also put up in my mind some illustrations by Mr. Hume and Mr. Ord. By the latter there was in particular a comparison of the savage manner of eating in Abyssinia with that of the Cyclops in Virgil. I then called on Crosbie and consulted with him about the mode of applying for a transportation pardon for John Reid. I talked with him too of the Abyssinian repast, and he illustrated it by mentioning a passage in Selden, *De jure naturae et gentium*.[4]

[1] The inscription (*Dulce bellum inexpertis*) which Hentzner in 1598 saw on the north side of the tomb was described in 1856 as illegible and almost obliterated.

[2] Robert Ord. "This respectable English judge will be long remembered in Scotland, where he built an elegant house and lived in it magnificently. His own ample fortune, with the addition of his salary, enabled him to be splendidly hospitable. . . . Lord Chief Baron Ord was on good terms with us all, in a country filled with jarring interests and keen parties" (*Hebrides*, 15 August 1773).

[3] In St. David Street, St. Andrew's Square, in the New Town.

[4] Both Selden and the Cyclops appear in Boswell's account in *The London Magazine*. Bruce's contemporaries were more interested in his description of

Mr. Longlands, Mr. William Macdonald, young Mr. Robert Syme, and Mr. Cummyng, the curious *Herald*[1] (for that is his chief designation), dined with me. We were well enough, and drank only three bottles of claret, which may be considered as a moderate quantity for a company of five Scotsmen. Mr. Syme indeed and Mr. Lawrie, my clerk, drank about a bottle of port. In the evening I dictated part of a paper for Lady Dundonald in her linen cause.

TUESDAY 16 AUGUST. Finished Lady Dundonald's paper before breakfast. Was busy all day dictating some account of Bruce's travels for *The London Magazine*. I made out, I think, twenty-four folio pages.[2] I was glad to find myself an useful partner, as I had received notice of my having a dividend of £15 odds of profit. Lady Dundonald and Lady Betty, Miss Roebuck, Captain and Mrs. Schaw drank tea. It was a very wet day.

WEDNESDAY 17 AUGUST. The weather continued to be very wet, which made me very lazy. In the morning Captain Schaw called and consulted me about the consequences of his wounding a horse in the Canongate, which had run off with a loaded cart and was running directly upon him at the head of the battalion. I went down to his house and examined a sergeant and two corporals as to the particulars. I made the Captain easy by assuring him that he would not be liable in damages; though I found in one of our old Acts of Parliament of Ro. 2 that where a beast was killed unintentionally the damage should be divided equally between the owner and the killer. There is an appearance of equity in this. But it is contrary to the maxim that everything perishes to its proper owner.

Mr. Lawrie was to go home to his father's for the autumn tomorrow. I therefore dictated all day papers which were to be finished

---

Abyssinian banquets of raw beef cut from living animals than in the more important portions of his heroic narrative. His veracity was generally doubted; in 1792 a sequel to Baron Munchausen's adventures was dedicated to him.

[1] James Cummyng, herald-painter, was Lyon Clerk Depute, 1770–1775. The Lyon Court has control over all matters pertaining to Scottish heraldry. Syme was a Writer to the Signet.

[2] His account appeared in two numbers of the magazine: August and September 1774.

immediately: a memorial for the Lyon Fiscal,[1] part of which was left unfinished, as I told Mr. Lawrie that I would be clerk myself; and a decreet arbitral (a matter of form) between the trustees for the fund for ministers' widows and the town of Kirkcaldy. After dinner I drank several glasses of old hock, just indulging in the gloomy rainy weather. After tea Steuart Hall[2] called and sat awhile. As I had never seen him but in the country, he brought strong upon my mind the dreary ideas of wet weather and weary nights which I have endured in Ayrshire, when all things appeared dismal. I have not had such a cloud of hypochondria this long time. I wish it may not press upon me in my old age.

THURSDAY 18 AUGUST. Mr. Lawrie set off in the fly at eight o'clock. I shall miss him much, as he goes errands, copies letters, and is very serviceable; but it is good for him to be at his father's in the vacation. As I began this summer to allow him the whole dues both of my first and second clerk—Matthew Dickie, who does nothing for me, being allowed to keep the full clerk's dues of all the consultations which he gives me—I am hopeful that Mr. Lawrie may by degrees make a competency in my service. He made about £24 this session, of which I put £5 for his behoof into Sir W. Forbes & Co.'s hands at £4 per cent interest, among the money lodged in my name. This was a fair beginning of Mr. Lawrie's fortune. I shall be happy if he is one day as rich as Stobie.[3]

I called on Michael Nasmith and he engaged to get my petition for John Reid well copied. I settled my account with the Bank of Scotland; sat awhile with Ilay Campbell about Bedlay.[4] Went to Heriot's Garden with my wife and Veronica, who is really a charming child. She began to walk by herself on Friday the 12th current. She could now cry "Papa" very distinctly.

I dined at Matthew Dickie's with Colonel Craufurd of Craufurd-

[1] William Black was at this time Fiscal (prosecutor) in the Lyon Office.

[2] Archibald Steuart of Steuart Hall.

[3] John Stobie had been clerk to Lord Auchinleck for many years.

[4] Archibald Roberton of Bedlay employed Boswell in a lawsuit against Capt. John Elphinstone of Cumbernauld, in regard to the relocation of a road which ran through Roberton's estate.

land and a Captain Drummond (a Macgregor),[1] formerly of Craufurd's regiment. Wallace of Holmstone[2] joined us at the glass after dinner. Notwithstanding my resolutions of sobriety, I was so great a man this day, and harangued with so much fluency, that I would needs indulge, and drank heartily of port and rum punch, which always hurts me. I was a good deal the worse. I may say, "Perdidi diem."[3] I drank tea with Grange. Hepburn, the Keeper of the Rolls, was with him.

FRIDAY 19 AUGUST. Mr. Charles Hay and I this day resumed our study of Erskine's *Institute*[4] where we left off last vacation. I went to his house then. He agreed to come to mine now. After we had read a portion, we fell to some of my Justiciary records, which took us up an hour, they were so interesting. I then called on Mr. Kincaid and sat half an hour with him. By neglect of the chairman employed to carry Mrs. Kincaid's burial letters, mine had been lost; so I was not at the burial. Mr. Kincaid[5] sent Brown the Librarian[6] to me this morning with a letter of apology. The visit which I now paid was a proper piece of attention to a very worthy gentlemanly man who has shown the greatest regard to all his wife's relations.[7] I found him in a composed and serene frame. He had lost a valuable spouse; but she had been long in bad health and was of so heavenly a mind that to die was great gain, the consideration of which really prevented one from regretting her departure. I resolved to continue that friendship with Mr. Kincaid which had always subsisted between our family and him, though we meet seldom.

1 Reputedly a ferocious and lawless clan, the Macgregors were forbidden to use their own name by an Act of Parliament of 1633. They took the names of other clans, many becoming Drummonds. The Act was annulled and the name restored in November 1774.

2 An elderly Writer to the Signet.

3 "I've lost a day"—a remark attributed by Suetonius to the Emperor Titus (*Lives of the Cæsars*, Book viii, § 1).

4 This famous work by the professor of Scots law John Erskine was published in 1773: *An Institute of the Law of Scotland*. See above, p. 234.

5 Alexander Kincaid, printer and Lord Provost of Edinburgh.

6 Of the Advocates' Library.

7 Kincaid's wife, the Hon. Caroline Ker, was, like Boswell, a great-grandchild of the second Earl of Kincardine.

Lord Dundonald's chaise came and carried my wife and me to dine with the Earl. His house at Belleville was getting some repairs; so he received us at the house of Mrs. Binning in St. Anne's Yards, who was now in London. This dinner was on account of Counsellor Archibald Macdonald, who had been very serviceable to the Earl's son James, in a dispute with the University of Oxford, or at least with Balliol College. I engaged Mr. Macdonald for this dinner. Lord Cochrane[1] was there; Captain and Mrs. Schaw, Colonel Webster, Mr. Henderson (Sir Robert's son), Lieutenant Vowel. The Earl was in extraordinary spirits. I drank very moderately. Lady Betty, my wife and I supped at Sir George Preston's. This was a day of luxury in eating. I both dined and supped on moor-fowl. ⚹[2]

SATURDAY 20 AUGUST. I have omitted a very pleasing incident. On Thursday forenoon Lord Pembroke called. I met him at the door. He said, "I set out tonight, and am come to ask Mrs. Boswell's commands for London." Mr. Graham of Balgowan[3] was with him. We went up to the dining-room. My bass fiddle was standing in a corner, I having begun again to play a little on it, remembering my father having told me that Lord Newhall resumed it and had one standing in his study. "What!" said Lord Pembroke, "are we brother bassers, as well as brother Corsicans?" His Lordship, it seems, plays upon it. My wife came and sat awhile, and we were easy and well. There was a polite attention in this visit which did honour to the Earl's disposition.

This morning I drew a petition to His Majesty for John Reid. I could think of nothing else; so Mr. Charles Hay and I read no law, but went with it to Michael Nasmith's, who was very much pleased with it, and undertook to have two fair copies on large paper ready to go by the post at night. Charles went with me to see John. His wife was with him. I adjured him not to say that he was innocent of the theft found proved against him if he was not so; that I had put into the

[1] Eldest living son of Lord Dundonald; succeeded his father in 1778.

[2] This symbol, which now appears in the Journal for the first time, probably indicates the resumption of conjugal relations between Boswell and his wife. Euphemia Boswell had been born three months before, on 20 May.

[3] See above, p. 116 *n. 3*.

petition what he said, but he would have as good, if not a better, chance by fairly confessing to His Majesty. Charles very properly said to him, "Take care and do not fill up the measure of your iniquity by telling a lie to your Sovereign." I in the strongest manner assured him that I thought the petition would have no effect—that I wrote it only because I had promised to do it; but that I really thought it would be better not to send it, as it might make him entertain vain hopes and prevent him from thinking seriously of death. John professed his conviction that the chance was hardly anything, but was for using the means. I could not therefore refuse him. Charles again addressed him as to his telling a lie, and said, "I may say, you are putting your salvation against one to ten thousand; nay, against nothing." John expressed his willingness to submit to what was *foreordained* for him. "John," said I, "this would not have been *foreordained* for you if you had not stolen sheep, and that was not *foreordained*. God does not foreordain wickedness. Your Bible tells you that." I then took it up and read from the Epistle of James, Chap. I, v. 13 and 14: "Let no man say when he is tempted, I am tempted of God; for God cannot be tempted with evil, neither tempteth he any man. But every man is tempted, when he is drawn away of his own lust, and enticed." This seemed to satisfy him. But people in his situation are very apt to become predestinarians. Dr. Daniel Macqueen, one of the ministers of Edinburgh, told me that when he was minister at Stirling, there was a man under sentence of death there whom some Cameronian or seceding minister had tutored deeply upon predestination till the man was positive that the crime which he had committed was decreed by his Maker; nor could Mr. Macqueen argue him out of this notion. When he came to the place of execution, the man was beginning to harangue the people upon this subject. Upon which, Mr. Macqueen, with his forcible and hurried manner, insisted with the magistrate to order the executioner to do his duty directly; and accordingly the man was thrown off, which prevented his mystical discourse. "He might have put more nonsense into their heads," said Macqueen, "than I could have driven out again in half a year." There was good sense in Mr. Macqueen's conduct; though his acquaintances do not fail in keeping up as a joke upon him his mode of opposing an argument.

Messrs. Charles Hay, Michael Nasmith, Alexander Innes[1] (for the first time), George Webster, Dr. Boswell, and Grange dined with me. We did not drink much. I took port and water. I had played at bowls[2] before dinner with Charles Hay, etc.

Between five and six Mr. Nasmith and George Webster accompanied me to the prison, when I read over the petition to John Reid, and he signed two copies of it. I again adjured him not to sign it if he was not innocent, and again pressed home upon him my conviction that his chance for life was hardly anything. I was wonderfully firm. I told him that I really thought it was happy for him that he was to die by a sentence of the law, as he had so much time to think seriously and prepare for death; whereas, if he was not stopped in that manner, his unhappy disposition to steal was such that it was to be feared he would have been cut off in the midst of his wickedness. I enclosed one copy of the petition to Lord Suffolk, Secretary of State for the Northern Department, and one to Lord Pembroke, and wrote a letter with each copy. I could not help entertaining some faint hope. John Reid's petition was business enough to me for one day.

[Boswell to the Earl of Pembroke]

Edinburgh, 20 August 1774

My Lord,—Presuming on your Lordship's goodness, I trouble you with the enclosed petition to His Majesty from John Reid, an unfortunate man under sentence of death. I have also transmitted a copy to my Lord Suffolk, Secretary of State for the Northern Department.

John Reid was my first client in criminal business when he was tried in 1766. I have therefore a particular concern in his fate and wish much that he should not be hanged.

May I beg that your Lordship may make me certain that the petition reaches His Majesty. There is a prejudice against the man in this country. It would therefore be happy if a transportation pardon could be obtained for him at once, his crime at any rate not being

[1] Another Writer to the Signet.

[2] See below, p. 291.

atrocious. I have the honour to be with very great regard, my Lord, your most obliged and obedient humble servant,

[JAMES BOSWELL].

EDITORIAL NOTE: Boswell's petition, after rehearsing the main lines of Reid's case, stressing the likelihood that it was Gardner who had stolen the sheep, and repeatedly mis-stating as fifteen the number of stolen sheep, concludes with a flourished compliment: "The prerogative of dispensing mercy is the brightest jewel in the British Crown, and several late instances of it in this part of the United Kingdom have endeared Your Majesty to your more northern subjects. Your petitioner flatters himself that he also shall have cause to bless the goodness of the King and shall not be singled out as a miserable exception from Your Majesty's beneficent lenity."

SUNDAY 21 AUGUST. My wife went with me to the New Church in the forenoon. Mr. Logan at Leith preached. I went alone in the afternoon. Dr. Dick preached. Mr. Nairne and I walked out to Lady Colville's to drink tea. She and Lady Anne were just going from home. They left us the key of the tea-chest, and we walked in the garden, pulled gooseberries, and then drank tea comfortably. The ladies returned and they and we walked agreeably. Captain Erskine was gone to Kellie. There came an invitation to Mr. Nairne to sup at Dr. Webster's with my wife and me, which he did. Sandy Webster was returned from a voyage to Russia.[1] Dr. Webster had no mercy on John Reid, because he had attempted to get witnesses to perjure themselves to bring him off. Said George: "This is what every man would do in his place. To preserve my life I would perjure all mankind. Nay, supposing all the stars in the firmament to be inhabited, I would perjure all their inhabitants." This was a sort of grand thought. But, to be sure, no thinking man of good principles would make even one person commit the crime of perjury, to save a short and uncertain life at the risk of salvation. There was a deal of warm conversation as usual; and Nairne was much pleased with the Websters, as they were with him.

[1] Mate of an East Indiaman, he died at sea in 1782.

MONDAY 22 AUGUST. The Law College went on. Mr. Hay and I walked before dinner on the Castle Hill with Mr. Andrew Balfour, newly made a Commissary of Edinburgh, and some peculiar kind of talk, the mode and manner only of which made it remarkable, was carried on. In the afternoon I read the first book of a treatise on taste which the late Reverend Dr. Wallace left behind him at his death, and of which his son, Mr. George Wallace, put a part into my hands in MS to peruse. The first book entertained me little, as it was just a repetition, somewhat varied, of what I had read in books on the same subject.

TUESDAY 23 AUGUST. The Law College went on, and must be understood to do so when I do not mention a cessation, Sundays excepted. We were interrupted twice today, for first Crosbie and then Cullen called. At one I called on Mr. George Wallace by appointment and walked in the Meadow with him, to talk of his father's book. I saw that he expected it would be a valuable property. I mentioned to him a few animadversions on what I had read, and I understood from him that the other parts of the book were almost all new. He promised to send me the chapter on historical composition. In the evening I read some of the first volume of Robertson's *Charles V*, which I had borrowed of Michael Nasmith. After dinner, being restless, I went to Dr. Webster's, and with the Colonel and George drank a bottle of port. Then tea. Dupont there.

WEDNESDAY 24 AUGUST. Mr. Hay and I played a stout match at bowls.[1] He gave me one, and I beat him three games. I dined at Nairne's, who had ten guests assembled without any kind of assortment, so that drinking only made the cement of the company. Nothing worth mentioning passed, except a fancy of my own upon Lochée's Military Academy at Chelsea, in which boys are made encamp, etc., to prepare them for war. I observed that it was absurd to make them suffer the hardships of a campaign without necessity. That they might as well be wounded and carried to an hospital, or even some of them be killed; and that the Master of the Academy would approve of their being distressed for want of provisions. I shall work

[1] In James Maidment's *Court of Session Garland* (1839) appears a verse *Epitaph on Charles Hay . . . who lies interred under the Bowling Green in Heriot's Garden.*

up this into an essay for *Rampager*, the designation which I assume as a signature to all my lively essays in *The Public Advertiser*.[1] A great deal of wine was drank today. I swallowed about a bottle of port, which inflamed me much, the weather being hot. I called at home; then sauntered in the streets; and then supped with my wife at Sir George Preston's, where I had sent four moor-fowl which I had in presents from Ayrshire, agreeable marks of kind remembrance from James Johnston in Cumnock and John Herbert in Auchencross. Dr. Webster and the Colonel and Mr. Wood, the surgeon, were at Sir George's. I devoured moor-fowl, and poured more port down my throat. I was sadly intoxicated. *Perdidi diem.*

THURSDAY 25 AUGUST. I was very sick and had a severe headache, and lay till between ten and eleven, when I grew better. There was no Law College today. Crosbie called on me in the forenoon, in great indignation at the Bailies of Edinburgh for having sentenced Henry McGraugh, an Irishman, to be imprisoned, whipped, and banished because he had called for victuals and drink in public houses and then told that he had not money to pay for them. Crosbie begged that I would inquire into the affair.[2]

I communicated to Crosbie a scheme which I had of making an experiment on John Reid, in case he was hanged, to try to recover him. I had mentioned it in secrecy to Charles Hay and Mr. Wood the surgeon, who promised me assistance. Crosbie told me that he had lately had a long conversation on the subject with Dr. Cullen, who thought it practicable. It was lucky that I spoke of it to Crosbie, for he was clear for trying it, and threw out many good hints as to what should be done. I resolved to wait on Dr. Cullen and get his instructions. I was this forenoon at the burial of a daughter of the late Mr. Sands, bookseller here. There is something usefully solemn in such a scene, and I make it a rule to attend every burial to which I am invited unless I have a sufficient excuse; as I expect that those who are invited to mine will pay their piece of decent attention.

I afterwards called at the prison, where I found Mr. Todd, Lady

[1] See above, p. 180 *n.* 2. Boswell's *Rampagers* during 1775–1779 deal much with the military aspect of American affairs.

[2] See above, pp. 207-8 and below, pp. 293–4, 323.

Maxwell's chaplain,[1] with John Reid. He seemed to be a weak, well-meaning young man. I again told John in his presence that there was hardly the least chance of a pardon and therefore that he ought to consider himself as a dying man. Yet I did now entertain a small additional glimpse of hope, because I saw in the newspapers that, a few days before, one Madan got a reprieve after he was at Tyburn, ready to be turned off, the man who really committed the robbery for which he was condemned having voluntarily appeared and owned it.[2] I thought this incident might make the Ministry more ready to listen to John Reid's story that Gardner was the real thief. John was looking gloomy today. He told me he had some bad dreams which made him believe he was now to die.

I then called for McGraugh, who was put into the cage, he was so violent a prisoner. He was a true Teague. I asked him why he was confined. He could give but a very confused account; but he assured me that he had neither stolen victuals and drink nor taken them by force, but only called for them. I asked him if he had stolen anything. "Only a paice (piece) of wood," said he; "but then, an't *plaise* your Honour, it was in the dark." "That will not make it better," said I. Afterwards, however, I saw that this odd saying of his, like all the Irish sayings at which we laugh as bulls or absurdities, had a meaning. For he meant that as he had taken the wood in the dark, it could not be known he had done it; so that it could be no part of the charge against

1 Lady Maxwell was Darcy Brisbane, who in 1760, at about the age of 17, was married to Sir Walter Maxwell of Pollock, Bt., and within two years was not only widowed but lost her infant son. A few years later she became a friend and correspondent of John Wesley, and thereafter, until her death in 1810, she led a life of extraordinary piety and was a prominent member of the Wesleyan Society at Edinburgh. Mr. Todd was apparently a household chaplain whom she is said to have employed for a short time—after which, "during the space of about forty years, Lady Maxwell was her own chaplain" (John Lancaster, *The Life of Darcy, Lady Maxwell*, London, 1826, p. 541).

2 Amos Merritt came forward at Tyburn on 19 August 1774 and declared that he himself had committed the crime of highway robbery for which Patrick Madan was about to be hanged. Madan was reprieved and later pardoned; he was present to bid farewell to Merritt when the latter was hanged for another crime on 10 January 1775.

him and consequently was no justification of the sentence of the magistrates. I promised to do what I could for him. I also saw one Macpherson, a young goldsmith confined for debt, from whom I had a letter telling me that a young woman had come into prison and lent him her clothes, in which he made his escape but was taken again; and that the *innocent* girl was imprisoned. I told him that breaking prison was a crime; that the girl had been aiding in the escape of a prisoner and therefore was not innocent; but that she would not be long confined.

My wife and I drank tea at Dr. Grant's. He was clear that a man who has hung ten minutes cannot be recovered; and he had dissected two. I was, however, resolved that the experiment should be tried. Dr. Grant carried me up to a very good library which he has and showed me a number of anatomical preparations.[1] The survey of skulls and other parts of the human body, and the reflection upon all of us being so frail and liable to so many painful diseases, made me dreary.

FRIDAY 26 AUGUST. Sir George and Lady Preston and Miss Preston, Colonel, George, and Sandy Websters, Mr. Wood the surgeon, and Mr. Bennet the Minister of Duddingston dined with us. I gave only port, being resolved to give claret seldom while I am not able to afford it commonly.[2] We were comfortable. I drank port and water, and did not discompose myself. I went to the Justiciary Office and wrote a bill of suspension with my own hand for McGraugh.[3]

SATURDAY 27 AUGUST. After our law, Charles Hay and I set

[1] Dr. Grant had been a candidate for the Chair of Physic in 1761; he gave lectures on the subject in 1770; he pursued the study of chemistry in his own house.

[2] Port was cheap because trade with Portugal was encouraged by a treaty; claret was produce of France and heavily taxed.

[3] The Lord of Justiciary whom Boswell petitioned suspended the sentence of whipping. The Procurator-Fiscal reclaimed, and McGraugh was detained in prison. (He had thrice previously been taken up on the same charge, twice dismissed on good behaviour, and the third time banished on his own plea, on pain of the punishments now imminent, if he returned.) On 4 February 1775 he was set at liberty on order of the Court of Justiciary, the Procurator-Fiscal having waived the whipping in view of his long confinement. *The Scots Magazine* (Appendix 1775, pp. 732–733) says that McGraugh's crime "has got the name of *sconcing*. *Sorning*, to which sconcing has an affinity, is the masterful taking meat, drink, and lodging".

out to dine at Leith, at Yeats the trumpeter's,[1] where we had dined before very well. I fixed it as a good Saturday's dining-place during our course of study, and fancied our tête-à-tête there to be like that of my grandfather and Lord Cullen on the Saturdays. As we walked down the street we met Crosbie and tried to prevail with him to go with us. But he was obstinate in a resolution to labour at law papers all this day. A heavy shower came on, and we went with him into John Balfour the bookseller's shop, where we chatted a good while. We then walked with him as far as his house, where we left him; and there we were joined by Ilay Campbell, who walked on with us. He insisted that we should go and dine with him at a little country-house which he had near Leith. We did so, and shared his family dinner with Mrs. Campbell and his children. It was a scene worth taking:[2] a family country dinner with the first writing lawyer at our bar. He told us that when Macqueen married, which was only about eighteen years ago, his practice did not exceed ——— a year, though he had since realised many thousands. Macqueen told him that one year he had made £1900. Ilay told us that he himself had made £1600 in a year in the ordinary course of business; and that a lawyer's labour is not increased in proportion with his gains, for that he now wrote less than he had done. This kind of conversation excited the solid coarse ambition of making money in the Court of Session. We drank a bottle of claret apiece and a fourth among us. We then drank tea, and Mr. Campbell walked with us a good [way] up as a convoy. I was not a bit intoxicated with what I had drank. Mr. Hay was engaged at home.

Last night Lord and Lady Dundonald and Lady Betty Cochrane, who had dined at our neighbour Captain Schaw's, called in for awhile. We had also a visit from the Laird of MacLeod, who had been in town a few days. I was exceedingly happy to see this excellent young chief in my house, and I cordially begged that he would make it his home. I called on him this forenoon, but he was abroad. He was engaged to sup with me tonight. I had also Lady Betty Cochrane, Crosbie, Dr. Grant, Nairne. Just as I was coming home, I overtook in the court Mrs.

[1] An inn kept by one of the trumpeters who rode before the Lords of Justiciary when they were on circuit.

[2] Drawing.

Schaw and Colonel Stopford. My wife suggested that we might have the Colonel and our neighbours. I accordingly went down and asked them to come up and take a share of a roasted chicken. They readily complied; and we passed really a pleasant evening. A curious thought struck me of having the Sheep-stealer's Progress in the manner of Hogarth's historical prints. We drank very little.

SUNDAY 28 AUGUST. It was a very wet day. I stayed at home in the forenoon, and read the Life of Carstares,[1] and a good part of the letters addressed to him. Mr. Crosbie had lent me the book, telling me there was nothing in it; and indeed I found it made up of ill-written uninteresting letters, and wondered how Lord Hailes had recommended the publication. I believe I had a prejudice against Carstares from his being King William's secretary. He seemed to me to be just an artful sagacious Presbyterian divine. My wife was not well and stayed at home all day. I went in the afternoon to the New Church. Mr. ——— preached. In the evening I continued to read Carstares's letters, still trying to find something worth while but in vain. Dr. Webster was gone to Fife. At five I was at the burial of a Miss Stewart of Shambellie. How little of true pious exercise had I this Sunday!

MONDAY 29 AUGUST. A very curious whim had come into my head: that I would have a portrait of John Reid as my first client in criminal business and as a very remarkable person in the annals of the Court of Justiciary. Keith Ralph,[2] a young painter who had studied under Runciman,[3] had drawn Mr. Lawrie's picture very like. I had him with me this forenoon, and he agreed to paint John. He desired to see him today, to have an idea of his face, to see what kind of light was in the room where he lay, and to judge what should be the size of the picture. Accordingly I went with him. I had before this given a hint of my design to Richard Lock, the inner turnkey, a very sensible, good

[1] *State-Papers and Letters Addressed to William Carstares . . . to Which Is Prefixed the Life of Mr. Carstares, Published from the Originals, by Joseph McCormick, D.D.*, Edinburgh, 1774.

[2] George Keith Ralph, born c. 1754, was later portrait-painter to the Duke of Clarence. He exhibited in London at the Academy from 1778 to 1811.

[3] Alexander Runciman, a Scots painter who had studied at Rome, was master of the academy of drawing newly established by the Board of Trustees for Manufactures. See below, p. 309.

kind of man; and he had no objection. Accordingly we went up. Mr. Ritchie, a kind of lay teacher who humanely attends all the people under sentence of death, was with John. I was acquainted with Mr. Ritchie, as he had called on me about my client Agnes Adam.[1] After standing a little and speaking a few words in a serious strain, I addressed myself to Ritchie in a kind of soft voice and mentioned my desire to have a remembrance of John Reid, by having a picture of him; that Mr. Ritchie and I could sit by and talk to him, and that I imagined John would have no objection, as it would not disturb him. Ritchie said he supposed John would have none; that he was so much obliged to me, he would do much more at my request; and he would come and be present. Next morning between nine and ten was fixed. Mr. Charles Hay, who waited in the street, went with me to Ralph's and saw some of his performances.

At four this afternoon Adam Bell was with me, along with Nimmo his landlord, consulting me to draw answers to a petition. I found myself much as in session time. Steuart Hall and Mr. Wood the surgeon drank tea. Wood dispelled the dreary country ideas which Steuart Hall would have raised. I took a walk with him to Drumsheugh and round by the New Town, and talked of the scheme of recovering John Reid. He said he did not think it practicable. But that he should give all the assistance in his power to have the experiment fairly tried.

TUESDAY 30 AUGUST. At ten o'clock I was with John Reid. Before I got there, Ralph was begun with his chalk and honest Ritchie was exhorting him quietly. I was happy to see that this whim of mine gave no trouble to John. One of his legs was fixed to a large iron goad, but he could rise very easily;[2] and he at any rate used to sit upon a

[1] See above, p. 208.

[2] "A round bar of iron, about the thickness of a man's arm above the elbow, crossed the apartment horizontally at the height of about six inches from the floor; and its extremities were strongly built into the wall at either end. Hatteraick's ankles were secured within shackles, which were connected by a chain at the distance of about four feet, with a large iron ring, which travelled upon the bar we have described. Thus a prisoner might shuffle along the length of the bar from one side of the room to another, but could not retreat farther from it in any other direction than the brief length of the chain admitted" (*Guy Mannering*, last chapter

form, so that he just kept his ordinary posture, and Ritchie and I conversed with him. He seemed to be quite composed, and said he had no hopes of life on account of the dreams which he had. That he dreamt he was riding on one white horse and leading another. "That," said he, "was too good a dream, and dreams are contrary." He said he also dreamt a great deal of being on the seashore and of passing deep waters. "However," said he, "I allwaye (always) get through them." "Well," said I, "John, I hope that shall not be contrary; but that you shall get through the great deep of death." I called for a dram of whisky. I had not thought how I should drink to John till I had the glass in my hand, and I felt some embarrassment. I could not say, "Your good health"; and "Here's to you" was too much in the style of hearty fellowship. I said, "John, I wish you well," or words pretty much the same, as "Wishing you well"—or some such phrase. The painter and Mr. Ritchie tasted the spirits. Richard the gaoler makes it a rule never to taste them within the walls of the prison.

John seemed to be the better of a dram. He told me that the Reids of Muiravonside had been there, he believed, for three hundred years; that they had been butchers for many generations. He could trace himself, his father, and grandfather in that business; that he never was worth £10 and never in much debt, so that he was always evens with the world. That in the year 1753 he enlisted in Sir Peter Halkett's regiment. But was taken up on an accusation of stealing two cows, for which he was tried at Glasgow and acquitted; after which, as his pay had run up to a considerable sum, the regiment let him alone, though he was several times taken up as a deserter at the instigation of ill-natured people; that he went up to London on foot and wrought there as a gardener for ——— till there was a hot press,[1] and then he came to Leith in a brig commanded by John Beatson. That after this he enlisted in Colonel Perry's regiment, but that a writer or agent whom he knew in Glasgow got him off by taking a bill from him for £11, for

---

but one). In a note Scott says, "This mode of securing prisoners was universally practised in Scotland after condemnation. When a man received sentence of death, he was put upon *the Gad,* as it was called. . . . The practice subsisted in Edinburgh till the old jail was taken down some years since."

[1] A special drive to press men into the service.

which he granted John a discharge which they concealed, so that the apparent debt above £10 kept him from being forced away; that he was employed for several years as a driver of cattle to England, particularly under Mr. Birtwhistle, the great English drover. That he was art and part in the theft of the sheep from the parish of Douglas, one of the articles in his trial in 1766. Graham, the man's herd, stole them and delivered them to him half a mile from the farm. That he did not steal the six score; that he married in 1759; that since his trial in 1766 he had led an honest, industrious life; that he received the sheep for which he was condemned from Gardner, and did not suspect them to be stolen. That his wife and children would be present at his death. I dissuaded him from this. He said his wife and he had lived comfortably fifteen years, and she said she would see him to the last and would *kep* him (i.e., receive his body when cut down); that his son, who was a boy of ten years of age, might forget it (meaning his execution) if he only heard of it, but that he would not readily forget it if he saw it. To hear a man talk of his own execution gave me a strange kind of feeling. He said he would be carried to his own burial-place at Muiravonside; that it was the second best in the kirkyard. There were symptoms of vanity in the long line of the Reids and the good burial-place; a proof that ideas of these kinds are natural and universal.

Ritchie and I sat awhile with him after the painter was gone, the first sitting being over. John said, "Death is no terror to me at present. I know not what it may be." Said Ritchie, "You must either be infatuated, or you have, by grace, a reliance on the merits of Jesus Christ." John said he trusted to the mercy of God in Christ; that he had been an unfortunate man, and insinuated that his fate was foreordained. Ritchie quoted the passage in James which I had quoted; but he seemed to be much hampered with Calvinistical notions about decrees, while he struggled to controvert John's wickedness being foreordained. Indeed the system of predestination includes all actions, bad as well as good. Ritchie pressed John much to make an authentic last speech. I told him that if he was guilty of the crime for which he was condemned, it was his duty to his country and the only reparation he could make, to acknowledge it, that his example might have a proper effect. He persisted in his denial, and did not seem willing to have any speech published. Ritchie said to me in his hearing that it was a perquisite for Richard, who had a great deal of trouble. I said we should get John to make a speech.

John complained much of Peter Reid for deceiving him by promising to swear as to the bargain between him and Gardner, and then drawing back. "For," said he, "if I had not trusted to him, I would not have told you that I could bring such proof, and then you could have done what you thought proper." He told me that he said to Peter in this very room: "Peter, mony (many) a lee (lie) I have telt (told) for you for which I repent"; and Peter said he would help him to the utmost on this occasion; and he did not think there was much harm in it, as it was to save a man's life; "though it was very wrang (wrong) to swear awa (away) a man's life." This was a kind of casuistical explanation of the ninth commandment: Thou shalt not bear false witness *against* thy neighbour. But—thou mayst do so *for* him. John cried a good deal when he told me this story of Peter Reid. He did not seem to be affected on any other occasion. I argued with him that it was happy that Peter Reid's conscience had checked him and prevented him from being guilty of perjury; that, to be sure, it was wrong in him to say that he would swear in John's support, but that it was better that he stopped than if he had gone on. John's system upon this subject was so crooked that he did not appear at all convinced.

It was a very wet day. I grew dreary and wanted either Charles Hay or Grange to dine with me, but neither of them could come. I took a little bowl of warm punch by myself, except a glass which Veronica drank. Her sweet little society was a gentle relief, but I was too dismal to enjoy it much. I had a letter from my brother David which was a cordial. I drank tea with Grange, but was gloomy. I had by sympathy sucked the dismal ideas of John Reid's situation, and as spirits or strong substance of any kind, when transferred to another body of a more delicate nature, will have much more influence than on the body from which it is transferred, so I suffered much more than John did. Grange very sensibly observed that we should keep at a distance from dreary objects; that we should shun what hurts the mind as we shun what disagrees with the stomach and hurts the body—a very good maxim for preserving a *mens sana*. At night Mr. Nairne called in and supped with us. He did me some good by his conversation.

WEDNESDAY 31 AUGUST. This was the second day of John Reid's sitting for his picture. Ralph the painter went through his part with perfect composure, hardly ever opening his mouth. He mentioned a Mr. Cochrane of Barbachlaw. John said he was a strange man. He used to drink hard, till he *squeeled* like a *nowt*. He would just play *bu*.[1] Strange that a creature under sentence of death should tell such an anecdote and seem entertained. I spoke to him of his execution, thinking it humane to familiarise his mind to it. I asked him if he was here when Murdison died.[2] He said no, and on my saying, "So you did not see him die," told me that he had never seen an execution. "No?" said I. "I wonder you never had the curiosity." He said he never had. That once, as he and some other drivers of cattle were coming from Yorkshire, they stopped at Penrith in Cumberland, where there was a man to be executed for murder next day; that some of his companions stayed to see it, but he and the rest did not. I then spoke of the way in England of having a cart and ours of having a ladder, and that it was said ours was the easiest way. "I take it, John," said I, "I shall die a severer death than you." "I dinna (do not) think," said he, "they can feel much; or that it can last ony (any) time; but there's nane (none)[3] of them to tell how it is." I mentioned Maggy Dickson, who had been hanged less than the usual time and was recovered, and said she felt no pain.[4] He told me he saw a Highlandman at Glasgow, a big strong

[1] Till he bellowed like an ox. He would just pretend to low.

[2] Alexander Murdison was convicted of sheep-stealing on 11 January 1773 and hanged on 24 March. See above, pp. 153, 156.

[3] Boswell's glosses upon quite easily interpreted Scots forms, not only here but elsewhere in the present volume, suggest that he has in mind some other audience than himself—an English-speaking audience.

[4] Margaret Dickson, a married woman separated from her husband, was hanged in Edinburgh for child-murder in 1724. According to the soberest account, her body was coffined at the foot of the gallows and put into a cart to be conveyed to Inveresk. On the way the men driving the cart stopped for a dram. When they came out of the public house, they heard a sound in the coffin, and on taking off the lid found her alive. She remained in a low state several days, complaining of a severe pain in her neck, but finally recovered, was reconciled to her husband, and bore him several children. She sold salt in the streets of Edinburgh, where she was generally known as "half-hangit Maggie".

man, who had escaped twice; first, the rope broke. "And," said John, "at that time it was thought they coudna (could not) hang them up again; and the second time, the gallows fell." He said his wife was resolved that he should die in white; that it was the custom in his part of the country to dress the dead body in linen, and she thought it would cost no more to do it when he was alive. He this day again averred the truth of his story that he got the sheep from Gardner. He said to me that there was something he had done a great many years ago, before any of his trials, that had followed him all this time. That it was not a great thing either, nor yet a small thing, and he would let me know it. This was somehow curious and awful. Honest Ritchie, from time to time, threw out serious reflections, as thus: "If any man sin, we have an advocate with the Father, even Christ the righteous. Christ is an advocate, indeed. Other advocates only plead for panels. But he takes upon him the offences of the panels and suffers in their stead." Ritchie also gave a particular account of the behaviour of Pickworth, and promised to give me a copy of a printed narrative of it which he wrote.[1] I did not know before that Ritchie was an author.

I mentioned that it was remarkable that there was always fine weather on execution days, and I asked Ritchie what was the meaning of pigeons flying when people were executed. He said that he thought the notions which some people entertained of that signifying good to the persons executed were *fablish*. John then told of a woman who was executed, who told that morning to a minister after awaking from a sound sleep, "If ye see some clear draps o' (drops of) rain faw (fall) on me after I'm custen owr (thrown over), I'm happy." And John said the clear drops did fall. All this was most suitable conversation for John. I asked him if he had ever seen the hangman. He said no. I said I had seen him this forenoon going into the office of the prison. "Ay," said John, "he'll be going about thinking there's something for him." He seemed to think of him with much aversion and declared he would

[1] *A Short Account of the Behaviour of William Pickworth, from His Condemnation to his Death: in a Letter from a Person Who Attended Him Often during That Time, to Which Is Annexed His Last Speech*, Edinburgh, 1771. He was a soldier in the Twenty-second Regiment of Foot, twenty-four years old, hanged in Edinburgh for robbery on 25 September 1771.

have no intercourse with him, one way or other; but he seemed somewhat reconciled when I told him that the hangman was a humane creature, and shed tears for unhappy people when they were to be executed. I inculcated upon John that he was now to have no hopes, since no answer had come to his application. He asked if there would not come an answer of some kind. I said not unless they were to grant something favourable, and that must have come before now had it been to come. He said he was thrown into a panic by hearing a horn blow in the street.[1] I was desirous to have his picture done *while under sentence of death* and was therefore rather desirous that, in case a respite was to come, it should not arrive till he had sat his full time. It was finished today and was a striking likeness, a gloomy head. He asked if it would not be better to have had on his bonnet, and said he should have had on a better waistcoat. He asked too if his name would be upon it. I said it would be on the back of it. Said he: "I thought it would have been on the fore (front) side of it." There was vanity again. As the painter advanced in doing it, I felt as if he had been raising a spectre. It was a strange thought. Here is a man sitting for his picture who is to be hanged this day eight days. John himself seemed to wonder somewhat at the operation, and said, "I'm sure you maun hae an unco (must have a strange) concern about this," or words to that purpose. When it was finished and hung upon a nail to dry, it swung, which looked ominous, and made an impression on my fancy. I gave John a dram of whisky today again. When I got home I found several vermin upon me which I had attracted while in the gaol. It was shocking. I changed all my clothes.

Lady Colville and Lady Anne Erskine drank tea with us, very agreeably. Mr. Hay and I had read no law today. When I came from the prison, we had gone to Heriot's Garden and played at bowls. Maclaurin was in town today, and played with us.

[Received c. 31 August, Lord Erroll to Boswell]

Slains Castle, 27 August 1774

SIR,—I have now lying before me yours of the tenth. I should be

[1] He thought perhaps of a post-horn.

very willing to show any favour in my power to a client of yours, but in the present case I am certain no application from me would be of any avail. I never had a good opinion of Mr. Clarke, although he was my tenant. And from your own account of Reid, I cannot find any reason for an indifferent person to apply in his favour. At the same [time] I cannot help applauding your doing so, as you are of opinion the jury condemned him on scrimp evidence, though I think a man being habit and repute of a bad character must always weigh with any jury. Lady Erroll joins me in best respects to you, and I am with very much esteem, Sir, your most obedient servant,

ERROLL.

THURSDAY 1 SEPTEMBER. I breakfasted at Mr. David Steuart's, Writer to the Signet, where was his father, Steuart Hall. At ten I called on Dr. Cullen to talk with him of recovering John Reid. He was gone abroad. I found his son, my brother lawyer, and trusted him with the secret, and he engaged to get me a meeting with his father. It came on a heavy rain; so I sat a good while with Cullen in his study, and had very good ideas presented to my mind about books and criminal law, etc. Every man has some peculiar views which seem new to another. After taking a tolerable dose of law, Mr. Hay and I went for a walk to Heriot's Garden, and then I dined with him. He had Dr. Monro and several more company with him, and it was concerted that we should get information from the Anatomical Professor as to recovering a hanged person,[1] which would be useful to Reid. Harry Erskine[2] was there, and talked so much that it was long before we could get Dr. Monro set upon the subject. He said in his opinion a man who is hanged suffers a great deal; that he is not at once stupefied by the shock, suffocation being a thing which must be gradual and

[1] There seems to have been a wide-spread interest at this time in the subject of recovering persons supposedly dead. The leading article in *The Scots Magazine* for September 1774 was an abstract of a French memoir, by M. Janin, published at Paris in 1773, "on the causes of sudden and violent death; wherein it is proved that persons who seemingly fall victims to it may be recovered." In 1774 the Humane Society, for the recovery of persons apparently drowned, was founded in London.

[2] See above, p. 207.

cannot be forced on instantaneously; so that a man is suffocated by hanging in a rope just as by having his respiration stopped by having a pillow pressed on the face, in Othello's way, or by stopping the mouth and nostrils, which one may try; and he said that for some time after a man is thrown over he is sensible and is conscious that he is *hanging*; but that in three minutes or so he is stupefied. He said that it was more difficult to recover a hanged person than a drowned, because hanging forces the blood up to the brain with more violence, there being a local compression at the neck; but that he thought the thing might be done by heat and rubbing to put the blood in motion, and by blowing air into the lungs; and he said the best way was to cut a hole in the throat, in the trachea, and introduce a pipe. I laid up all this for service in case it should be necessary. He told me that ten or twelve of his students had, unknown to him, tried to recover my clients Brown and Wilson,[1] but had only blown with their own breaths into the mouths of the *subjects*, which was not sufficient. He said some people had applied to him for leave to put on fires and make preparations for recovering Lieutenant Ogilvy in his class. That he thought it would be very wrong in him to allow it, and told them he should have no objection if Lord Justice-Clerk gave his consent. That he spoke to Lord Justice-Clerk, who said that if such a thing was allowed, the College of Edinburgh should never again get a body from the Court of Justiciary. Indeed it would have been counteracting their sentence. He said he dissected Ogilvy publicly, and that there was no hurt on his head by the fall from the gibbet.[2]

I sat here today, thinking myself well employed in listening to Dr. Monro, whom I seldom met. He asked me to sup with him next day with the Laird of MacLeod. I drank rather more than a bottle of Madeira. It was about ten when we parted. I made a good deal of impression on the company in favour of John Reid's innocence. As I

[1] Hanged on 15 September 1773. See above, pp. 201-2.

[2] This notorious case has been given a volume in the Famous Scots Trials. Lieutenant Patrick Ogilvy became the lover of the young wife of his brother, the Laird of Eastmiln, and connived with her in poisoning him. Mrs. Ogilvy (a niece of Boswell's friend William Nairne) escaped from prison and got to France, but Patrick was hanged—in a bungling manner—on 13 November 1765.

considered him as now a gone man, I resolved to know the truth by being with him to the very last moment of his life, even to walk a step or two up the ladder and ask him *then*, just before his going off, what was the real matter of fact; for if he should deny *then*, I could not resist the conviction.

FRIDAY 2 SEPTEMBER. I lay till near ten. A little after I rose and was at breakfast and Mr. Hay was come, while the tea-things were standing, I was called out to a man—and who was this but Richard Lock, who informed me that John Reid had got a respite for fourteen days;[1] that Captain Fraser had been up with him and read it to him, and that he teared more now than he had ever seen him. I was put into great agitation. All my nerves started. I instantly dressed, and Mr. Hay and I walked out, met Michael Nasmith, who had seen the respite in the Council Chamber, and he went thither with us, when Bailie Brown showed us it.[2] Wright, the stationer, who was at the time ———,[3] cried out with a kind of unfeeling sneer, "It will be lang (long) life and ill health;" and all the people in the Chamber seemed against poor John. We then went up to John, whom we found in a dreadful state. He was quite unhinged. His knees knocked against each other, he trembled so; and he cried bitterly. I spoke to him in most earnest manner and told him, since the respite was only for fourteen days, the judges would be consulted and they would report

[1] The respite (Public Record Office, Scottish Entry Book, Criminal) is dated at St. James's 26 August and signed by Lord Rochford. On the same date Lord Rochford, "in the absence of Lord Suffolk", sent the Lord Justice-Clerk John Reid's petition and Boswell's accompanying letter, requesting a report "whether and how far the said John Reid may appear . . . to be an object of His Majesty's Royal Mercy." "But if your Lordship shall be fully satisfied with the verdict and shall not have discovered any favourable circumstances in the convict's case, I am to desire your Lordship to return the said respite to me when your Lordship transmits your report." On 17 October Boswell heard from the Justice-Clerk's brother that the respite had thus been optional—"that Lord Rochford sent the respite to him with a power to deliver it, or put it in the fire as he should judge proper."

[2] Perhaps the same as "Buckram" Brown, below, p. 314.

[3] Charles Wright was Dean of Guild, a lay judge, elected by the tradesmen of the city, with jurisdiction in mercantile causes and over building regulations. On this occasion he was apparently officiating in some such capacity as "chairman" or "president" within the Council Chamber, and Boswell cannot recall the exact word.

against him. He must therefore consider that he had just fourteen days more allowed him to prepare for his awful change. He moaned and spoke of his being "cut off after all, with a hale (whole) heart." I said he must compose himself. He said he hoped he should, if it pleased GOD to continue him in his senses, as he had hitherto done. I said, "You *would* make this application, though I told you I thought it would have no effect. If you suffer from it, it is owing to yourself." It was striking to see a man who had been quite composed when he thought his execution certain become so weak and so much agitated by a respite. My wife put a construction on his conduct which seemed probable. She said it was plain he had all along been expecting a pardon and therefore was composed, but that now when he found that only a respite for fourteen days had come and that inquiry was to be made at the judges, he for the first time had the view of death. But if I can judge of human nature by close observation, I think he was before this time reconciled to his fate, and that the respite affected him by throwing him into a wretched state of incertainty. I gave him a shilling to get some spirits as a cordial. Messrs. Hay and Nasmith went with me to the Justiciary Office, but we could learn nothing there but that John Davidson, the Crown Agent, had applied for an extract of the trial on Monday.[1] The respite therefore must have been kept up some days.

I was quite agitated, partly by feeling for Reid, whom I had seen in so miserable a condition, partly by keeness for my own consequence, that I should not fail in what I had undertaken, but get a transportation pardon for my client, since a respite had come. I resolved to walk a little in the fresh air in the Meadow. Hay and Nasmith accompanied me and helped me to calm myself. I thought of applying to Lord Advocate. They were for my taking a chaise and going directly to his country-house at the Whim, which was but fourteen miles off. I thought it would be better to send an express to him with a letter, as I could write in stronger terms than I could speak; and I would ask a transportation pardon from him as a favour which I should consider as a

[1] "The Justice-Clerk . . . though he sent up his own opinion, sent also up a full copy of the trial that it might be judged of by the King in Council" (Journal, 17 October 1774).

serious obligation for life. I determined that we should call on worthy Nairne and take his advice. He humanely said that since I had obtained a respite, he wished I might save Reid from execution; and he gave it as his opinion that I had better go to Lord Advocate in person. Honest Charles Hay would not leave me in my distress, but accompanied me, as honest Kent did Lear.

We got a chaise at Peter Ramsay's directly, and set off. Charles agreed to wait at an inn not far from the Advocate's, as he was ill-dressed, and it would be better I should wait on the Advocate alone. We talked or rather raved of all the possibilities as to John Reid's affair as we drove along, and Mr. Hay was by this time grown almost as eager to save him as I was. He stopped at an inn at Howgate three miles from the Whim. I was uneasy when by myself, restless and impatient. When I arrived at the house, I was told my Lord was gone to Sir James Clerk's at Penicuik. I drove back to Howgate, where Hay had dined. I took a glass of port and a bit of bread, and then we got into the chaise again and drove to Penicuik. We put up our horses at the inn. He walked with me half way to Sir James's and promised to wait at the village. It was now between five and six. As I approached the house, I saw Sir James and Lord Advocate and some other gentlemen taking a walk after dinner. I had dined here before with Sir James. After making my bow to him, I said, "My Lord Advocate, I am in quest of your Lordship. I have been at the Whim. May I beg to speak with you?" We went aside. He immediately started the subject, answering, "About your friend John Reid." I spoke to him very earnestly. He told me he had seen the respite and my letter to Lord Suffolk and the petition for John. He expressed his unwillingness to have an execution after a respite, but said that the respite here had been compelled by the application coming so late. That the King's business required that an example should be made of this man, and if it were to be asked at him, he could not say that Reid was a proper object of mercy. But that he was to give no opinion one way or other. He made for a little a kind of secret of what was doing. But upon my urging him, he said it lay with the judges, and I must apply to them. I said I did not like to apply to them, and I told him with great sincerity that he was the only man employed by the Crown in the Justiciary

Court who had not a strong bias against the panels. I said the Justice-Clerk stood in a very delicate situation here, as he had attacked Reid after being acquitted by his country,[1] and would be supposed to be much prejudiced against him. If I were in his place, I would not wish to make a severe report in such circumstances. The Advocate smiled. He gave me full time and never seemed inclined to go in, but walked on the lawn with a complacent easy behaviour. I showed him that I was really very much concerned here and begged he would assist me; that I should never forget the obligation. He said it would be improper for him to interfere.

Sir James sent and invited me to tea. I went in with Lord Advocate and drank some coffee and eat a crumb of biscuit. I went and looked at Runciman's paintings in Ossian's Hall,[2] and was much pleased. Sir James was extremely polite to me. Lord Advocate carried me in his coach to the village, but as he had a gentleman and lady with him I could get but little said. I however resumed my solicitation and said, "Well, my Lord, you'll think of it." He with a pleasing tone said something to this purpose: "Then as King William said, 'You must not think no more of it.' " Though I did not distinctly hear what he said, it appeared to me that he had an intention to do something for me. He pressed me much to go home with him, but I told him I was

[1] In giving his judgment in the Douglas Cause, in another court and several months after Reid's acquittal, the Lord Justice-Clerk indulged in an *obiter dictum* which was reported as follows: "We have indeed seen cases where there was a moral impossibility of the prisoner's innocence, and yet we have seen juries acquit such a one. Such a case was that of Reid, who was lately tried before the criminal Court, for the crime of *sheep-stealing*. . . . A counsel at that bar, who likes to distinguish himself upon such occasions, patronized the prisoner's defence and notwithstanding the clearest and most positive evidence of all the facts which I have mentioned, 'The jury acquitted the prisoner' " (*A Summary of the Speeches, Arguments, and Determinations of . . . the Lords of . . . Session* [in the Douglas Cause], London, 1767, pp. 323–324).

[2] A series of twelve paintings of scenes from Ossian's poems, on the ceiling of a large room designed for a picture gallery, with smaller paintings to complete the design. This room was one of the most important commissions given to Runciman on his return from Rome (see above, p. 296) by Sir James Clerk and other patrons. The paintings, finished in 1773, were highly esteemed, but perished when the house was destroyed by fire in 1899.

engaged in town. Mr. Hay and I drank a pint of white wine and eat a bit of biscuit and then took our chaise again. I observed how curious it was that two beings who were not sure of their own lives a day should be driving about in this manner to preserve the life of a wretch a little longer. Said Charles: "Can we be better employed?" On my coming home, and Mr. Hay with me, my wife, who never favoured John Reid and who was sorry to see me so much interested about him, told me that she had heard some decent-looking men talking tonight on the street against him. One of them said, "I think no laws will get leave to stand now. I wish the law of Moses may get leave to stand." She delivered me a letter from Lord Pembroke in most polite terms. mentioning that he had written to Lord Rochford and urged the affair strongly. This revived my hopes. I went to Dr. Monro's. Colonel Campbell of Finab and his family and the Laird of MacLeod and some other company were there. I played awhile at loo and lost only 18d. We supped very genteelly. I was in a very good frame, had taken a liking to claret and drank a bottle of it. I was pleased at this acquisition to the number of my convivial acquaintances.

[Received 2 September, Lord Pembroke to Boswell]

[Wilton] 29 August 1774

Sir,—I have received your commands and shall execute them as well as I can, with the greatest pleasure. As I cannot be in town to give the petition myself, and as I understand you have applied to Lord Suffolk, I have wrote to the other Secretary, Lord Rochford, and have urged the affair strongly to him.

I beg to make my compliments acceptable to Mrs. Boswell, and am, Sir, with the greatest truth and regard, your most obedient humble servant,

Pembroke.

[Michael Nasmith to Boswell]

[Edinburgh] almost 11, 2 September [1774]

Dear Sir,—I don't know whether you are returned. If—Do give me a hint of your hopes. I am engaged or would have waited on you.

John's wife was with me this afternoon. I gave her a letter to the messenger who apprehended,[1] with three or four queries, but begged him to come to town immediately to give you every information.

She tells me that after John heard the report against him, he had frequent conferences with Gardner, who lived (but was under hiding for the housebreaking) within thirty yards of John, anent the sheep. That the very moment John was taken he told the messenger that he had received the sheep from Gardner, and asked him whether he could not also apprehend him. The messenger, giving his hip a clap, said, "I can, I have a warrand in my pocket against him," and Gardner, within ten minutes after John, was also taken into custody, and they were in company as prisoners for some time. Gardner was sent to Stirling. These are facts you were totally ignorant of. I have begged the messenger's information what passed betwixt John and Gardner while in company. From this something good or bad may be learned. The messenger, if he has any bias, it will be in John's favour. Old acquaintances. I expect the messenger here on Sunday or a letter on Monday. What hopes now have you? Ever yours most sincerely,

M. NASMITH.

SATURDAY 3 SEPTEMBER. I had an opportunity of doing a great kindness to a friend[2] by lending him £50. My wife very handsomely was clear for my doing it, and the gratitude which he expressed in a line which he wrote to me was valuable.[3]

SUNDAY 4 SEPTEMBER. I was at the New Church all day; Dr. Blair in the forenoon, Mr. Walker in the afternoon. Nothing remarkable was impressed upon me. My wife and I took our Sunday's supper at Dr. Webster's. I had drank tea at Lady Colville's, as she was going to Fife next day to stay till October. Before supper I walked in the garden with the Colonel, who was warm for John Reid, while his father was strenuous against him. It occurred to me that the Colonel's

[1] He was a "messenger-at-arms", accompanied by a party of dragoons.

[2] Probably Andrew Erskine, who, when applying to Boswell in 1777 for a loan of £50, referred to it as "the old sum".

[3] Boswell here left nearly half a page blank, perhaps to record more events of this day when he remembered them, perhaps to copy in his "friend's" grateful note.

interest with Lord Cornwallis, who is intimate with the King and whose uncle is Archbishop of Canterbury, might be effectual. I asked the Colonel, "Does he know the narrowness of this damned country?" COLONEL. "Yes; was a year in it; despises it, hates it." "Then," said I, " 'twill do." The Colonel agreed to write to him, and I was to write at the same time. We went to the Colonel's room and he instantly began to flourish away in a letter to the Earl, of which he scrolled[1] a part. I saw him quite in the train. At supper we had Lieutenant Wellwood and Grant Seton. George was high in liquor and harangued wonderfully. I roared against him. He said, "Noise is upon both sides. Better fire the half-moon in the Castle.[2] Governor Wemyss has the best argument. There is no answering the great guns." Dr. Webster, the Colonel, and I drank a bottle of port apiece. I was so full of John Reid, Lord Cornwallis, etc., that the ordinary Sunday supper ideas were forgotten. Both the Colonel and I loved a glass tonight.[3]

MONDAY 5 SEPTEMBER. The Law College went on pretty well. It helped to quiet me. At two I went to Colonel Webster. I suggested to him to mention the prejudice of the judges in this narrow country on some occasions, which he did excellently well. For a moment I considered that it was not right that the supreme judges of a country should be censured by a young colonel whose letter might have influence. But then I thought, since they really have a bias to severity, it should be checked. And now there is much at stake: the life of a man whom I think innocent, and my own fame. In the evening the Colonel and Michael Nasmith came and sat by me while I wrote to Lord Cornwallis and a second time to Lord Pembroke, in which I not only mentioned my own anxiety but that I should be sorry to have it thought in this country that his Lordship had failed. The Colonel threw in flashes into my letter to Lord Cornwallis. Mr. Nasmith was quite pleased with the Colonel. He said I was cool in comparison of him. Before I got to the post-office the London mail was upon the horse. I

[1] Drafted. See below, p. 320.

[2] A bastion in the shape of a half-moon, with a battery of cannon from which salutes were and are still fired on official occasions.

[3] Another sentence of perhaps eight words follows in the manuscript, but it has been carefully deleted by Boswell, and remains undeciphered.

would not trust the post-boy with two such important packets. I therefore sent them by an express from the post-office to Haddington, which cost me £7.9. But one day's sooner arrival was well worth the money. Mr. Nasmith came home and supped with me.

[Boswell to Lord Pembroke]

Edinburgh, 5 September 1774

My Lord,—Your Lordship's most obliging letter has confirmed me in the opinion which I formed of your humanity. A respite for fourteen days has come for John Reid. But I understand that some of the judges are desired to make a report concerning him, and as I already hinted to your Lordship that there are prejudices against him in this narrow country which it would take some time to explain, I dread that the report may be unfavourable. If that shall be the case and he shall be yet ordered for execution, his situation will be deplorable, and the application made in his behalf will only serve to augment his misery. I must therefore again intrude upon your Lordship and beg in the most earnest manner that you may make a point of having his sentence changed to transportation. As I have mentioned my obligations to your Lordship for interposing in this affair, I should be sorry to have it thought in this country that Lord Pembroke *strongly urged* a petition for mercy in the case of a simple theft, supposing the charge true, and failed in obtaining it. The cruelty of an execution after respite is equal to many deaths, and therefore there is rarely an instance of it. This poor wretch, even if guilty, does not merit such severity. I am so much distressed with this wretched case that your Lordship will relieve me as well as my client by getting the sentence mitigated, and believe me, my Lord, I shall be most sincerely grateful for the obligation. Colonel Webster has written to Lord Cornwallis in favour of the unhappy man, whom I do really believe innocent of the theft for which he is condemned, and I would fain hope that I shall be made easy by having his life saved. It would be improper for me to suggest to your Lordship in what manner to secure a pardon. But I flatter myself that in the circumstances in which the affair now is, your Lordship will take effectual measures to obtain it. I shall be in great anxiety till I receive a few lines from your Lordship. My wife joins me in most respectful compliments, and I have the honour to be with unfeigned warmth your Lordship's much obliged humble servant,

[JAMES BOSWELL].

TUESDAY 6 SEPTEMBER. Dined at Mr. Donaldson's, where were Mr. Brown, who has the appellation of *Buckram* Brown,[1] who said all the books on trade—Child, Davenant, etc.—were nonsense, except Sir Matthew Decker's treatise.[2] We had also Mr. Mylne, the architect of Blackfriars Bridge, who told me that Mr. Johnson had begun again to drink wine and to speak in praise of doing so, which put me in the humour of it.[3] Also Captain Charles Douglas of the Navy, who had drank no fermented liquor for several years and said he was much healthier and stronger, could bear more fatigue, fast longer, and added four hours in the twenty-four to his existence, as he required less sleep. He preached up his system. But Mylne, who had tried it, said it would not answer with his constitution; and to this Mr. McDowall, the woollen-cloth manufacturer, who was there, assented cordially. Donaldson gave us very good claret. I loved the liquor, sucked it, and found it salutary. We had good stout conversation about the Bostonians and taxes, and trials for life or death. I removed part of the prejudice against John Reid. We drank tea. Brown said smuggling was not criminal. It was gaming—running the risk of certain penalties; and suppose all our own subjects should let it alone and we should see the Dutch getting all the profits of it, would not a man do well to try to get a part for himself? I answered that suppose all our own subjects should give over robbing on the highway and none but Dutchmen follow that occupation, would a man do well to try to

[1] "From his stiffness of temper and manners" (*Boswelliana*, p. 281). He was a china-merchant and magistrate of Edinburgh.

[2] Sir Matthew's *Essay on the Causes of the Decline of the Foreign Trade* appeared in 1744. Adam Smith did not think so well of it as Mr. Brown.

[3] There is no reason for doubting Mylne's testimony, but it does not appear that Johnson's use of wine after 1765 was more than sparing and sporadic.

get a part of the guineas, and not let them be carried out of the kingdom by the *Mynheers*? This got me the laugh of the company on my side.

[Michael Nasmith to Boswell]

Edinburgh, 6 September 1774

DEAR SIR,—Do you think it would be proper to transmit to Mr. Wilson, writer in Glasgow, that part of John's last speech respecting Gardner? I think it would be at any rate a matter of satisfaction to us to have Gardner, before he goes, examined upon every particular. If you think it proper, you may send me the speech to have the excerpt made, or you may cause my clerk do it, as perhaps you may not like to let the speech, as it stands, go out of your own possession. I am most sincerely, dear Sir, yours,

M. NASMITH.

[Michael Nasmith to Boswell]

Edinburgh, 6 September 1774

DEAR SIR,—Wilson is a fellow of spirit, and I wish him to know how matters stand. And sincerely I think I have told him nothing but real truth. But you'll let me know whether any thing is improper. There are such a world of questions to be asked at Gardner. If there be any truth in John's speech, I am sure we'll have some of it from Gardner, if he is not possessed of superlative cunning. I am, dear Sir, yours,

M. NASMITH.

The more I think of this matter the less I am disposed to think that the verdict is just, be Reid innocent or guilty.

[Michael Nasmith to John Wilson, Jr., Writer in Glasgow]

Edinburgh, 6 September 1774

DEAR JOHNNY,—You must know something more about poor John Reid's situation.

In 1766, when tried here for sheep-stealing, when the verdict of the jury was read finding him innocent, some of the judges took the liberty to give a different opinion, and the Lord Justice-Clerk in his speech in the Douglas Cause took some striking liberties with poor John's character. Upon these grounds, notwithstanding the verdict, all mankind were authorised by the Court to hold him guilty.

In last indictment habit and repute was libelled. Mr. Boswell opposed this with great spirit. In the proof, the Advocate by a minute admitted what had been said by the judges at last trial, and the speeches in the Douglas Cause were produced. The proof amounted to this: that eighteen were stolen, and that five of these were found in John's possession. John could not prove he purchased them, nor could he prove that he had not himself brought them home. Nor could he prove he was at home the night before they arrived. Of about twenty-five witnesses who were summoned for him, not one of them could say a word, and one of the Crown witnesses swore that he imagined (being Reid's next neighbour) that the sheep was brought home by John early before daylight in the morning, although John avers, and his wife too, that he was in his bed all that night, and that Russel, a lad employed by Gardner, brought them. The habit and repute bore everything before it. Five of the nineteen were found in his possession. Ergo the libel was found proved. Such a conclusion perchance may be right, but I defy mortal creature to say it is. Boswell was great. There never was a charge made with greater dignity and judgment. Had Corsica been at stake, he could not have stood forth with greater firmness, and at the same time with all that respect which was necessary, to show that the former trial could not influence in the present question. He implored the jury to disentangle themselves from all prejudices. The Lord Justice-Clerk complained loudly to the jury he and the Court had been arraigned. The verdict was returned finding the indictment proved.

A respite, I told you last night, has been obtained for fourteen days, but we now understand His Majesty wishes to have the Justiciary Court's report whether the poor man ought to die or live. You see where we are. We fear the Lord Justice-Clerk. The battle is betwixt

Boswell and the Court. He is opposing all his interest. He is all humanity. Reid is his oldest client in the Justiciary Court. He wishes not to see him die where the proof is not conclusive, nor any man where the proof is no more than that five stolen sheep are found in his possession. A simple act of theft, and that only supported by presumption. Is it not hard?

Before the respite came, John's last speech was framed. It has been put into Mr. Boswell's possession. Enclosed is a copy of that part of it respecting Gardner. It may be true. If it is, what a direful thing in this country of knowledge, and all the rest of it, for the poor man to be hung up!

If Gardner be gone to Greenock and not off, you'll follow him and make every enquiry. Your letter perhaps may be a sufficient answer to the Lord Justice-Clerk's report to His Majesty. Enquire as to the poinding[1]—if there was any such person as Russel—as to the letter. Feign that we have the letter. You need no instructions. When Boswell or I can serve you, command. I am, etc.,

M. NASMITH.[2]

EDITORIAL NOTE: The broadside *Last Speech, Confession, and Dying Words of John Reid . . . given to Richard Lock, Inner Turnkey of the Tolbooth, Edinburgh . . . Printed by H. Galbraith* was not published until after 21 September. (See below, Appendix A.) But the text of this broadside taken with the letter just presented makes it clear that Boswell and Nasmith were by now in possession of a statement by Reid to the effect that, about ten days before the "melancholy affair" for which Reid was to suffer, Gardner had arranged with Reid to deliver to him a parcel of sheep for slaughter on Tuesday 4 October. Gardner did not, however, actually deliver the sheep on that day. Instead, on Thursday "thereafter, early in the morning before I had got out of bed, a young man named Thomas Russel chapped at my door and told me that Gardner had sent me nineteen sheep and at same time delivered me a line from him, in which he informed me that he

[1] Distraining a person's goods; pronounced "pinding".

[2] The letter is a copy in Nasmith's hand.

could not come on the Tuesday as he had promised, as he had been employed in poinding a man that was owing him some money."

WEDNESDAY 7 SEPTEMBER. Mr. Nasmith called with a letter from Brown, the messenger who had taken up John Reid, addressed to John, and mentioning that, as they were upon the road, John asked him if he could apprehend anyone else and mentioned Gardner, who was accordingly apprehended. From this letter it appeared to me and Messrs. Hay and Nasmith that John had been lying; for if he had got the sheep from Gardner without suspicion, would not he, when accused of stealing them, have instantly accused Gardner, loudly and keenly? No law was read today, we talked so long of John Reid. I determined to try again to know the truth.

I went up to John a little before two, with the messenger's letter in my hand. Seeing me have a paper, he gave an earnest look, I suppose in expectation that it was his pardon. But I at once accosted him as a dying man, upbraided him with having imposed on me, and said to him what I and Mr. Nasmith had concluded from perusal of the letter. He calmly explained his conduct. "Sir," said he, "Gardner had before this time come to my house and owned to me that he had stolen the sheep, and promised me great rewards if I would not discover him. Therefore, when I was taken up, I would not speak out against him, but wanted him to be apprehended, that he and I might concert what was to be done to keep ourselves safe. But he was but a very little time with me, and then was carried to Stirling." I was not much convinced by this account of the matter. I had wrought myself into a passion against John for deceiving me, and spoke violently to him, not feeling for him at the time. I had chosen my time so as to be with him when two o'clock struck. "John," said I, "you hear that clock strike. You hear that bell. If this does not move you, nothing will. That you are to consider as your last bell. You remember your sentence. On Wednesday the 7 of September. This is the day. Between the hours of two and four in the afternoon; this is that very time. After this day you are to look upon yourself as a dead man; as a man in a middle state between the two worlds. You are not in eternity, because you are still in the body; but you are not properly alive, because this is the day appointed for your death. You are to look on this fortnight as so much time allowed to you to repent of all your wickedness, and particularly of your lying to me in such a way as you have done. Think that this day fortnight by four o'clock you will be rendering an account to your Maker. I am afraid that you are encouraged by your wife to persist in obstinacy, not to disgrace her and your children. But that is a small consideration to a man going into eternity. I think it your duty to own your being guilty on this occasion if you be really so, which I cannot but think is the case. By doing so you will make all the atonement in your power to society. But at any rate I beseech you not to deny your guilt contrary to truth." This was as vehement and solemn a harangue as could be made upon any occasion. The circumstance of the clock striking and the two o'clock bell ringing were finely adapted to touch the imagination. But John seemed to be very unfeeling today. He persisted in his tale. There was something approaching to the ludicrous when, in the middle of my speech to him about his not being properly alive, he said very gravely, "Ay; I'm dead in law." I was too violent with him. I said, "With what face can you go into the other world?" And: "If your ghost should come and tell me this, I would not believe it." This last sentence made me frightened, as I have faith in apparitions, and had a kind of idea that perhaps his ghost might come to me and tell me that I had been unjust to him. I concluded with saying, "You have paper, pen, and ink there. Let me have a real account of everything." He said he would. Richard Lock had come into the room before I was done speaking. I desired him to advise John to be candid.

Mr. Nasmith met me when I came out of prison and was very impatient to hear about John. In telling him John's explanation of his behaviour when taken up, I became impressed that it might be true, and enlarged on the uncertainty of circumstantial evidence. Nasmith was convinced too, and said, "We are as much in the dark as ever." I took him home with me to dinner; and, after drinking a bottle of port between us, a curious thought struck me that I would write the case of John Reid as if dictated by himself on this the day fixed for his execution. I accordingly did it, and hit off very well the thoughts and style of what such a case would have been. Nasmith suggested the idea of Gardner confessing in America. He took it home to get it copied, and undertook to send it to Galbraith, a printer, that it might be hawked about the streets this very night; which would have a striking effect, as it called on his readers to think that it was his *ghost* speaking to them.

And now let me mention some circumstances omitted in my Journal. John's vanity appeared while his picture was drawing, by his asking me if his name would be put upon it. I said it would be put on the back of it. Said he: "I thought it would have been on the fore (front) side."[1] His predestinarian belief appeared from his observing, when I spoke of the wonderful escape of Andrews, etc., from Paisley,[2] "Their time was not come." His wife had been with me since the respite came. I gave her no hopes, but bid her have a cart to carry away his body. "Ay," said she, "there shall be a cart if there's occasion for it"; so I saw that all I could say did not prevent her from imagining that he had a pretty good chance for life.

The Answers for Nimmo were wanted soon. I found that I put them off from day to day. So one evening last week I sent for Adam Bell and made him sit by me while I revised the scroll[3] of the Answers before the Lord Ordinary; corrected, added, wrote papers apart, and so obliged myself, by labouring in his presence both before and after supper, to complete my task, all but a few pages, which I afterwards did. Mr. Lawrie had been a jaunt to Stirling and Perth. He came to Edinburgh on Sunday. I met him at the Cross on Sunday evening. He breakfasted with me on Monday and went home again that day. My wife and I supped this night at Captain Schaw's with Lady Dundonald, Lady Betty, Colonel Stopford, etc., very well.

[1] Boswell had actually not omitted this. See above, p. 303.

[2] See above, p. 209, the unexpectedly successful effort of Boswell and Crosbie defending John Andrews and others in a trial in March 1774 for arson committed at Paisley.

[3] See above, p. 312.

[Received c. 7 September, John Wilson, Jr., to Michael Nasmith]

Glasgow, 6 September 1774

DEAR SIR,—This day I received yours of yesterday[1] about the case of John Reid, who hath received His Majesty's respite of his capital punishment for fourteen days. I see Mr. Boswell and you are still employed in the cause of humanity, nay, could our politicians see it, of good policy also—rescuing the lives of the lieges from destruction appointed too frequently by the barbarous laws of a civilised nation. Can any sober thinking person believe it that in a country which boasts so much of its knowledge and refinement there should exist a law assigning death as the punishment of the crime of stealing eighteen sheep? *Ninety and nine* sheep, which once were less valued than one lost and recovered, are less valuable than the life of any of His Majesty's subjects. What pity it is that the sentiments of that excellent philosopher and politician the Marquis Beccaria have not hitherto been capable of opening the eyes of our legislators, who can suffer the laws on so slight occasions to murder the citizens with a formal pageantry.—I am truly sorry that I can add no information from Gardner, from whom you say Reid maintains he bought the sheep, he having above three weeks ago stayed a night only here in his passage to transportation. I am, dear Sir, your most obedient servant.

JOHN WILSON, JR.

THE MOURNFUL CASE OF POOR MISFORTUNATE AND UNHAPPY JOHN REID, Now lying under sentence of death in the Tolbooth of Edinburgh, dated Wednesday night, the 7th of September 1774.

This is the very day on which I was doomed to die; and had it not been for the mercy of our most gracious Sovereign, whom GOD long bless and preserve, I should by this time have been a miserable spectacle, and my last speech crying dolefully through the streets of this city. O! listen then unto me, while I am yet in the land of the living, and think that it is my GHOST speaking unto you!

Much cry has been made against me by small and great. And how can a poor man like me withstand it? But before I go hence and be no

[1] Nasmith's first letter to Wilson, written apparently the day before the one presented above, pp. 315–17, has not been found.

more, I trust you will hear the words of truth, and peradventure your minds may be changed.

I am condemned because some of these sheep were found in my flesh-house and I could not bring downright probation of him from whom I came by them. But I say now, as I told my lawyer, who said it unto the Lords and will say unto the end, that William Gardner, and none else, was the man, and he is now a transported thief, though he was loose when I was seized and caused him for to be taen, that he might answer therefor and I not be the sufferer. John Brown the messenger in Linlithgow can attest this; and many an honest man has no witnesses present when he receives goods. But I see that my being tried two times before, though cleared by juries, many of whom, now alive, can bear testimony for me, has made me be thought guilty at all events.

I hope none of you shall by malicious report of enemies be brought to trial, since it is all one whatever is the fate thereof.

What will you say when Gardner's conscience smites him in America and he owns that I got the sheep honestly from him, and I am gone and cannot be recalled?

May all good Christians, then, charitably pray that as the King's heart is in the hand of the Lord, and he turneth it whithersoever he will, it may please him to save me from an ignominious death, which can do harm to no man.[1]

THURSDAY 8 SEPTEMBER. Mr. Donaldson and his son, Mr. Mylne the architect, Balbarton, Sir George and Lady Preston and Miss Preston dined with us. My servant James had a child ill of the small-pox. He would not agree to stay away from it; and as I was afraid that my little Effie might be infected, I would not allow him to come into my house; so I was now without a manservant. I saw that a married servant would not do in a family where only one is kept, and therefore I gave him warning to provide himself against the term. It gave me some uneasiness to think that a poor man should be dismissed because he had strong natural affection; but I considered that a man in his station of life is bound to submit to many disadvantages, and if he

[1] From a draft in Boswell's hand. See below, p. 332.

cannot do so, he is at least unfit for being the sole manservant in a family; and I hoped that he would get a good place somewhere else. Sir George's ladies went home early. He and the rest of the company drank tea. I had taken too much claret. I strolled in the streets a long time.[1] I supped at Sir George's with my wife. Mrs. Wellwood[2] was there. I drank too much strong port negus. After I came home I was monstrously passionate.

FRIDAY 9 SEPTEMBER. After our law Mr. Hay and I had a game at bowls. He dined with me and drank tea. I was now become a man of high estimation in the prison, in so much that prisoners applied to me by petition: "Unto the Honourable James Boswell, Esq., Advocate, The Petition of ——— Humbly Showeth." I did them what service I could. Henry McGraugh's case was now become an object of great attention, the newspapers having many letters about it. Some of them I wrote myself. Galbraith had not printed John Reid's case.[3] On Saturday last Mr. Ritchie called on me in the afternoon and showed me part of a dying speech which he had drawn up from what John said to him. I asked Ritchie of what religious profession he was. He said, "I belong to a few *meeters* in the Potterrow." It seems he was an Independent, but had separated from Dr. Boswell's people on some difference about discipline.[4] I promised to consider what he had drawn up. Dr. Young drank tea with us. He thought hanging a quick death, there being violence besides suffocation.

[Received c. 9 September, "Tyburn" to Boswell]

SIR,—I understand your design. John Reid will steal for you, and

[1] Here occurs an indistinct private symbol, apparently consisting of two characters, the first a Greek letter π.

[2] Sir George Preston's eldest daughter, mother of Lieutenant Robert.

[3] See above, p. 320. On 8 September Nasmith had written to Boswell as follows: "Last night the composition was re-copied and a note added: 'Print this for me immediately to be sent about.' An address was put upon the back, and the letter was given to a porter. About ten another porter was dispatched to have the matter distributed. Nothing has appeared. Perhaps '*print this* for *me*' has carried the thing into a wrong channel, to the centre of the city. We'll afterwards learn."

[4] Dr. Boswell belonged to the Glassites or Sandemanians, a Presbyterian sect which opposed the principle of established churches and national covenants.

the Irishman shall then have plenty from your table. You know that good mutton is pleasant to the Faculty of Advocates: yea, although you know it to be stolen; and if the Irishman had done to you as he has done to others, you and Andrew would be———[1] indeed. The case is truly this: the Irishman and Crosbie, Boswell and John Reid, is all alike guilty.

TYBURN.

SATURDAY 10 SEPTEMBER. Captain Robert Preston had arrived last night. I called for him this morning at Sir George's, missed him, but found him at Dr. Webster's. He then came to my house and sat a little. He was engaged all this day. After breakfast Mr. Nasmith called, which interrupted the Law College. Mr. Hay and he agreed with me that as I was to transmit a memorial on the evidence against John Reid, showing its insufficiency, it would be proper to send along with it a declaration by his wife that he was in his own house the night when the theft was committed, and for several nights before. This the woman all along affirmed, and her testimony was the only proof that in the circumstances of the case could be had. I drew a short petition to the Magistrates which Mr. Nasmith got John to sign, and then presented it. Bailie Torry, who then officiated, was timorous, and some clerk advised that it should be intimated to the King's Advocate, Solicitor, or Crown Agent. The Bailie gave judgement accordingly. They were all out of town; and at any rate would have opposed it, though in reality they had no concern with it. The trial was over. The declaration was only a piece of evidence, perhaps not strictly legal, but which might have weight with His Majesty, after a respite had been granted. Bailie Macqueen, to whom Mr. Nasmith spoke first, very gravely said that taking the declaration would be to destroy a trial by jury. We were now in a dilemma. We thought of trying a Justice of Peace, but we could not bear being refused again. Mr. ——— suggested that the declaration might be taken before two notaries public. We sallied forth into the street to look for another notary to join Mr. Nasmith. We met Andrew Dick, Writer to the

[1] Word undeciphered: it appears to read *C-ge* or *Co-ge*. The writer seems to be fairly literate.

Signet. He would not be concerned in the matter; and said with a dull sort of sneer, "He may prepare himself for Wednesday come eight days." I was angry at the animal, and told him before Messieurs Hay and Nasmith that John told me that Mr. Andrew Dick and he were fourth cousins. This the creature could not deny; and to have it known mortified him not a little. It occurred that perhaps a commissary might take the declaration. We walked out to George's Square, and I called on Commissary Smollett[1] and laid the matter before him. He said that, as a commissary was not *virtute officii* a Justice of Peace all over the country like the Lords of Session and Barons of Exchequer, and had no criminal jurisdiction, he could not take the declaration. I then suggested that a protest might be taken against the Bailie for delaying it. He thought this right, and said that along with the protest a petition from the poor woman might be sent, setting forth what she would have declared had she not been prevented; which would probably not have been the case in our neighbouring country, affidavits being readily taken by magistrates in England.

Messieurs Hay and Nasmith waited for me in the Square, and we went and dined together at Baptie's in Bruntsfield Links, very soberly, and came to the resolution of taking no protest, as that would occasion a noise, but just having the declaration certified by two notaries public. We came in to town, sauntered at the Cross, anxious for another notary to join Mr. Nasmith. One Tyrie appeared but declined to give his assistance. We were in a great dilemma. At last I found Matthew Dickie. We went into Hutchinson's and had a bottle of claret for ourselves and a bottle of porter for Mrs. Reid and Richard Lock, who brought her. I then exhorted her to tell nothing but truth; said I was not a judge, so could not administer an oath to her; but that solemnly to declare what was not true would be a great sin. She said, "I am in the presence of God." Her declaration then was taken, and she really seemed to speak what was genuine truth. Mr. Dickie went home. I and my two zealous coadjutors drank tea, and I wrote two letters to Lord Rochford: one as to the Secretary of State and another as to the private nobleman; and I put them, with a memorial and the

[1] James Smollett of Bonhill, first cousin of the novelist Tobias; he was a brother-in-law of Sir James Clerk of Penicuik.

declaration, into the post-office with my own hand, as I have done every letter concerning John Reid. Messieurs Hay and Nasmith came home and supped with me. This was a day of much agitation. I was quite exhausted. We drank little.

[Boswell to the Earl of Rochford]

Edinburgh, 10 September 1774

My Lord,—A respite having arrived from your Lordship's office for John Reid, under sentence of death here, I think it my duty in justice to the unhappy man, for whom I was counsel, and whose trial was attended with very peculiar circumstances, to transmit to your Lordship a memorial upon the evidence and a solemn declaration taken since the trial; as I am indeed anxious that the royal clemency may not be intercepted when it is my serious opinion that it is proper to grant it. I have the honour to be, my Lord, your Lordship's most obedient, humble servant,

[James Boswell].

Editorial Note: Boswell's "memorial" argued that one proof of Reid's innocence in receiving the sheep from Gardner was his complete carelessness in allowing the sheep to graze in the park near his house, and in failing to remove the heads of two of the sheep in his slaughter-house or in any way to remove or deface the marks of identification on any of the sheep. (Precautions of that sort had had great weight in establishing guilt in the noted trial of Murdison and Miller the previous year.) He suggested that the cross-examination of William Black had shown the "rashness" of this witness, "who endeavoured to swear as strongly as he could against the prisoner." In both the memorial and his letter to Rochford "as to the private nobleman," Boswell advertised the illiberality which prevailed in his own country. "This poor man had formerly suffered a severe imprisonment upon an accusation of the same nature, though when brought to trial he was acquitted by a verdict of his country. There was therefore no wonder that he should endeavour [by running away] to avoid such a hardship upon this occasion. And it may be added that he was alarmed from a consideration of what it is to be feared has been the consequence, that in a narrow country the prejudice created against him by his being formerly tried, though acquitted, might insensibly operate upon the minds of a jury. . . ." It is to be hoped that this prejudice "will be disregarded by liberal minds who think justly of a trial by jury."

He began his personal letter to Lord Rochford with an appeal to his own political past. "Perhaps your Lordship may have heard of my name on occasion of my humble efforts in behalf of the brave and unfortunate Corsicans. I shall only say that although I have not the honour to be personally known to Lord Rochford, I have often felt the warmest regard for him, knowing his spirited and generous conduct at the Court of France at a time when the interposition of Great Britain in the manner devised by your Lordship would have saved that gallant little nation from severe oppression."

[Declaration of Janet Reid]

At Edinburgh, 10 September in the year of Our Lord 1774 of the reign of our Sovereign Lord George, by the Grace of God of Great Britain, France, and Ireland King, the fourteenth year, in presence of us Matthew Dickie and Michael Nasmith, one of the clerks to His Majesty's Signet, and both of us notars public admitted by royal authority and also by authority of the Lords of Council and Session conform to Act of Parliament, being duly sworn into the said office:

Appeared Janet the wife of John Reid, now lying under sentence of death in the prison of Edinburgh, and solemnly declared and affirmed that her said husband sleeped at home in his own house upon the nights of the sixth and seventh of October last, the last of which is the night on which it is alleged that he committed the theft for which he is condemned, and that he sleeped both those nights in the bed with the declarant, which he also did during every other night of that week, and during the three last nights of the week preceding. That they went regularly to bed each of these nights at or before eleven of the clock, being their usual time of going to bed, and they lay till sun-rising, except upon Thursday's morning, when her husband was called up about an hour before sun-rising to receive a parcel of sheep from William Gardner. And all that she has now solemnly declared and affirmed she is ready and willing to attest upon oath before any of His Majesty's judges. In testimony whereof she hereto adhibits her subscription in our presence and in presence of Charles Hay, Esq., advocate, and Matthew Montgomery, writer in Edinburgh.

(Signed) JANET REID, *præmissa attestor*
Veritas MATTHEW DICKIE, No. Pub.
M. NASMITH, N. P.
CHA. HAY, Witness
M. MONTGOMERIE, Witness[1]

SUNDAY 11 SEPTEMBER. I stayed at home all forenoon. My wife and I dined quietly by ourselves. In the afternoon I walked about the King's Park. Called on Lord Dundonald. Drank a large glass of Madeira with him, and then drank tea with the ladies. My wife and I supped at Sir George Preston's, where [were] the Websters, all but the Colonel and Annie, who were in the country. Captain Robert became warm for John Reid; said he would write a letter to Bamber Gascoyne,[2] who had a great deal to say with Lord Rochford; and he would pay the half of an express to carry it. I was to call on him next morning to get it. We had a deal of jovial roaring, and drank till two in the morning.

MONDAY 12 SEPTEMBER. I was very ill with last night's riot. Between eight and nine, Captain Preston had a message for me. I went to him. He made me write while he dictated a very strong letter indeed, to which he put his name. It was agreed that it would go soon enough by the post. Sir George and all the family set off this morning for Valleyfield. Matthew Dickie dined with me. I began to consider that Captain Preston's letter being in my handwriting might appear to Lord Rochford to have been framed by me; and I really could not vouch its contents. I therefore resolved not send it, but wrote to the Captain that if he pleased to send me a letter in his own handwriting, in

1 A copy in an unknown hand.

2 M.P. for Weobly 1770–1774, eldest son of Sir Crisp Gascoyne, Lord Mayor of London in 1752.

time for Tuesday's post,[1] it would do. He did not think it necessary, for none came.

TUESDAY 13 SEPTEMBER. The Laird of Dundas[2] had asked me to eat turtle with him this day at Fortune's. After a good match at bowls with Mr. Hay, I went to Fortune's, but found the feast was put off till next day; but as it had not been notified to me, I resolved not to attend next day. Charles Hay had told me that he had excellent mutton to dinner today; so I hastened to his house, but found dinner over and him eating some of the mutton by himself. I joined him and dined heartily, and saw I was made very welcome. He and I and his brother[3] drank a bottle of Madeira and a bottle of claret. I then, for the first time for many months, played at whist, Maclaurin and I having freed each other from a bet of five guineas who should first play again. I won, and also drank tea.

[Boswell to the printer of *The London Chronicle*][4]

Edinburgh, 13 September 1774

SIR,—The rigour of our present penal laws has been long the subject of complaint. It is to be hoped that the legislature will at last see fit to relax it. In the meantime, the utmost care should be taken that there should at least be full evidence against an unhappy man before he is dragged to a violent death for theft or any of those lesser crimes which are at present capital by law in England and by practice in Scotland. We have at present in this city a remarkable man lying under sentence of death, being convicted of the theft of a few sheep. His name is John Reid. He is remarkable because he was formerly

[1] London mail left Edinburgh every night except Wednesday and Sunday at half-past eight.

[2] James Dundas, a distant cousin of the Lord President and the Solicitor-General.

[3] James Hay.

[4] This letter, which Boswell does not mention in the Journal till several days later, appeared in *The London Chronicle* for 17–20 September, and led to his receiving on 6 October a letter from the son of the Lord Justice-Clerk offering the alternatives of public apology or a duel. The uncomfortable incident which ensued is narrated in the next volume of this series.

tried and acquitted by a very worthy jury, notwithstanding which some persons in high office publicly represented him as guilty. In particular one great man of the law exclaimed against him in his speech in the great Douglas Cause. This is a striking specimen of what goes on in this narrow country. A strong prejudice was raised against him, and now he was condemned upon circumstantial evidence which several impartial gentlemen of very good skill were of opinion was inconclusive. He has uniformly affirmed that, although the sheep were found in his possession, he had obtained them by a fair and honest bargain from another man. His case is very much similar to that of Madan, who was lately in the cart at Tyburn just going to be turned off, as guilty of a robbery upon circumstantial evidence, when Merritt appeared and confessed that he was the man who had committed the crime. But the man from whom Reid got the sheep has not as yet been so conscientious as Merritt. He has maintained an obstinate denial; but having been transported for housebreaking, he will probably confess in America.

A respite for fourteen days was sent to Reid from the office of Lord Rochford, from whence Madan's respite also was sent. But, according to my information, an opinion from Scotland was desired upon the case: an opinion from that very man who exclaimed in the Civil Court against a man acquitted by a jury in the Criminal Court, when his life was staked upon the issue.

The determination of the Sovereign is expected here with anxiety. I wish to avoid strong expressions. I would turn my mind only towards mercy. This will reach you on Saturday. It is entreated that you may insert it directly, as it may perhaps have influence in some manner that we cannot exactly foresee, and an express with a pardon, or with another respite till there can be time to hear from America, will prevent what I am afraid would have a wretched appearance in the annals of this country. I am, Sir, your constant reader,

A Royalist.

WEDNESDAY 14 SEPTEMBER. Having gone out to the Justiciary Office in the morning, Mr. Hay had called and missed me; so we had no law. I called at the bank for Maclaurin, and he and I took a walk in the Meadow. After dinner Ritchie called on me and said he was very desirous that John Reid should declare what he had committed long ago, which he thought had followed him. I promised to come to the prison, and accordingly went.

John was very sedate. He told Mr. Ritchie and me that, before his first trial, one night he drank hard and lay all night at the side of a sheep-fold; that when he awaked the devil put it into his head (or some such expression) and he drove off all the sheep in the fold (the "*hail hirsle*"); that before he was off the farm to which they belonged, he came to a water, and there he separated four of them, which he took home, killed, and sold; and he said it was alleged that he had taken five, but it never came to any trial. This was but a small matter. John said he would have it published. His owning this theft made me give more credit to his denial of that for which he was condemned, for why should he deny the one and confess the other? I told him that now I believed him, and I acknowledged that I had been too violent with him this day eight days. He seemed to be grateful to me; and said that few would have done so much for a brother, though a twin, as I had done for him. He said that he had always had something heavy about his mind since his last trial and never could be merry as formerly. He said that last night he had strange dreams. He saw a wonderful moon with many streamers. And he and a man who died some time ago, he imagined were walking together, and the man had a gun in his hand; that two eagles—two pretty speckled birds—lighted on a tree. (*I* had very near said that these signified Lord Cornwallis and Lord Pembroke, who were his friends; but I checked myself.) He called to the man to shoot, but he did not; and one of the eagles flew into the man's arms, who gave it to John, and he carried it. Ritchie very foolishly smiled, and said, "Maybe, John, it may be a messenger of good news to you." This might have given him hopes. "No," said I. "Had it been a *dow* (dove), I should have thought it good; but an eagle is a bad bird." "Ay," said John earnestly, "a ravenous bird." "But," said Ritchie, "it did not fly on John, but on the other man, who gave it to John." "Well," said I, "that is to say, the bad news will come to Captain Fraser, and he'll deliver it to John."

I asked John if he ever saw anything in the iron room where he lay.

He said no; but that he heard yesterday at nine in the morning a noise upon the form,[1] as if something had fallen upon it with a *clash*. Ritchie and he seemed to consider this as some sort of warning. He said he had heard such a noise in the corner of the room a little before his respite came. And he said that the night before James Brown's pardon came, Brown was asleep, and he was awake, and heard like swine running from the door, round a part of the room, and *grumphling*.[2] He seemed to be in a very composed frame. I said it was an awful thought that this day sennight at this time he would be in eternity. I said I hoped his repentance was sincere and his faith in Christ sincere, and that he would be saved through the merits of the Saviour, and perhaps he might this day eight days be looking down with pity on Mr. Ritchie and me. I found that he had hardly written anything.

I should have observed that on Saturday we sent for George Reid the printer to Hutchinson's, and he undertook to get the case which I had drawn in John Reid's style printed and cried, to conciliate the lower populace. It was accordingly done; but old Robertson had put in "*taken from his own mouth*", which was a lie. Richard Lock told me that John was very angry at this case. I said it could do no harm.[3]

Colonel Webster and Annie, who were now returned, and George came and supped with me. My wife was indisposed. We roared and drank, both too much.

THURSDAY 15 SEPTEMBER. After a game at bowls, I dined at Lord Dundonald's. Commissioner Cochrane and George Webster were there. George and I drank rather too much port. He walked home with me. A bottle of claret was standing out. I insisted on our drinking it, which we did pleasantly, and then drank tea with my wife.

FRIDAY 16 SEPTEMBER. Charles Hay and I this day completed our course of Erskine's *Institutes*. I dined with him, with Maclaurin,

[1] The bench on which Reid sat. See above, p. 298.

[2] See above, pp. 208–9, Boswell's defence of James Brown in a trial for horse-stealing, 7 February 1774.

[3] See above, p. 322. A printed copy of this broadside among the Boswell papers differs from the copy in Boswell's hand (see our text above, pp. 321–2) only in the heading, which has been altered to read: ". . . taken from his own mouth on Wednesday night, the 7th of September 1774, being the day fixed for his execution."

who was in good spirits but offended me by a kind of profaneness in quoting Scripture. He was of opinion that it was wrong to apply for John Reid; and when I asserted that he was innocent, Maclaurin had a pretty good simile. He said I had worked up my mind upon the subject. That the mind of man might be worked up from little or nothing like soap suds, till the basin is overflowed. We drank moderately, and then played at whist. I went home at night, and was in a strange wearied humour; so went directly to bed.

SATURDAY 17 SEPTEMBER. Mr. Robert Boswell and I breakfasted at my uncle the Doctor's. Richard Lock came in the morning, after my return from the Doctor's, and told me, "It is all over with John Reid. He dies on Wednesday. There's a letter come that no farther respite is to be granted."[1] I was struck with concern. Mr. Hay came, and he and I walked a little on the Castle Hill and then called on Mr. Nasmith. We agreed to dine together at Leith to relieve our vexation at the bad news. I first went up a little to John Reid. His wife was with him. He was not much affected with the bad news, as he had not been indulging hopes. I again exhorted him to tell nothing but truth.

Messieurs Hay, Nasmith, and I walked down to Leith, and dined at Trumpeter Yeats's. We were fain to fly to wine to get rid of the uneasiness which we felt that, after all that had been done, poor John Reid should fall a victim. I thought myself like Duncan Forbes.[2] We drank two bottles of port each. I was not satisfied with this, but stopped at a shop in Leith and insisted that we should drink some gin. Mr. Nasmith and one Ronald, the master of the shop, and I drank each a gill. Nasmith was very drunk, Mr. Hay and I quite in our senses. We all walked up some way or other. Mr. Hay came home with me. I

[1] "The law must take its course. . . . I cannot help regretting with your Lordship that Mr. Boswell did not endeavour to learn your Lordship's opinion before he wrote to this office, as in all probability if he had done so, he would not have occasioned the hopes which the respite may have given the poor man, and he would have been convinced that your Lordship entirely agreed with the rest of the judges of the Court of Justiciary in the sentence which they pronounced" (Lord Suffolk to the Lord Justice-Clerk, 9 September 1774: Public Record Office, Scottish Entry Book, Criminal).

[2] See above, p. 237.

found a letter from Lord Pembroke which gave me still hopes, for he said he would go to town and see the King himself; and I flattered myself that his Lordship might procure an alteration of the doom. Mr. Hay left me. I grew monstrously drunk, and was in a state of mingled frenzy and stupefaction. I do not recollect what passed.

[Hugh Warrender to James Tait, one of the town clerks of Edinburgh]

Edinburgh, 17 September 1774

Sir,—The Earl of Suffolk, Secretary of State, by his letter to the Lords of Justiciary dated from St. James's the nine instant, and of which I have been just now acquainted, writes that the extract of the trial of John Reid had been laid before the King, and, as there did not appear to be any favourable circumstance in that unhappy man's case, that no further respite would be granted, and that the law must take its course after the expiration of the respite formerly sent and notified to the Magistrates of Edinburgh.

This I thought it my duty to notify as soon as possible, that the unhappy man may not be allowed to continue longer under any false hopes that he may have been led to entertain.

I am in the absence of John Davidson, Sir, your most obedient humble servant,

Hugh Warrender,
City Clerk of Edinburgh.[1]

[Received 17 September, Lord Pembroke to Boswell]

Wilton House, 11 September 1774

I dare say, my dear Sir, that Lord Rochford has done the poor man's business, but, in case of any mistake, I will go up to town and see the King myself on Thursday next, the usual day of Court in the summer, if nothing prevents His Majesty's coming to town.

[1] This letter is a copy in Boswell's hand. John Davidson (see above, p. 307) was Crown Agent in Edinburgh and Warrender was his clerk. The style "City Clerk of Edinburgh", which Warrender assumes as Davidson's deputy, appears not to have been official.

My best compliments wait on Mrs. Boswell. I am, Sir, with the greatest truth and regard, your most obedient humble servant,

PEMBROKE.

SUNDAY 18 SEPTEMBER. It gave me much concern to be informed by my dear wife that I had been quite outrageous in my drunkenness the night before; that I had cursed her in a shocking manner and even thrown a candlestick with a lighted candle at her. It made me shudder to hear such an account of my behaviour to one whom I have so much reason to love and regard; and I considered that, since drinking has so violent an effect on me, there is no knowing what dreadful crime I may commit. I therefore most firmly resolved to be sober. I was very ill today. Both Mr. Hay and Mr. Nasmith called on me. About twelve I called on Grange, and he and I walked out by the West Kirk and round by Watson's Hospital, which did me much good. I found my uncle the Doctor when I got home. He dined with us. I stayed at home in the afternoon as I had done in the forenoon. Mr. Hay came after church, and he and I walked in Heriot's Garden. Lady Dundonald and Lady Betty Cochrane drank tea with us.

MONDAY 19 SEPTEMBER. Between seven and eight I was with the Doctor by appointment, and he and I walked out to Sir James Foulis's at Colinton, where we breakfasted. It was melancholy to see an ancient respectable family in decay. Sir James has much curious knowledge,[1] but his whim and want of dignity displeased me. We saw his lady and youngest daughter. He walked with us to Dreghorn (Mr. Maclaurin's), where I was engaged to dine and play at bowls. Charles Hay and his sister came. It was a wet day, but we had a stout bowling match. Sir James went home. We dined very well and drank little. Then Maclaurin, Hay, and I took a rubber, Hay playing the dead man. Maclaurin told me that I had the character of speaking ill of my companions, but that he did not believe it. Hay justified me, owning at the same time that I would have my joke on them when it could not really hurt them. I said I certainly did speak freely of those of whom I had not a good opinion, but I did not live with them as companions.

[1] He was a Celtic scholar, engaged in research on the place names of Scotland and the origin of the Scots.

Maclaurin said I carried that too far. It gave me some sort of uneasiness to hear that I was misrepresented; but then my full consciousness of my real goodness made me easy. We drank tea; and then the Doctor and I came off in a hackney-coach which my wife sent for us. By the road he disputed warmly for his particular tenets as to the Christian religion: salvation by faith alone, etc. I felt some pain when I found how ill I could argue on the most important of all subjects, and cold clouds of doubt went athwart my mind.

When I got home I found letters for me from Lord Rochford, Lord Pembroke, Mr. Eden, Under-Secretary in Lord Suffolk's office, and the Duke of Queensberry, and was finally assured that John Reid would be executed. I was hurt, and also felt an indignation at the Justice-Clerk, whose violent report had prevented my obtaining for John Reid the royal mercy; but I resolved not to write against him till time had cooled me. Mr. Hay called, and was much concerned. He and I went to Mr. Nasmith, who was very impatient. We all agreed that it was a shocking affair. The last resort now was the scheme of recovering John. Mr. Hay promised to call at my house next morning to talk of it. Mr. Nasmith and I went to see Mr. Wood. He was not at home. We found him at Mrs. Alison's in New Street, Canongate, at supper, got him into a room, and spoke with him. He said that a house must be found as near the place of execution as possible, for that the rumbling of a cart would destroy John altogether. He said a stable or any place would do. He would attend and have the proper apparatus, and get Mr. Innes, Dr. Monro's dissector, to attend. I was much agitated tonight. It rained very heavily. I wished it might do so on Wednesday, that the execution might perhaps be hastened.

[Received 19 September, William Eden[1] to Boswell]

St. James's, 13 September 1774

SIR,—I am directed by Lord Suffolk to acknowledge your letter to

[1] William Eden, Under-Secretary of State for the North, 1772–1778, was in 1793 created Baron Auckland in the peerage of Great Britain. He was a younger son of Sir Robert Eden, third Baronet of West Auckland, County Durham. The former Prime Minister of Great Britain, Sir Anthony Eden, is descended from another son of Sir Robert.

THOMAS MILLER (1717–1789),
Lord Justice-Clerk; later Lord President and baronet. From an oil painting reputedly by Sir Joshua Reynolds, sold at Christie's in 1927. Photograph courtesy of the Frick Art Reference Library

his Lordship enclosing a petition to the King from the unfortunate convict John Reid, and to assure you that every attention has been given to your wishes that the nature of the case would admit. In the result, it was with much concern that his Lordship, after obtaining the fullest information and laying it before the King, found it his duty to leave the law to take its course. I am, Sir, your most obedient, humble servant,

WM. EDEN.

[Received 19 September, Lord Rochford to Boswell]

St. James's, 15 September 1774

SIR,—Your two letters of the tenth instant, with the enclosures, were received yesterday, and at the same time I had a letter from Lord Cornwallis, enclosing one to his Lordship from you on the case of John Reid; and I am very sorry to be under the necessity of acquainting you that after the fullest informations taken on the proceedings of that trial, which have been laid before the King, together with the report of Lord Justice-Clerk, it has been determined that the law should take its course. I am, Sir, your most obedient, humble servant,

ROCHFORD.

[Received 19 September, Lord Pembroke to Boswell]

St. James's, Thursday 15 September 1774

I came up this morning on purpose to speak to His Majesty, my dear Sir, as you wished, and I am very sorry not to have been more successful. Lord Cornwallis also has applied in favour of Reid, but the judge's report, which I saw, is so very strong against him that the man's guilt is looked upon here in the most atrocious light possible. Lord Rochford would have urged for mercy had he been able to do it, but he and the King too indeed think the judge must resign if, after his report, any mitigation of the sentence should take place.[1] I am very

[1] "The King was certainly disposed to transport, but the judge's report was too strong. Indeed, I never read anything more so, or so positive" (Lord Pembroke to Boswell, 2 October 1774).

much concerned at my ill success, and shall be more so if it debars me from receiving your orders on any future occasion where you can make me useful.

I am, Sir, with the greatest truth and regard, your most obedient, humble servant,

PEMBROKE.

TUESDAY 20 SEPTEMBER. Before breakfast I received a very good letter from Mr. Nasmith dissuading me from the scheme of recovering John Reid, but he did not persuade me. Mr. Hay came and he and I called on Mr. Nasmith and took him with us to look for a place where the corpse might be deposited. We walked about the Grassmarket and Portsburgh, and saw some small houses to let. Mr. Nasmith proposed that we might take one till Martinmas; but then it occurred that the landlord would make a noise if a hanged man was put into it. In short, we were in a dilemma. I thought of the Canongate Kilwinning Lodge, of which I was Master and could excuse myself to the brethren for taking liberty with it; but it was too far off. I did not think it right to trust a caddie, or any low man, with the secret. I asked John Robertson the chairman if he could find a house that would take in the corpse till the mob dispersed. He thought none would do it. Mr. Nasmith went out of town. Mr. Hay, after a short party at bowls, went with me and called for Mr. Innes,[1] Dr. Monro's dissector. Mr. Wood had not yet spoken to him; but he very readily agreed to give his help. He however could not help us to get a house. I called on Wood. Neither could he help us as to that article; and he began to doubt of the propriety of the scheme. I however remained firm to it, and Mr. Hay stood by me. Mr. Innes suggested one George Macfarlane, a stabler, where a puppet-show had been kept. Mr. Hay and I went to the Grassmarket, where he lived. But first it occurred to me that there was one Andrew Bennet, a stabler, whom I had lately got out of prison. We went to him. He had no family but his wife, and they were both fools. They were prodigiously grateful to me, called

[1] His *Short Description of the Human Muscles, Chiefly As They Appear on Dissection*, 1776, was used in dissecting rooms at Edinburgh for fifty years after his death in 1777.

me *his Grace*, Andrew having reproved his wife for calling me only *his Honour*. I told them that the friends of the poor man who was to be executed next day were anxious to lodge his body in some place till the mob should disperse, and, as he was a client of mine, I was desirous to assist them; so I hoped Andrew would let them have his stable for that purpose. He agreed to it, though his wife made some objection, and though he said he would rather let his *craig* (throat) be cut than allow it, unless to oblige me. I sounded them as to letting the body into their house; but Mrs. Bennet screamed, and Andrew said very justly that nobody would come to it any more if that was done.[1] It is amazing what difficulty I found in such a place as Edinburgh to get a place for my purpose. The stable here entered by a close next entry to the door of the house, and had no communication with the house; so that the operators must be obliged to take their stations in the stable some time before the execution was over. It was a small stable, and there was a smith's shop just at the door of it; so that we could not be private enough. However, I was glad to have secured any place.

Mr. Hay and I then went to George Macfarlane's. He was not in. We had not dined, as we did not choose to see my wife while we were about such a project, which I had communicated to her and which shocked her. We called for punch and bread and cheese, all of which proved wretched. We sat about an hour, waiting for the landlord's coming in, that we might have tried if he would let us have a better place, but he did not come. I observed that we were reduced to do the meanest and most disagreeable things for this strange scheme, as much so as candidates in a borough election.

I called at home at five, Hay having gone to a coffee-house and engaged to meet me at the Cross at six. I found my wife so shocked that I left her immediately and went down to the prison. I was now more firmly impressed with a belief of John Reid's innocence, the Reverend Dr. Dick having come to the bowling-green in the forenoon and told me that, as he was to attend him to his execution, he had talked with him very seriously, and (the Doctor used a very good expression) had got behind all the subterfuges of such a mind as his, such as his thinking it right to deny, to leave a better character for the

[1] It was probably a tavern.

sake of his wife and children, and had found him firm and consistent in his declaration that he was not guilty. The Doctor said this affair gave him great uneasiness; and he told me that the Reverend Dr. Macqueen was to go along with him to attend at the execution; that he also had been with John, and was of the same opinion. I begged that he and Dr. Macqueen would be particularly attentive to investigate the truth as much as possible, as I really believed he was condemned on insufficient evidence, and, from his solemn averments of his innocence, thought him not guilty of the crime for which he was condemned; such averments being in my opinion an overbalance not for positive, or even strong circumstantial, evidence, but for such evidence as was brought against him, which I thought could produce no more than suspicion.

When I came to the prison I found that John Reid's wife and children were with him. The door of the iron room was now left open and they were allowed to go and come as they pleased. He was very composed. His daughter Janet was a girl about fifteen, his eldest son Benjamin about ten, his youngest son Daniel between two and three. It was a striking scene to see John on the last night of his life surrounded by his family. His wife and two eldest children behaved very quietly. It was really curious to see the young child Daniel, who knew nothing of the melancholy situation of his father, jumping upon him with great fondness, laughing and calling to him with vivacity. The contrast was remarkable between the father in chains and in gloom and the child quite free and frolicsome. John took him on his knee with affection. He said to me that his daughter Jenny was the only one of his children whom he had named after any relation; and he went over all the names of the rest. They had almost all Old Testament names. They were seven in all. I again exhorted him to truth. One Miln in Leith Wynd, a kind of lay teacher, and Mr. Ritchie were with him; and he was to have some good Christians to sit up with him all night.

Mr. Hay went with me again to Mr. Innes, who was satisfied with Bennet's stable and desired that there should be a blanket and a good quantity of warm salt prepared. We went again to Bennet's, and took a dram of whisky of his own distilling; and he and his wife promised to have the blanket and the salt in readiness, I having said that some surgeon had advised his friends to rub the body with warm salt to preserve it, as it was to be carried to the country. Bennet, though a fool, had smoked what was intended; for he said, "Could they not cut him down living?" I said that would be wrong. I should have observed, when I was with John this evening, it gave me some uneasiness to think that he was solemnly preparing for an awful eternity while at the same time I was to try to keep him back. He spoke himself very calmly of *the corpse*, by which he meant his own dead body; for I spoke to his wife before him about it: that I had secured a place for it, but I wished she could get a better place for it to be laid in till the mob dispersed. She said she would try Mrs. Walker at the sign of the Bishop in the Grassmarket, who was very friendly to her. It was a comfort to me that neither John nor his wife had the least idea of any attempt to recover him.

Mr. Hay and I met my worthy friend Grange in the Grassmarket tonight. He was much against the attempt. After supper Mr. Wood called and told me that he had the proper apparatus ready; that he had also engaged Mr. Aitkin, another surgeon, to attend, and that, if I insisted on it, he was willing to make the experiment, but that as a friend he could not but advise me against it; that it would be impossible to conceal it; the mob would press upon us, and continue looking in at the door. A great clamour would be made against me as defying the laws and as doing a ridiculous thing, and that a man in business must pay attention in prudence to the voice of mankind; that the chance of success was hardly anything, and this was to be put in the scale against a certainty of so many disagreeable consequences. But he suggested another thought which had great weight with me. "This man," said he, "has got over the bitterness of death; he is resigned to his fate. He will have got over the pain of death. He may curse you for bringing him back. He may tell you that you kept him from heaven." I determined to give up the scheme. Wood got into a disagreeable kind of sceptical conversation about the soul being material, from all that we could observe. It is hard that our most valuable articles of belief are rather the effects of sentiment than of demonstration. I disliked Wood because he revived doubts in my mind which

I could not at once dispel. Yet he had no bad meaning, but was honestly and in confidence expressing his own uneasiness. He said that the fear of death sometimes distressed him in the night. He seemed to have formed no principles upon the subject, but just had ideas, sometimes of one kind, sometimes of another, floating in his mind. He had a notion, which I have heard the Reverend Mr. Wyvill support, that only some souls were designed for immortality. What a blessing it is to have steady religious sentiments.

[Michael Nasmith to Boswell]

Edinburgh, 20 September 1774

My dear Sir,—This is a matter of secrecy. We have properly speaking no person to advise with. The proposed attempt appears to be attended with so much humanity that the moment any of our friends may have it in confidence they may find themselves in the same situation we ourselves are. I have been therefore deliberating with myself how far the world may think we have acted a worthy part in having attempted to preserve his life.

The jury have returned an unanimous verdict finding him guilty. The Court of Justiciary have been unanimous in finding him worthy of death. Our Sovereign has given it as his opinion that the interests of society are at stake if he is suffered to escape. The voice of the whole people approves. In short, everything sacred in society seems to forbid the attempt.

Humanity and a strong belief of John's innocence have already impelled you to do much for him, but let us cast our eyes forward and see what effects the attempt may have upon the poor wretches who may hereafter be condemned to lose their lives. Death is already sufficiently terrible. I fear much that the proposed attempt, be the event what it will, may be attended with the worst consequences, consequences that neither of us would wish to be the authors of. In the awful approach of eternity the mind is disposed to grasp at every shadow. Few will hereafter come to suffer in this country to whose ears John's story may not have reached. If he is brought to life, they will hold it up as full evidence that they too may—and that there may be a Boswell at hand the moment they are cut down. If the experiment proves ineffectual, they will solace themselves with such thoughts as these: that he was old—that he had been desperately wicked—that though the experiment did not succeed upon him, the world is every day getting more knowledge, it may upon them—that heaven may have foreseen that they could not be otherways reclaimed than by suspending them in a rope and allowing them thereafter to return to life. To step out of this world in such a situation, without repentance, confession, and resignation is a dismal thought.

To me the affair at present appears in these points of view and is not unworthy of the most cool deliberation. What do you think of talking to Mrs. Boswell, who, if I am a right judge, possesses both judgement and humanity in abundance? I am, dear Sir, yours sincerely,

M. NASMITH.

WEDNESDAY 21 SEPTEMBER. John Reid's wife called on me before breakfast and told me that Mrs. Walker said she was welcome to the best room in her house for the corpse; but that afterwards her landlord had sent to her that she must quit his house if she allowed such a thing. I said that there would be no occasion for any place. The mob would not trouble the corpse; and it might be put directly on the cart that she expected was to come for it. After breakfast Mr. Nasmith came, and was pleased to find that the scheme of recovery was given up. He and I went to Bennet's and told him there was no use for his stable. We walked backwards and forwards in the Grassmarket, looking at the gallows and talking of John Reid. Mr. Nasmith said he imagined he would yet confess; for his wife had said this morning that he had something to tell me which he had as yet told to no mortal. We went to the prison about half an hour after twelve. He was now released from the iron about his leg. The Reverend Dr. Webster and Mr. Ritchie were with him. We waited in the hall along with his wife, who had white linen clothes with black ribbons in a bundle, ready to put on him before he should go out to execution. There was a deep settled grief in her countenance. She was resolved to attend him to the last; but Richard whispered me that the

Magistrates had given orders that she should be detained in the prison till the execution was over. I dissuaded her from going and she agreed to take my advice; and then Richard told her the orders of the Magistrates. I said aloud I was glad to hear of it. The Reverend Dr. Macqueen, who afterwards came in, told her it would be a tempting of Providence to go; that it might affect her so as to render her incapable to take care of her fatherless children; and Mr. Ritchie said that the best thing she could do was to remain in the prison and pray for her husband. Dr. Macqueen said to me he was so much impressed with the poor man's innocence that he had some difficulty whether he ought to attend the execution and authorise it by his presence. I said he certainly should attend, for it was *legal*; and, besides, supposing it ever so unjust, it was humane to attend an unhappy man in his last moments. "But," said Dr. Macqueen, "I will not pray for him as a guilty man." "You would be very much in the wrong to do so," said I, "if you think him not guilty." Dr. Webster and I had no conversation as he passed through the hall except inquiring at each other how we did.

John's wife then went up to him for a little, having been told both by me and Mr. Nasmith that she could not hope for the blessing of Providence on her and her children if by her advice John went out of the world with a lie in his mouth. I followed in a little, and found him in his usual dress, standing at the window. I told him I understood he had something to mention to me. He said he *would* mention it. He had since his trial in 1766 stolen a few sheep (I think five), of which he never was suspected. "John," said I, "it gives me concern to find that even such a warning as you got then did not prevent you from stealing. I really imagine that if you had now got off you might again have been guilty, such influence has Satan over you." He said he did not know but he might. Then I observed that his untimely death might be a mercy to him, as he had time for repentance. He seemed to admit that it might be so. He said that what he had now told me he had not mentioned even to his wife; and I might let it rest. I called up Mr. Nasmith, with whom came Mr. Ritchie. I said he might acknowledge this fact to them, which he did. I asked him, if I saw it proper to mention it as making his denial of the theft for which he was condemned more probable, I might be at liberty to do so? He said I might dispose of it as I thought proper. But he persisted in denying the theft for which he was condemned. He now began to put on his white dress, and we left him. Some time after, his wife came down and begged that we would go up to him, that he might not be alone. Dress has a wonderful impression on the fancy. I was not much affected when I saw him this morning in his usual dress. But now he was all in white, with a high nightcap on, and he appeared much taller, and upon the whole struck me with a kind of tremor. He was praying; but stopped when we came in. I bid him not be disturbed, but go on with his devotions. He did so, and prayed with decent fervency, while his wife, Mr. Nasmith, and I stood close around him. He prayed in particular, "Grant, O Lord, through the merits of my Saviour, that this the day of my death may be the day of my birth unto life eternal." Poor man, I felt now a kind of regard for him. He said calmly, "I think I'll be in eternity in about an hour." His wife said something from which he saw that she was not to attend him to his execution; and he said, "So you're no (not) to be wi' me." I satisfied him that it was right she should not go. I said, "I suppose, John, you know that the executioner is down in the hall." He said no. I told him that he was there and would tie his arms before he went out. "Ay," said his wife, "to keep him from catching at the *tow* (rope)." "Yes," said I, "that it may be easier for him." John said he would submit to everything.

I once more conjured him to tell the truth. "John," said I, "you must excuse me for still entertaining some doubt, as you know you have formerly deceived me in some particulars. I have done more for you in this world than ever was done for any man in your circumstances. I beseech you let me be of some use to you for the next world. Consider what a shocking thing it is to go out of the world with a lie in your mouth. How can you expect mercy, if you are in rebellion against the GOD of truth?" I thus pressed him; and while he stood in his dead clothes, on the very brink of the grave, with his knees knocking together, partly from the cold occasioned by his linen clothes, partly from an awful apprehension of death, he most solemnly averred that what he had told concerning the present alleged crime was the truth. Before this, I had at Mr. Ritchie's desire read over his last speech to him, which was rather an irksome task as it was very long; and he said it was all right except some immaterial circumstance about his meeting Wilson with the six score of sheep. Vulgar minds, and indeed all minds, will be more struck with some unusual thought than with the most awful consideration which they have often heard. I tried John thus: "We are all mortal. Our life is uncertain. I may perhaps die in a week hence. Now, John, consider how terrible it would be if I should come into the other world and find" (looking him steadfastly in the face) "that you have been imposing on me." He was roused by this, but still persisted. "Then," said I, "John, I shall trouble you no more upon this head. I believe you. God forbid that I should not believe the word of a fellow man in your awful situation, when there is no strong evidence against it, as I should hope to be believed myself in the same situation. But remember, John, it is trusting to you that I believe. It is between God and your own conscience if you have told the truth; and you should not allow me to believe if it is not true." He adhered. I asked him if he had anything more to tell. He said he had been guilty of one other act of sheep-stealing. I think he said of seven sheep; but I think he did not mention precisely when. As he shivered, his wife took off her green cloth cloak and threw it about his shoulders. It was curious to see such care taken to keep from a little cold one who was so soon to be violently put to death. He desired she might think no more of him, and let his children push their way in the world. "The eldest boy," said he, "is reading very well. Take care that he reads the word of God." He desired her to keep a New Testament and a psalm-book which he had got in a present from Mr. Ritchie and which he was to take with him to the scaffold.[1] He was quite sensible and judicious. He had written a kind of circular letter to all his friends on whom he could depend, begging them to be kind to his family.

[1] Boswell also seems to have given him some book of devotion on the occasion of his former trial. Among the Boswell papers at Yale is a scrap of paper bearing the unfinished draft of an inscription: "To John Reid, an unhappy prisoner, from James Boswell, one of his counsel; who, if he cannot save him from punishment in this world, hopes to assist him in obtaining mercy in the world which is to come and hea . . ."

Two o'clock struck. I said, with a solemn tone, "There's two o'clock." In a little Richard came up. The sound of his feet on the stair struck me. He said calmly, "Will you come awa now?" This was a striking period. John said yes, and readily prepared to go down. Mr. Nasmith and I went down a little before him. A pretty, well-dressed young woman and her maid were in a small closet off the hall; and a number of prisoners formed a kind of audience, being placed as spectators in a sort of loft looking down to the hall. There was a dead silence, all waiting to see the dying man appear. The sound of his steps coming down the stair affected me like what one fancies to be the impression of a supernatural grave noise before any solemn event. When he stepped into the hall, it was quite the appearance of a ghost. The hangman, who was in a small room off the hall, then came forth. He took off his hat and made a low bow to the prisoner. John bowed his head towards him. They stood looking at each other with an awkward uneasy attention. I interfered, and said, "John, you are to have no resentment against this poor man. He only does his duty." "I only do my duty," repeated the hangman. "I have no resentment against him," said John. "I desire to forgive all mankind." "Well, John," said I, "you are leaving the world with a very proper disposition: forgiving as you hope to be forgiven." I forgot to mention that before he left the iron room Mr. Ritchie said to him, "Our merciful King was hindered from pardoning you by a representation against you; but you are going before the King of Heaven, who knows all things and whose mercy cannot be prevented by any representation." The hangman advanced and *pinioned* him, as the phrase is; that is, tied his arms with a small cord. John stood quiet and undisturbed. I said, "Richard, give him another glass of wine." Captain Fraser, the gaoler, had sent him the night before a bottle of claret, part of which Richard had given him, warmed with sugar, early in the morning, two glasses of it in the forenoon, and now he gave him another. John drank to us. He then paused a little, then kissed his wife with a sad adieu, then Mr. Ritchie kissed him. I then took him by the hand with both mine, saying, "John, it is not yet too late. If you have anything to acknowledge, do it at the last to the reverend gentlemen, Dr. Macqueen and Dr. Dick, to whom you are much obliged. Farewell, and I pray God may be merciful to you." He seemed faint and deep in thought. The prison door then opened and he stepped away with the hangman behind him, and the door was instantly shut. His wife then cried, "O Richard, let me up," and got to the window and looked earnestly out till he was out of sight. Mr. Nasmith and I went to a window more to the west, and saw him stalking forward in the gloomy procession.[1] I

[1] The procession went west up the Lawnmarket and down the West Bow. See the map opposite p. xi. The following account, dated a few months later, seems to be actually a reminiscence, accurate in all but a few details, by another eye-witness of Reid's execution. Reid's was apparently the only execution that occurred at Edinburgh during this period.

"The town of Edinburgh, from the amazing height of its buildings, seems peculiarly formed to make a spectacle of this kind solemn and affecting. The houses, from the bottom up to the top, were lined with people, every window crowded with spectators to see the unfortunate man pass by. At one o'clock the City Guard went to the door of the Tolbooth, the common gaol here, to receive and conduct their prisoner to the place of execution, which is always in the Grassmarket, at a very great distance from the prison. All the remaining length of the High Street was filled with people, not only from the town itself, but the country around, whom the novelty of the sight had brought together. On the Guard knocking at the door of the Tolbooth, the unhappy criminal made his appearance. He was dressed in a white waistcoat and breeches, usual on these occasions, bound with black ribands, and a night-cap tied with the same. His white hairs, which were spread over his face, made his appearance still more pitiable. Two clergymen walked on each side of him, and were discoursing with him on subjects of religion. The executioner, who seemed ashamed of the meanness of his office, followed muffled up in a great coat, and the City Guards, with their arms ready, marched around him. The criminal, whose hands were tied behind him, and the rope about his neck, walked up the remaining part of the street. It is the custom in this country for the criminal to walk to the gallows, which has something much more decent in it than being thrown into a cart, as in England, and carried, like a beast, to slaughter. The slow, pensive, melancholy step of a man in these circumstances has something in it that seems to accord with affliction, and affects the mind forcibly with its distress. . . .

"When the criminal had descended three parts of the hill which leads to the Grassmarket, he beheld the crowd waiting for his coming, and the instrument of execution at the end of it. He made a short stop here, naturally shocked at such a sight, and the people seemed to sympathize with his affliction" (Edward Topham, *Letters from Edinburgh, Written in the Years 1774 and 1775*, London, 1776, pp. 59–61: 9 December 1774).

then desired his wife to retire and pray that he might be supported in this his hour of trial. Captain Fraser gave her four shillings. It was very agreeable to see such humanity in the gaoler, and indeed the tenderness with which the last hours of a convict were soothed pleased me much.

The mob were gone from the prison door in a moment. Mr. Nasmith and I walked through the Parliament Close, down the Back Stairs and up the Cowgate, both of us satisfied of John Reid's innocence, and Mr. Nasmith observing the littleness of human justice, that could not reach a man for the crimes which he committed but punished him for what he did not commit.

We got to the place of execution about the time that the procession did. We would not go upon the scaffold nor be seen by John, lest it should be thought that we prevented him from confessing. It was a fine day. The sun shone bright. We stood close to the scaffold on the south side between two of the Town Guard. There were fewer people present than upon any such occasion that I ever saw. He behaved with great calmness and piety. Just as he was going to mount the ladder, he desired to see his wife and children; but was told they were taken care of. There was his sister and his daughter near to the gibbet, but they were removed. Dr. Dick asked him if what he had said was the truth. He said it was. Just as he was going off, he made an attempt to speak. Somebody on the scaffold called, "Pull up his cap." The executioner did so. He then said, "Take warning. Mine is an unjust sentence." Then his cap was pulled down and he went off. He catched the ladder; but soon quitted his hold. To me it sounded as if he said, "just sentence"; and the people were divided, some crying, "He says his sentence is *just*." Some: "No. He says *unjust*." Mr. Laing, clerk to Mr. Tait, one of the town clerks, put me out of doubt, by telling me he had asked the executioner, who said it was *unjust*. I was not at all shocked with this execution at the time. John died seemingly without much pain. He was effectually hanged, the rope having fixed upon his neck very firmly, and he was allowed to hang near three quarters of an hour; so that any attempt to recover him would have been in vain. I comforted myself in thinking that by giving up the scheme I had avoided much anxiety and uneasiness.

We waited till he was cut down; and then walked to the Greyfriars Churchyard, in the office of which his corpse was deposited by porters whom Mr. Nasmith and I paid, no cart having come for his body. A considerable mob gathered about the office. Mr. Nasmith went to Hutchinson's to bespeak some dinner and write a note to *The Courant* that there would be a paragraph tonight giving an account of the execution; for we agreed that a recent account would make a strong impression. I walked seriously backwards and forwards a considerable time in the churchyard waiting for John Reid's wife coming, that I might resign the corpse to her charge. I at last wearied, and then went to the office of the prison. There I asked the executioner myself what had passed. He told me that John first spoke to him on the ladder and said he suffered wrongfully; and then called to the people that his sentence was unjust. John's sister came here, and returned me many thanks for what I had done for her brother. She was for burying him in the Greyfriars Churchyard, since no cart had come. "No," said I, "the will of the dead shall be fulfilled. He was anxious to be laid in his own burying-place, and it shall be done." I then desired Richard to see if he could get a cart to hire, and bid him bring John's wife to Hutchinson's. Mr. Nasmith and I eat some cold beef and cold fowl and drank some port, and then I wrote a paragraph to be inserted in the newspapers. Mr. Nasmith threw in a few words. I made two copies of it, and, both to the printer of *The Courant* and *Mercury*, subjoined my name to be kept as the authority. Richard brought John's wife and daughter. "Well," said I, "Mrs. Reid, I have the satisfaction to tell you that your husband behaved as well as we could wish." "And that is a great satisfaction," said she. We made her eat a little and take a glass, but she was, though not violently or very tenderly affected, in a kind of dull grief. The girl did not seem moved. She eat heartily. I told Mrs. Reid that I insisted that John should be buried at home; and as I found that as yet no carter would undertake to go but at an extravagant price, the corpse might lie till tomorrow night, and then perhaps a reasonable carter might be had. Mr. Nasmith went to *The Courant* with the paragraph, and I to *The Mercury*. I sat till it was printed. It was liberal in Robertson,[1] who

[1] John Robertson was publisher of *The Caledonian Mercury*. The account in the

was himself one of the jury, to admit it; and he corrected the press.

It was now about eight in the evening, and gloom came upon me. I went home and found my wife no comforter, as she thought I had carried my zeal for John too far, might hurt my own character and interest by it, and as she thought him guilty. I was so affrighted that I started every now and then and durst hardly rise from my chair at the fireside. I sent for Grange, but he was not at home. I however got Dr. Webster, who came and supped, and he and I drank a bottle of claret. But still I was quite dismal.

[The Burial of John Reid]

THURSDAY 22 SEPTEMBER. I had passed the night much better than I expected and was easier in the morning. Charles Hay called and after I had given him a detail of all my conduct towards poor John, he said emphatically, "Well, GOD has blessed you with one of the best hearts that ever man had." Luckily for me, Bedlay had come to town anxious to get a bill of suspension drawn by me instantly. This diverted the gloom, for I kept him by me, and I wrote while both he and I dictated, and had it finished by dinner time. He drank tea with me. To touch a fee again was pleasant. Ritchie had secured a cart, and John's wife took leave of me at night when she set out with the corpse.

FRIDAY 23 SEPTEMBER. Yesterday morning I had a visit from Mr. George McQueen, one of the bailies of Edinburgh. As I had attacked his sentence about Henry McGraugh, I imagined that he was come to find fault with my conduct in some strange manner, as I was not acquainted with him. But I was agreeably surprised when he asked me to dine with him on Wednesday next with Dr. Macqueen and Dr. Dick. I then saw that our connexion was on account of John Reid, the Bailie having been one of the former jury who voted to acquit him, and being convinced of his innocence on the last occasion. I told him I was sorry that my defending McGraugh was interpreted as disrespectful to the Magistrates. I thought the sentence too severe and did

papers led to a proposal by Gordon, the chancellor of the jury, that Boswell be prosecuted. With added introduction and conclusion, it was republished by Boswell in *The London Chronicle* for 27–29 September.

what in my opinion was right, as the Bailie had done in pronouncing the sentence. We were at once on an easy footing. He told me that he had been quite unmanned at John Reid's execution, as he really believed him to be an innocent man; and he was even under some difficulty how to act. To be sure, the case was nice—to be authorising as a magistrate what a man believed to be unjust. But private judgement must submit in public administration. He said the Justice-Clerk had behaved as he always does: cruelly. And he said he had great peace in his mind when he reflected on the verdict of which he had a share. This evening the Reverend Dr. Ewing, who was returned[1] and on his way to London, Dr. Webster, Miss Webster, Sandy Webster, and Mr. Nasmith supped with us. I was now pretty easy. My wife made a very good application of a passage in *Douglas, a Tragedy*, saying that John Reid was now gone, but that his jury, fifteen men upon oath, were alive. By my speaking strongly of the injustice of the sentence, I did John no good and in some measure attacked them.

> The *living* claim some duty; vainly thou
> Bestow'st thy care upon the silent dead.[2]

I drank tea with Mr. Donaldson this afternoon. ✕[3]

[Alexander Ritchie to Boswell]

Edinburgh, 24 September 1774

Sir,—I intended to have called on you yesterday to have given you the particulars as to John Reid's burial, but I was disappointed, for the carter that carried his corpse to the place of interment did not return home till late in the evening, and when I knew he was come, I sent for him, and he told me that the body was buried in a place belonging to his forefathers, but that the poor widow was in great distress because one of the heritors had declared that, although all the parish should consent to his lying there, yet he would not allow it. She

[1] See above, p. 230. He had been travelling in Ireland during the summer.

[2] John Home's *Douglas*, I, i; original has "cares".

[3] See above, p. 287 *n*. 2.

therefore begs your assistance in this critical matter. I apprehend that an order from one of the Lords forbidding the heritors and Session to meddle any further with the corpse of John Reid but to allow them[1] to lie in the burying place belonging to his ancestors—that I apprehend would end the matter, but I do not pretend to direct you. I have the honour to be, Sir, your most obedient servant,

ALEXR. RITCHIE.

P.S. I intend to wait on you about ten o'clock and give you an instance of female courage and unshaken love.

SATURDAY 24 SEPTEMBER. Mr. Ritchie called and informed me that when John Reid's wife came to Muiravonside churchyard, she could not get the key. Therefore she and some women and the carter laid the coffin on the dyke (wall), and, some of them being on one side, some on the other, they lifted it over. They then had to send two miles for a spade, and then the carter dug a grave and buried the corpse. I got afterwards a circumstantial account of the burial in a letter from the schoolmaster of the parish, Mr. Ritchie having written to him that I was informed that the corpse was to be lifted, and that they who did it should be prosecuted. It would have been a curious question on the right of sepulture. John had, no doubt, a piece of burying-ground, but the voice of the country is that a malefactor cannot be laid in an usual burying-place, though in a churchyard. Yet there is no law as to that.

[Alexander Ritchie to Thomas Greenhill, Senior Clerk in the parish of Muiravonside]

Edinburgh, 24 September 1774

SIR,—I am desired to inform you that Mr. James Boswell, being acquainted that an opposition being made by some persons against admitting the corpse of John Reid into his burying-place, and his wife and some others, being obliged to force their way in with great difficulty, got him interred but are in great apprehension of the body

[1] "Corpse" (generally spelled "corps") was often treated as a plural in eighteenth-century Scotland and northern England.

being lifted out of the burying-place of his ancestors by some headstrong persons, contrary to any law that yet exists, for as he has fulfilled the law, there is no reason why he may not be laid in the burying-place of his ancestors—you'll be so good as notify to the Session and heritors that if any violent measures be taken, whoever takes such will be prosecuted in due course of law and be obliged to rebury the said corpse in said place at their own expense. You may show this to all concerned, both Session and others, and I remain yours, etc.,

ALEXR. RITCHIE.[1]

[Alexander Ritchie to Janet Reid]

Edinburgh, 27 September 1774

JANET,—You know I told you before and after your husband's death that you would meet with opposition, in burying him in the churchyard belonging to the parish, from some persons. Your answer to me was that the Session had given you liberty. But I understand now that you could not get so much as the key of the churchyard door nor obtain a spade or shovel from any in that neighbourhood, till you was obliged to bring them from a considerable distance. I further understand that none of your friends gave you any assistance or countenance at that time. Thus you may see how vain it is to trust in man, for they commonly misgive us in the time of our greatest distress. The use you should make of a disappointment from friends is that you should trust in the Lord, for He will not disappoint the expectations of any who trust in Him. I would now advise you that if any persons have removed the corpse and buried them in another place or intend to do it, you must quietly submit, as you are a poor widow and unable to withstand them. And as your husband's soul is now in an unalterable state, and what happens to his body cannot touch his noble part, this may compose your mind. You have fulfilled the promise you made to him in laying him in his fathers' burying-ground, and the whole parish will know that you have not sold him to the surgeons, as some were pleased to report. I entreat you therefore to compose

[1] Ritchie's original letter somehow found its way into Boswell's collection.

yourself and take care of your fatherless children and instruct them in the knowledge of the word of God and set a good example before them, that they may shun the paths that lead to destruction, for you have the part both of father and mother to fulfil towards them, and that you cannot do unless God enable you. Seek Him, and He will not forsake you. I entreat you at the same time not to quarrel with any person whom you think has wronged your husband or yourself, but rather forgive and pray for them and commit your whole cause to God, who judgeth righteously. As to Mr. James Boswell, you know what great trouble he put himself to in endeavouring to save your husband's life. This was attended with great expense, and although he did not succeed according to his wishes, that was not his fault, and after your husband's death, he was at the expense of causing him to be carried to the place of interment. But I apprehend it would be very improper for you to desire Mr. Boswell to enter into a law plea with the heritors and Session of Muiravonside about where that piece of dead clay should lie. I expect therefore you will give him no more trouble. I remain yours, a friend to the afflicted,

ALEXR. RITCHIE.

P.S. You may show this letter to any of your friends you please.[1]

[Thomas Greenhill to Alexander Ritchie, "to be communicated to Mr. James Boswell"]

Muiravonside School, 1 October 1774

SIR,—I was favoured with yours yesterday, dated the twenty-fourth of September last, anent John Reid's corpse. The history of that matter is thus, that his wife after his getting a reprieve for fourteen days applied to the Session anent having him interred in the churchyard amongst his relations, but as the affair was entirely new to the Session, and that there was no occasion for her transporting his corpse at such a distance, the Session told her against that day fourteen days they should inform her what was their resolution, but she never came nigh them, and they agreed that upon her applying to the heritors, they saw nothing to oppose it, in regard that the man was to satisfy

[1] The letter is a copy, in Ritchie's own hand, with his signature.

what the law required. It is true that his wife brought out his corpse very early on Friday morning before the minister was up to get the keys, and or ever she called for either minister or elder, she had put him in over the gates, and thereafter she got some spades and digged a grave for him in another person's burying-place at her own hand. And upon that person's entering a complaint anent it to the minister, the minister did all he could by advising the man to let Reid lie, since he was now buried, for it would still be called Reid's grave. Besides, I told the man it was not prudent to move Reid's corpse, and before he could get proper evidence of the mistake, Reid's corpse would be in such a condition that it was dangerous to move him, upon which the man was satisfied. But Reid's relict, finding that she had mistaken the burying-place of her husband, did upon Wednesday last lift his corpse and reburied him above two of his own children and left the other grave open and did not cover Reid's corpse decently, upon which the minister and I caused our beadle cover him properly and fill up the other grave distinctly. And although some people whose heads have been as light as their feet have made a great deal of noise anent the matter, yet no people of sense or character would or will give Reid's corpse any disturbance, and it has been greatly owing to the forwardness of his relict that there has been so much idle tattle anent the matter. And I can assure you that neither heritor or Session will give any disturbance. I have troubled you with this history at large, as I find Mr. James Boswell has been complained to, that he may know there will be no more trouble anent that affair and am, Sir, your very humble servant,

THOS. GREENHILL.

APPENDIX A

THE LAST SPEECH, CONFESSION, AND DYING WORDS OF JOHN REID, Flesher in Hillend, near Avonbridge, who was execute in the Grassmarket of Edinburgh, on Wednesday the twenty-first[1] day of September, 1774, for the crime of sheep-stealing.

I, John Reid, aged forty-eight years past the twenty-second day of November last, born in the shire of Stirling, in the parish of Muiravonside, and brought up there: I was determined once to make no speech, but being informed that one would be made in my name and the public imposed on thereby, I thought it proper to give the following account, which may be depended on from me as a dying man. My parents were in low circumstances, and I was sent to the herding when eight years of age, by which means I got but small education. However, afterwards I learned to read and write a little. The masters I served with were William Bryce in Blacktown, John Taylor in Getlandertown, John Taylor in Kenmore, John Taylor in Candie, John Calder in Hill; and since I was married, served John Brock in Hillend, who had a very great regard for me, as all my former masters had. As to my occupation, I learned with my father to be a flesher, which trade him and his forefathers followed for several generations, and, as I was informed, always maintained good characters.

My father and mother died with unblemished characters, and when I got a little money, I began to do business for myself, and sometimes was apt to fall into company and drink too much. And one evening in coming from the town of Linlithgow, along with a comrade, being pretty drunk, we went into a fold belonging to John Bell and turned out his whole flock of sheep, of which flock I carried off four and left all the rest on the ground at a little distance from the fold. The sheep being a-missing, the next week thereafter John Bell came and

[1] The text reads "22d".

laid hold on me and affirmed that I had taken five of his sheep and carried me before Mr. John Macleod to be examined; upon which I was liberate, as no evident proof came out against me. This happened in the month of June 1752. But in the month of December thereafter, John Bell and me being at a wedding together, and some of the company there, particularly Alexander Andrew in Linlithgow, William Miller, and William Marshall, advised and assisted him in apprehending me again for the said four sheep and carried me to Stirling. But I there enlisted to be a soldier and so got clear of John Bell. But I must acknowledge that I was actually guilty in taking these four sheep, which was the beginning of my great misery and laid the foundation for this my fatal end.

After I was enlisted, they neglecting to give me my pay regularly, I therefore got friends and so got clear of them. Notwithstanding, I was taken up seventeen different times as a deserter, and I was always willing to go along with them, providing they would give me my pay from the first day I was enlisted. But their not complying with this my just demand, I always got clear of them as before.

The next remarkable thing that befell me was in the year 1753, when I was indicted before the Lords Drummore and Strichen at Glasgow for stealing two cows and selling them to Mr. Gilbert, a flesher in Leith. But that charge against me was false, for I proved by Mr. Gilbert and his servant that these two cows I sold him were delivered to him twelve days before the pursuer's cows were a-missing; upon which I was dismissed, after a very short trial.

After this I went to London and stayed there some short time, but, there being a hard press for men, I returned again to Scotland and followed my trade as a flesher, as formerly. And soon thereafter I became acquainted with Mr. John Birtwhistle, an eminent English drover, who employed me for many years in driving his cattle from the north of Scotland to England and also in taking grass-parks for them. I have had eleven or twelve hundred head of cattle of his under my care at one time, and there was never any of them a-missing that was committed to my charge. He likewise entrusted me with large sums of money for clearing his accounts and paying the servants' wages who I employed to assist in driving his cattle, of which I always give him an honest account. This he will acknowledge if he is yet alive. And had I followed his advice when he wanted me to move my family into England, I might have been happy in his service to this day, for he was an excellent master and dealt well with me on every occasion, as he did with every other person with whom he had any dealings.

I have served several other drovers. I had always their approbation for an honest servant. Notwithstanding, I had the misfortune of having many things laid to my charge of which I was innocent, and they themselves were convinced of that afterwards. Of this I shall give you one instance. Bailie John Addison in Borrowstounness having a parcel of sheep about the number of thirty, they happened to stray from the park in the winter season, and he was advised to get a warrant to apprehend me upon suspicion of having stolen these sheep. But the sheep being found, he declared that he was sorry that he had impeached me, and indeed I was innocent. But it is not very easy to wipe off the clamour in the country when once raised.

The next remarkable thing that happened to me worthy of notice was that before the Lords of Justiciary in the year 1766, when I was indicted for stealing six score of sheep, the property of Mr. Laidlaw at Kingledoors. The circumstances as to this are as follows: I had been in England with a drove of cattle for Mr. Birtwhistle, and on my return home I met with a man on the way who called himself Wilson and asked me if I would drive that parcel of sheep to a place near Glasgow, for he had a mind to sell them to the fleshers there. And as he had business by the way, he desired me to go on, and he would come up with me against Saturday. He likewise mentioned the price he would sell them at and desired me at the same time to sell them if I found merchants. Accordingly I agreed to take them under my charge and drove them full three days and arrived at the place appointed on Saturday, when I gave information to the fleshers in Glasgow, some of whom saw the sheep but would not come up to the price set upon them (being five guineas the score, they only offering five pounds the score); so that I was not at liberty to make a final bargain. I then went to look after my employer, but he not coming up according to his promise, I asked a friend what I should do in the matter, who advised me to leave the sheep, as they would be safe in the park till the owner came up himself. His advice I followed and left the sheep on the sabbath morning and went to my own house and never saw my employer till about four years after my trial was over, in a public market. I was determined to seize him, but he prevented me by his sudden disappearing, so that I never saw him since. I got the charge of these sheep about ten miles distance from Kingledoors, but did not know them to be the property of Mr. Laidlaw till I heard of it some time afterwards. And of that whole six score of sheep, I disposed of none of them but one which fell lame by the way and could not travel. That one I sold to my landlord where I lodged one night, and to the best of my knowledge I received for it 5s. 6d. This is a true account of this matter concerning the six score sheep.

But another branch in that trial: I was accused of stealing twenty-seven ewes in 1763 from the farm of Maidengill[1] in the parish of Douglas. As to this the fact was that I did not steal them, as my jury found, but I confess that I was in concert with another man who stole them and delivered them to me at a little distance from the farm to carry away. Who that man was I have mentioned to my lawyer for his satisfaction but do not choose to publish it to the world, as I hope that he has repented. I must, however, inform the public that previous to my trial I paid for all these sheep that I made use of. And the owners would not have prosecute me if they had not been constrained to do it. After I was assoilzied and dismissed from the bar, I went home and followed my business in the flesher way as formerly.

But as I am now condemned to die an ignominious death for stealing or resetting nineteen sheep, knowing them to be stolen, the property of Alexander Gray tenant in Lyne, in the county of Peebles, I shall give the particulars of this matter: to wit, one of my neighbours, William Gardner, with whom I had many transactions in buying and selling both horses, cows, and sheep, and I had been several times employed by him in the way of my business as a flesher and has[2] sold his meat for him several times and drawn the money, for which he always

[1] Supplied from the 1766 indictment. The broadside text has Maidweenhead, apparently by confusion with the Medwenhead in Peeblesshire of the 1774 indictment. The parish of Douglas is in Lanarkshire.

[2] Scots grammar for "have". See above, p. 220 *n.* 3.

paid me discreetly for my trouble. But about ten days before this melancholy affair happened for which I am now soon to suffer, he came to me and told me that he had a parcel of sheep which he had bought and which he intended to give me to sell for him. As he had told me that he was to get them in exchange, he was afraid they would not be a bargain for me, but that I must kill and sell them for him to the best advantage, and that he would pay me for my trouble. And as I knew that he had several transactions in that part of the country which he mentioned, I the more readily believed him, and he had brought two sheep home some time before, which I killed for his own use, and which confirmed me of the truth of his having more to bring. Gardner and me parted at that time, and he promised to bring the sheep as on the Tuesday thereafter, that I might kill and sell them directly, as he wanted the money to go to a market that was to be the week thereafter. But the sheep did not come at the time appointed, but on the Thursday thereafter, early in the morning before I had got out of bed, a young man named Thomas Russel chapped at my door and told me that Gardner had sent me nineteen sheep and at same time delivered me a line from him, in which he informed me that he could not come on the Tuesday as he had promised, as he had been employed in poinding a man that was owing him some money, but that he would endeavour to see me as soon as possible. And he further desired me to begin to kill and prepare the sheep for the market, which accordingly I did. And on the morrow thereafter Gardner called at my house and communed with me about a bargain, and he told me if I was to sell the sheep on my own risk, the price would be £6. 10s., 30s. of which I paid him directly, the other £5 I was to give him on the Tuesday thereafter providing that I had made a tolerable profit on them, and if not, I was to give him what money they drew, and he was to pay me for my trouble. Upon this Gardner went away home and took one of the carcasses of the sheep along with him. And the next morning being Saturday, I went to Falkirk and sold eight of the carcasses in the public market.

But on the Monday after, Alexander Gray's herd came inquiring after the sheep, and he found two of them dead in my flesh-house, and three living ones in a park near to my house. The rest I had sold amongst my neighbours. I make no doubt but these were all the property of Alexander Gray, but I knew nothing of that till this very time. The discovery of the sheep on the Monday prevented Gardner from calling for his money on the Tuesday, as he had promised, and I on the other hand was filled with terror and kept myself secret but slept in my own house every night for several weeks. And about four weeks after the discovery, Gardner came to me and informed me how he came by the sheep and entreated me not to discover him and he would do all in his power to serve me.

However, my fears increasing, I went straight to the north of England, where I remained several weeks and then was so infatuate as to think of returning home. And in my way home, I was informed that Alexander Gray would trouble himself no further about the sheep, and that the rumour would soon die away. I went to my own house, where I kept myself secret for several weeks, but some of my neighbours gave intelligence that I was at home. A messenger with a party of dragoons came and apprehended me before I had got out of bed, and when I found I was taken, I caused Gardner to be taken also, as I knew that he was the mainspring of the whole action. But I did not tell at that time that he sent the sheep to me, or that I had received a line from him along with them, for I expected that we would be kept prisoners together and I might have an opportunity of clearing myself in his presence. But in this I was disappointed, for he was soon removed from me by a warrant against him for several other crimes, for which he is now banished to America; and Thomas Russel, who brought the sheep to me, has left the country also, so that I am left to suffer for all.

As to the witnesses who appeared on my trial, there was some contradictions among them, but I shall now pass them over. But as to my friend William Black in Hillend, he fell into some mistakes which were of fatal consequences to me, but I shall not trouble the public with them. I wish the Lord may forgive him and may grant me a heart to forgive him and all who have wished me evil.

As to the jury, I doubt not but my former character and the two forementioned trials made an impression upon their minds. But as both judges and jury are only accountable to the righteous Judge of all the earth, I shall quietly submit to my awful fate.

I acknowledge I have sinned against God in many ways, but I have been very much comforted with many passages of the Holy Scripture, by which I see that He is great in mercy and rich in love to the chief of sinners, even to such as me. He has declared that he has no delight in the death of the sinner. O that He would be graciously pleased to open my heart to receive the Lord Jesus Christ as my only Saviour, that when I come to be deprived of this my natural life by sentence of the law, I may be delivered from the power of the second death and may have a part among the ransomed and redeemed of the Lord, who shall praise Him for His redeeming love. I lament my poor wife, with whom I have lived these sixteen years in great harmony and comfort. None needs impute any part of my misfortunes to her advice or counsel, for she has given me all the good instructions that was in her power, especially since my trial in the year 1766, and she has often told me that my connexion with Gardner would be of bad consequences. (And indeed he has helped me to the gallows, for which I wish he may be forgiven.) I am sorry for my poor helpless children, but I recommend them to the Lord, who is the orphans' help from His holy habitation and is only able to take care of them. I return my hearty thanks to my benefactors and in an especial manner to the honourable gentleman who has plead my cause once and again without fee or reward from me and has further ministered to my necessities and after all has taken every step to save my life at last. (But God, that rules all things, has not seen it meet that it should be so.) I wish that all his lawful undertakings in behalf of unfortunate panels may prosper, and that when he comes to leave the earthly bar, he may find a welcome reception from the righteous Advocate at the Father's right hand, and then he will be fully rewarded for the services done to fellow men in their afflictions. Adieu, vain world.

JOHN REID.

JAMES ANDERSON, Witness.
PATRICK ANDERSON, Witness.

The above declaration was given to Richard Lock, inner turnkey of the Tolbooth, Edinburgh, by the above John Reid.

[Edinburgh: printed by H. Galbraith. Price one penny.]

APPENDIX B

The Scottish Courts and Legal System

1769–1774[1]

On 26 July 1766, James Boswell was admitted to the Faculty of Advocates and three days afterwards he began to practise in the Scottish courts. For the next twenty years, with complete regularity and a fair degree of assiduity, he followed his professional career in Scotland, not abandoning it until early in 1786, when, in fulfilment of a long-cherished dream, he was admitted to the English bar and took up residence in London. Since so much of his daily life from 1766 onwards was spent in and about courts, especially the Court of Session in Edinburgh, the reader may find himself helped by an extended note on the principal features of the Scottish judicial system.

Both in its law and in its court procedure, the Scottish system differed widely from the usage of England.[2] The basis of Scots law was the Roman civil law as expounded by the Dutch commentators, which

[1] This sketch is an expansion of a draft offered to the editors by a good friend and encourager of the Yale Editions of the Private Papers of James Boswell, Mr. N. S. Curnow of Johannesburg, South Africa.

[2] Since the purpose of this appendix is merely to elucidate Boswell's text, we have used the past tense throughout, though a good deal of the information here given would be as true for the present century as for the eighteenth. Our main sources are Hugo Arnot, *The History of Edinburgh*, 1788; Robert Bell, *A Dictionary of the Law of Scotland*, 2 vols., 1807; [James Boswell] *A Letter to . . . Lord Braxfield*, 1780; George Brunton and David Haig, *An Historical Account of the Senators of the College of Justice*, 1832; Henry Cockburn, *Memorials of His Time*, 1856; Sir Francis J. Grant, *The Faculty of Advocates in Scotland, 1532–1943*, Scottish Record Society, 1944; C. A. Malcolm, "The Parliament House and its Antecedents", in Stair Society *Publications*, xx, 449–458; and *The Royal Kalendar or Complete and Correct Annual Register . . . for the Year 1774*.

explains why so many Scots advocates, including Boswell, his father, and his grandfather, studied for a time in Dutch universities. In one respect, though following a different nomenclature, the Scots professional arrangements agreed with those of England as opposed to those of the United States. In America, the vast majority of lawyers today are members of the bar and hence are qualified to plead in court, as well as to advise clients, to draw documents, and to manage cases (*causes* is the correct Scots terminology). In England there is a sharp division between *solicitors*, who prepare and manage cases, and *barristers*, who plead them; and the same distinction obtained in Scotland, though the terminology there was *writers* and *advocates*. (A Writer to the Signet was a writer whose membership in an ancient legal society entitled him to certain privileges.) Boswell was an advocate, which means that he was commonly engaged and briefed by a writer who was managing the case. Advocates and Writers to the Signet were as a rule members of the same social class—upper middle, many, indeed, being of the aristocracy—but the profession of advocate was considered rather more ambitious and "liberal" than that of writer.

The principal courts in which Boswell appeared during the period of his Scottish practice were the Court of Session, the High Court of Justiciary, which sat in Edinburgh and at circuit towns in the country, the General Assembly of the Church of Scotland, and the House of Lords—the last-named, of course, being situated in London.

The Court of Session was the supreme court for civil cases in Scotland. It sat in its own rooms in the Parliament House in Edinburgh on all week-days except Monday from 12 June to 11 August (Summer Session) and from 12 November to 11 March (Winter Session), with a short recess at Christmas. The Bench consisted of fifteen judges, known as Senators of the College of Justice or Lords of Council and Session: fourteen Ordinary Lords and a fifteenth or presiding judge who was styled the Lord President. Each judge bore the style of Lord, his further designation being usually that of his country estate. (Thus Alexander Boswell was styled Lord Auchinleck; James Burnett, Lord Monboddo. All judges, however, signed their Christian and family names, even to official acts.) By custom only advocates of considerable experience in the Court of Session were appointed judges, and such eventual promotion was the aim of most advocates. In 1774 the stated salary of the Lord President was £1300 a year and that of the Ordinary Lords £700.[1]

The business of the Court was transacted in two divisions known as the Outer House and the Inner House. The court-room of the Outer House was the Parliament Hall, the stately apartment in which the Scots Parliament had sat from 1639 until the Union of 1707. Each week, in turn, one of the Ordinary Lords sat as a single judge in what had been the Sovereign's throne, and summarily decided the simpler legal actions. When his verdict was not acceptable to one of the parties, appeal was made to the Inner House, where the Court of Session, headed by the Lord President, sat to review the judgements of the Ordinaries. The proceedings in the Court of Session were carried on very largely in writing, advocates having to present their cases and arguments by way of minutes, representations, informations, memorials, replies, etc.—often in printed form—for the judges to consider. Only rarely, in cases of special importance, did the Court order a hearing in presence, that is, permit the opposing advocates to argue the cause *viva voce*. All cases in this court were tried without juries. Appeal could be taken to the House of Lords from its final judgement. The Lords of Session wore gowns of purple cloth with cape and facings of crimson velvet. On the cape and facings were knots of cloth which had formerly been bows for tying the halves of the gown together in front. Eighteenth-century portraits indicate that full-bottomed wigs and long white cravats were normal accessories.

Six of the Lords of Session held dual appointments, and constituted the High Court of Justiciary, the supreme court of Scotland for criminal cases. This court was in theory headed by the Lord Justice-General, a peer of exalted rank (the Duke of Queensberry held the office during the period covered by this volume). But if the Lord Justice-General did not hold the office as a pure sinecure, he no longer took part in trials and may for our purposes be ignored. The actual

[1] Arnot says (p. 479) that, though the stated salary remained unchanged, Lord President Dundas was given an addition for his lifetime of £300 annually, beginning in 1769.

head of the Court was the Lord Justice-Clerk, one of the fifteen, who received an addition of £500 to his salary as Lord of Session. The other five Lords or Commissioners of Justiciary received an addition of £200 each. They met in their own room in the Council House adjoining the Parliament Hall at its north-west end (the site now occupied by the lobby of the Signet Library) during the terms of the Court of Session, Mondays being entirely reserved for Justiciary business. Prosecutions for the Crown were conducted by His Majesty's Advocate for Scotland (commonly styled the Lord Advocate) and the Solicitor-General, generally assisted by other advocates. Criminal cases were tried before juries of fifteen citizens, a majority of votes being sufficient for a verdict. Scots law permitted not two but three verdicts: Guilty, Not Guilty, and Not Proven, the last being no less a full acquittal from the pains of the law than Not Guilty. The Lords of Justiciary wore scarlet gowns with cape and facings of white. Generally speaking, an appointment as Ordinary Lord of Session was terminated only by death or total incapacity to act, but a Justiciary Lord commonly relinquished his office on finding that age or infirmity was reducing his capacity for work.

Some time in the spring after the rising of the Court of Session, and again in September, the Lords of Justiciary went on circuit: that is, presided at criminal courts at various stated towns in three areas into which Scotland was divided. The Western Circuit sat at Stirling, Glasgow, and Inveraray; the Northern at Perth, Aberdeen, and Inverness; the Southern at Jedburgh, Dumfries, and Ayr. Two judges were appointed for each circuit, but the duty was often actually performed by one. Each judge was allowed from £300 to £360 a year for circuit expenses, which included fairly lavish hospitality in circuit towns. Young lawyers acquired practice by "going the circuits"; older and better established lawyers were less likely to take the trouble.

No appeal lay from the sentence of the High Court of Justiciary, and a prisoner capitally convicted in that court could hope for reversal or mitigation of sentence only by exercise of the royal mercy. To allow time for appeal to the Crown, no capital sentence could be carried into execution to the south of the Forth within less than thirty days, or to the north of the Forth within less than forty.

APPENDIX B

There were only two changes in the Bench from the time of Boswell's admission to the bar to the end of the period covered by this volume. James Burnett, Lord Monboddo, was made Lord of Session on 12 February 1767 to succeed Andrew Fletcher, Lord Milton, deceased; and on 16 November 1769 Robert Bruce, Lord Kennet, replaced Andrew Pringle, Lord Alemoor, as Lord of Justiciary, Alemoor continuing as Lord of Session. The following table gives the complete roster of the "Fifteen" from the latter date to 15 February 1775. Lords of Justiciary are indicated by asterisks.

Judicial Title	*Family Name*	*Born/Died*	*Appointed Judge*
Lord President	Robert Dundas	1713–1787	1760
*Lord Justice-Clerk	Thomas Miller	1717–1789	1766
Lord Alemoor	Andrew Pringle	d. 1776	1759
Lord Alva	James Erskine	1722–1796	1761
*Lord Auchinleck	Alexander Boswell	1707–1782	1754
*Lord Coalston	George Brown	d. 1776	1756
Lord Elliock	James Veitch	1712–1793	1761
Lord Gardenstone	Francis Garden	1721–1793	1764
Lord Hailes	Sir David Dalrymple	1726–1792	1766
*Lord Kames	Henry Home	1696–1782	1752
*Lord Kennet	Robert Bruce	1718–1785	1764
Lord Monboddo	James Burnett	1714–1799	1767
*Lord Pitfour	James Ferguson	1700–1777	1764
Lord Stonefield	John Campbell	d. 1801	1763
Lord Strichen	Alexander Fraser	1699–1775	1760

The Lord Advocate from 1766–1775 was James Montgomery (1721–1803), the Solicitor-General, Henry Dundas (1742–1811).

The judges of another Scottish court receive frequent mention in Boswell's Journal, but he himself did little or no business there. The Court of Exchequer tried cases relating to customs, excise, and other matters concerning Crown revenue. It consisted of a Lord Chief Baron and four other Barons. This court followed the forms of English law, and English barristers as well as Scots advocates were eligible for appointment to its Bench. The salaries of three of the

Barons were the same as those of the Ordinary Lords of Session, but Baron Winn received £1200 and the Lord Chief Baron received £2000 annually. The judges in 1774 were as follows:

Lord Chief Baron	Robert Ord (d. 1778)
Baron	John Grant (d. 1776)
Baron	John Maule (1706–1781)
Baron	William Mure (1718–1776)
Baron	George Winn (1725–1798, resigned appointment 1776)

Boswell went every day during term to the Parliament House, arriving at nine o'clock. (See above, 12 August 1774.) If he had no case to plead, he joined the other advocates in the Parliament Hall, where they paced back and forth in the Outer House, which was promenade and waiting-room as well as court-room. (An area at the north end, fenced off by a slight wooden partition running half way to the ceiling, was occupied by the stalls of stationers and booksellers, later of jewellers and cutlers.) Scots advocates did not have offices or chambers distinct from their dwellings. Boswell dictated his papers at home and made appointments with clients in a tavern. As will be seen from the dates given above, the sessions of the courts covered only six months of the year. During the long vacations, the professional demands on an advocate were few. If he were ambitious and prudent, he studied law then, for the Scots bar was crowded and a commanding practice had to be fought for. As the present volume demonstrates, Boswell did study law with his father in the autumn vacation of 1771 and with his fellow advocate Charles Hay during the spring and autumn vacations of 1774. He had an appeal case in the House of Lords as an excuse for his London jaunt of 1772. But he had no such excuse for that of 1773; and he also spent the entire autumn vacation of that year in a tour to the Hebrides with Dr. Johnson. He would come more and more to feel that he had a right to rush off to London as soon as the court rose in the spring. But from 1766 to 1783 he did not once absent himself from Scotland during term time.

The fact that it cut into vacation may have been one of the reasons why he came to entertain such hearty dislike for the business of the General Assembly of the Church of Scotland. This, the supreme ecclesiastical court of the kingdom, sat each May in an apartment appropriated to its use in St. Giles's Church. It was made up of ministers and elders elected annually from each presbytery, was presided over by a Moderator chosen at each Assembly from its own members, and was attended by a Lord High Commissioner representing the King. The best known of Boswell's cases in this court concerned a clergyman who was refused induction and ordination because of previous immoral behaviour. (See above, 5 April 1772.) Most of his cases appear to have dealt with the then very lively issue of patronage: whether the chief landholder of a parish could present ministers, or whether they should come at the direct call of the parish.

The House of Lords of the Parliament of Great Britain, besides being a House of the legislature, was also the final court of appeal from most of the courts in Great Britain though not (as has already been mentioned) from the criminal courts of Scotland.[1] It sat as a court on stated days of the week throughout the legal year, even during the prorogation or dissolution of Parliament. Any Member of the House (all the peers of England and of Great Britain, sixteen representative Scots peers, and twenty-six bishops) could attend and could vote on an appeal, and Members sometimes exercised this privilege (see above, 11 April 1773), but the decisions were usually left to the "Law Lords," that is, to the Lord Chancellor and the judges of the supreme courts of England who held the rank of peers. In 1772 there were only two Law Lords: Lord Apsley, the Chancellor, and Lord Mansfield, Lord Chief Justice of the King's Bench. Lord Mansfield deputised for Lord Apsley and sat alone from 4 April to 1 May of that year. Cases in the House of Lords were managed by solicitors and pleaded by advocates or barristers. The respective cases of the appellant and the respondent, forming the subject-matter of the appeal, were printed and bound in a considerable number of copies at the expense of the appellant and lodged with the House in advance of the trial; some of

[1] The sources for this part of the sketch are mainly Michael Macdonagh, *The Book of Parliament*, 1897, and Sir Frank MacKinnon, "The Law and the Lawyers", in *Johnson's England*, ed. A. S. Turberville, 2 vols., 1933.

these were bound in purple cloth for the use of the Law Lords. Only two counsel could be heard on each side. Further details of the procedure are given above, pp. 118–19.

Glossary of Legal Terms

Assoilzie (*pronounced* assoilyie *or* assoilly). To acquit by sentence of a court.

Bill of Suspension. An appeal in form to a judge to prohibit execution of a sentence until further hearings have been held; a request for an injunction.

Compear. To appear in court personally or by attorney.

Decern. To decree or adjudge.

Decreet Arbitral. The judgement of an arbiter in a private judicial proceeding.

Habit and Repute. Having the general reputation of being.

Information. A written pleading ordered by the Lord Ordinary when he takes a cause to report to the Inner House.

Interlocutor. The judgement of the Court, or of the Lord Ordinary, which, unless reclaimed or appealed, has the effect of deciding the cause.

Libel. Generally speaking, the part of the indictment stating the grounds of the charge on which a civil or criminal prosecution takes place. As a verb, to institute proceedings by filing a libel, or complaint.

Memorial. A statement of facts drawn up to be submitted for counsel's opinion. Also, an advocate's brief.

Minute. A notice of intention presented to the Court by a party to a suit.

Panel. The defendant (accused) in a criminal action.

Poinding (*pronounced* pînding). The process by which a creditor seizes a debtor's property so as to become vested with the title and right of sale or appropriation in satisfaction of his debt.

Precognition. A preliminary examination of witnesses by the Lord Ordinary or by Justices of the Peace, in a criminal cause; also, the evidence uncovered in this examination.

Pursuer. The plaintiff or prosecutor.

Reclaiming Petition. A written pleading stating the grounds on which a judgement of the Lord Ordinary or whole Court is expected to be altered.

Relevancy. In criminal actions, the correctness or propriety of the indictment.

Representation. A written pleading presented to the Lord Ordinary when his judgement is brought under review.

Reset of Theft. Receiving goods knowing them to be stolen.

INDEX

This is in general an index of proper names with analysis of actions, opinions, and personal relationships under the important names. Under Edinburgh and London the buildings, streets, and other locations in the cities are listed. Observations on a person are ordinarily listed under that person; for example, Boswell's characterisation of Lord Mansfield will be found under Mansfield and not under Boswell. An exception is made in the case of Samuel Johnson, whose opinions on various people are listed in Part III of the article under his name, and are not always specified under the names of the persons in question. Sovereigns appear under their Christian names; noblemen and Lords of Session under their titles. The titles are usually those proper to the period 1769–1774. Maiden names of married women are given in parentheses. Titles of books are listed under the name of the author. Locations on the maps of Edinburgh, and London are indicated by letters and numbers in parentheses after names. The letters A to D (A2, D3, etc.) refer to the London map. The letter E, whether singly (E) or with a number (E4), refers to the map of the City of Edinburgh, (Env.) to the map of the Environs of Edinburgh, both at following p.x. Habitations of persons mentioned in the text are located on the maps if Boswell reports visits to them. The following abbreviations are used: D. (Duke), M. (Marquess), E. (Earl), V. (Viscount), B. (Baron), Bt. (Baronet), W.S. (Writer to the Signet) JB (James Boswell), SJ (Samuel Johnson).

INDEX

INDEX

INDEX

INDEX

P

INDEX